Truth through Proof

# Truth through Proof

## A Formalist Foundation for Mathematics

Alan Weir

CLARENDON PRESS · OXFORD

# OXFORD
**UNIVERSITY PRESS**

Great Clarendon Street, Oxford OX2 6DP

Oxford University Press is a department of the University of Oxford.
It furthers the University's objective of excellence in research, scholarship,
and education by publishing worldwide in

Oxford New York

Auckland Cape Town Dar es Salaam Hong Kong Karachi
Kuala Lumpur Madrid Melbourne Mexico City Nairobi
New Delhi Shanghai Taipei Toronto

With offices in

Argentina Austria Brazil Chile Czech Republic France Greece
Guatemala Hungary Italy Japan Poland Portugal Singapore
South Korea Switzerland Thailand Turkey Ukraine Vietnam

Oxford is a registered trade mark of Oxford University Press
in the UK and in certain other countries

Published in the United States
by Oxford University Press Inc., New York

British Library Cataloguing in Publication Data
Data available

Library of Congress Cataloging in Publication Data
Data available

Typeset by SPI Publisher Services, Pondicherry, India
Printed in Great Britain
on acid-free paper by
MPG Books Group, Bodmin and King's Lynn

ISBN 978-0-19-954149-2

1 3 5 7 9 10 8 6 4 2

# Preface

This book has taken a long time to make it into print. I hope that means that it has been maturing and improving like a top-class malt, and not that it has slowly been going off, like food which has been left too long. Certainly I would like to have taken longer. But however long one works at a book, still more improvements are possible; the murky notion of the potential infinite has some purchase here. One has to call a halt at some point, one hopes before the stage when more errors than improvements are added by further alteration.

It is not difficult for me to find excuses for the length of time it has taken to complete the book. Pressure of heavy teaching and administration loads, the hefty and dispiriting rise in bureaucracy and form-filling which contemporary academics have been faced with—not to mention having to take arms daily against a tsunami of emails—all these, I might claim, have conspired to slow down progress on this work. I might claim that, I think with a little justification, but overall this is only a very partial explanation of my rather stately progress towards completing the task I set myself at the outset.

A weightier reason for the slow maturation of the book is the sheer difficulty of the subject matter, philosophy of mathematics. It is an area where many of the deepest philosophical problems, in areas such as metaphysics, epistemology, and language, can be treated in a particularly pure form and where the dark fog of pretentious waffle and obscurantism is exposed and swiftly dispelled in the clear sunlight. But not only is the area a challenging one, it has also attracted many fine philosophers who have set very high standards in the quality of recent work in this area. I would like to say that, having worked on the book for some time, this has enabled me to take full account of all this excellent recent work. But almost the opposite has been the case—as the years have rolled on and more and more good work has come out, it has become harder, not easier, to keep up with it whilst attending to other duties.

Thus apologies are due to those whose work, if I had known of it, or known it better, would have informed and improved the argument of this monograph. It makes no attempt, I should say, at any kind of survey of the existing state of play in philosophy of mathematics but sets off on its own course. Not a new one to be sure, in fact one that most philosophers, if not mathematicians, think leads straight on to the rocks. In philosophy, at any rate, to be called a 'formalist' is usually an accusation, rather than a commendation, though thankfully it does not bring with it the kind of dangers Shostakovich faced when accused of musical formalism in Stalin's Soviet Union. What is presented here is not, however, a rehash of the derided pre-Hilbertian game formalism but a new, and I hope improved, variant.

I also wish to acknowledge at this point all those who have influenced me in my intellectual development, as I optimistically hope it has proven to be. Perforce this ought to be a long list, for the sort of reasons already given, though I fear that the vagaries and patchiness of my memory mean it is much shorter than it should be—apologies, then, to those who should have been on it but are not. (Perhaps apologies are also due to those who are on it but wish they were not!)

To start fairly near the beginning, my earliest inspiration in turning to philosophy of mathematics was Neil Tennant, who, as a young lecturer, turned my head away from Bradley towards Quine (though later reflection discerns more in common between the two than I initially would have suspected); towards logic (implanting a firm bias in favour of the Gentzen/Prawitz approach); and towards philosophy of mathematics. I hope he does not count his work with me as a failure because I remained, then and now, immune to the attractions of intuitionism and relevantism. Following a widespread tradition, I bite the hand which fed me in Chapter 6, where I criticize the kind of appeal to idealization which Neil makes in accounting for our mathematical knowledge. In my postgraduate work I was very fortunate to have two very attentive supervisors in L. J. Cohen and Michael Woods, alas both no longer with us. Jon Cohen was a tremendous support in my early career, including supporting me in the initial stages of work on this book.

My first tenured job was at Queen's University, Belfast, where I taught from 1985 to 2006. These were somewhat abnormal times, especially in the earlier years, but I joined a very supportive department, one which recognized that not all projects can bring instantaneous results. The late Christopher McKnight, in particular, patiently and carefully read many early drafts of sections of the book.

From my earliest teaching days, as a temporary lecturer in Scotland, Crispin Wright was a dominant figure on the scene, particularly for philosophers of mathematics. His encouragement encompassed both work of mine critical of his own neo-logicist project as well as more sympathetic themes. The extraordinary Arché Centre at St Andrews he directed has provided a tremendous boost to Scotland's profile on the contemporary philosophical scene and set a great example and challenge for other Scottish universities to follow. It was on one of my visits there that I first met Stewart Shapiro and he has been a source of sound advice, both philosophical and technical. Well before his connection with Arché, Graham Priest's powerful critique of orthodoxy on the paradoxes strongly influenced me, though not to the extent of embracing dialetheism. I eventually decided against trying to tackle the problems of interpreting set theory in this book; one at a time is the prudent approach, when it comes to attempts to revive philosophies which appeared in the obituary sections of the journals some time ago. Finally, in the matter of acknowledging philosophical colleagues, my heartfelt thanks go to Glasgow University for inviting me to take up a chair at a wonderful and highly collegiate department.

I am very grateful also to Oxford University Press and in particular to its Philosophy editor, St. Peter Momtchiloff, for his uncountably infinite patience in waiting on this product, and then publishing it. Thanks are especially owed to the press for continuing, among their many and varied publishing endeavours, to reserve a significant space for books whose likely impact on the price and sales of video games, or on the net income of the tourist industry, or on average life expectancy, is zero (except insofar as it has lowered my own). I very much hope, of course, that the book will have an academic impact. Even here we should be open about the fact that the vast bulk of the output of nearly all academics will be almost totally forgotten in a few decades' time. But in the UK at least (though these trends seem to be quite widespread at the moment) it is non-academic 'impact' which poses the greatest threat to scholarly endeavour and the pursuit of academic excellence.

Theoretical breakthroughs have, of course, had phenomenal impact on human life, usually indirect and unforeseen, though sometimes more immediately and directly. Despite this, we are now forced to defend the principle that money which is set aside to support pure research should not be distributed, in any part, on the basis of non-academic factors evaluated by non-academic judges, whether these non-academic factors be the political or religious opinions of the recipients, their golf handicaps, or the non-academic impact they have (which in many areas is probably inversely correlated with academic merit).

Alas, precisely this sort of non-academic evaluation of research quality is what is being proposed in the UK and it is especially dispiriting that so many academics have adopted a policy of appeasement toward the Impacters. The pragmatists have argued that if we engage with the bureaucrats we can push down the proportion of the non-academic component used to 'measure' research excellence, from 25 per cent to something lower, say 15 per cent (something which may well have been in the minds of the bureaucrats anyway, when they made their opening gambit). Compare and contrast, if you can: the government proposes that 25 per cent of a student's degree grade be determined by parental income (or body mass index or some such); the 'pragmatists' agree but argue the proportion should be lowered to 15 per cent.

Frege, Russell, and Gödel did not embark on their investigations into the nature of logic, philosophy of mathematics, formal languages, and proof systems in order to write software for mechanical or electronic computers. Yet their bluest of blue sky research certainly had impact: it led to the world of information technology, led to a total transformation of the technology humans live by, in other words. It is a nice counterfactual question how quickly the computer revolution, the programming languages and software in particular, would have arisen if by the 1930s the engineering knowledge was as it actually was but mathematical logic was at pre-Fregean levels. Doubtless the pure mathematicians would at some point have come up with formal languages and recursive function theory, but only because they stand on the shoulders of previous giants devoted to pure disinterested research.

The chances of this book leading, as an unintended consequence, to a similar technological revolution are exceedingly small, indeed vanishingly small. Philosophers (other than, perhaps, applied philosophers), and the publishing houses who publish them should not attempt to justify what they do in extrinsic terms but be open about the fact that we pursue philosophy as an end in itself.

This is no reason in itself, it is true, for these activities, however much they grip us, to be funded by the taxpayer, any more than the golf fanatic should be funded in order to work on reducing her handicap. But whilst few taxpayers would agree to the latter, many support the maintenance and nourishment of the intellectual traditions passed down to us from previous generations just as they support and approve of the transmission and preservation of our cultural heritage. Moreover, given what we know of intellectual history, we can be pretty confident that if our hunter-gatherer ancestors had all been Gradgrinds primed to inquire only after readily determinable data, and were followed in this by their descendants, then hunter-gatherers we would have remained to this day. And that is reason enough to give to the more hard-nosed taxpayer for maintaining, at some reasonable level or other, a community of researchers, an interlinked network evaluating academic worth according to their own criteria. The record of history very strongly suggests that it is much more probable that technological advance will emerge from the work of such a community, though the likelihood for each component is very small, than if no such pure research community, of scholars, universities, and publishing houses exists.

I alluded to the idea that the academic community is not a scattered and discrete fusion of isolated and unconnected islands but rather is much more like a Quinean interlinked network with no, or only a few, individual elements having an extra-academic effect on their own. That is surely particularly evident in the case of philosophy. Most philosophers are philosophers of X, for at least one other discipline X; in the present case, X being mathematics. Yet I have to confess that I am not an 'interdisciplinary' philosopher of mathematics. I am a philosopher, and only a philosopher, by training. There are philosophers of mathematics, those behind the 'real mathematics' movement, who see dangers in this. Philosophy of mathematics, they hold, has concentrated far too much on a narrow diet of examples from areas most familiar to non-mathematicians, or those most congenial to logician/philosophers: set theory, arithmetic, analysis. This, they feel, may lead to a distorted view of what mathematics is; for a correct perspective we have to look at mathematics as it is actually practised, not in high school, nor even in undergraduate curricula, but at the coal face of the latest research monographs and journals.

In this book, as will be quickly seen, only the usual suspects are paraded before you, the aforementioned number theory and set theory in particular; moreover there is no investigation of what cutting-edge mathematicians in these areas do, only a look at standard axiomatizations, simple theorems, and the like. I do not say this is a virtue. Clearly the more mathematics a philosopher of mathematics knows, the more X a philosopher of X knows, the better, *ceteris paribus*. But *ceteris* is almost never *paribus*, and human limitations mean that the more mathematics one knows the less philosophy one knows, in particular the less engagement one has with philosophers outside philosophy of mathematics (one needs to emphasize 'engagement' because doing philosophy is more than just reading and writing philosophy). The epistemology of philosophy, like the epistemology of science, is holistic at least to the extent that stances one takes, explicitly or implicitly, in one sub-area will have significant implications, perceived or not, in others. In this book, for example, I make use of some ideas from philosophy of language and engage in forays into topics such as projectivism and the treatment of fiction; perhaps rashly, but I think these are risks one has to take if one is properly to test the strengths and weaknesses of a philosophical standpoint.

What is more likely to lead one away from a correct view of the nature of mathematics (assuming, as I do, that there is such a thing)? Insufficient knowledge of mathematics? Or lack of familiarity with debates and ideas from more distant areas of philosophy? No one can know in advance. But it is here that the chains of interconnection among academics are so important. I rely, in gauging whether my account of mathematics will hold in full generality, on discussions with philosophers with more mathematical training than I. They are better able to engage, and do often engage, with top-flight mathematicians with philosophical leanings; who in turn are directly involved in working with the mathematical community in general, and so on.

Philosophy is a team game, in which the team includes not just philosophers but, in principle, thinkers from any and every serious intellectual discipline. (Of course where the boundaries lie here is both vague and contentious; I say a little on the question of how much deference philosophers should show toward other disciplines, linguistics in particular, in Chapter 3). But that does not mean that all philosophers should be interdisciplinary, in the sense of studying with, and writing with, practitioners from outside philosophy. I said earlier that the 'impact' agenda posed the greatest threat to intellectual standards today, but perhaps not, perhaps the 'interdisciplinary' agenda is at least as dangerous (what is it about 'I' words today!).

For there is abroad just now a movement which one might describe as 'Academic Esperantoism'. The Esperantoists thought that a single human brain, or group of brains, could produce, in a short space of time, linguistic and conceptual structures to rival in power those of natural languages which evolved through countless generations and involved the (uncoordinated) interaction of millions. Similarly, the Academic Esperantoists think that a committee of well-meaning academics can swiftly generate structures, practices, and traditions comparable in intellectual worth to the existing disciplines which have emerged through generations, in some cases millennia, of activity by scholars. The Esperantoists complain that existing disciplines constitute 'silos' blocking worthwhile cross-disciplinary work. The boundaries, however, have always been partially permeable yet sufficiently non-porous to generate a useful filtration mechanism, newly emerging disciplines proving their worth by surviving the (essential) tests imposed by existing, disciplinary boundaries. In the boundary-less world to which we seem to be heading, we risk wasting enormous amounts of time and money creating large numbers of transient pick-and-mix pseudo-disciplines which are sterile mules with no staying power at all.

All credit to OUP, then, for reserving a space for the individual scholar (who is not in the least, as I emphasized above, a 'lone' scholar) in traditional disciplines; long may this continue. The OUP operation is also, of course, a team effort and as well as Peter Momtchiloff my grateful thanks go to the others involved in bringing the project to fruition, in particular Catherine Berry, Elmandi du Toit, Nigel Hope, and Sarah Parker. Earlier in the process three readers, two glorying under the names 'X' and 'Y', and one under the name 'Stewart Shapiro', provided enormously helpful comments, the last-named going way beyond the call of duty, and I am very grateful for the time they spent on this task, a largely unsung role but an extremely important one.

Last but not least, I wish to acknowledge my debt to my family. Obviously without one's parents one would not produce any work at all. But the total and unstinting support and encouragement I received from my parents represents an endowment far beyond anything merely genetic. My father did not live to see this book emerge into the daylight, a sad but not unexpected or atypical development, given the vagaries of old age and the length of gestation of the book. What was not expected was that my sister Sharman would not live to see it either, dying in childbirth, at the end of the twentieth century, in a modern hospital. In the lengthy Fatal Accident Inquiry which followed I had cause to reflect on the differences between following a career in clinical medicine and a career in an abstruse and unpractical area such as theoretical philosophy. One thing which struck forcibly was the direct relevance, for example in the debate between classical statisticians and Bayesians, or the debate about the rationality of double blind clinical trials, of theoretical philosophy to life-and-death matters. There are indeed areas where philosophy could have a beneficial impact, but not of course if the philosophy is of poor quality, its worth judged on irrelevant criteria.

The regret that I feel in not being able to say, triumphantly 'there, I got it finished at last', is, needless to say, a trifling one in the context. My sister would have taken great interest in the book, it is true, more than I did in her distinguished career in business and the arts, and that failing is a more serious regret. But these are not the important counterfactuals one dwells on in situations such as these.

Even philosophers who have not been confronted by such a stark contrast between abstract philosophy and harsh reality must sometimes have doubts about the value of their calling. It must, one hopes, be a rare philosopher who never thinks 'what am I doing here' or 'what use is all this stuff' whilst doing philosophy—listening to some rarefied discussion which seems very far removed from the pressing concerns which have weighed down the vast majority of our fellows throughout history and which show no signs of abating, and may indeed become worse. But most of us, on reflection, overcome such thoughts; we should then have the courage to stand up for our profession, its intrinsic worth and the value of public support for it in societies rich enough to afford an intellectual life. Or if we do not convince ourselves of this, give up philosophy and become doctors or gardeners, or whatever, instead.

An alternative profession may have provided more 'street cred' for my children, but they seem to have been not quite as embarrassed at having a philosopher father as I supposed they might. They have grown up, pretty much, along with the book; but the trials and joys of working on a book do not quite match, in their extremes, those of bringing up children. As regards my long-suffering wife Ann, what can I say? Whilst all around expressed scepticism about whether the book would ever appear so, too, did she; thus vindicating my faith in her essential good sense, notwithstanding the counterexample provided by her marrying me.

I have resisted the temptation to fill the book with excerpts from those of my papers which, in part, represented work in progress, with but a few exceptions. For these, I am grateful to the publishers for permission to include passages from the following works. To Oxford University Press for permission to include in Chapter 5 a paragraph which closely follows one in 'Quine on Indeterminacy' in Ernest Lepore and Barry C. Smith (eds.), *The Oxford Handbook of Philosophy of Language*, (OUP, 2006), ch. 11, pp. 233–49, and in Chapter 8 for a couple of paragraphs taken from 'Naïve Truth and Sophisticated Logic' in *Deflationism and Paradox* (OUP, 2008), pp. 218–49. Secondly, I am grateful to Professor Jean Paul van Bendegem, editor of *Logique et Analyse*, for permission to include a paragraph or so from 'Naïve Set Theory, Paraconsistency and Indeterminacy I', *Logique et Analyse* (1998), pp. 219–66. My struggles with naïve set theory, in fact, provide one last excuse for delay since it was only comparatively late in the day that I decided my attempts to develop (by contrast with Graham Priest's dialetheism) a consistent but still powerful naïve set theory require a separate treatment. This I intend to do next, but nobody who knows me is holding their breath!

To my mother and in memory of my father and sister Sharman

# Contents

# Introduction

The doctrine of mathematical realism, or 'platonism' as it is often called, has many attractions, not least among them being simplicity. For platonism takes mathematics very much at face value and then reads the obvious semantics into mathematical theses. Thus a mathematical sentence such as '3 is prime' is superficially very similar in structure to a sentence such as 'Calum is tall'. Just as the latter sentence ascribes a property to an individual so too, it seems, does the former, if surface grammar is to be taken for our guide. Since it is fairly clear that numbers are not denizens of the ordinary spatio-temporal world, such mathematical sentences, for the platonist, describe a timeless world of abstract particulars whose interrelationships are immune from the vicissitudes of our life amidst the causal flux.

As well as simplicity, platonism would seem to have the additional virtue of explanatory power. For its realist stance enables it to account for the independence of mathematical domains from the cognitive abilities of those who introduce them—discover them, the platonist would say. In any interesting mathematical structure, an unending succession of new and often surprising facts emerges from ongoing mathematical investigation and a limitless supply of questions remains to be answered (with no mechanical decision procedure for providing answers to each and every one of them). This is as we would expect, if the mathematical realm is completely independent of us and our intellectual powers. Moreover, mathematical truths are necessary truths, or so it has traditionally been held. At any rate, their epistemic status seems qualitatively distinct from even the most well-attested empirical truth. Platonism can seem to explain this, if one supposes that abstract objects, being immutable, are necessary existents.

The platonistic conception of mathematics as providing knowledge of the immutable also has, for some, a quasi-religious attraction. Bertrand Russell wrote of the consolation mathematics seemed to offer him, in early life, when beset with the woes of our ephemeral and careworn world. Mathematics, wrote Russell, is '[r]emote from human passions, remote even from the pitiful facts of nature' and a realm 'where pure thought can dwell as in its natural home, and where one, at least, of our nobler impulses can escape from the dreary exile of the actual world"[1].

But there is also a strong intuitive pull away from platonism. It is not difficult to find the idea that mathematics provides us with details of a realm of causally inert, timeless, and non-localized objects hard to swallow. For those of an empiricist or naturalist bent, in particular, the thesis that we can have knowledge of objects and properties which stand in no causal or spatio-temporal relation towards us has often seemed implausible or downright incoherent. Furthermore, the platonist has difficulties explaining how mathematics has managed to be so spectacularly applicable to the physical world, if it charts an entirely different realm.

The epistemological difficulties which attend platonism are well known (see Benacerraf 1973); but we need presuppose no special epistemological theory (a causal theory of knowledge, for instance) to see the problem. It is evident if one looks at the matter from the perspective of naturalized epistemology (Quine 1969), whether or not one views this as the whole of legitimate epistemology. Assume that a world of abstract mathematical items exists—or, for comparison, assume that a world of trees, stones, and rivers exists—but bracket one's belief, if one has it, that one *knows* (or justifiably believes) that such entities exist. Now attempt, using any element of one's overall world-view—for the naturalist, this will be the world-view provided by contemporary natural science—to account for this knowledge. Clearly this test would be far too stringent if we required a complete account of our knowledge; we cannot even do that for our knowledge of trees and stones, never mind transcendental or transfinite numbers. From the other direction, it would be near-trivial if all that was required was that the claim to know our theory of the world, including its mathematical aspects, was consistent with that theory. Assuming our overall theory T is logically consistent (and says nothing about knowledge) then ⌜T & we know that T⌝[2] is logically consistent.

But a knowledge claim, though not flatly inconsistent with our overall theory, may introduce a gap into our picture of the workings of the world which we have no idea at all how to fill. For naturalists, this is the case with Cartesian dualism, and in particular its conception of other minds. That is, suppose we add to our theory of the workings of the physical world, including our body and brains, the idea that conscious awareness is an attribute or mode of a non-physical soul and do not seek to question how, in the first-personal case, brain and soul interact. How, though, do we acquire knowledge of the attributes and events going on in other minds? It is hard to

---

[1]    From 'The Study of Mathematics' in *The New Quarterly* 1907, quoted in Russell (1959, p. 210).

[2]    Here ⌜ and ⌝ are Quinean corner quotes indicating quasi-quotation as in his *Mathematical Logic* (1940, §6). Each string book-ended by these signs represents a non-empty set S of concatenations, each of the same length as the string. If the *i*th term of the string is a metalinguistic name of an expression, this expression is the *i*th term of each of the concatenations in S. Variables range over all non-logical or mathematical constants. Assigning a constant to each such variable yields a singular term standing for a member of S and only members of S can be arrived at in this way.

see how we could have any such knowledge unless there is interaction, relatively invariant in its form, between the bodies which we perceive by ordinary means on the one hand, and changes in souls on the other, though each of these souls is completely lacking in any spatial location.[3] This is something utterly inexplicable from the perspective of current physical science; there is no well-confirmed and explanatorily successful theory charting regularities or correlations relating brain states and soul states.

The hypothesis of the existence of mind-independent trees and stones suffers from no such gaping chasm. It is true that we lack a fully comprehensive theory of how we can know, through perception for example, of the existence and properties of trees and stones. It is still a highly contentious matter whether a naturalistic account of perception and consciousness is even coherent. But we possess, from within a naturalistic framework, an increasingly detailed account of how the properties of trees and stones interact, in a systematic and structure-preserving way, with changes in our sensory organs and then in our brains. So, in the absence of a complete theory of mind (which no philosophical position can, at the moment, offer), our common sense conception of a world of mind-independent macroscopic objects is in pretty good epistemic shape. We have journeyed a little way into the brain, as it were, and have seen how it can reliably track certain features and changes in the surrounding environment. I do not mean to suggest that we can simply dismiss traditional scepticism completely in favour of naturalized epistemology. The point is that naturalized epistemology imposes a non-trivial test of internal stability which some world-views pass fairly easily and others seem to stumble over. It may be, though, that further, more stringent tests, are legitimate or even obligatory.

Now how does mathematical platonism fare, when put to the test by naturalized epistemology? Very badly I suggest. This is particularly true if one focuses not so much on *justificatory* matters, as has usually been the case in discussions in the philosophy of mathematics, that is on questions of our entitlement to believe or claim to know mathematical theses; the problem for platonism is considerably more severe when one turns to *conceptual* questions which arise in what one might call *naturalized semantics*, that is the naturalized epistemology of that very special knowledge we have when we know the meanings of expressions. How do we even grasp the concept of a prime number, or a transcendental number, or an harmonic function? For our grasp of the concept of a tree or a stone we might make a start by appealing to discriminatory abilities we can display towards stones and trees of various different characters. It is evident that platonism cannot get off the starting blocks at all in any such way. The platonist response is often to appeal to some form of semantic holism. Our grasp of mathematical concepts, just like that of theoretical concepts in the physical sciences (indeed, for extreme holists, even concepts such as those of 'tree' or 'stone') is not to be

---

[3] Indeed, even if there is such co-variance, it is still hard to see how we could grasp the concept of other minds on the Cartesian view of minds.

explained one-by-one in terms of recognitional abilities. Rather we understand each member of a vast system of concepts by our grasp of whole theories, and in particular of the logical interconnections among the syntactic components of the theory.

I will attack this picture of mathematical understanding, and indeed theoretical understanding in general, in Chapter 5, §III. If these attacks are well-founded, then platonism looks highly suspect, at least as suspect as Cartesian dualism, from a naturalistic perspective.[4] Arguably, indeed, it is in worse shape. Difficult though it may be to see how Cartesian souls can interact with physical bodies, since they persist and change through time such interaction does at least make some sort of sense, certainly on broadly Humean notions of causality. Since I accept, as a general methodological maxim, the prescription that one should push a naturalistic approach as far as it will go, I take this epistemological problem with platonism to be a powerful motivation in favour of anti-platonism in mathematics.

But all is not plain sailing for naturalism. I have talked freely thus far of this 'ism' but of course the term, like all such, can be used in different ways with different shades of meaning, even in a fairly limited context like philosophy of mathematics. I would distinguish two broad strands of naturalism: *methodological naturalism* and *ontological naturalism*.[5] The methodological naturalist assumes there is a fairly definite set of rules, maxims or prescriptions at work in the 'natural' sciences, such as physics, chemistry and molecular biology, this constituting 'Scientific Method'. There is no algorithm which tells one in all cases how to apply this method. Nonetheless there is a body of workers—the scientific community—who generally agree on whether the method is applied correctly or not. Whatever exactly the method is—such virtues as simplicity, elegance, familiarity, scope, and fecundity appear in many accounts—it involves centrally an appeal to observation and experiment. Correct applications of the method, the methodological naturalist goes on, have enormously increased our knowledge, understanding, technological powers, and control of the world around us to an extent which would scarcely be imaginable to generations living prior to the age of modern science. The methodological naturalist therefore prescribes that one ought to follow scientific method, at a level of sophistication appropriate to the problem at hand, whenever attempting to find out the truth about anything and whenever attempting to understand any phenomenon.

The paradigm of an anti-naturalist in the methodological domain is someone who holds a view on the basis of an appeal to an authority whose credentials are not in turn based on experiment or observation. The authority of religious leaders and sacred texts is the standard example as this does not typically seem to rest on observation or experiment in the usual sense. A related anti-naturalist method is appeal to internal 'intuition' or some mystical form of revelation or apprehension, distinct from

---

[4] Neo-logicists such as Hale and Wright (2001) will disagree. I pose some further difficulties for platonism, including their brand, in Chapter 4, §II.5*.

[5] Cf. Weir (2005a).

ordinary sense perception, in order to justify a belief or attitude whose object is supposed to be an external entity or phenomenon.

The ontological naturalist holds first of all that the ontology of the natural sciences consists of physical objects and perhaps also physical properties and relations. Explaining just exactly what these are is a somewhat delicate matter, even in the case of physical objects. The most obvious account in the latter case is a Cartesian or quasi-Cartesian one. Physical objects are extended in space and time; they occupy a region of space and an interval in time, or in post-Einsteinian terms, occupy a region of spacetime. Even that is not entirely unproblematic given interpretations of quantum mechanics in which it is said that fundamental particles lack definite position. Explicating what it is for a property to be physical is more tricky still.[6] At any rate, let us concede to the ontological naturalist that we have a rough idea of what is meant by a physical ontology. The ontological naturalist's position is then straightforward: everything which exists is physical, either a physical object or, if such entities are countenanced, a physical property or relation.[7] Such a naturalist, then, will reject platonism, consigning it to the intellectual junkyard along with Cartesian dualism. I have suggested that she has strong epistemological reasons for doing so.

However, naturalists of either stamp, by their very nature, place great reliance on the physical sciences. But these are thoroughly saturated with mathematics. Moreover, mathematics, on the surface at any rate, provides a counter-example to methodological naturalism, a veritable Trojan Horse in the naturalist's citadel. The central mathematical method of proof from axioms shares one feature with empirical science, namely the key role of deduction of conclusions from premises; indeed this role is far more central to mathematics than science. But there is a crucial difference. Whereas the ultimate premises in science are hypotheses and conjectures ripe for testing against experiment, in mathematics they are 'axioms', known a priori. For those in the Kantian tradition, this knowledge arises through some form of intuitive awareness. The epistemic role of the axioms in mathematics, then, seems uncomfortably close to that played by the insights of a mystic.

On the ontological side, we have seen that mathematics seems to commit us to an ontology even more unnatural than that of the substance dualist. It is not at all clear that the ontological naturalist can simply reject the platonistic philosophy of mathematics without also losing rational entitlement to the results of mathematics itself. Quine and Putnam (Putnam, 1972—for discussion see Colyvan, 2001) have argued that, since the mathematical and empirical components of the sciences cannot be extricated, we are committed to the existential consequences of our mathematical as well as our physical theories, and thus to an infinity of mathematical entities which surely cannot be identified with physical objects, properties, or functions. Ontological

---

[6] Cf. Weir (2003b) for some suggestions.

[7] I set to one side, as not particularly relevant to the current issue, more varied or baroque ontological categorizations invoking events, or tropes or states of affairs, conceived of as distinct from objects, properties, and relations.

naturalists, therefore, have to respond either by denying the indispensability of mathematics to science, as does Hartry Field (Field, 1980) or by somehow trying to neutralize the apparent ontological commitment to a vast array of abstract entities inherent in mathematics, pure and applied. It is the latter course I will follow, since I think that mathematics, even if theoretically dispensable as an inference engine in the sciences, is conceptually indispensable in generating our theoretical concepts (Chapter 5, §III). I will aim, in other words, for an anti-realist but 'face-value' reading of mathematics in which we take all its theorems, including those asserting the existence of vast infinite realms of mathematical entities, to be true yet without commitment to the existence of any mathematical objects at all, in mind-independent reality.

How can this be? How can we have our cake and eat it in this fashion? My approach requires a *heterogeneous* conception of assertoric language. That is, where some see all assertions as working in essentially the same way, as representing, correctly or incorrectly, the way things are in a reality independent of us—what things there are, what properties and interrelationships they have—I side with those who see assertion as more variegated. There are various modes of assertion ('assertion' being used in a minimally theoretical sense). All have in common the existence of a non-subjective distinction between correct and incorrect assertion. All are true when it would be correct to assert them,[8] false otherwise. But not all assertions work by representing the world. Other non-representational *modes of assertion* might work by, for example, expressing or projecting our internal attitudes on to the world. Even in these cases, there are correct ways to do so, resulting in true assertions, and incorrect ways, resulting in untrue ones. And in the mathematical case, I will discern a further, distinctive mode of non-representational assertion.

In Chapter 1, then, after isolating some aspects of the thorny notion of 'realism' which are of interest, I defend this multi-mode notion of assertion by appeal to a key distinction, between the *informational content* of utterances of sentences on the one hand and their *metaphysical content* on the other. The first is roughly speaking what philosophers have meant by 'literal content' or 'cognitive content'; it is in the same ballpark as Frege's *Sinn*. The second sets out the circumstances which make-true (or make-false) the utterances,[9] circumstances which may not feature in the informational content. The metaphysical content should explain, in some sense, what it is which makes the utterances true when they are true, though the concepts invoked in this explanation need not be ones which the utterers themselves are aware of.

---

[8] I do not take it as following from this that we must be capable of verifying whether or not an assertion is true or false; 'correctness' will be explicated in a way devoid of rational normativity, so that a completely unjustified 'lucky guess' can nonetheless be a correct assertion.

[9] One might talk here of the 'truth-makers' for the utterances but I would be wary of this talk unless it is made clear that one is not thereby committed to 'situations', 'states of affairs', 'facts', or similar, propositionally structured, entities which some hold (dubiously in my view) to be ingredients of reality.

I illustrate these ideas in Chapter 2 with, firstly, a version of projectivism and then with an anti-realist but non-projective approach to discourse about fiction. These are used to introduce and to motivate the informational/metaphysical distinction and as evidence that it is not ad hoc; however, my account of mathematical assertions will not take a projectivist form at all. Rather, I will attempt to revive 'formalism', indeed a formalism of a pre-Hilbertian sort often referred to as 'game formalism'. After the assault on this kind of view by Frege in his *Grundgesetze* II, §§86–137 (Frege 1903/80), formalism has fallen into disrepute. In its original form, it deserves no better. Its revisionary conception of mathematical utterances as never used to make truth-valued assertions is, I agree, untenable. I will argue, however, that we have thrown the proverbial baby out with the bathwater and will attempt to resuscitate and nurture to maturity an intellectual offspring of the formalist movement using the ideas of different modes of assertion and of distinctions in the type of content a sentence can have.

For a mathematical claim like Kant's time-honoured '$7 + 5 = 12$' '*neo-formalism*', as I will call my revised version of formalism, proffers no non-trivial synonym or illuminating paraphrase or analysis. The theory is a 'hermeneutic one', in the terminology of Burgess and Rosen in their invaluable book on nominalism (1997, pp. 6–7) and has nothing much to say at the level of informational content. However, the metaphysical content, the content which explains the conditions which make an utterance true, or make it false, is non-representational. What makes such utterances true is the existence of proofs of them, what makes them false is the existence of refutations. But though competent speakers must therefore be sensitive to the provability or refutability of mathematical claims, this awareness need not be very explicit or reflective and the notions of provability and refutability form no part (in general) of the informational content of mathematical judgements. The mode of assertion of such judgements, I will say, is *formal*, not representational.

In this way, the apparent inconsistency of face-value mathematical anti-realism is to be resolved. There are infinitely many primes, such an anti-realist avers (face-value acceptance of mathematics), although of course there are no primes at all (ontological anti-realism). The existence claim is made in formal mode, and what makes it true is the existence of proofs of strings which express the infinitude of the primes. The negative claim is made in representational mode and what makes it true is the absence in the world of any entities such as numbers, construed as platonists construe them, and of properties of numbers such as primeness.[10] As an aid to clarity I will often adapt a convention attributed to Putnam[11] and write claims which I deem to be in

[10] This is a somewhat stronger claim than the neo-formalist needs to press. The key idea is that mathematical theorems can be true or useful whether or not there are any abstract entities which correspond to the traditional conception of mathematical objects.

[11] I am following here Terence Horgan (1994, p. 316) and Hilary Putnam, from whom Horgan borrows the device of writing words in small capitals when intending to 'be talking about denizens of the mind-independent, discourse-independent world'.

representational mode—and which concern the existence or otherwise of abstract entities—in SMALL CAPITALS.[12] Thus the neo-formalist contentions take the form seen in:

There are infinitely many primes but THERE ARE NO prime numbers.

It may seem that this requires the neo-formalist to discern an ambiguity in uses of 'exist' and similar terms in English. However I argue in Chapter 2, §III and in Chapter 3, §II.1, §III.2 that, if there is ambiguity here at all, the ambiguity is not one of the usual sort investigated by linguists. It is not lexical, nor an ambiguity of scope nor deep-structural ambiguity; it is not an ambiguity at the level of informational content at all.

Now one of the classic criticisms of formalism is that by explaining mathematics in terms of the existence of proofs and refutations of mathematical sentences the formalist gains no appreciable ontological advantage over the platonist. For there are infinitely many sentences, proofs, and disproofs. Therefore, since there are only finitely many concrete utterances, the ontology of syntax and proof theory is an ontology of abstract entities—symbol types and sequences thereof—just as much as is that of mathematics (cf. Dummett 1991a, p. 225). This is widely (and rightly) held to be a compelling refutation of traditional game formalism.

In response, the neo-formalist has to explicate all the syntactic notions which figure in the metaphysical content of mathematical utterances in purely concrete physical terms. The ontology of neo-formalist syntax is an ontology of concrete tokens. Hence the metaphysical content of an utterance of '7 + 5 = 12' is that it is made-true just in CASE THERE EXISTS a concrete structure which IS, (or could be interpreted as) a proof of a token of '7 + 5 = 12' according to the rules which we use in our ordinary arithmetical calculations. In this way, mathematics and naturalism are reconciled. We can make true assertions (in formal mode) whose metaphysical content carries no ontological commitment to abstract objects. The metatheorist can explain what makes the assertions true by appealing only to relations between mathematicians (sophisticated or otherwise) and concrete tokens.

Clearly such an account incurs an obligation to explain proofhood in purely concrete or nominalistic terms (and to provide an assurance that the modal element 'could be interpreted' harbours no hidden commitment to abstract objects). This obligation is discharged but not until Chapter 6 since the specification of the nature of concrete proof makes little sense except when set in the context of an account of the formal structure of syntax and proof theory. This is given in Chapter 3, in terms of the existence of proofs and refutations, rather than the EXISTENCE of concrete proofs and concrete refutations. The reader is asked, therefore, to accept this apparently platonistic talk in Chapters 3–5 until the pledge to cash it all out in concrete terms is redeemed in Chapter 6.

---

[12] Often but not always, for to attempt to do so would be (a) difficult and (b) sore on the eyes! I will use small capitals when wanting to emphasize the representational nature of the existence claims.

In Chapter 4 I look at some fairly obvious objections to neo-formalism and compare it in relevant aspects to certain rival positions, platonist and non-platonist. Knowledge of some of the contemporary literature will be useful in following the dialectic of Section II.5* and I have starred it (and Chapter 5, §II*) to indicate this. Similarly I have starred two sections in Chapter 8 which require more than the usual knowledge of logic and basic set theory which most analytic philosophers acquire. These sections, however, are not essential to grasping the nature of neo-formalism and I have tried to present the rest of the book at a level which will be understood by anyone with basic knowledge of logic and the traditional questions and positions in philosophy of mathematics.[13]

In Chapter 5 I address a crucial problem for any philosophy of mathematics—explaining how mathematics, prima facie an a priori, non-empirical subject, can be so astonishingly useful in its application to understanding, predicting, and controlling the physical world. The neo-formalist answer invokes another mode of assertion, a 'mixed' mode which occurs when we combine purely mathematical and empirical vocabulary—'the number of apples in the bowl is even'. The metaphysical contents of such assertions invoke (in general) twin sources of truth; on the one hand, true, purely empirical, claims, made-true by the external physical world and possessing representational metaphysical contents. The other source is the body of formally true mathematical principles, including 'bridge' principles linking mathematical and non-mathematical vocabulary. In the starred Section §II*, I compare neo-formalism's account of applications with one which has heavily influenced it, Hartry Field's fictionalism, arguing for the superiority of the neo-formalist account.

As remarked, Chapter 6 attempts to redeem the pledge to provide purely concrete accounts of proof and of metaphysical content for mathematical judgements in general. A purely concrete ontology of tokens, however, particularly if they are all supposed to be comprehensible to humans, would seem to generate enormous difficulty in accounting for mathematics. Many utterances, including perfectly comprehensible ones, are plausibly thought of as having no concrete proofs or disproofs purely because there is not enough material or time in the universe to construct them. It is clearly necessary, then, to invoke some form of idealization to get round this problem. I contrast two different ways to do this. In slogan form, one way is to 'idealize the person', to imagine mathematicians with powers and capacities which no human, indeed arguably no physical being, could have. The second part of Chapter 6 attacks this common tendency to talk of 'ideal beings' and 'in principle possibility' as being no more acceptable to a naturalist than appeal to supernatural beings in explaining the emergence of life.

Chapter 7 offers a rival and, I argue, better account of the nature of idealization in syntax and proof theory. In slogan form one idealizes the language rather than the person. Somewhat less cryptically, one idealizes by asserting the existence of a function

---

[13] For an excellent introduction to philosophy of mathematics, see Shapiro (2000c).

from the concrete tokens of actual mathematical utterances into the infinite structures of the syntax of formal languages. The 'existence' assertion here is a normal font one rather than a small capitals EXISTENCE one; for such mathematical existence claims have metaphysical content which is partly formal and not purely representational. True, such an existence claim is a piece of *applied*, not pure, mathematics. Its truth is partly based on truths about EXISTING things, namely concrete tokens; but only partly. The idea is that one assesses the correct norms for logic and inference in mathematics, for example the extent to which instances of the law of excluded middle (P $\vee$ $\sim$P) hold, by reference to theoretical investigations of formal languages, not by reference to physiological, as it were, considerations of actual capacities, memory spans, etc. So long as THERE EXIST concrete tokens of the theorems (including the existential theorems) of the applied mathematics which one needs in the idealization, then it is permissible for a neo-formalist to use the theorems of the idealizing theory. It is argued that this not only enables us to escape the clutches of debilitatingly strong forms of finitism in mathematics, it also reveals that the emphasis on the finite nature of proof, which took hold in logic after Gödel's work in the 1930s, is a harmful prejudice which should be abandoned. There should be no size limit on the abstract structures which can be invoked in idealizations of our finite corpus of mathematical utterances.

The matter of idealization in syntactic theory is thus tangled up with logical issues. Is neo-formalism, for example, compatible with espousal of classical logic, or at least with holding it is acceptable to use it in mathematics? This raises very deep and important questions about the nature of logic which are too weighty to be tackled as a side issue in a monograph devoted to a separate topic. In Chapter 8, I present a system of logic, weaker than classical logic in lacking the law of excluded middle but nonetheless still quite powerful (it contains the rule of double negation elimination, for example, which is rejected by the intuitionists). Justification or vindication of this logic as correct is out of place here (the whole question of what correctness amounts to in logic would have to be addressed, for one thing). Rather, the logic is used to investigate the extent to which the neo-formalist is entitled to reason classically in standard mathematical disciplines such as arithmetic, analysis and set theory. Since the neo-formalist ties truth closely to provability (at the idealized theoretical level), provability has to conform to a 'primality constraint'. If a sentence (A $\vee$ B) is true and thus provable, one of the disjuncts must be true (here I presuppose the falsity of supervaluationism). Thus either disjunct A or disjunct B must be provable. In the case where B = $\sim$A—the law of excluded middle—this can only be upheld for 'decidable' sentences A, sentences such that either A or its negation is provable. (Where this holds for all A, we have 'negation-completeness'.) For the more interesting classical theories this is not the case in the usual formalizations. Chapter 8 argues that a correct idealization using the resources of infinitary logic shows the usual formulations to be unnecessarily weak; negation-complete versions of arithmetic, analysis, simple type theory and a highly idealized set theory are presented. It is acknowledged that for the most part these theories are not part of 'really existing mathematics' but it is argued, by appeal to prime or negation-complete extensions of standard theories, that use of classical logic in these cases can be justified in these 'real' cases too, though with some question marks hanging over the higher flights of set theory. Neo-formalism emerges then as doctrine with teeth but for the most part one which does not bite, a non-revisionary viewpoint in which classical practice in the standard mathematical areas needed in the sciences is vindicated but without the problematic ontological commitments of platonism.

A final chapter summarizes the conclusions arrived at, attempting to evaluate what has been achieved by the neo-formalist and what problems still remain.

# 1

# Metaphysics

## §I  Traditional Realism

In the first few sentences of this book I introduced, without much ceremony, the doctrine of 'mathematical realism'. However it is a well-known feature of many debates about 'ism' words that they have a tendency to degenerate into fruitless terminological disputes. Although terminological matters are of secondary importance, still some attention has to be paid to clarification of what one means by 'realism', for it has been particularly bruised and battered in this way. As Crispin Wright has illustrated (Wright 1992), there are in fact multiple strands to the notion of realism as it crops up in contemporary philosophical debates. I will not attempt to provide an alternative mapping of this conceptual terrain, rather I want to separate out two particular aspects of realism and set in place a (fairly orthodox) semantic framework in terms of which these aspects can be investigated.

But though sufficient clarity regarding the meaning of expressions like 'realism' and 'anti-realism' in the ensuing discussion is the most important desideratum, nonetheless when dealing with an expression with a distinguished philosophical history there will be a tendency for readers to interpret the word in traditional ways. For this reason my aim will be to get an optimal pay-off between fidelity to historical usage, or a central element of historical usage, and presentation of a doctrine which is interesting and plausible in the current philosophical climate. In particular, one should avoid interpretations of 'realism' which render the doctrine trivial or absurd. Realism is trivial if it is simply the negation of theses such as 'everything is in the human mind' or 'nothing exists unless humans perceive it'. Only the insane believe such things and it is a grave injustice to saddle philosophers such as Berkeley with theses of that kind. Nor is much gained by defining realism in terms of kindred, and similarly obscure notions, such as objectivity, without giving an independent account of the latter. Even worse are hand-waving attempts to characterize the notion using virtually meaningless formulae—the realist believes the world is really out there, and so on.[1]

By the same token, one should not encumber realists with absurdities which no serious member of the realist tradition actually maintained. One example to be avoided is characterizing realism as the view that we can compare our theories with an unconceptualized reality to check for fit.[2] Only extreme empiricists, some of the positivists perhaps, could plausibly be interpreted as holding such a view, and they could hardly be termed realists.

If one attempts to employ the word in a way consonant with its historical usage, one finds two specific forms of realism are often distinguished: (i) medieval realism regarding the existence of properties; (ii) the dispute between direct realists on the one hand and phenomenalists and representationalists on the other. The first dispute resurfaced, no doubt in a rather mangled and distorted fashion, in twentieth-century philosophy, for example in the 'debate' between Quine's McX and his Wyman in 'On what there is' (Quine 1948/53). Realists in this debate argue that predicates such as 'is wise' stand for mind-independent correlates—here the property of wisdom—just as names such as 'Socrates' stand for independently existing objects. Their opponents, the 'nominalists' in the medieval sense,[3] argue that 'is wise' applies meaningfully and truly to some mind-independent objects and fails to apply to others without it being the case that it too stands for some mind-independent entity distinct from the objects it is true of.[4] Insofar as predicates designate anything at all, they designate mind-dependent entities such as concepts.

As for the other main historic form of realism, that found in the philosophy of mind, the direct realists emphasize the distinction between the act of perceiving and its object.[5] The latter, where it exists, is a mind-independent entity, the direct realist maintains, whereas the act of perceiving (and perhaps also its content, if any) are clearly mind-dependent. The real core of direct realism, however, consists in the (not unproblematic) idea that there is no intermediary between perceiver and perceived. The most extreme opponents of direct realism reject (or fail to see) the distinction

---

[1] Nor, contrary to an apparently widespread perception, are 'really out there' or ' "really" out there' any clearer than 'really out there'.

[2] As Putnam seems to suggest—Putnam (1981, p. 130); cf. Devitt (1984, p. 193).

[3] Not to be confused with the modern sense in which nominalism consists in the rejection of abstract *objects* or *particulars*. The modern view is neutral on the nature and existence of *properties* or *universals*. 'Concretism' is perhaps a better name for the modern doctrine.

[4] There is no doubt that the concept of mind-independence is a complex, problematic, and contested one, in almost as much need of clarification as 'realism' or 'objectivity'. I add a few bystander comments on the issue in §II.3, but a full elucidation of the notion would require a substantial engagement with general metaphysics which is out of place here. I think there is enough common understanding of the meaning of the term among the contestants for my use of it to be clear enough for the purposes of this section.

[5] Twardowski (1894) argued for a tripartite structure of act, content (e.g. that a tree is in front of one), and finally the object. But introduction of content will be unwelcome to some direct realists. The direct realists were rather patronizingly called naïve realists when the sense-datum theory was in vogue but the 'naïve realist' tag is now being worn as a badge of pride by those who reject any representational intermediary in perception and who will thus be wary of the very idea of perceptual content.

between the object of perception and the act. They are thus inevitably forced to the conclusion that the immediate objects of perception are mind-dependent entities—ideas, sense data, or what have you.[6]

Leaving aside, though, the merits or otherwise of these two traditional forms of realism, what is it that they have in common? What makes them both species of realism? Well, in both disputes, realism about universals versus nominalism and conceptualism, direct realism versus phenomenalism and representationalism, the general pattern seems to be that realism affirms the mind-independent existence of some sort of entity (properties, or objects of perception), whereas idealism or anti-realism denies it. There is an essential ontological element in realism, in other words, an affirmation of the existence of certain types of thing outwith the mind. What form, though, does the dispute take in current philosophy?

## §II  Contemporary Realism

### §II.1

In contemporary analytical philosophy the 'realism versus anti-realism' dichotomy seems to be used to cover two somewhat different sets of problems, only one of which seems closely related to the traditional disputes. The more traditional set of problems arises in the philosophy of science where the realism/anti-realism dichotomy is often drawn in terms of scientific realism versus instrumentalism. The instrumentalist distinguishes between observational and theoretical sectors of language and maintains that only sentences of the former sector are objectively true or false. Theoretical sentences are instrumentalistically useful to the extent that their observational consequences turn out to be true but, insofar as the instrumentalist allows that sentences of the theoretical sector can be true or false at all,[7] this can consist in nothing more than such predictive utility or disutility. A more nuanced position adds to predictive power other theoretical virtues such as simplicity, elegance, perhaps even beauty. It is notoriously difficult to see how such factors can be other than anthropocentric. If there can be underdetermination of theory by evidence[8] then the instrumentalist is pushed strongly in the direction of a relativistic view of truth for scientific theory, though if it is required that underdetermined theories must not merely entail the same observational consequences but also tie on such factors as degree of confirmation, or on the other virtues such as simplicity and beauty, the drive to relativism (if not the drive to anti-realism) is perhaps weaker.

---

[6] For a rejection of any element of representation in perception, see Weir (2004c).

[7] An instrumentalist who accepts a deflationary notion of truth and is prepared to assert theoretical sentences she believes to be instrumentalistically useful will allow that scientific sentences are true or false but still maintain the asymmetry with the observational sector.

[8] See Weir (2006b, §III) and references therein.

For the scientific realist, by contrast, even if one can draw a significant distinction between observational and theoretical sectors, which some doubt, there is no asymmetry in respect of truth and in particular in terms of what makes sentences true (or false). Sentences from either sector are rendered absolutely true or false by a mind-independent world. Scientific realism is also often taken to include the anti-sceptical view that science, if correctly pursued, progresses closer and closer to the truth, and that the theoretical terms of current science are not empty but refer to mind-independent entities with natures of roughly the same type as those we ascribe to them.[9] It may be conceded that progress towards truth is not inevitable but rather that assiduous application of scientific method makes such progress 'highly likely', 'well-confirmed', or the like. The notion of probability here cannot be utterly subjective and personalist if this aspect of scientific realism is to have any bite.

Scientific realism, then, in its orientation towards ontological questions concerning the existence of theoretical entities, seems to be a realism in much the same sense as the traditional doctrines in metaphysics and philosophy of mind. But 'realism' is also currently used as a name for certain fallibilistic doctrines. And the linguistic turn in much modern philosophy has led in turn to fallibilism being interpreted as, at least in part, a semantic, not an ontological, doctrine. *Truth* for sentences is not determined by the evidence in favour of the propositions they express; truth is 'verification-transcendent' or 'evidence-transcendent', as Crispin Wright has put it (Wright 1993, pp. 3–10 and *passim*). Both Michael Dummett and Hilary Putnam, for example, take realism to be a semantic-cum-epistemic doctrine upholding this evidence-transcendence of truth. Dummett writes (1963/78, p. 146):[10]

Realism I characterise as the belief that statements . . . possess an objective truth value, independently of our means of knowing it.[11]

---

[9] Cf. Newton-Smith (1981, p. 39), Boyd (1983, p. 45). This optimistic anti-sceptical theme obviously sits in great tension with the notion of mind-independence, if the latter is construed in the sceptical fashion discussed later. A realist about science who takes the sceptical line on mind-independence will deny that there is any rational guarantee of convergence to truth.

[10] Though he also adds immediately a clause incorporating a belief in a mind-independent reality as part of realism. But it is clear from e.g. the preface to *Truth and Other Enigmas* (1978, pp. xxviii–xxix) that he thinks that the 'cash value' of this mind-independence phrase is to be found in the connection, or lack of it, between truth and epistemic notions.

[11] For Dummett the Law of Bivalence—every proposition is either true or false—is crucial to 'realism'. In his earlier writings, indeed, bivalence was not viewed as an essential ingredient of realism. For he allowed that there are reasons a realist might have for not affirming bivalence in a certain area (cf. Dummett 1978, pp. xliii–xliv), and one might think that reasons relating to topics such as vagueness and 'empty' names give one reason to abandon bivalence without abandoning realism. However, in later writings (e.g. 1982/92, pp. 264–6; 1993, pp. 467–8), Dummett abandons this view and argues instead that it is necessary for a realist about a particular region of discourse to uphold bivalence for this region, though this is not sufficient to establish one's credentials as a bona fide realist. It is also necessary that *truth* and *reference* play an explanatory role in the *theory of meaning* proffered by the realist. This would rule out the combination of deflationism and realism but there seems nothing in the historical usage of the term 'realism' to justify such as a stipulation. See further Dummett (1981b, ch. 20), (1991a, ch. 20), (1993, ch. 20).

Putnam in a similar vein (1978, p. 125) has the metaphysical realist hold that truth is

*radically non-epistemic*—we might be 'brains in a vat' and so the theory that is 'ideal' from the point of view of operational utility, inner beauty and elegance, 'plausibility', simplicity, 'conservatism', etc., *might be false* [italics and scare quotes in the original].

Against this, he himself thinks (1983, p. 210, see also 1990, pp. 110–11) that

truth becomes a radically epistemic notion.

But what can it mean to say that truth is radically non-epistemic? To say only that humans get some things wrong, hold some false beliefs, is utterly platitudinous and uninteresting. To say that everything we believe might be wrong, by contrast, is very radical. Even if we narrow our attention to a restricted area of discourse, fallibilistic formulations such as Putnam's above suggest taking realism about a specific area of discourse, about the external physical world say, to amount to the view that we can never be certain about the truth-value of sentences in that area, not even sentences such as 'there are trees' or 'there are stones'. But this is surely to take us very far from historical realists—they were not radical sceptics. Indeed, as remarked above, in the case of scientific realists, we can discern a very strong anti-sceptical bent.[12] Realists in the traditional sense are typically as certain as Dr Johnson of the existence of spatio-temporal relations, physical objects, trees, people etc. without in any way impugning their realist attitude towards these entities.

So we might try a second way to interpret the epistemic conception of anti-realism, one which is, paradoxically, more metaphysical. According to this second 'metaphysical fallibilist' construal of realism, the possibility of error is read in a non-epistemic, 'metaphysical' way. Metaphysical possibility deals in ways the world might have developed, even though it actually did not. Not so ⌜It is epistemically possible that $p$⌝; this means that the actual truth of $p$ is compatible with what I (or the community to which I belong) know. This contrast between epistemic and non-epistemic possibility is, I believe, relatively unproblematic, and is comprehensible to every first-year philosophy undergraduate.[13] I know I am in Belfast just now and was not in Sydney, Australia five minutes ago; there is no epistemic possibility of it being the other way round. Yet it could have turned out, even though I know it has not, that I was in Sydney, not Belfast, at this time. This 'could have turned out', is non-epistemic possibility. It is true that there are more obscure and problematic cases: can a human person be a dot-sized, fertilized cell, is backwards causation possible, and so on? But we can allow that the question of whether a view is realist or not, under this construal of possibility, may not always be perfectly determinate or clear.

Having given the notion of metaphysical possibility a relatively clean bill of health, how do we use it to explicate realism? The idea is that sentence $s$ of a given

---

[12] Cf. Wright (1993, pp. 4–5), Heal (1989, pp. 16–17).
[13] Well, that was true when I first started writing this book anyway.

community's language has realist truth-conditions iff it is a metaphysical possibility that everyone in the community grasps *s* (with its actual meaning) but fails to believe it even though it is true; or else that there is a similar possibility that they fail to disbelieve it though it is false. So one can be a realist about 'the universe existed more than five minutes ago' even if one is certain that it did and one is aware of that certainty, even if one is not prepared to say 'the universe might, for aught I know, be only five minutes old'. One is realist if, for example, one allows the metaphysical possibility of a universe whose initial state is identical to that of our universe five minutes ago and whose future states—including the states which constitute our understanding sentences the way we do and believing in the sentences we do believe in—succeed earlier ones in exactly the way ours do.

To make sense of this idea we need in addition to the notion of metaphysical possibility also the notion of truth. But only a relatively neutral aspect of this notion is required, essentially just satisfaction of the Tarskian T-schema for the relevant fragment of discourse under discussion, a schema with instances such as:

> 'The universe is more than five minutes old' is true iff the universe is more than five minutes old.

Now deflationists hold that conformity with the Tarskian 'disquotational' schema is all there is to the notion of truth (though the paradoxes do cause problems here, see Weir 2005*b*); or perhaps that the naïve rules for truth[14] exhaust the notion or (for those happy with the notion of analyticity) are analytic of the notion of truth. But even those who think there is more to the concept of truth than this ought to accept that conformity with the schema is at least partly constitutive of truth.

It will be rightly objected, however, that the 'metaphysically fallibilist' characterization of realism is too weak if it amounts to nothing more than the mere admission that there is a (non-epistemic) possibility of error for *some* (or even many) sentences (of a given, significant region of discourse).[15] This much is platitudinous and so should not be used to define a contentious metaphysical position such as realism. One standard way round this, in epistemic accounts of realism, is to take the realist to be committed to the possibility of error even in optimal conditions for belief formation. The realist about a certain class of beliefs holds that such beliefs, even if arrived at in the best conditions for arriving at beliefs of that type, can (non-epistemically) be wholly false. Putnam's supposedly 'neo-Kantian' perspective, contra such realism, is that

the only sort of truth we can have an idea of, or use for, is *assertibility* (by creatures with our rational natures) *under optimal conditions* (as determined by our sensible natures).

---

[14] Allowing us to derive the left-hand side of instances of the T-schema from the right-hand side, and vice versa.

[15] Reading the modal operator as having wider scope than the quantifier, i.e. with the reading $\Diamond(\exists s$: we believe $s$ but $s$ is not true).

(Putnam, 1983, p. 210, author's italics, see also the preface to that collection *Realism and Reason*, pp. xvii–xviii)

However, characterizing optimal belief situations is quite a tricky matter. Clearly truth is identical with optimal belief where an optimal belief is simply defined as one which happens to be true. But while this notion of 'optimal belief' can be ruled out of court, it is not so easy to substitute a more acceptable and informative account. One might simply say with Putnam (e.g. 1990, pp. vii–ix) that it is not possible to give an informative characterization but that nonetheless the notion of better or worse epistemic situations makes sense. We can often add more informative detail in particular cases without ever being able to *reduce* truth for a sentence *s* to some other notion, usually, indeed, presupposing the truth of other sentences in specifying optimal situations for *s*. But this position is rather unsatisfactory. Putnam seems to be claiming that there is, for each sentence, a more or less a priori link between its being true and its being verifiable in conditions which are optimal for that type of sentence. But why, unless one hoped (contra the deflationist) for some non-trivial analysis or specification of truth in epistemic terms, believe in this link any more than believe in an *a priori* link between being true and being *wished for* in some optimal emotional state (calm, reflective etc.)?

## §II.2

At any rate, if we can indeed make the notion of optimal conditions sufficiently clear (whether through explications of the above sort or not) then we can fine tune the idea of 'metaphysical fallibilism'. We can distinguish, first of all, the '*strong fallibilist realist*', who holds that being true and being verifiable (justifiable, warranted or whatever) in optimal circumstances are not 'metaphysically equivalent', from the *weak fallibilist*, who drops the qualifications about optimal circumstances. Strong fallibilism is a form of anti-verificationism: for the strong fallibilist, there are, or at least there might be, some true propositions which could not be verified (under the metaphysical reading of 'could not') even in optimal circumstances for investigating that type of proposition. The anti-realist, that is the opponent of realism in the above sense, is, therefore, a verificationist.

What I am now calling weak fallibilism was earlier dismissed as uninterestingly platitudinous, it being obvious that we could go wrong, in some circumstance or other, for *some* (or even many) sentences of any philosophically interesting region of discourse. However, introducing the notion of optimal circumstances is not the only response one could make to restore interest: another is to strengthen the embedded quantifier to a universal one. As noted above, the view that we might be wrong about *everything* is very radical, indeed I would say literally incredible, where 'might' is read epistemically. Is there a believable doctrine to be had, when we change the modality to the metaphysical one? We now have two parameters to play with: firstly the strong/weak one, with the former invoking epistemically optimal circumstances, and now a second distinction between versions of fallibilism restricted to a subset of sentences, and unrestricted versions. Since realism is often relativized to particular areas of discourse, we can consider only 'relatively unrestricted' theses, where we universally generalize not over all sentences of a speaker or community's language, but all sentences of an area of discourse.

This gives us the following clutch of related theses:

*Unrestricted Strong Fallibilism* (about region of discourse R): For *every* sentence *s* in R it is (metaphysically) possible for speakers to believe *s* in optimal conditions though it is not true or disbelieve *s*, again in optimal conditions, though it is not false.

*Restricted Strong Fallibilism*: For *some* sentences *s* in R it is (metaphysically) possible for speakers to believe *s* in optimal conditions though it is not true or disbelieve *s*, in optimal conditions, though it is not false.

There are parallel weaker versions:

*Unrestricted Weak Fallibilism*: For *every* sentence *s* in R it is (metaphysically) possible for speakers to believe *s* though it is not true or disbelieve *s*, though it is not false.

*Restricted Weak Fallibilism*: For *some* sentences *s* in R it is (metaphysically) possible for speakers to believe *s* though it is not true or disbelieve *s* though it is not false.

Of course restricted fallibilism relative to region of discourse R transmutes into unrestricted fallibilism relative to region $R^* \subset R$, if we shrink R down to an $R^*$ which contains only sentences speakers can go wrong about, in the appropriate way, in R. So the restricted/unrestricted distinction is only significant if it is granted that there are fairly natural divisions of language into different, salient and interesting, kinds of discourse—the language of physics, or folk psychology say. Unrestricted versions of fallibilism will be of little interest if relativized to a region which is artificial or gerrymandered.

Now how does strong fallibilism relate to the popular account of realism as the denial of the equivalence of *p* with *p* is knowable, with anti-realism thus defined as affirmation of $p \leftrightarrow \Diamond Kp$?[16] Such anti-realism has well-known defects. As Fitch showed, one can prove from this the absurd conclusion that every truth is known, in an ordinary sense of 'known', granted only fairly weak assumptions about the epistemic 'logic' of 'known' (specifically that K*p* entails *p* and K(*p*&*q*) entails (K*p*&K*q*)) plus very basic modal propositional logic.[17] One can, indeed, escape absurdity by denying the distributivity of knowledge over conjunction or by rejecting classical logic in favour of intuitionist logic, accepting $p \rightarrow \sim \sim Kp$ under intuitionist construals of $\rightarrow$ and $\sim$. But both these moves are rather desperate.

---

[16] This is ambiguous of course, depending on which person or group one takes to be the knowers and how one construes the notion of possibility involved.

[17] See Timothy Williamson (1982; 2000, ch. 11). We need only the standard definition of $\Diamond$ and the rule that the necessitations of theorems are theorems.

However it is not clear that the anti-realist of the above stamp is committed to $p \leftrightarrow \Diamond Kp$. Suppose, for instance, one identifies truth for a sentence with there being better grounds for it than its negation (or perhaps with its having higher probability than its negation) in all, or most, anyway, optimal cases. Then it does not follow that if a sentence is true there could have been a situation in which it was known (as opposed to merely being reasonably thought to be probable). What does follow is only that we cannot have truth for $s$ where in (most) optimal circumstances we would disbelieve $s$, nor falsity where in the ideal case we would believe it. Even so, verificationism still has trouble with 'blindspot' propositions (Sorensen 1988) such as 'there is non-sentient plant life in another galaxy and no conscious being will ever have good grounds for believing this'. It would seem that the verificationist simply has to say that no such proposition can be determinately true, a very counter-intuitive course.[18]

Many other problems arise with verificationism, of course, even sophisticated forms which eschew anything like phenomenalist or operationalist reductionism. The verificationist is committed to the coherence of some such notion as justified assertion, warranted assertion, or whatever, where justification and warrant for a sentence must come to more than just widespread communal assent or high subjective probability, if verificationism is not to degenerate into unbridled relativism. For what is to count as a community with a shared norm of warrantedness? If it is only a shared understanding of language and a propensity to arrive at similar verdicts, then to identify truth with a high degree of warranted belief in the 'community' is to allow that pretty much everything is true, relative to some community or other, with no grounds for privileging one community over another except parochial or egotistical prejudice in favour of one's own current band of like-minded peers.

The verificationist, therefore, in order to avoid an extreme and pernicious relativism, has to adopt a highly credulous attitude towards notions such as 'rational warrantedness relative to the evidence' or 'objective epistemic probability'. The idea that the notion of objective rational warrant is a more secure notion than the (fallibilist) realist's conception of truth is, to be blunt, a nonsense, as the history of attempts to make sense of objective but non-statistical notions of probability highlights. Simple frequency theories and, less simply, propensity theories of probability, interpret probabilistic judgements in a broadly statistical fashion. Thus interpreted, they make claims about the universe (94.75 per cent of all ravens, past, present and future, are black) which are as objective as non-statistical claims which equally transcend current evidence. Is there a measure of the *rational credibility* of such claims, relative to the given evidence, a measure with the same objectivity as claims about logical entailment (whatever exactly that is—no easy question)? Carnap's investigations into inductive

---

[18] These propositions are a subspecies of the type Tennant calls 'Anti-Cartesian', a category which includes, for example, propositions such that judging them to be true requires their falsity (e.g. the proposition that there are no thinkers). He argues (1997*b*, pp. 272–6) that the truth = knowability equation only applies to Cartesian propositions and maintains that this restriction not only leaves a substantial, non-trivial principle in its wake but in addition, and more contentiously, is not ad hoc.

logic and similar programmes attempted to show there is such a probabilistic measure, but I think the consensus is that no such programme has shown any signs of succeeding.[19] This should make us very wary of the anti-realist's notion of 'rational warrant' or 'assertibility conditions' for they seem to occupy the same territory.[20]

One might, nonetheless, have confidence that the problems of verificationism could be met (and what theory does not have problems?) if the arguments in its favour were compelling. But, on the contrary, the best-known arguments in favour seem to depend on an outmoded empiricist epistemology. One highly empiricist approach to sentence meaning starts from the idea that the meanings transmitted and learnt in language-learning (and made manifest in one's linguistic outpourings) cannot *transcend* the empirical circumstances of the learning. Such strong empiricism leads some verificationists to their identification or replacement of the notion of truth with epistemic notions such as verifiability or justified assertibility and to their denial that beliefs arrived at in optimal circumstances can be false. Critics of such views counter that far from resting metaphysics on the secure foundational base of philosophy of language, verificationism has been founded on an outmoded epistemology, specifically a crude empiricist theory of the acquisition and transmission of knowledge of linguistic meaning. The Chomskyans will say, for instance, that the empirical circumstances of language learning may act only as a catalyst activating a largely innate cognitive state of understanding which can transcend its experiential inputs.

## §II.3

Anti-realists deny any such dependence of their views on crude epistemology or on a 'reductionist' view of mind; I am sceptical about the denial. But whatever the merits or demerits of the verificationist anti-realist's case, it still seems to me unfruitful to characterize realism, about a particular area of discourse, in strong fallibilist terms— as rejection of some sort of 'ideal verifiability' theory for the sentences of that region; and for essentially the same reason as in the weak fallibilist cases. Unrestricted strong fallibilism, applied to any interesting region of discourse, is a much stronger doctrine than is historically associated with the term 'realism'. Indeed this is the case even for unrestricted weak fallibilism. For there are plenty of sentences which are such that a realist, in a fairly traditional sense, would deny that there is even a metaphysical possibility of error in any circumstances, including optimal ones. For example, someone with a strongly naturalist view of the mind will reject the metaphysical possibility that the sentence 'there are physical bodies' could be false but believed true. Add in a Humean view of belief as not under the direct control of the will together with the claim that a belief in physical bodies is inescapable and one is led to conclude that there is likewise no non-epistemic possibility of believing that there are no physical bodies (though a Cartesian might delude herself into falsely

---

[19] Though see Jon Williamson (2005, ch. 5).
[20] Cf. also Timothy Williamson (2000, §4.8) and Weir (1986c, p. 472).

thinking she can choose to believe this).[21] A philosopher who holds these naturalistic-cum-Humean views about bodies and beliefs may well bridle at the suggestion that she is an anti-realist about physical bodies.

On less contentious assumptions, 'there are believers' poses a similar problem.[22] One can be a realist about the existence of believers and yet deny that an entire community could ever think, certainly in optimal conditions, that there are none; and, of course, 'there are believers' could not be falsely believed (whatever eliminativists may say).

Traditional realists are convinced that there are minds, human bodies, spatio-temporal relations, and so on. They, or many of them anyway, reject even the metaphysical possibility that we could be in error about these matters and yet are realists about all these entities (or about propositions concerning these entities if one wishes to put this in a more Dummettian form). So even weak fallibilism of the unrestricted type, a fortiori the stronger version, seems more sceptical a position than traditional realism with respect to regions such as discourse about the physical world or ordinary folk psychology. Since restricted weak fallibilism is too weak, this suggests restricted strong fallibilism as the best candidate for a Dummett/Putnam style characterization of realism. But is even this in keeping with philosophical tradition? Consider discourse about the physical sizes, shapes, and distances between objects in our everyday macroscopic world. Clearly we can be in error as to whether Seán is taller than Iain or not. But in optimal circumstances? Insofar as one can make sense of optimality here, this might be disputed by many philosophers. But do they *ipso facto* reject the reality of the properties and relations of shape, distance, and so forth which obtain among the everyday objects we deal with? This does not seem right and this in turn tells against fallibilistic formulations as a way of making sense of the traditional realism debate.

Hence, though of course one is free to use 'realism' as one pleases, I find myself in sympathy with Devitt in wishing to return to a traditional 'ontological' characterization of realism as belief in mind-independent existence. Devitt writes, for instance (1984, p. 3):

I urge: *Maxim 2* Distinguish the metaphysical (ontological) issue of realism from any semantic issue.

He characterizes common-sense realism as the belief that most common-sense objects 'objectively exist independently of the mental' (ibid., p. 22).[23]

---

[21] Admittedly it is unclear whether this is a 'metaphysical' impossibility. As noted earlier, the notion of metaphysical possibility is somewhat obscure and hence sometimes leads to problematic cases in characterizing realism, and this type of sentence might well be one of them.

[22] Devitt (1984, pp. 13–14) formulates realism as belief in an objective *non-mental* world. But he acknowledges that one can be realist about minds, excluding this from his account of realism because of the complications it would generate for him.

[23] Robert Burns, in his poem 'The Dream', wrote 'Facts are chiels that winna ding and downa be disputed'. This seems to link robust realism with an *anti*-fallibilist attitude. There is no room for

On the other hand, I noted in §I the problematic nature of 'mind-independent'. Putnam comments (1990, p. 30):

What does it mean, apart from a certain philosophical controversy, to speak of 'mind-independence'?

Devitt recognizes himself (ibid., p. 4) that an epistemic element comes into the characterization of 'mind-independence'. The Putnam/Dummett elucidation of mind-independence in terms of fallibilism does chime with many themes in the realist tradition. To reject fallibility (at the optimal limit) is to engage in a sort of species vanity, a refusal to accept that reality might far outreach our cognitive limits. The rhetoric is familiar. We are insignificant in the cosmic scale of things, products of billions of years of evolution on a planet surrounding a very ordinary star in an ordinary galaxy, one of billions of such galaxies. Natural selection has ensured we represent the world accurately enough to survive (thus far), but why think it bestows on us the ability to penetrate into the innermost secrets of the cosmos, past, present, and future, to penetrate to the basic physical workings of the most far-flung regions?[24] This is preposterous anthropocentrism which we should have thrown off after the Copernican revolution.[25]

Such rhetoric does strike a chord with many realists. Certainly it does in this author's case. The anti-realist might attempt to deflect accusations of species vanity by identifying truth with the ideal belief of a cognitive subject who need not be human. However, the accusation of 'thinker-vanity', an overestimation of the powers of cognitively endowed, thinking beings such as ourselves but including also any extraterrestrials there may be (who, from a naturalistic perspective, would also have to have evolved from simpler materials), can be set forward in almost the same terms as

---

disagreement and uncertainty where facts are concerned, for Burns, and in this he is perhaps expressing a widespread attitude among non-philosophers and also those philosophers for whom convergence in an area of discourse is a mark of realism.

[24] But why should natural selection have given us even the ability to *speculate* plausibly about theoretical matters far removed from immediate survival value or to develop pure mathematics? And why has pure mathematics been so useful in theoretical applications? Eugene Wigner (1967) and Mark Steiner (1998) discuss this. Thomas Nagel's realism extends beyond accepting that there can be evident-transcendent propositions to embracing the likelihood that there are aspects of the universe which we cannot even conceptualize (Nagel 1986, ch. 6). This too chimes well with the rejection of species vanity.

[25] Neil Tennant makes the counter-charge that the realist displays 'semantic hubris' in claiming to grasp evidence-transcendent propositions (1997b, p. 49). This is a strange charge. Propositions are on the mind side of the mind/world divide. There is no hubristic over-stretching in claiming to be able to reach as far as them but not necessarily on out into the world, to whatever grounds their truth or falsity. Similarly there is no hubris in claiming to be able to imagine or conceptualize running a mile in a minute, but there is in claiming to be able to do it. To claim to have a more extensive conceptual system than some other community (or species), to claim that they can only grasp an 'evidence-immanent' subset of the propositions you can grasp, is to make a claim of semantic superiority. But clearly some conceptual systems among communities and species on earth do extend or go beyond others. Only the claim that one's own system was at least as extensive as that of god-like beings could be classed as hubristic. As is the claim that the human mind can lay bare any of the hidden features of the universe, in any region of spacetime however large or small, however distant.

for human thinkers. (And what would this putative cognitive subject and its powers have to do with the truth-conditions of sentences of our language?)

Can we effect a compromise, a Devitt-style 'ontological' characterization of realism with respect to a given set of entities as constituted by a belief in their mind-independent existence, where mind-independence is, in turn, characterized in fallibilist terms à la Putnam and Dummett? And can we do this without saddling the realist with radical scepticism or an unattractive conception of what is naturally or 'metaphysically' possible?

The simplest such proposal would characterize a realist with respect to Xs as someone who holds, firstly, that some areas of discourse are evidence-transcendent, in the Dummettian sense, so adopting a modest estimation of the relation between mind and world, and who secondly affirms that Xs exist. The first strand I will call the metaphysical element, the second the ontological.[26] These are the two strands which I mentioned at the outset I wished to distinguish. However we need to tie the two strands together more closely if we wish to achieve a plausible characterization of what it is to affirm the mind-independent existence of Xs. Someone who holds to evidence-transcendent truth and affirms that Xs exist should not count as a realist about Xs if the affirmation of the existence of Xs, though sincere, should not be taken at face value or else should not be read in a straight, representational fashion.

To illustrate the first case, someone might affirm that there were three witches who appeared before Macbeth and affirm this as sincerely as she avers that there were three Allied leaders who met at Potsdam at the end of the Second World War. Yet such a person need not be a realist about witches. Even if she believes in evidence-transcendent truths, she is not a realist about such beings if, in other contexts, she denies that witches exist. One way she can exculpate herself from the charge of inconsistency is by saying that 'There were three witches who appeared to Macbeth' should not be taken literally but is really elliptical for: 'It follows from the text of Shakespeare's play that three witches appeared to Macbeth'. Whether this is a good account of fictional discourse is not what is at issue here (I say a little more on this in Chapter 2, §1.2–3). The point is rather that this is a fairly clear way in which affirmation of ⌜X's exist⌝ should not, in all circumstances, be taken as indicative of a realist attitude towards Xs.

For a more complicated but more relevant example of this type of anti-realism consider the 'modal constructivism' of Charles Chihara (1990). In this theory, a sentence such as 'Prime numbers exist' is mapped onto a different modal one. The modal correlate expresses the claim that it is possible to construct a second-order open sentence of a particular type—a 'cardinality attribute' (ibid., p. 81)—intuitively

---

[26] Devitt, as we have seen, runs 'metaphysical' and 'ontological' together, in contrast with 'semantic'. But I have agreed sufficiently with Dummett on mind-independence to tie the metaphysical and semantic closely together and contrast them with ontological questions of existential commitment. This separation of ontological versus metaphysical aspects is quite common, cf. Miller (2008), Brock and Mares (2007), and Shapiro's 'realism in truth-value' versus 'realism in ontology, (2000c, ch. 2.2).

attributing a cardinality to the property expressed by a first-order sentence. This second-order sentence in turn satisfies a third-order sentence (corresponding to the property of being prime). The modal sentence, Chihara says, can be true even though there are no abstract objects. The notions of possibility and satisfaction essential to his account are best thought of, he says, as primitive, susceptible to no illuminating, non-trivial analysis. Nor should we suppose that in talking of the possibility of construction we refer to any real capabilities which we have (Chihara 1990, p. 46). Chihara acknowledges that his constructibility sentences do not mean the same as the mathematical theses they are associated with. The idea is that they can perform the same function in everyday life and in science.

Clearly Chihara should not be interpreted as a mathematical realist (in a sense including the ontological element). Even though Chihara is prepared to assert mathematical existence claims and also, as I understand him, to allow that some of these can be evidence-transcendent, the existence claims have to be 'de-coded' into another language in which it turns out that they are not existence claims at all.

So the realist about Xs, we should say, not only countenances mind-independent truths and affirms that Xs exist, but we require further that she does not cancel the existential affirmation in some way, for instance by insisting it should be read non-literally. Even if we think the literal/non-literal distinction is determinate enough to filter out uninteresting ontological realisms, this however is not the only, nor the most interesting, way in which apparent existential commitment should be written off as merely apparent. For the more interesting case I turn to a rather different strand of 'reductionist' anti-realism.

## §III Sense, Circumstance, World

### §III.1

The scare-quoting of 'reductionist' was deliberate, for sometimes this term is used as little more than a derogatory epithet, often by opponents of some form of identity thesis. But an identity claim is not a reduction, since the identity relation is symmetrical, whereas reduction is asymmetric. It might be said that if one claims all members of some category F are identical with members of a proper subcategory of category G, *but not* vice versa, we have a reduction. So the claim that mental states are a subcategory of the category of physical states is reductionist, since not all physical states are mental. On the other hand, if this subsumption of the mental and the physical were true then for any subclass of the mental states, the pains say, we can expect there to be a physical predicate, say a predicate N of neurology, no doubt inordinately complex and disjunctive, which picks out just those mental states,[27] the pains. Hence the N states are a proper subcategory of the mental states, but not all mental states are N states. We

---

[27] Using this broadly to cover processes and events too.

therefore have a reduction in the other direction, of certain neural states or processes, the N states, into the mental. But this goes against the exceptionless nature of the asymmetry between mental and physical we usually have in mind when talking of reduction of the mental to the physical. (Not to mention the fact that on this view we get the rather odd result that males 'reduce' to humans, as do females, the copper coins in my pocket reduce to the totality of all the coins in my pocket, and so on for a host of other such cases.)

Little wonder, then, that analyses of the concept of reduction usually take it to be not a purely ontological notion but rather one which holds, at least in the first instance, between theories, the *reducing* theory and the *reduced* theory. In the simplest case, the mapping relating the two is said to preserve truth-value: if the map $\mu$ takes A from the reduced theory to $\mu(A)$ in the reducing theory, then A and $\mu(A)$ are either both true or both false (or perhaps both neither). (It might also be held that in a good reduction, the reducing theory is true, or approximately true.) But, taking theories to be closed under logical consequence and thus infinite, there are always such truth-preserving mappings between two theories (expressed in languages of the same cardinality), if both lack false consequences or both have false consequences. Hence we need to look for more subtle and structured mappings and an account of why the mappings are in some interesting sense asymmetric—from reduced theory to reducing, rather than conversely. Such accounts are found in Kemeny and Oppenheim (1956), Nagel (1961, ch. 11) and Mostowski, Robinson, and Tarski (1953).

I want to develop a somewhat different notion of ontological, rather than linguistic, reduction, which I will apply to the mathematical case. A key building block is a distinction between different aspects of meaning which I will dub *informational content* on the one hand versus *metaphysical content* on the other, a distinction which will be crucial to the whole argument of the book. By 'informational content' I intend something similar to the notion or notions others have expressed by terms such as 'cognitive content', 'literal content', or—by Frege—'*Sinn*'.[28] Needless to say, these phrases are not entirely precise in their 'meaning', and will not be used in exactly the same way by different theorists to express one and the same idea. Frege's notion, in particular, is often held to be overloaded, used by Frege to fulfil too many disparate semantic functions.[29] I take the basic idea, still with Frege as guiding light, to be that informational content is abstracted from an equivalence relation among sentences specified in terms of *epistemic* attitudes such as assent and dissent or believing true/believing false. Two sentences have the same informational content if, holding context fixed, speakers would assent to (dissent from) the one iff they would assent to (dissent from) the other.[30] Parts of sentences can be assigned the same informational content

---

[28] I used the terms 'literal content' and 'explanatory truth-conditions' to describe the dichotomy in Weir (1993, pp. 261–2), but now think the current terminology less misleading.

[29] See John Skorupski (1984, esp. pp. 228–36) and John Perry (1979).

[30] The modal element 'would' is crucial, see Peacocke (1992). I intend nothing Quinean here: there is no reference to stimulation and keying of response to stimulation; as remarked, I take the idea to be broadly

if substitution of one for the other in any sentence leaves informational content unchanged.[31] Thus informational content is a relatively transparent aspect of language: if two terms have the same informational content for speakers then with a little reflection they should be able to see this.[32]

Thus I take 'Iain kicked Seán' and 'Seán was kicked by Iain' to have the same informational content. Holding context fixed, we competent speakers would assent to (dissent from) one just when we would assent to (dissent from) the other. The same goes for sentences related by very obvious logical transformations, a sentence and its double negation (at least for those espousing classical and related logics) or a sentence and its self-conjunction, for example. Another case might be substitution of an obvious and widely accepted synonym for a word or phrase. (Even one who rejects the analytic/synthetic distinction, or the epistemological slant put on it anyway, could accept that, as a matter of fact, there are pairs of sentences related in such ways to which speakers match their verdicts, in any context.)

What it is for context to remain fixed is not a precise matter. Moreover, I have no analysis, certainly no tight, non-trivial necessary, and sufficient conditions, for 'sameness of context'. Similarly I do not doubt that the ingenious can dream up situations in which competent speakers assent to a sentence but not to its passive transformation or vice versa, or more generally differentiate epistemically two sentences of the sort which I have claimed share informational content. But these would be highly atypical situations, and not relevant to our understanding of the meaning of the sentence. Again, I have no analysis in terms of necessary and sufficient conditions of what counts as a 'typical' situation in this context. One must rely on one's competence in the language and one's common-sense judgement as to what is typical and what extreme. Some unfortunates lack such judgement and perhaps sometimes in philosophy others merely pretend to lack it.

Now philosophers of language have seen fit both to draw finer distinctions, breaking up sentences, or at least sentence utterances, with the same informational content into distinct subcategories, and also grouping expressions more broadly, equating expressions with distinct informational content according to some wider

---

Fregean in inspiration. The condition given, moreover, is only a sufficient one for the existence of the equivalence relation: cf. Gareth Evans's 'Intuitive Criterion of Difference' for thoughts (Evans 1982, p. 18). Ambiguity blocks extension of the criterion to a necessary condition. We do not want to say that in an utterance of 'that is a crane' directed at a bird, 'crane' has the same informational content as in an utterance directed at a lifting apparatus. But we cannot apply the epistemic attitude test since we cannot hold the context fixed. However, I do not, for present purposes, need a complete theory of informational content. All I need is to make it plausible that some such notion is coherent and important in philosophy of language, and is to be differentiated from what I am calling 'metaphysical content'.

[31] Quotational contexts, and the like, threaten to wreck this criterion, but I would take them to be excluded by the 'context fixed' clause.

[32] This is not an absolute matter. For those whose beliefs, at least in a particular area, are rather opaque to them, it may not be clear that they would assent to (dissent from) $s$ just when assenting to (dissenting from) $s'$. But the notion of informational content, as will become clear, is a lot nearer to the surface, as it were, than that of metaphysical content.

criterion.[33] But the other key notion I wish to introduce, the notion of metaphysical content, is orthogonal, in conceptual space, to these sorts of concepts. It has its home in a *metatheoretic* account of speakers' language in which one hopes to shed some explanatory light on what it is for a speaker to grasp or understand a particular expression. An important feature of such accounts is that a metatheorist will often have to appeal, in explaining grasp of expression $\varphi$, to concepts which form no part of the informational content of $\varphi$ and of which the speaker herself may lack reflective awareness.

For a simple example, consider the following account of what it is to grasp sentences in which 'this' or 'that' occurs demonstratively. Suppose we try to explain our knowledge of their meaning in terms of salience. ⌐That $\varphi$ is a $\psi$⌐ holds in a context of utterance, one might claim, just when the most salient (for the utterer) $\varphi$ in that context is a $\psi$. To know the meaning of such utterances is to know this, in some sense. But what sense? For one might grasp ⌐that $\varphi$ is a $\psi$⌐ without having the concept of salience itself.

For the beginnings of an answer we can say that speakers might judge that utterances of such sentences are true just when, allowing for explicable error, they judge that $\alpha$ has the property designated by the substitution for $\psi$, where $\alpha$ is the $\varphi$ most salient for them in the context of utterance—most salient *according to the metatheorist's conception of salience*. Here the *analysandum* does not have the same meaning in the intuitive sense as the *analysans* (and the main philosophical work, for those who follow this approach, will go into explaining further the notion of salience). Since competent users of 'that' need not have the concept of salience, the *analysandum*, in conformity with our intuitions about meaning, does not have the same informational content as the *analysans*. One can believe the former without even being able to grasp the latter.

Informational and metaphysical content can come apart even for speakers who have the concepts which the metatheorist employs in order to explain how they use their words meaningfully (when the metatheorist theorizes on her own language, for example). This can be seen if we look at propositional attitude, modal, or temporal contexts. Thus the speaker may accept

one hour ago, that table was in the storeroom

on any of the readings which she finds natural but on at least one reading of

one hour ago, the most salient table was in the storeroom

---

[33] A broader notion is that of having the same truth-conditions. The usual understanding is that $p$ and $q$ have the same truth-conditions just when they are materially equivalent or else perhaps when they are necessarily equivalent. The latter are *strict* truth-conditions in Martin Davies's phrase—Davies (1981, p. 28). He challenges the identification of truth-conditions and Fregean sense at p. 40. Sameness of informational content, however, is certainly a more fine-grained relation than having the same strict truth-conditions.

not accept the latter sentence. She may know that the table which was most salient to her and her audience an hour ago is a different one from the one which is salient now but was in the storeroom an hour ago.

Two further illustrations.[34] Some philosophers have hoped to give, or sketch, an account of vague language in a precise, or more precise, metalanguage; and some have tried to give an account of indexical and related context-dependent discourse—use of tense, personal pronouns, etc.—in a context-independent (or less context-dependent) metalanguage.[35] In each case, I claim, the project requires us to distinguish informational content from metaphysical content. 'I had a headache yesterday' does not have the same sense or informational content as 'the utterer has a headache the day before the utterance'. However the latter sentence not only gives the circumstances under which utterances of the former are true but does so in an illuminating fashion; or so proponents of such an approach will argue. A competent user of the first-person pronoun and of tense must grasp the sensitivity of truth-value to the earlier facts about the utterer, whether or not she can theorize about that grasp. For example, she must modulate her verdicts to, on the one hand, ⌜I had property $\varphi$⌝ as uttered by S just now and, on the other, ⌜N has property $\varphi$ before $t$⌝ in such a way that, where she believes 'N' refers to the individual S before her now, grasps the general idea of times, and believes it is now $t$, the two verdicts agree.

So much for illustrative examples. Can something more general be said in characterization of 'metaphysical content'? I intend that it play a role in a theoretical framework which shares this much with truth-conditional theories of meaning: to give the metaphysical content for a sentence is to specify, for all the contexts in which it might be uttered, those circumstances which render it true, as uttered, and those which render it false (and to specify them in a context-independent, or at least less context-dependent, fashion). Since the vast majority of the sentences we utter are context-dependent, sentences capturing, in a general way, truth-conditions for such sentences will not be synonymous with (share informational content with) the sentences whose truth-conditions they give. Furthermore the conditions we set out should *explain*, or at least be part of an explanation of, what it is for us to grasp the expression. They must not specify conditions which 'accidentally', as it were, correspond to the conditions under which the sentence is true and those under which it is false. Rather they must illuminate the linguistic abilities which must be displayed by speakers competently using the phrase or term (speakers who might not reflectively be aware of this illuminating account). It is in this way that the metatheoretic account

---

[34] In giving these illustrations I am not intending to provide a substantial and compelling argument in favour of the semantic ideas underlying them, though in fact I find those ideas plausible. The point, rather, is more to provide examples of semantic theories which have *some* degree of plausibility and which show how one might appeal to truth-conditions which are not part of a sentence's informational content as part of an explanation of grasp of the relevant sentences.

[35] 'Presentists' will deny that a fully context-independent language is possible just as Williamson casts doubt on the possibility of a 'citadel' of vagueness-free language from which to carry through the semantic metatheory (Williamson 1994, p. 169).

brings out the sense in which speakers know, e.g. that certain types of demonstrative pick out salient items in the environment, even if they lack the concept of salience.

This notion of explanatoriness is not precise, of course, since there can be disagreement not only over whether an account explains our grasp of the informational content of some class of sentences but even over whether it is a candidate explanation. One person's good explanation can fail even to be a bad one, to someone else. But it is no more a failing in a characterization of a notion that not everyone agrees on when it applies than it is a failing in a philosophical doctrine that not everyone can be brought to agree with it.

What, then, is the difference between a sentence which sets out metaphysical content and a sentence which specifies disquotational truth-conditions? Let us say that the metaphysical content tells us the conditions under which the sentence is '*made-true*' and '*made-false*'. How could it be that s is made-true iff P holds unless P holds iff s is true? The notions can come apart in more complex contexts—such as propositional attitude, modal, and temporal contexts. If we suppose a given context held fixed, a context in which the referents of indexicals and demonstratives are held constant and relative to which tenses are determined, then:

> 'One hour ago, that table was in the storeroom' is true iff
> one hour ago that table was in the storeroom iff
> one hour ago 'that table is in the storeroom' was true.

But though it holds in our fixed context (supposing the salience account of demonstratives is right) that 'that table is in the storeroom' is made-true iff the most salient table is in the storeroom, nonetheless even continuing to hold context fixed:

> 'One hour ago, that table was in the storeroom' is *not* made-true iff
> one hour ago, 'the most salient table is in the storeroom' was made-true.

Informational content thus comes apart from metaphysical content.[36]

---

[36] This is the kind of example which led Kamp to revise Montague-style semantics in the direction of 'double indexing' (Kamp 1971; cf. Kaplan 1989, pp. 509–10). In 'He made a mistake which will cause a lot of problems' we cannot analyse the sentence along the lines '[In the past]: (he makes an $x$: (Mistake($x$) & [In the future]: ($x$ causes problems)))' since that does not ensure the problems are in the future of any utterance of the sentence. Operators like (In the past), or similar locations, can shift the values of some context-dependent terms, but others—'now' and 'actually' in many usages—'jump out' of the scope of any such operators and have their semantic value fixed by the context of the overall utterance. Similarly, 'that table' has wide scope with respect to such operators, whereas 'the most salient table' does not. I am suggesting that a good way to handle this, and shed light on the nature of the different linguistic behaviour of different terms, is through the informational/metaphysical distinction. Now the literature on these topics tends to be replete with heavy ontological commitment to entities such as possible worlds (which tend to feature in the 'circumstances of evaluation' of the shifty operators the latter distinguished from 'context of use', specifying details of token utterances). Indeed for some it is only modal, and not for example temporal, locutions which should be analysed as operators on circumstances of evaluation. Perhaps such commitment to non-actual entities can be explained away; perhaps. However I will use the notion of metaphysical content in such a way that it is 'metaphysically light' and does not commit us to such things as possible worlds in handling the phenomena which led to the idea of 'double indexing'.

## §III.2

The general theoretical framework in which the two notions come apart might be characterized as that of SCW theories of meaning with 'S' for Sense or *Sinn*, the informational content of sentences; 'C' for Circumstance (or context); and W for 'World', construed as independent, in general, of linguistic entities and linguistic acts. Versions of such theories are widely, but not universally, adopted especially by those who remain broadly within the Fregean tradition but recognize that Frege tried to pack too much into his notion of *Sinn*.

For early in his career, Frege seems to have held that to any complete utterance which we understand there corresponds, at time *t* of utterance, a *Sinn*, specifically a thought, this being a complete proposition with a unique truth-value at *t*. The sentence utterance expresses a proposition, something grasped by our minds. It asks a complete question of the world; the world supplies the answer, true or false, whether we know the answer or not. As a result context-dependent utterances, for example those containing demonstratives, personal pronouns, tensed verbs, and the like, Frege has to treat as elliptical for fuller sentences which speakers could, if asked, come up with and which express the complete proposition associated with the utterance.[37]

No one believes this now. De-contextualized sentences often do not have the same sense as the original. I could believe it is sunny without believing it is sunny in Glasgow at such a date and time. I might not know the date or time or, if sufficiently befuddled, even know where I am. This cognitive difference shows there is a difference in sense between the context-sensitive words and the 'insensitive' ones. Particularly clear counterexamples are provided by the role which indexical thoughts play in action.[38]

The first-person pronoun provides an obvious example here. I hear the airport announcer that the driver of a Fiat Punto registration RCZ9894 parked illegally out front must move the car immediately as it is about to be towed away; I smirk to myself and declare that it serves the idiot right for parking his or her car there. A sudden pang of anxiety causes me to look at the key fob of the car I just rented and I realize 'That's *my* car they are about to tow away!'. Suddenly I move faster than has been observed for many a long year.

What causes the change in my behaviour? Clearly a change in belief. But I did not burst for the exit because I had just formed the belief that Fiat Punto registration RCZ9894 is to be towed away just after 11.23 GMT on 19 October 2009 from outside the airport on the outskirts of Glasgow, Scotland, Earth, Solar System, the Universe. For I believed *that* (if I knew the date and time) while I was smugly smirking. What causes me to get moving is that I come to believe 'I am that driver!' and this is an *essentially* indexical thought. The 'I' (and the implicit now in 'about to tow away') cannot be eliminated in favour of some Fregean sense. If there are descriptive

---

[37] '[T]he same sentence does not always express the same thought, because the words need to be supplemented in order to get a complete sense' (Frege 1979, p. 135).

[38] Cf. Perry (1979).

conditions free of indexical elements which uniquely pick out me, still no such condition is operative in the thinking which underpins my action. So the Fregean idea that each utterance expresses an 'Archimedean' thought, one which can be grasped and communicated to anyone, at any place and time, is false.[39]

The SCW response to this (which can be allied to a position in philosophy of language which is otherwise Fregean) goes as follows. We start from sentences, or more concretely from utterances of sentences.[40] Utterances of declarative sentences are typically true or false, and what makes them one or the other is, in general, a triple product of firstly the *Sinn* or informational content they express, secondly the circumstances of the utterance, and finally the way the world is. The informational content of the declarative sentence we grasp by understanding the fragment of language to which it belongs; it does not in general consist in a complete thought, does not yet pose a definitive question to the world. That only happens when the world, as it were, fills in the gaps in the incomplete thought[41] (hence there is, on this way of thinking, an inherently external aspect to the complete thoughts expressed by, for example, indexical utterances). Thus 'the world' plays two distinct roles on SCW theories: it (a) completes the semantic content of utterances to yield propositions—the C-part— and (b) determines whether the resulting propositions are true or false—the W-part.

This is a somewhat surprising combination of duties which 'the world', or external objects, properties, relations, events, or whatever, perform. How is it done? Not by magic, certainly, and it is the task of (neo-Fregean) philosophy of language to come up with a satisfactory explanation of how it happens. This must involve relating words and circumstances to the linguistic practices of speakers in some illuminating way. The middle term of the triad—Circumstances—stands for a bridging aspect, neither entirely linguistic/conceptual nor entirely mind-independent but constituted by relations between certain linguistic terms (perhaps including 'unpronounced' or covert constituents) and bits of the world. The characterization of circumstances sets out which specific bits of the world are specially related to those constituents of the sentence which lack context-independent semantic value. 'The World', as it is in itself, stands independent of all links and relations to mind and language; or rather mind, language, and their links to other bits of the world are merely one grouping of aspects of the world, of no especially ontological significance, among others.

A general account of how the three layers, of context-independent *Sinn* or informational content, then relational, bridging Circumstance, and finally the World, as it is in itself, interrelate is beyond the scope of this study. I will try to give some indications

---

[39] Frege, indeed, came to acknowledge this at least in the case of first-personal thoughts. In his late article 'Thought' he talks of each of us being 'presented to himself in a special way, in which he is presented to no one else' (Frege (1918/97) p. 333), a way which cannot be communicated to others.

[40] Or from something rather more abstract generated by doing some linguistic work on concrete tokens. cf. Predelli's 'clauses', in Predelli (2005, pp. 3–6, 14ff.).

[41] This type of idea is most clearly endorsed by 'indexicalists' who think that items from the external world 'saturate' indexical parameters (which can be implicit—'unpronounced'—as well as explicit parts of the grammatical structure) in the utterance in a way constrained by semantic, rather than pragmatic, principles.

of how such an account might go in particular cases, most especially of course in the case of mathematical discourse. Here I am concerned only to reserve for the notion of 'metaphysical content' the role of recording the conditions whose obtaining or otherwise in the world *make-true* utterances made in a particular circumstance. A goal of an explanatory theory of meaning is to show how our grasp of language ensures that these conditions are generated from the informational content of the utterance and the circumstance of utterance. Thus, to be a little less abstract, in the case of the proto-theory of demonstratives, the work of philosophers of language pro-pounding a salience-type theory will be to give us a general account of what salience is and how it functions to determine the referent of demonstratives. A theory like this, though philosophical rather than empirical, does have to meet empirical constraints. The property of salience attributed must be one it makes sense to think creatures like us can empirically detect, and empirical psychology may bear on whether that is true. Salience will figure in the account of the bridging language/world relations which complete informational content in the case of context-dependent sentences; the result will be made-true or false by the world in ways encapsulated by metaphysical content.

It is important to emphasize, then, that a specific metaphysical content is a proposition; not a language-independent part of the world, but a representation of (in general) such a thing.[42] This way of approaching matters enables one to be relatively neutral on ontological matters since differences in how to read the ontological commitments of sentences specifying metaphysical content (should the predicates be taken to refer to universals, for example?) can be set to one side. Of course some ontological aspects will be explicit—if the metaphysical content ascribed to a given sentence in a particular circumstance by semantic theory T entails that there are abstract objects, then the sentence's truth is incompatible, according to T, with concretism. But the neutrality of the notion of metaphysical content means that different metatheorists can apply it in different ways. The sentence

'I might have been a great footballer'

as uttered by Weir on 19 October 2009 has the metaphysical content 'Weir might have been a great footballer'. This can be read 'homophonically' by one theorist, that is simply as 'Weir might have been a great footballer' whilst another might gloss this further as: 'there is a (fairly distant) possible world in which Weir is a great footballer'.

In sum, 'informational content' stands for, roughly speaking, the conventional meaning of expressions; 'Circumstances' represent especially highlighted, as it were, aspects of reality which figure in the theory of the language/world relations and which are involved in completing the sense of a sentence so that it can ask a question of the

---

[42] But not, however, a 'deep structure' or 'logical form'. There is no implication that the metaphysical content of a sentence need be in the speaker's mind, either explicitly or implicitly, not those parts of the mind which supervene on the brain anyway.

world; and metaphysical content specifies what makes true and makes false a sentence in a circumstance.

The SCW framework, or something quite like it, is a pretty widespread one; for example, the informational content/metaphysical content distinction is clearly in the same conceptual neighbourhood as Kaplan's character versus content distinction.[43] But not everyone agrees. Contextualists, 'radical contextualists' in particular such as Searle (1979, esp. ch. 5) and Travis (1997), in effect deny there is such a thing as informational content, something belonging to words and phrases independently of context which is grasped by competent speakers and which non-trivially helps determine the proposition expressed by utterances on occasion in tandem with features of the occasion.

Now it is only necessary for the purposes of this study that the radical contextualists be wrong about the special case of mathematical discourse (clearly one of the least context-sensitive areas of language). Nonetheless, the view of mathematics to be defended will be better grounded if it flows from a general account of language. Since this is not an essay in the philosophy of language, I can do little more here than record my disagreement with the radical contextualists and sketch the direction my criticism of it would take. In particular, I side with those who hold that radical contextualism makes language grasp a mystery, who hold that the radical view renders it inexplicable how speakers can grasp the content of any utterance;[44] and secondly, I side with those who hold that the radical contextualists underestimate the effect that the pervasiveness of vagueness in language has. Outside of mathematics, most if not all terms are vague (and arguably even inside mathematics there are areas of indeterminacy). If one rejects epistemicism and the 'glut' theory of the dialetheist, then this means that for most terms or phrases there are indefinitely many situations in which they lack a definite truth-value. Still there is this much truth in the glut theory: often it will be natural in such situations to make out a case for saying the phrase truly applies and equally find a way of reading it as falsely applying.

And this is how I would respond to the radical contextualists. The examples they point to are cases, or more usually pairs of cases, in which a term, a predicate usually, neither determinately applies nor fails to apply, though in one there may be greater pragmatic reason to assert or apply it than the other. For example, my local, 'The Drouthie Thrapple', is a smallish pub with a maximum capacity of about forty.

---

[43] Kaplan (1989, §VI (i) and (ii)); metaphysical content is most closely analogous to Kaplan's second sense of 'content' discussed in fn. 28, p. 503. The pair 'that table was in the storeroom' and 'the most salient table was in the storeroom' bears evident analogies to Kripke's pair 'Aristotle was fond of dogs' versus 'the last great philosopher was fond of dogs' (Kripke 1972/80, pp. 6–7). Appeal to the informational content/metaphysical content distinction can, I believe, account for the phenomena Kripke appeals to in support of his anti-Fregean account of singular terms and rigid designation whilst remaining within a broadly Fregean approach. But this is too large a thesis to defend here.

[44] Of course since many radical contextualists are Wittgensteinians they will happily embrace the deep intellectual nihilism, the opposition to searching for general theories of language understanding which I am taking to be a highly unattractive feature of the contextualist view.

I conjecture that, with five or fewer in the pub, one would get a consensus among English speakers that 'there are many in the pub' is false. Half-full, indeed perhaps even less, say with fifteen in the pub, it would be agreed that there are many in the pub. Assume with the indeterminist that when there are, say, between six and fourteen in the pub it is neither determinately true nor false that there are many in the pub.[45]

But now suppose that Seán has heard that the pub will be boycotted tonight because it has stopped selling 'Old Speckled Hen'; he expects that only Iain will break the boycott because he has heard this too and likes to be different. The boycott rumour is, however, false: in fact there are fourteen in the pub. Seán phones Iain and asks 'are there many in the pub?'. Iain, whose battery is about to run out on his mobile, replies briefly 'Yes there are'. At the same time, Agnes is phoning Senga. They have both heard that the pub will probably be so packed that it will have to close its doors because of a (false) rumour that St Mirren's new celebrity signing Donaldo is going to turn up. Senga, but not Agnes, has managed to get to the pub and Agnes asks the same question of her. But Senga, similarly pushed for time, replies 'no, there aren't many here'.

I think one should not say in this case that Iain and Senga spoke truly, nor say that they spoke falsely. Their claims lack determinate truth-value but there were good pragmatic (in an ordinary, non-theoretical sense) reasons for them to say what they did; there is nothing blameworthy in their (speech) actions. Against this, Rothschild and Segal say, of a somewhat similar case,[46] 'the effect is dramatic enough not to be attributable to ordinary vagueness'. Well maybe not a very ordinary case; but I take the pub example, at any rate, to be a case of vagueness nonetheless.

Furthermore, even granted that there are indefinitely many cases where such phrases lack determinate value, it does not follow in the least that these are the norm. On the contrary, it may well be that the more typical circumstances of use of simple English phrases are ones in which they have a determinate truth-value, one determined in part by the informational content of the expressions involved. Certainly on many perfectly ordinary occasions of utterance of 'Canada is bigger than the Island

---

[45] Here we see the problem which the epistemicist such as Williamson raises for indeterminist accounts, especially if they take the form of positing truth-value gaps. Any such account seems to replace a single sharp boundary between two jointly exhaustive positive and negative extensions with two sharp boundaries between, firstly, the positive extension set against the union of the borderline cases and the negative extension and then, on the negative side, between the union of borderline cases and the positive extension set against the negative extension. Proliferating more of these boundaries, in a many-valued system, does not seem to ease the problem (and supervaluationism seems no better on this score either). I do not think this poses an insurmountable problem for indeterminism, but that would require a lot of arguing. Still, to the extent that one is dubious about both epistemicism and dialetheism one is likely to find an indeterminist approach of some sort attractive; I suggest to such philosophers that one can subsume contextualist examples of the sort discussed above under the heading of vagueness thus construed.

[46] Rothschild and Segal (2009, p. 468). Their example concerns a watermelon green on the outside, red inside, of which a greengrocer says it is red and a painter says it is not red. In that particular example, it is tempting to say that the greengrocer's remark is elliptical for 'it's red inside', but I agree that ellipsis (and ambiguity) are not going to cope with all the sorts of examples the radical contextualist comes up with in challenging the SCW framework. Travis (1997, p. 91) also expresses scepticism that an appeal to vagueness can answer the contextualist challenge.

of Bute', 'John is taller than Jean', 'That tile is not red' etc., through sentence after sentence of ordinary English, the utterances will be determinately true or determinately false. Of course the contextualist does not deny that utterances in contexts can be true or false. But if it is said that this cannot in part be determined by some context-invariant *Sinn* which is brought to occasion of use—for why then are there cases of indeterminacy?—this can be set aside as a mere dogmatic refusal to accept genuine indeterminacy, to accept that senses can determine positive and negative extensions which do not exhaust their domain. To be sure, controversy still rages as to how we can explain this phenomenon but this itself shows that we are not bereft of any ideas about how to explain indeterminacy. It is bad philosophical methodology to abandon a philosophical framework, here the SCW framework, even where it seems to provide an attractive and intuitive way to approach an important phenomenon, just because it has consequences or presuppositions over which there is no consensus. That way lies the death of philosophy.

Even if the SCW account can meet the radical contextualist challenge, there is a challenge to at least its more ambitious versions from an opposite quarter, the 'minimalism' of Cappelen and Lepore (2005). According to them, the only relativity to context is that determined by grammatical expressions belonging to a fairly traditional 'Basic Set' (ibid., pp. 1–2) of contextually sensitive items such as pronouns, demonstratives, words or morphological components expressing tense, adverbs such as 'here' and 'now', and so forth. Cappelen and Lepore give three tests for determining (fallibly—they are not put forward as jointly providing necessary and sufficient conditions) whether or not a sentence is genuinely context-sensitive. They argue that these tests do indeed settle on something like the Basic Set as the class of context-sensitive expressions.

There is an obvious response to make here. Cappelen and Lepore are interested in what one might call 'superficial sensitivity', in expressions whose linguistic workings are relatively transparent to language users:

If expression *e* is context-sensitive, then it's *obviously* context-sensitive. Speakers should *not* have to theorize about it in order to realise that it is context sensitive. . . .

We're highlighting these obvious features of communication [fast and unreflective] in order to register a very simple point: If an expression *e* has its semantic value fixed in a context of utterance, that had better be obvious to all of us. (ibid., p. 112, italics in original)

But it is not at all obvious that all the (semantic) workings of language have to be obvious to language users (any more than it has to be obvious to someone whose decision-making broadly follows the pattern of maximizing expected utility which decision theory enjoins that her decision-making does follow this pattern). So it may be that they have indeed alighted upon a particularly transparent form of relativity of semantic value to circumstance, one which deserves to be called context-relativity because it is triggered by overt constituents of utterances with that role (perhaps additionally via some 'unvoiced' but nonetheless articulated constituents of the utterance whose reality is well vouched for in linguistic theory). This, however, is a proper subset of the relativity of semantic value to something broader than context, something I have been calling 'circumstance'.

This sort of strategy they describe (pp. 8–9) as an appeal to 'unarticulated constituents' and suggest that language competence becomes sheer magic on such a view.[47] It would certainly be puzzling if a relativity to circumstance was triggered by a *constituent* of the utterance but one which was neither an overt syntactic one nor one which could plausibly be thought of as 'unpronounced'. The mention of 'constituents' perhaps shows that they are in the grip of the view that all sensitivity to context must be triggered by subsentential components rather than by systematic keying of sentence to sentence or something similar (compare 'contextual definition'). Nevertheless the challenge to provide a non-magical account of how that systematic sensitivity can be grounded in linguistic practice remains and is a powerful and legitimate one.[48] I will try to sketch how this can be done for some test cases outside of mathematics in the next chapter before going on to a detailed account for mathematics in the rest of the book. The surface or transparent informational content of sentences will be systematically linked with the metaphysical content which reveals what makes those sentences true or false.

The terrain, then, is on the borders between metaphysics and philosophy of language. (I reject the rather strict separation of the two found in Cappelen and Lepore 2005, pp. 159ff.) However, as remarked earlier, I intend to remain in the border regions and not stray into full-scale metaphysics. In particular, the metaphysical content of a sentence is not to be viewed as something 'worldly', as a situation or state of affairs (cf. Armstrong's 'truth-makers', Armstrong 1997, pp. 128ff., 150; 2004), 'tropes' (Mulligan, Simons, and Smith 1984) or whatever. I wish to be neutral here as to whether such entities exist.[49] (In fact I do not believe in such things, but nothing in the account of mathematics I will give hinges on this rejection.) If we give as the metaphysical content of 'it's raining', as uttered in Glasgow on 19 October 2009, that it is raining in Glasgow on 19 October 2009, the metaphysics of 'it is raining in Glasgow on 19 October 2009' is still unsettled. Do predicates in sentences specifying metaphysical content stand for properties? If so, do all do or just some, and so forth? Once we broach these sorts of questions we have embarked on full-scale metaphysics and we do not need to do this to shed light on the workings of language.

But even the limited metaphysical ambitions lying behind the introduction of the notion of metaphysical content do have the potential to make some philosophical and indeed metaphysical waves. For one thing, failure to differentiate sharply between

---

[47] Cf. their criticism (Cappelen and Lepore 2005, p. 159) concerning a case in which they say 'the quantifier magically occurs (as with Perry's unarticulated constituents)'.

[48] Though presumably not for Chomskyans, who would reject as positivistic or 'operationalist' the idea that linguistic structure should not be posited unless it can be mirrored somehow in practice or linguistic behaviour.

[49] I do not see an ontology of state of affairs as essential to realism, contra Brock and Mares (2007, ch. 1).

metaphysical content and the informational content or sense of sentences has, I believe, contributed to the disrepute into which the classic enterprise of analytic philosophy—conceptual analysis—has fallen. Whilst little philosophical mileage is to be had, in general, out of providing non-trivial synonyms or tight necessary and sufficient conditions for philosophically interesting concepts, it is a different matter when analysis is seen as providing plausible metaphysical contents.

Furthermore, the distinction can be applied with good effect to deal with the problems with the notion of ontological reduction which were raised at the beginning of §III. Metaphorically, we can see the Circumstances in the SCW triad as forming a structure of reflecting mirrors set in a frame. For sentences with certain kinds of informational content, the frame directs a single mirror outwards to track, all being well (and *pace* Rorty), the nature of the external world; these are the sentences with realist truth-conditions. For other types of informational content, some or all of the mirrors are directed inward yielding a representation which behaves just like a sentence with realist truth-conditions; the 'phenomenology' of grasping the sentence is exactly the same as for those with realist, representational truth-conditions. However, in these cases, the sentence lacks realist truth-conditions, truth being partly or wholly determined by something non-external.

In the next chapter I will try to illustrate these ideas less metaphorically with some test cases from outside mathematics before concluding with an overview of the semantic framework to be applied to mathematics and a final determination of how the notion of 'realism' is to be understood in the remainder of the work.

# 2

# Ontological Reductionism

## §I. Projectivism in the SCW Framework

In this chapter I apply the SCW framework and the informational/metaphysical distinction to projectivism in order to illustrate how it can be used to develop an anti-realist reductionism; this is followed by a sketchier application to fictional discourse. The chapter concludes with an attempt to intertwine the two metaphysical and ontological strands of realism to yield a form of reductionist anti-realism which can be occupied, it will be the task of the rest of the book to argue, by an anti-platonist position in mathematics recognizably descended from classic formalism.

I will be largely concerned here with applying projectivist ideas to taste, aesthetic value, humour, and subjective probability.[1] A central theme in projectivism for all such areas is the existence of a fairly sharp bifurcation between mind-independent reality on the one hand, and human constructs projected onto that reality, on the other. This, for example, is what a fervent anti-projectivist such as Hilary Putnam finds so objectionable (1990, p. 90):

What has collapsed is the attempt to divide mundane reality, the reality of the *Lebenswelt*, into Real Reality and Projection.

For Putnam, projectivists are, as it were, Stalinist metaphysicians blithely trying to ignore the collapse of a philosophical Berlin Wall. In the other camp, the projectivist project has been championed by Simon Blackburn (1984, ch. 6; 1993*a*) who traces its ancestry back to Hume's idea that we have a 'productive faculty' prone to 'gilding and staining all natural objects with the colours borrowed from internal sentiment' (1751/1975, p. 294) and his claim that 'the mind has a great propensity to spread itself on external objects' (1739/1888, p. 167).[2]

---

[1] The most heavily discussed application of projectivism, of course, has been to moral discourse but as I find that the least plausible application I will largely focus on the others mentioned above.

[2] We can see this as in turn an extrapolation (and also significant alteration) of Francis Hutcheson's moral sense theory (in turn indebted to Shaftesbury) beyond the moral realm.

What is important for current purposes is that projectivism can be developed as a theory in which the metaphysical content of certain sentences not only diverges from the informational content of the sentences but serves to endow them with a non-realist semantics. The central idea is that competent users of certain sentences (in certain contexts) *key* (sincere) utterances of the sentences to the presence of internal attitudes though the sentences do not *say* that the attitudes obtain. So, for example, projectivist accounts of 'tasty', 'probable', 'funny', and 'cool'[3] (in the non-thermal sense), might link assertion of simple sentences containing these words to the attitudes indicated in the table below.

| | | |
|---|---|---|
| *x* is tasty | is keyed to | The utterer desires to eat more of *x* |
| *p* is probable | is keyed to | The utterer has a strong degree of belief in *p* |
| *x* is funny | is keyed to | The utterer has a strong inclination to laugh when confronted with *x* |
| *x* is cool | is keyed to | The utterer's peer group are keen on *x* |

The sentences on the right, that is, form part of the explanation for what makes-true the sentences on the left on a given occasion of utterance but they are not part of their literal content. By 'keying', I mean that competent speakers will pattern their verbal responses in such a way that (sincere) assent verdicts to sentences on the left-hand side occur (explicable error aside) just when the sentences on the right are true. We do not understand the words in the left column unless we apply them sincerely just when the corresponding attitudes hold. (The most obvious way this could happen is if the presence of the attitudes is transparent to us; but we could display such sensitivity even if not always reflectively aware of having the attitudes.) The links set out in the table are meaning-constitutive, in other words, according to this form of projectivism.

Of course the explanatory conditions just given are too simple. A minor point is that I might well think the haggis very tasty but have no desire to eat any more because I have stuffed my belly full of it.[4] We can perhaps meet this by adding to the metaphysical content 'or the utterer enjoyed eating it just now'. More importantly, the claimed agreement between assent on the left and truth in the right, in each equation, does not always obtain, even allowing for slips of the tongue, confusion, etc. A competent speaker might well sincerely agree that the haggis is tasty even though she never had any desire to eat it at the time of agreeing this nor did she enjoy it, and

---

[3] The example of 'cool' in its use as a term of commendation, particularly of matters of fashion and style as evaluated by the peer group one belongs to (or longs to belong to), is found in the work of Sally Haslanger (1995, p. 98). As she notes, these kinds of fashion-bound linguistic usages tend to date; indeed, in my lifetime this use of 'cool' has gone out of fashion and come back in again and now seems to be 'uncool' once more. Perhaps it is destined to wax and wane cyclically into the indefinite future.

[4] And of course fine-grained aesthetic judgements of works of art are much more complex and richer in structure than the notion of 'tasty' considered above, involving a more complicated mix of empirical and evaluative elements.

even though she is well aware of this. She might aver that it is probable that an asteroid will hit the earth in the next few decades yet have no strong belief that one will. The most obvious way (compatible with a projectivist approach) this might happen is if the speaker believes that others (or herself in a different physical condition) would have enjoyed the haggis, or if she thinks others believe in the asteroid impact. If projectivism is to work for concepts like 'tasty' and 'probable', this deference to an implicit peer group (a deference I have made explicit in the 'cool' example) has to be the only way divergence of verdict can occur when the verdict is made in an optimal situation for judgements of that sort. If this is right, however, then the projectivist can allow an element of objectivity, or rather intersubjectivity, in the ascription of such predicates, and greatly increase the plausibility of projectivism thereby.[5]

That is, ascriptions of 'tasty', 'funny' 'probable', and 'cool' are evaluable as correct or incorrect despite their non-realist nature. They can be incorrect because we often modify our attitudes on realizing they are deviant, as compared with some peer group we identity with (or in the light of our knowledge of our own stable attitudes). Failure to modify can bring forth correction from the peer group. The idea, then, is that a correct attitude, and hence a correct projective sentence[6]—'this haggis is tasty', 'a large asteroid will probably hit us soon', or whatever—is one that would be held reflectively, in a (metaphorically) 'cool' moment, and when the speaker is sensitive to the attitudes of the gustatory or doxastic communities she belongs to (with respect to those sentences; she need not be aware that she is sensitive to those attitudes nor have reflective knowledge of what those communities are). Here belonging to the community will entail some significant tendency for one's attitudes to converge on those dominant in the community, when one registers, perhaps not fully reflectively, those communal attitudes. If the T-schema holds of projective sentences and if 'correctness' distributes across 'iff' then for any projective sentence $s$, $\ulcorner s$ is true$\urcorner$ will be correct iff $p$ is[7] (where substituends for '$s$' name substituends for '$p$').

Of course projective predicates can be applied to names which pick out items to which we cannot directly strike attitudes. We can construct sentences such as 'sunsets

---

[5] Generalizing this projectivism account of 'tasty' to 'good' as in 'desirable' yields a theory which, in its alignment of desire and the corresponding projective belief (via the claim that $\ulcorner x$ is desirable$\urcorner$ is keyed to $\ulcorner$ I desire $x\urcorner$), seems to resemble the 'Simple anti-Humeanism' attacked by David Lewis (1988, 1996). But the qualifications noted above mean there is no universal identity of degree of belief in $\ulcorner$ it is good that $p$ obtain$\urcorner$ with the degree to which the subject desires that $p$ even when the degrees are one or zero. Nor need the projectivist be committed to intermediate degrees of belief and desire. Even if she is, the credence a subject places in $\ulcorner$ It is good that $p$ obtain$\urcorner$ will not even have a tendency to co-vary with the degree to which the subject desires that $p$. If the latter is 0.5, for example (supposing the scale of values bounded and normalized between 0 and 1), her degree of belief in $\ulcorner$ It is good that $p$ obtain$\urcorner$ (as opposed to $\ulcorner$ It is good to degree 0.5 that $p$ obtain$\urcorner$) will, for a reflectively aware subject, go to zero.

[6] That is, a sentence which the projectivist thinks is suitable for a projectivist treatment.

[7] This distributivity presupposes that the notion of 'correct' remains constant across the biconditional. Thus an utterance of 'John is tall' may be factually correct but the utterance of '"John is tall" is true' prudentially incorrect if a psychopathic anti-semanticist with a pathological loathing of the word 'true', and all those who utter it, is in the audience.

on planet Gliese 581d are beautiful'. The obvious way to extend the projective treatment to these cases is to hold that such a sentence is true if the item in question, here the sunsets on this planet, have a (mind-independent) property which, applied to items we do strike attitudes towards, would cause us to adopt the attitude which 'is beautiful' projects (unlikely as the star Gliese 581 is a red dwarf).

Now strident anti-deflationists will object to application of the T-schema to projective sentences. A correspondence theorist may grant that it is correct in a given situation to utter 'this painting is beautiful' but wrong to assert that ' "this painting is beautiful" is true', hence refuse to assert the corresponding instance of the T-schema. If, that is, our theorist does not admit the existence of aesthetic facts then aesthetic sentences cannot be true (or false) for lack of facts for them to correspond (or fail to correspond) to.

Even a correspondence theorist, however, should admit (leaving aside problems with the paradoxes anyway) that we can introduce a purely disquotational notion of truth. If this consorts with a fairly deflationary notion of assertion in the way sketched below then perhaps even such a theorist can accept the 'ontology-free' view of mathematics to be defended. Note also that adopting a deflationistic view of truth and assertion is by no means to adopt a deflationary view of metaphysics, if the latter means a quietist eschewal of systematic theorizing in metaphysics. It is just that the metaphysical action will take place somewhere else, for instance in connection with the notion of 'metaphysical content'. By a deflationary account of 'assertion' I mean that I intend throughout to use 'assert' and related terms in a non-theoretical, everyday sense. To assert that $p$ is just to say that $p$ (except that perhaps 'assert' has connotations of a more forceful saying) and 'saying that' is an ordinary enough notion.[8]

The key claim of this study—that mathematical existence claims can be true though there are no mathematical facts, states of affairs, objects, or properties in mind-independent reality—must be false if a full-blown correspondence theory of truth is true (corresponds to the philosophical facts, such a theorist would say). Conversely, if one is a deflationist and applies the T-schema or naïve truth rules (Chapter 1, §II.1) to indicative sentences in general, or at any rate to any sentences which can be used to make assertions in some relatively everyday atheoretical notion of assertion,[9] then the key claim is at least still a live option. But one does not have to go all the way with deflationism to accept the view that we should not import highly specific metaphysical content, e.g. realism, into the concept of truth itself. It is because the notion of truth is relatively neutral, metaphysically, that philosophers can have non-trivial debates about the nature of the truth-conditions of philosophically interesting sentences. We do

---

[8] What the criteria are for when two sayings are sayings of the same thing is a very tricky matter. It is tempting to think of there being two different criteria, one in which direct quotation of the utterance or a strict translation thereof yields a 'same-saying' utterance, and another criterion or bunch of criteria related to indirect quotation, which are considerably looser. But I do not think this issue impinges on the viability of the SCW framework or the informational content/metaphysical content distinction.

[9] See §III below.

need, then, to move some distance away from a correspondence theory to make sense of truth-evaluable projective utterances; but not all the way to deflationism. (For those tempted towards correspondence-type views I urge: construe the argument of the book as conditional; if a relatively deflationary approach to truth works, then a reductionism which evacuates mathematics of ontological commitment is feasible. Those who find the consequent philosophically attractive may then be moved to reconsider their scepticism.)

Turning, now, in more detail to the actual work of projectivism's leading champion Simon Blackburn, his earlier formulations introduced it as, at least for the most part, a *non-cognitivist* theory of areas such as morals and aesthetics. Utterances in these domains lack truth-values, although our practice is such as to make it useful to treat them *as if* they effect truth-valued assertions. In later work—'fast-track' projectivism (Blackburn 1993a, pp. 185–6) and in particular his 'inclusive projectivism' (1993b, pp. 366–7)—he is more sympathetic to the idea that they really are genuine truth-apt assertions. This brings his position closer to Crispin Wright's *minimalist* view.[10] Wright holds that declarative utterances in regions of discourse such as aesthetics and judgements about humour typically are assertoric; moreover, a minimal notion of truth, devoid of realist metaphysical commitment, applies to all assertions. Thus 'Euthyphronic' statements are evaluable as true or false.[11]

Nonetheless Blackburn still harbours some doubts about minimalistic treatments of truth, doubts which do not rest on allegiance to correspondence theories of truth. He worries (2006, pp. 249–50) that someone may use indicative conditionals (which are, indeed, indicatives) in the disciplined and non-random way specified in Adams's assertibility theory, thus satisfying minimalistic conditions on the applicability of a truth predicate. But we cannot straightway assume they have truth-conditions, specified homophonically by the T-schema so as to coincide with Adams's assertibility conditions. For we cannot so swiftly dispose of Lewis's demonstration (1976) that, aside from trivial cases, there is no conditional whose probability of truth is equal to the conditional probability which determines assertibility, on the assertibility theory; hence no such truth-valued conditional.

---

[10] Wright (1992, pp. 79–80, 108–39), though in Wright's minimalism there is far less emphasis on the need to 'earn the right' (Blackburn 1993b, p. 367) to treat grammatically declarative utterances for which there are standards of correct and incorrect utterance as genuine assertions.

[11] See also the notion of 'response-dependency' in, for example, Mark Johnston (1992). What makes the metaphysics of aesthetic statements or judgements of funniness anti-realist for Wright (if, indeed, it is) is the 'Euthyphro Contrast'. These judgements do not *track* a property but rather *constitute* the property. He proposes a successively more complex battery of biconditionals and conditionalized biconditionals as criteria for determining whether attribution of predicates on the basis of internal attitudes merely reliably detects an objective property or whether, by contrast, there is no objective property but only 'projection' of internal attitudes. I will attempt to side-step these criteria by assuming firstly, in the projective case, an essentially analytic connection between awareness of, or sensitivity to, the internal attitude and readiness to apply the predicate, and secondly by locating the distinction between realist and anti-realist judgements in the metaphysical content of the judgements. I also leave aside here the differences between Wright's minimalism and full-blown deflationism (Wright 1992, pp. 18–24).

The worry is a legitimate one and shows that whilst it may be relatively straightforward to apply the truth predicate to a purely atomistic sublanguage, in the interesting case of a language with serious syntactic and semantic structure this structure will impose constraints which have to be met if the complex sentences are to have truth-conditions. It will then be a non-trivial question whether a set of practices with superficially declarative sentences can meet those constraints and can therefore generate truth-apt sentences. In the next chapter, we shall come across a problem of exactly this sort with respect to the version of formalism to be advocated for mathematics.

However, I will leave such worries to one side for now and concentrate on this cognitivist version of projectivist theories, in which projective utterances have truth-values, as it is far superior to its non-cognitivist cousin. For if projective sentences have truth-values and we can respond to the worries raised two paragraphs ago then they can form subcomponents of logically complex sentences also bearing truth-values. It would be a mistake, in that case, to suppose that such complex sentences must have their meaning in turn explained projectively.[12] The basic projective sentences have truth-values and truth-functors apply indiscriminately to any sentences bearing truth-values, however it is that those truth-values are bestowed or acquired. The meaning of any such sentence should be seen as a structured whole, with the meaning of the component projective sentences (determined by their use in simple contexts) forming part and the meaning of the logical operators forming another, independent, part. The difference between the variant forms of projectivism can be expressed in terms of the difference between minimal, disquotational truth-conditions and metaphysical contents. The simple 'non-cognitivist' projectivist refuses to apply the truth predicate to projectivist sentences. A slightly more subtle 'quasi-non-cognitivist' is prepared to apply the truth predicate (or at least simulate doing so), adhering to the Tarskian scheme, at least for the area of discourse in question. But she does not view the logical operators as having a topic-neutral sense common to projectivist and non-projectivist utterances. Such a projectivist might, for example, give independent metaphysical contents for negations:

'$x$ is funny' is made-true by $a$[13] iff I have a strong tendency to laugh at $a$;
'$x$ is not funny' is made-true by $a$ iff I have a strong tendency to groan at $a$.

Hence although for disquotational 'true' we have

---

[12] No need, that is, for Blackburn's search for separate projectivist meaning for logical operators (1984, pp. 189–96)—in response to 'Frege's problem', as raised by Geach (1965) (see also Dummett 1981*a*, pp. 348–53). This is the problem that we draw *logical* inferences from compound sentences with mixed projective and factual components. If some of these sentences are not evaluable as true or false, by dint of having components which lack truth-value, then it makes no sense to evaluate the argument as valid and thus *truth*-preserving. For a critique of Blackburn's 'slow-track' or 'contrastive' projectivist programme of developing a 'logic' for a language only some of whose sentences have truth-values, see Hale (1984) and (1993) and for Blackburn's response see Blackburn (1993*b*).

[13] i.e. with $a$ assigned as the value of variable $x$.

'that joke was not funny' is true iff it is not the case that 'that joke was funny' is true iff that joke was not funny

we do not have, according to the quasi-non-cognitivist

'that joke was not funny' is made-true iff it is not the case that 'that joke was funny' is made-true iff that joke was not funny.

For if we neither incline to laugh at the joke nor groan at it, then neither 'that joke was funny' nor 'that joke was not funny' is made-true.

The notion of 'make-true' would have nothing to do with truth, the last four letters would be a mere typographical quirk, unless for the simplest sentences at least we have an equation between 'make-true' and 'true', or rather between being made true and being true in the circumstances incorporated into the metaphysical content. The term of art 'make-true' is in fact partly defined by its use in biconditionals generating metaphysical contents for sentences relative to circumstances. Hence since 'that joke was funny' is not made-true (in the case envisaged at the end of the last paragraph) this sentence is not true. The quasi-non-cognitivist, applying the Tarskian disquotational scheme to negations, concludes that 'that joke was not funny' is true, although in the case envisaged it is not made-true. 'True' and 'made-true' come apart even for very elementary logical compounds of simple sentences and now the Frege/Geach problem threatens to return. For the quasi-non-cognitivist's account of the metaphysical content of complex sentences is an idle cog unless the meaning of the logical operators, and thereby the ground for the validity of logical rules, is determined by what is made-true, not by what is true. But the 'logic' which will result will not agree on the logical consequence relation determined by the disquotational notion of truth, and so the quasi-non-cognitivist is committed to the implausible view that the latter is not the 'real' logical consequence relation.

Things are much smoother for the 'cognitivist' projectivist who views the logical operators as having autonomous, topic-neutral meanings. She gives a 'homophonic' account of the metaphysical contents for logical compounds of sentences containing projective components:

'$x$ is not funny' is made-true by $a$ iff it is not the case that '$x$ is funny' is made true by $a$.

If 'that joke was funny' is not made-true then 'that joke was not funny' is both true and made-true. (Such a projectivist may perhaps distinguish 'not funny' from 'unfunny' giving the latter truth-conditions in terms of inclinations to groan.) The complex sentence should not be seen as an abbreviation for a logically non-complex sentence whose meaning is given in some direct way corresponding to the meaning of the basic constituents; to think this way is to fail to see the autonomy of the logical operators. This breed of projectivist has no problem with logical inferences involving 'mixed' sentences, with both projective and non-projective components, at least if the only logical operators involved are ones for which a homophonic account like the above one is given. In valid inferences disquotational truth is transmitted from premisses to conclusion in the usual way (and disquotational falsity transmitted upwards from conclusion to premiss, in the single premiss case too). Moreover, 'makes-true' will distribute over logical compounds just as disquotational truth does.

From now on, then, 'projectivism' is to be read as 'cognitivist projectivism', unless contra-indicated. If the superiority of cognitivist to non-cognitivist projectivism is accepted then here is a reason for projectivists to accept that there is a deflationary notion of truth, one which consorts with 'make-true', that is with metaphysical content, in such a way (which will involve all the complexities which indexicality and its indexing by circumstances bring) that sentences of the appropriate sort can be true without commitment to realms of naturalistically puzzling properties.

The example in question, humour, calls to mind another important objection to the projectivist project, at least when conceived in a naturalistic framework. John McDowell (1998, p. 158) objects to the projectivist account of ⌜x is funny⌝, given in terms of keying to dispositions to laugh, on the grounds that one might laugh, at a friend's stand-up comedy routine say, for two different reasons: (a) because it is funny, or, (b), contrastingly, out of nervous embarrassment because it is humiliatingly unfunny. The projectivist account of humour will go wrong, then, unless it ties ascriptions of funniness to a to dispositions to laugh *because a is found to be funny*. But now we can clearly no longer give a non-trivial analysis of funniness in terms of human responses. The responses have been 'contaminated', in Blackburn's phrase (Blackburn 1993b, p. 373) because they are defined in terms of a response to the very property we are trying to 'analyse away'. Similarly it is no use explaining our use of ⌜x is tasty⌝ in terms of keying to the response of 'discerning tastiness in the food'.

It is crucial to projectivism that McDowell's challenge be met head on, that the projectivist find a way (it need not be the only way) of specifying the response which gives the metaphysical content of humour judgements without commitment to properties of funniness.[14] It is crucial, at any rate, if projectivism is to be a naturalistic project intent on explaining our grasp of aesthetic and other regions of discourse without invoking any property unknown to the physical sciences. Since humour is not our main topic here, I will leave this challenge to one side, but a similar challenge will be faced by the (non-projectivist) reductionist anti-realism about mathematics which is the main theme of the book.

To see how reductionism fits in here, it perhaps helps to enter into the Metaphysics Room temporarily and assume moderate realism about properties: i.e. assume some

---

[14] If the response is specified by a propositional attitude ⌜a is funny⌝ glossed along the lines of ⌜x thinks that a is funny⌝ then there is no reason to suppose that there must arise commitment to a property of funniness on the part of the metatheorist, no more than providing a metatheory for ⌜x believes that unicorns exist⌝ will inevitably lead to commitment to unicorns. But the account is now viciously circular as an account of speaker's understanding since it presupposes grasp of the concept in question *by the speaker*, and not just by the metatheorist.

predicates stand for or designate properties. Suppose for example one thought that a simple atomic predication could not be true unless the predicate designated a property. It would seem, then, that if one was hostile to aesthetic properties or funniness or 'coolness' then one will have to adopt an error theory about sentences ascribing such properties. Not so, if one gives the metaphysical content of such sentences in projective fashion. What makes 'this haggis is tasty' true is that I have certain conative relations with the haggis (as it were). Given the metaphysical stance we have assumed *pro tem* this might be taken to populate the world with certain (naturalistically unproblematic) attitudes or relations between humans and objects; but not properties of tastiness—we have reduced those away.

But before examining in more detail the nature of this sort of ontological reduction, it is necessary to look a little more carefully at the connections between the truth an utterance and what I have called with no qualification its 'correctness'. 'Makes-true' locutions are simply a way of expressing correctness conditions. Sentence $s$, as uttered in circumstances $c$, is made-true in conditions $p$ iff $p$ specify when sentence an assertion of $s$ in such circumstances is correct (which, I will argue, is independent of whether or not it is rational to assert $s$). What does this correctness amount to? Is it a normative notion?

## §II. Snapshot Dispositions, Correction, Fiction

Central to the projectivist project, as I have conceived it, is the deflationary idea that 'non-factual' utterances can be true without corresponding to any mind-independent state of affairs; that, for example, simple subject/predicate utterances can be correct even though the predicate designates no property or the singular term no object. If such correspondence is not what makes an utterance of the form ⌜$a$ is tasty⌝ or ⌜$a$ is funny⌝ true or correct, what does? The suggestion might be that truth is determined by conformity with a *norm* which embodies standards of correctness, standards with prescriptive or similar force. The norm in the projective case, moreover, is not given by a prescription that one ought to represent the facts, the states of affairs. The norm, rather, is that one modulate assent and dissent to the presence in oneself (or the relevant peer group) of the relevant attitudes. This might seem to lead us in the direction of some sort of assertibility theory of meaning, for projective sentences at least. Grasp of the meaning of sentences is constituted by rules which prescribe when to assert and when to deny. A sentence is assertible, read as 'may be asserted', iff asserting it does not violate norm N. And a sentence is true iff assertible. Which norm is in question will vary from one projective notion—'tasty', 'probable'—or whatever, to another.

But a single utterance is typically subject to a great many different sorts of norm. Thus, on being introduced to my host for dinner I may, in the grip of a misguided maxim of maximal informativeness, utter sincerely the thought which immediately comes into my mind: 'Your wig is cheap and obvious'. Mine host may indeed be wearing a cheap and obvious wig, so my utterance is correct in that it represents accurately this property of my host. On the other hand my utterance would, in all normal circumstances, be a very rude one. It may also be a very imprudent one if, for example, my follicly challenged host holds the purse strings on which my department depends. So we may say that the utterance satisfies representational or factual norms but violates norms of prudence and etiquette. Should we say, then (following a norm of theoretical semantics perhaps), that the utterance is true$_R$ because assertible relative to representational norms but false$_P$ and false$_E$ because asserting it would violate norms of prudence and etiquette? Should we distinguish three different types of truth here: factual truth, prudential truth, and etiquette truth?

This cannot be right: given the variety of norms, this threatens to multiply types of truth uncontrollably. It is simply not plausible that there are all these different types of truth. One line of response is to single out a special norm as the norm which determines truth and falsity conditions, a *semantic* norm (perhaps appealing to the, far from clear, semantic/pragmatics distinction). I share, however, the scepticism of those who doubt whether one can single out something which is both determinative of truth-conditions and normative.[15]

For one thing, I take it that for something to count as a norm, it must embody or be tied or linked to practices of criticism. But suppose I assert to myself a proposition *p* which I fairly strongly believe on the basis of perception or of a compelling hunch which turns out, however, to be false. Assume further that I have found no evidence against *p* even though I have not been negligent in gathering or assessing evidence. No whiff of criticism attends me in these cases, even though there is no other obligation, absolute or prima facie, which trumps or cancels out my supposed obligation to utter the sentence expressing *p* only when *p*. Hence the semantic incorrectness of asserting *p* is not an example of violation of a genuine norm.

It might be objected that there clearly has been violation of a norm here, namely the prescription to assert only what one has good evidence for (Clifford 1877/1999), to proportion, with the wise man, one's belief to the evidence (Hume 1748/1975, p. 110). Affirming something is not reasonable simply because one lacks contrary evidence, it will be said, else lots of crazy existential claims (about giant teapots orbiting distant exoplanets and the like) will have to be classed as rationally assertible.

This response rests on a hubristically ambitious conception of the scope and powers of human reason and fails to take into account the threefold dichotomy between the rationally obligatory, the rationally forbidden, and the rationally neutral. The third group comprises that vast body of propositions which are neither enjoined by reason nor precluded; into this group falls my blameless assertion of *p*.[16] The overweening

---

[15] See for example, Boghossian (2005), Hattiangadi (2006), Miller (2006), Glüer and Wikforss (2009). For a contrary view, see Whiting (2007).

[16] Compare the classic deontic division of actions into obligatory, forbidden and, in the middle, permitted but not obligatory; cf. von Wright (1951, p. 1).

conception of the scope of reason encapsulated in the idea that all determinate propositions fall into two categories, of rationally enjoined or rationally forbidden, is not only false but dangerous since it invites irrationalist overreactions to its bloated and readily punctured claims.

Well, suppose we accept this[17]—it still leaves us no further forward on the question of semantic (non-normative) correctness. I suggest that on dropping the notion of semantic normativity, even in the highly anti-realist case of projectivist utterances, we should return to something like a traditional notion of analytic or meaning-constitutive principles governing our use of terms.[18] By an analytic principle governing an expression $e$ in a natural language $L$ I mean a non-trivial biconditional of the form:

> Speaker S understands one of the meanings which $e$ has, as it occurs in $L$, iff the speaker has abilities $A_1, \ldots A_n$ made manifest by engagement in practices $P_1, \ldots P_m$.

This yields one non-normative sense of 'correct' in language. Failure to use the word in accordance with the given practices betrays failure to grasp the meaning of the word in the language, and so is incorrect as an example of performance in language L. But a competent speaker, exhibiting no incorrectness in that sense, can make erroneous assertions. If it is not to be the case that everything which seems right is right, then among the abilities and practices which constitute grasp of words there must occur *correctional practices*. For instance, as well as assenting or dissenting to 'there goes a rabbit' from occasion to occasion in a suitable manner—we might class these as *'snapshot'* linguistic dispositions—speakers will have dispositions (largely unactualized) to assent or dissent to sentences such as 'that wasn't after all a rabbit over there a moment ago' and so forth. It may be possible, using plausible principles governing meaning, to distil from the totality of such counterfactual verdicts, perhaps with suitable weighting, the set of rabbits as the extension of 'rabbit', even if, on some occasions, optimal for evaluation of the bare sentence 'there's a rabbit', speakers may give 'snapshot' assent when no rabbit is present, or dissent when one is. And this yields the crucial notion of non-normative correctness which can be exhibited by fully competent speakers: applying a word to an item which does not belong to its extension, the latter determined after the fashion above. We can rephrase this using the 'made-true' terminology: specifications of the extension of a predicate, as determined above, set out what makes-true (and makes-false) application of the predicate in each case, the idea generalizing to other syntactic categories.

---

[17] A rather Humean position, though it seems on the surface anyway to sit uneasily with the quotation just given from the *Enquiry concerning Human Understanding*. A lot hinges on how to read 'wise' of course.

[18] Such a move will be abjured by the hard-line Quineans, but I suspect they are a dying breed. I argue against the coherence of Quine's more extreme rejection of the analytic/synthetic distinction (particularly where he extends it to basic logical rules as opposed to theses) in Weir (2005a, pp. 463–4). I say a little more on this in Chapter 5, §III.

Even leaving aside the problem of ontological relativity, and the worry that the extension of 'rabbit' is seriously underdetermined by such practices, any such account of objective content as based on analytic or meaning-constitutive practices faces formidable obstacles. For example, it seems hard to square it with a 'molecular' account of language[19] according to which there is a partial ordering of sentences, or sets of sentences, of the language. The partial order relation holds between sets of sentences S and S′ just when grasp of any sentence in S′ requires grasp of all in S, but grasp of none in S requires grasp of any in S′. The relation is well-founded, winding down to a bedrock of primitive sentences, 'Lo, a rabbit', perhaps, whose meaning is 'atomistic' and dependent on no others.[20]

Molecularism is highly attractive to all those not sunk in nihilistic despair with respect to the prospects of an explanation of language grasp. It is hard to see how we can isolate, for each expression, a set of practices which constitute grasp of meaning if 'holism', at least in the sense of the negation of molecularism, is true (cf. Weir 1986a). But if our explanation of grasp of atomic sentences involving 'rabbit' invokes meaning-constitutive correctional practices towards more complex sentences such as 'that was a rabbit over there just a moment ago', molecularity seems to go out the window; this would seem to mean there are ineliminable loops in the semantic dependency relation among members of any partition of the language into sentence sets.

I will not attempt to make any substantial headway with this difficulty here, for language in general.[21] It will suffice if some plausible analytic principles, divided roughly into 'snapshot' and 'correctional' principles, can be proffered for certain areas of discourse, notably here projective utterances, but I will also touch on discourse about fiction and of course ultimately mathematics. These principles should sustain the informational content/metaphysical content distinction and bolster an anti-realist treatment of the regions in question.

Nor will I attempt to answer Quinean scepticism. I will, rather, traffic heavily in notions—understanding, meaning—which the Quinean rejects. Yet even the non-Quinean might be sceptical. What are the non-trivial specifications of the abilities which constitute grasp of words such as 'unsteadily', 'table', 'sings'? We have all learnt, of course, the Fregean slogan that only in the context of a sentence does a word have meaning (Frege, 1884/1953, p. x, §§60, 62, 106). But what are the abilities constitutive of grasp of sentences like 'that table is brown' or 'Hamish is walking unsteadily' even for someone who understands the expressions other than 'table' and 'unsteadily'? Certainly there are no particular vocal or other movements that a competent speaker who understands 'that table is brown' must make, or fail to make, in any given context, as was made clear by Geach (1957, pp. 8ff.) and Chisholm (1957, ch. 11).

---

[19] Cf. Dummett (1976, p. 79).

[20] Quine's observation sentences, on one of his two (or more) rather different definitions of observation sentence, have this character.

[21] For a fuller discussion, see Weir (2003b).

Mental states do not issue in pieces of non-mentalistically described behaviour one by one.

Thankfully, since it is clearly hopeless, atomistic behaviourism is not the only route to non-trivial explication of mental abilities. Still, even rejecting it and helping ourselves fairly liberally to mentalistic notions, what non-trivial conditions are essential to grasp of 'that table is brown'? That one sincerely assent to the sentence as queried, if only to oneself, just when one believes that the referent of 'that table' is brown? This condition has all the appearance of a trivial analytic truth linking 'sincere assent' and 'belief'; not, then, something able to serve a substantial role in a genuinely explanatory account of meaning grasp. Moreover, helping oneself to the notion of believing that $p$, where $p$ gives the content of the sentence whose grasp one is trying to explain, is far too liberal for any theorist who is not convinced that thought is independent of and prior to language, who is not convinced that one can explain what it is to believe $p$, for $p$ with content of arbitrary complexity, independently of an account of linguistic competence.

A potentially much more informative condition is that one give sincere assent to utterances of 'that table is brown' just when one is confronted with a brown table, in some direct perceptual sense. But of course we return again to 'seems right' $\neq$ 'is right'; the possibility of error falsifies this account. An important tradition in philosophy of language seeks to stay within the spirit of this approach, whilst avoiding the simple refutation above, by restricting consideration, in specifying meaning-constitutive practices, to judgements made in 'optimal conditions'. This tradition, however, runs into all the difficulties with optimality canvassed in Chapter 1, §II.1. Arguably, even in our most directly empirical (particular) judgements about the world we always, *pace* the anti-realist, run the risk of error—and that even in non-trivially specified 'optimal' cases (see on this Williamson 2000, ch. 4). As indicated earlier, it is here that appeal to 'correctional practices' in addition to 'snapshot dispositions' is essential and the difficulties with molecularism sketched above simply have to be met head on in a full account.

But, less generally, let us look at the projectivist case I have been running with. My 'cognitive projectivist' claims that it is analytic of 'tasty' (in one of its meanings) that (to take only some cases):

> whenever one has tasted a sample of some food $a$ when one is in a reflective, cool moment, not fully sated, in full possession of one's faculties, and well-informed about the gustatory attitudes of one's peers, then:
> one affirms ⌈t is tasty⌉, where t is a singular term you grasp and are aware refers to $a$, just when one desires to go on eating more of $a$.

A more comprehensive account, one which can ground an 'intersubjective' notion of taste, will replace the clause about peer attitudes with specification of correctional practices. Those who have a notion of 'tasty' which is not utterly subjective have dispositions to retract earlier verdicts as to whether $a$ was tasty at a given time in the light of their beliefs about the (current) attitudes of peer groups. And what makes a particular group G the peer group for a given speaker with respect to the attitude in question is that she amends the attitude which the predicate 'tasty' projects in response to her beliefs about the attitudes of members of G.

Let us try for a little more generality and turn from projectivism so see whether any similarly anti-realist appeal to snapshot-plus-correctional practices can be applied elsewhere, specifically to discourse about fiction. Consider this preliminary stab at snapshot meaning-constitutive principles for 'Dmitry Karamazov has at least two half-brothers' (in the context of discussions of Dostoyevsky's *The Brothers Karamazov*, rather than in the context of an utterance among language users who know of a real individual with that name):

> It is constitutive of grasp of 'Dmitry Karamazov has at least two half-brothers', in the context of discussion of a given English translation of *The Brothers Karamazov*, that one sincerely assent (if only 'privately') to the sentence iff one believes that the sentence 'flows from' the translated text.

(Clearly, at the least, the scare-quoted 'flows from' requires much further elucidation, of which some will be given below.)

Here we have a purely subjective notion of fictional truth in which assent is tied to the belief states of book-readers. To get a more objective (but not necessarily realist) notion, we need the practices which constitute grasp of the sentence to include some sort of correctional abilities which are sensitive to the actual text. A satisfactory account, in fact, would have to encompass an explanatory account of our grasp of purely representational sentences describing the content of books—no mean task. We need the correctional abilities for fictional discourse sentences to be closely linked to those for purely representational sentences about fiction; these abilities should fix on the details of the text itself rather than speakers' beliefs about the text, as that which the corrected verdicts settle on. This would explain why the metaphysical content of sentences such as 'Dmitry Karamazov has at least two half-brothers' is given by what 'flows' from the text, not what utterers believe flows from the text. However, the crucial claim here is that the difference in informational content between the Karamazov sentence and a sentence explicitly about what flows from the text explains why the former sentence is not a representational one.

If the idea of there being a combination of snapshot and correctional practices which are meaning-constitutive for an expression can be made out, we get a non-normative reading of the sense in which utterances, in matters of taste, probability, discourse about fiction, and so forth, are correct or incorrect. They are *semantically correct* or 'made-true' if and only if a proposition which encapsulates the metaphysical content of the utterance obtains. What determines the metaphysical content of an utterance are the meaning-constitutive practices, snapshot and correctional, for that practice together with general 'metaphysical' principles, analytic of the concept of 'meaning', which determine how metaphysical content is related to the meaning-constitutive practices for utterances of that class. The upshot, in the fiction case, is that irrespective of whether it would be polite, moral, prudent, and so forth to assent to an utterance of 'Svidrigailov died accidentally under the wheels of a horse carriage'[22] in the context of a discussion of *Crime and Punishment*, the utterance is true just when the proposition that he died under the wheels of a horse carriage flows from (a given translation of) the text. But this is no part of the informational content of the sentence, as can be seen by, for example, the very different behaviour of the sentence and its metaphysical content in intensional and modal contexts.

What determines what the supposed meaning-constitutive, snapshot, and correctional practices are, for a given expression or class of expressions? And what determines what the 'metaphysical' principles are which relate metaphysical content to meaning-constitutive or analytic practices? These questions have to be separated from the epistemic question of how we might know whether a particular claim about metaphysical principles or meaning-constitutive practices for an expression is true or not. In the epistemic case, a fairly holistic epistemology is appropriate. One must look at the claim in the context of a broader framework one finds plausible, a framework which might well include one's 'intuitions' about the meaning of the expression, one's pre-theoretical beliefs about it that is. But by no means only these intuitions. In addition, the framework will include other particular claims one finds plausible about meaning-constitutive principles together with more general accounts of the nature of meaning, theories about the nature of mind in general, scientific theories about the nature of the human organism, a general metaphysical outlook, and so on. One then estimates how well the claim about analytic principles for the expression fits in to this broader framework and how coherent the overall framework is.

As to the first 'metaphysical' or non-epistemological question, the answer here depends on what the truth is concerning the nature of meaning, or the aspect or aspects of meaning relevant to truth and falsity (which I have claimed include both informational and metaphysical content). The phrase 'the nature of meaning' I would gloss further as meaning-constitutive or analytic principles governing 'meaning'. But I will not delve further into such very general debates in the philosophy of language. It will be sufficient for present purposes if it is plausible that there are some meaning-constitutive abilities, roughly on the lines outlined and including 'snapshot' and 'correctional' practices and abilities, and which are true of some types of utterance for which an anti-realist 'ontological reductionist' reading makes sense. The dialectical

---

[22] One might think it immoral to utter this truth about fiction if one is in the company of someone who has recently lost a loved one to suicide; or if not immoral, one might feel uneasy about averring that that is how he died. Or rather how he died 'in the story'. This last sentence, the use of the pronoun in particular, cannot be accounted for in the relatively simple way suggested above, since it does not flow from Dostoyevsky's text that Svidrigailov is a character in a story who meets a particular end. Clearly a proper treatment of fiction on the anti-realist lines sketched here would require a much more extensive treatment; I touch very briefly on some of the more complex cases, 'faction' for example, below and in Chapter 5, §II*.

strategy is then to use this as a foothold to argue for formalistic principles as analytic for typical mathematical utterances.

The foothold will be firm to the extent that it is plausible that the informational/metaphysical content distinction can be made sense of and can be put to use in developing a form of anti-realism in cases such as projectivism and discourse about fiction. It will doubtless be felt, very reasonably, that more work is required to establish sufficient plausibility in those areas. For example, I scare-quoted a crucial idea in the sketch I gave of an anti-realist account of discourse about fiction (which I take, contra 'make-believe' theories, to be, in general, genuinely assertoric[23]). The metaphysical content (but not informational content) of 'Dmitry Karamazov has at least two half-brothers', in the context of the discussion of Dostoyevsky's *The Brothers Karamazov*, is that this sentence 'flows from' the text of the novel. This notion is tricky for it cannot be identified with that of being entailed by the text. For what if the text is inconsistent, as may often be the case in a complex book? Appeal to a narrow notion of relevant or paraconsistent entailment will not work in all cases for there may, as a result of authorial oversight or printer errors say, be simple and blatant contradictions: 'Mac-Sporran was present at the murder' on one page, 'MacSporran was not present at the murder' on another. Or what if the novel contains a sentence of the form ⌜Professor MacSporran proved that $p$⌝ where $p$ is some logical or mathematical impossiblity, the negation of Fermat's Last Theorem for example?

A looser and more subtle notion is needed. Perhaps something along the lines of what experienced readers would, on reflective consideration, judge must form part of the story if it is to make overall sense.[24] What makes-true fictional discourse, in other words, are counterfactual truths about what would emerge when experienced readers try to fill out the text to generate a more complete world. We might call this a 'hermeneutical' account of truth in fiction. It is determined by the practices of readers as they try to interpret the text, but we situate this inside an SCW framework in such a way that the metaphysical content which spells out the interpretational practices is not part of the *Sinn* of the utterances; hence they are not made-true by their informational content mirroring features of the World. The attribution of metaphysical contents to the fictional discourse of a group of speakers will be arbitrary and non-explanatory, however, unless it is true of them (or at any rate, those to whom they defer in these matters) that, in the right circumstances, they could be the experienced readers and their verdicts of fictional discourse would alter, if need be, to conform with the outcome of any such reflection on the text.

---

[23] But since my use of 'assertion' is very lightweight, theoretically, perhaps there is not such a sharp difference here.

[24] Or perhaps what readers would come up with if they were to 'make-believe' the fiction were true and try to fill it out in a coherent way; the role of pretence being emphasized by theorists such as Currie (1990) and Walton (1990). However, on the current account, statements about fiction are not make-believe but genuine assertions.

Even this explication of 'flows from the text' may not work for works which are *deliberately inconsistent* and portray events from two different perspectives, say (Hogg's *The Private Memoirs and Confessions of a Justified Sinner*, for example). There we may have to relativize truth not just to the novel but to the various perspectives in the novel.[25] But the important point is that this view, though anti-realist, entails that statements about works of fiction (including the statements in the text itself) can be non-elliptically true, contra elliptical accounts of fiction and in opposition also to error-theoretic treatments. The latter contend that though it may be pragmatically useful to assert that Sherlock Holmes lived in London, the proposition is actually false. Against these the 'hermeneutic' non-elliptical, anti-error theory sketched above is a form of 'face-value fictional anti-realism', though one which depends on a prior account of representational discourse. For judging what makes sense of the story requires treating the sentences of the work of fiction as meaningful, not simply syntactic strings on which derivations can be performed. Hence for the hermeneutic theory, the meaning of fictional utterances is parasitic on a non-fictional representational meaning which the utterances (or at least most terms of the utterance, not all proper names perhaps) have.[26]

An interesting subcase, with analogies to the problem for formalists in handling applied mathematics, is 'faction'. What does the hermeneutic view have to say about truth and falsity in mixed factual/fictional pieces of literature? In Scott's *Waverley*, the fictional Edward Waverley interacts with a real individual, Bonnie Prince Charlie. The Wizard of the North would not get any purely factual matters wrong, of course. But suppose he did, suppose in the novel he had the Young Pretender born in Paris rather than Rome, because he falsely believed that was the case. Is the sentence in the novel false? I think we have to say no here, for it has a different meaning from its use in assertoric discourse outside novels. If a literary critic, in a commentary, asserts he was born in Paris, has he spoken falsely?[27] Perhaps there is no determinate answer in that case. (In general there will be much indeterminacy in fictional discourse, since the counterfactual metaphysical contents which ground their correctness will often be indeterminate.)

---

[25] There may, moreover, be more than one group of readers relevant to the reading even of a specific token, two groups who would come to different verdicts say. This will introduce an additional relativity to circumstance; and an additional vagueness, since it will be vague who is in the group of readers. Thanks to an audience at the University of Edinburgh for helpful comments and criticisms of this proposed treatment of fiction.

[26] Thanks to Andrew Jorgensen for emphasizing this to me.

[27] Even in the theoretically light use I wish to make of the notion of 'assertion', it seems to me implausible to suppose that utterances inside fiction, poems, novels, plays, etc. are themselves assertoric (as opposed to critical pronouncements, these seem to pass all surface tests for being assertions). There may be some exceptions where there is a dual use. Consider the announcements the BBC made to British spies in the Second World War. Imagine they were not read out as bizarre sentences in special bulletins but inserted in radio plays. During the play someone may say 'John Jones has been ordered to embark on the project for which he had been preparing for months'. In this special case we may have something which is an assertion directed at spy code-named John Jones as well as a non-superfluous part of the play.

Many further problems for the position arise from the kinds of assertions which critics make. They often refer to 'fictional characters' as if they are real—'A certain fictional detective is more famous than any real detective' (Parsons 1982, p. 83)—or make comparisons across different works of fiction. This often seems to make sense—it seems right to say that Fyodor Karamazov is more of a rogue than Stepan Oblonsky, Anna Karenina's brother. If what makes claims about fictional works true or false is determined always and only by coherence within the story (or substory) then, implausibly, none of these claims can be true. Can the hermeneutic theory handle such problems? I say a little on this in Chapter 5, §II* but undoubtedly not enough. I am not, it should be said, prepared to go to the stake for this view of discourse about fiction anyway, since my main target is mathematical realism. Perhaps the view that such discourse is elliptical—

'Dmitry Karamazov has at least two half-brothers' is elliptical for 'In Dostoyevsky's novel, things are said which entail that he had at least two half-brothers'.

—is after all superior, though I find that very doubtful. More promising is the fairly standard line that such sentences are false but can often usefully and appropriately be asserted. If, however, the view I have proffered has at least some plausibility then that will give independent support to the claim that we can make true existential claims whilst, in some interesting sense, avoiding commitment to an ontology.

## §III. Reduction

But what can this interesting sense be? This returns us to the metaphysics in 'metaphysical content'. I have emphasized that associating sentences which spell out metaphysical content with their 'target' sentences in the object language whose metaphysical content they give does not, on its own, bring with it any heavy metaphysical commitment. I held out the promise, though, that this can shed light on ontology, ontological reduction in particular. To see how, let us return to projectivism.

The advantages of projectivism are that it avoids the obvious flaws in subjectivism—saying the haggis is tasty, that the joke is funny, or that rain is probable is to say nothing about oneself—whilst hoping to give a wholly naturalistic account of these concepts. As Blackburn (1984, p. 182) puts it, projectivism 'asks no more than this: a natural world and patterns of reaction to it'. So in what sense is projectivism reductionist? Can we say more here than was said at the end of §I?

We need to look at this from the perspective of the metatheorist (and note that the metatheory should apply to the object-language speakers regardless of those speakers' own metaphysical views, though of course metatheorist and object language speaker can be one and the same). For illustrative purposes imagine that the metatheorist is a realist about properties, at least where some sort of causal punch is involved. That is, if she believes it true that the substance dissolved because, in part, of its chemical structure she will believe it has chemical properties which cause dissolving. Now suppose our metatheorist is considering an utterance by one of the speech community under investigation to the effect that Hamish drank from the glass because he thought it probably contained Old Speckled Hen beer and he thinks this beer is very good. Must our *metatheorist*, in explaining how such utterances can be true or false, also embrace a commitment to properties of goodness, or goodness-for-beer, and properties of high probability, applicable to events, or perhaps states of affairs?

Not if she is a projectivist. For in that case, according to her account, in ascriptions of goodness and high probability the predicates which appear to ascribe these properties do not function in a straight, referential way picking out mind-independent properties of a mysterious sort but rather are correctly applied (in simple, unembedded contexts) just when internal attitudes, of desire or of degree of belief, obtain. We need suppose only that human attitudes exist to account for tastiness and probability (at least in the epistemic, non-statistical sense of credibility) so that the projective truth-conditions are in a clear sense non-realist. (Of course if, with Putnam, one doubts whether one can give a naturalistic account of attitudes then it is hard to see how anything is to be gained from projectivism. Projectivism only makes sense from within a fairly naturalistic metaphysics.)

Projectivism is not only an anti-realist position, it also seems clearly to be a relativistic doctrine. One and the same piece of music may be truly described as sublime by one person and falsely so by another (insincerely pretending to find it sublime perhaps), because the aesthetic standards they (and their respective peer groups) project differ. But we should not be so quick to discern relativism, for may it not be the case that 'that piece was sublime' expresses different propositions on different lips, in which case there is no relativism? The absolutist can allow that 'that crane is 106 metres tall' can be true in the context of a discussion of the non-biblical Samson, the gantry crane in Harland and Wolff shipyard Belfast, and false as uttered by a bird-watcher, because they are expressing different propositions in each case.

Nonetheless it is quite intuitive to think that words like 'sublime' and 'tasty' retain the same informational content in different contexts, just as it seems natural to say that personal pronouns or indicators like 'here' and 'now' do (cf. Kaplan on 'character', 1989, §VI (ii)). Ambiguity blocks intercontextual disquotation and the 'Collective Descriptions' test, two of Cappelen and Lepore's indexicality tests (Cappelen and Lepore 2005, pp. 88–9 and 99–101). Similarly, if both Niamh and Orla, despite their somewhat differing aesthetic sensibilities, say 'Beethoven's String Quartet Opus 130 is sublime', then it is perfectly acceptable for Calum, who differs radically from both in his musical tastes, to say in a different context 'Niamh and Orla both said Beethoven's Opus 130 quartet is sublime', indirectly quoting intercontextually and collectively both Niamh and Orla. This suggests that there is no ambiguity, no change of informational content, in the use of 'sublime' by all three speakers, though the metaphysical content of sentences they utter containing the term will differ. Projecti-vism, then, is a good candidate for a relativistic anti-realist reductionism. But the relativism is not essential to the reductionism. There need be no relativity in a critic's description of the 'facts' of a novel, the plot say (or the 'facts' of one of the narratives of a multi-narrative novel). And, I will argue below (Chapter 3, §II.4), neo-formalism in mathematics gives us another example of a reductionist, but non-relativistic, anti-realism.[28]

The general reductionist idea, then, is this. Our subject S (S may be one of us) espouses a theory T with existential consequences such as that there exist φs. T is ontologically committed to φs, that is; as is S by dint of espousing T.[29] But in our metatheory, we are able to account for S's understanding of T without ourselves being committed to the existence of φs. Our metatheory does not entail the existence of Fs, for any predicate F which translates the object language φ. In the interesting, genuinely reductive, cases we can even account for the truth of T without being committed to φs. The position is reductionist because the existential consequences of the metatheory M are weaker (perhaps leaving aside commitment to various entities needed in syntax and semantics, irrelevant to theory T) than those of the object theory T. T entails, let us say, that tastiness exists whilst M does not have this entailment. M may indeed entail that there is no such property but does, consistently with this, aim to explain how we manage to make assertions, some of which are true, by using the expression 'is tasty'.

Thus in this 'cognitivist' version of projectivism we make assertions, correct or incorrect, when we discourse on what is, or is not, funny, tasty, cool, probable, and so forth. These are every bit as much assertions as those we make when we argue about the shape of a particular island or its distance from the mainland. However, only in the latter case are we 'limning reality', are we *representing*, rightly or wrongly, a reality independently of us. In these cases the metatheory will utilize the basic notions of traditional semantics, a domain of discourse (its members being real existing entities, according to the background theory of the world espoused by the metatheorist), a relation of reference between singular terms and objects in the domain, perhaps also between predicates and properties to which the metatheorist is committed, and so forth.[30] The projectivist mode of assertion, by contrast, is *non-representational*. It does

---

[28]  Thus I wish to resist Kölbel's suggestion (2002) that rejection of realism must drive us towards relativity concerning truth.

[29]  By the ontological commitments of a theory, then, I mean simply the existential consequences—sentences of the form 'there exists an F' or 'there exist Fs'—and not the original Quinean notion specified in terms of the existential quantifier. I will also equate 'there exists' and 'there are'. Some distinguish the 'being consequences' from the 'existential consequences', for example by taking the latter to be a narrower set. This seems highly implausible to me as a fact about English. For those for whom it is not implausible, distinguish ontological commitment (Existence) from ontological commitment (Being); the argument below is essen-tially unaffected, except that we have two forms of ontological reduction instead of one.

[30]  Though generally speaking it will not be purely homophonic: it will not be homophonic with respect to classically contextual expressions from Cappelen and Lepore's 'Basic Set'. For example, 'I' will not occur, in general, in the metaphysical content explicating what makes true a particular utterance 'I am pain' at a given time and place.

not depict the world but projects our attitudes on to the world, though of course those attitudes themselves are part of reality too.

Now what, in general, is the difference between a representational mode of assertion and a non-representational one? It cannot be that in the former case the metaphysical contents never involve humans or other conscious beings.[31] We can represent the facts about our own biology or mental states. Unpicking the 'our' can help. I can make assertions about your biological make-up or mental state and what makes-true or makes-false my utterance is nothing to do with my internal states or even with those of the peer group to which I defer on these matters, for you may not belong to it. So these biological or psychological utterances are clearly in representational mode. Less directly, I can make representational claims about *my own* biology or psychology if

(a) you could make those claims, suitably altered to allow for changes of context which affect the 'Basic' context-sensitive terms;

(b) this suitably altered utterance has, with its ordinary meaning, the same metaphysical content as my utterance had, and

(c) your claims are representational in the previous, more direct, sense.

Thus when I say 'I have a headache' this is representational because if you had said 'he has a headache' what would make that utterance true or false is the very same state which makes my utterance true or false; but the truth-makers, for you, do not involve your internal states. However, if I say 'that haggis is tasty' and you uttered the same sentence, directed at the same plate of haggis and with its usual meaning, then (b) and (c) above cannot both be true. Perhaps if we defer to exactly the same peer group and have the same sort of internal constitution, then a single sentence can give the metaphysical content for your utterance and mine. But in that case, condition (c) fails. The assertion is therefore in non-representational mode.

What, though, of generalizations over all humans or perhaps even all conscious beings: 'all conscious beings are unhappy', 'all conscious beings are DNA-based', and so forth? There is no relevant contextuality involved here and yet when you utter such sentences what makes them true or false is the same as what makes them true or false in my mouth but includes, in part, your own internal states, as well as mine. Yet intuitively they represent states of the world every bit as much as 'females have ovaries' as uttered by a male.

One strategy for handling such cases is to note that the sentences are structured, complex ones. If we can make sense of the idea that each part is in some sense representational, then we can count the whole as representational too. Thus the examples given are universal generalizations. If the correct semantics for the quantifier in 'all conscious beings are DNA-based' is exactly the same as that in 'all red giant stars

---

[31] That is, it is not the case that the sentences which give the truth-makers never contain terms referring to or designate humans or properties and relations specific to humans.

are older than the Sun' and if the latter sentence in its usual use is representational in the simpler sense, then thus far we have no reason to deny representational status to 'all conscious beings are DNA-based'. We need to look at how 'conscious being' and 'DNA-based' are working in the generalization. If the predicate '$x$ is a conscious being' is correctly given the same semantics in the generalization (or formal paraphrase rather) as in 'John is a conscious being', as uttered by someone other than John and that utterance is in representational mode in the simpler sentence, then again the occurrence of 'conscious being' in our target sentence does not impugn its representational status. If we can do that for all the constituents of the sentence, then utterances (in some imagined typical context) are in representational mode, if not (consider 'all human beings are ugly') then it is not. By such a strategy, then, I think we may generalize the notion of representational and non-representational modes of assertion to cover these trickier cases.

The resultant form of (cognitivist) projectivism is not only an anti-realist position, it is also reductionist, at least if we assume realism about properties, if we assume that some predicates designate mind-independent non-particular aspects of reality—hexagonality, being further from $x$ than from $y$—just as some singular terms designate particulars. It enables us to 'reduce' tastiness but not hexagonality if, on the one hand, our theory can explain what makes-true or makes-false ascriptions of 'tasty' without entailing that tastiness exists whilst, on the other, it appeals to the existence of hexagonality in explaining what it is about $a$ that makes 'is a hexagon' true or false of it.

Is there an example of this brand of realism/anti-realism debate which turns on subject terms and objects, rather than predicates and properties? Yes, the hermeneutical anti-realism concerning fictional discourse is an example, for according to it

Sherlock Holmes lived in Baker Street at the turn of the twentieth century

is true. Nonetheless, when turning our attention to an inventory of those human beings who have lived in the last couple of hundred years, Sherlock Holmes, as described in the novels, will not feature. The hermeneutical anti-realist about fictional character, whilst affirming that Sherlock Holmes existed in London around the end of the nineteenth century and smoked a pipe also, apparently inconsistently, denies that Holmes ever existed. The conflict is to be resolved by denying in (one hopes) a consistent semantic metatheory that the detective exists whilst nonetheless providing a non-referential semantics which explains how 'Holmes smokes a pipe' and 'Sherlock Holmes existed in London around the end of the nineteenth century' have metaphysical contents under which the sentences are 'semantically correct', are made-true by the appropriate conditions in the world, and thus, on a disquotational reading of 'true', are true. These conditions have to do with sentences in Conan Doyle's novels, what their representational meaning is (under which most are false), and what propositions cohere, and what do not, with those sentences, as would be judged by an appropriate group of readers and interpreters of the novels.

How exactly does this resolve the apparent inconsistency? One way to do this is to say that 'Holmes exists' is true when our mode of assertion is fictional but false when it is representational. To keep tabs on which mode of assertion is in play we might use some marker, for instance varying fonts. As remarked in the Introduction, I will use small capitals to indicate representational mode when this needs emphasizing. Thus our hermeneuticist holds both that Sherlock Holmes existed and lived in London and also that HOLMES NEVER EXISTED.

It is an arbitrary matter, however, whether our marker is change of font, or change of spelling, or use of a distinctive vocabulary—'subsists' versus 'exists' for example, *Der Bestand* versus *Die Existenz*. But the latter notational option suggests that I am discerning an ambiguity in 'exists' (and braving the wrath of the Quinean, who deprecates such proliferation of meanings for 'exist' as 'double talk' (Quine 1960, p. 242)). Is 'exist' ambiguous between 'mere existence' and '*really, truly* existing'? In which case we are back with scare-quoting, italicizing, and general banging-shoes-on-the-table behaviour. What is it to be: is there a plurality of 'modes of assertion'—representational versus various non-representational sub-varieties such as projective or fictive? Or is consistency between 'Holmes exists' and 'Holmes does not exist' to be restored by discerning a change of meaning in 'exists' from one sentence to the next so that there is a merely terminological contradiction?

If there is an ambiguity between 'exists' and 'EXISTS' it is not an ordinary sort of ambiguity between occurrences of words in representational mode.[32] We do not have a case like 'crane' as applied to the long-legged bird versus 'crane' as applied to the apparatus for lifting things, or other such stereotypical ambiguity. It is not the case that language users (as opposed to theorists) will typically be able, perhaps under suitable prompting, to come up with two non-synonymous disambiguations. Nor is it the sort of ambiguity to attract the attention of the linguists, ambiguity of scope or deep-structural ambiguity, for example, since the differences between the usages occur at the level of metaphysical content, rather than at the level of informational content (and since they do not depend on systematic syntactic relationships between the object sentence and metatheoretic sentence which gives the metaphysical content).

On the other side, though what we have here are differing modes of assertion, they are all equally forms of assertion. When someone says that the sunset is beautiful or that Holmes smoked a pipe, her utterances will typically look, walk, and quack like assertions. I see nothing in the ordinary notion of assertion to justify withholding the title of 'assertion' from such utterances. As remarked in §I, I use 'assert' and related terms in a non-theoretical, everyday sense.

Although it is not impossible that we are systematically mistaken in our application of our ordinary concept of assertion, the assumption that we are I find highly

---

[32] A long and patient intervention by Stewart Shapiro convinced me that it was best to have no truck with lexical ambiguity at all whilst Crispin Wright convinced me it was hopeless to rest all the weight of avoiding contradiction on the notion of mode of assertion.

implausible. So not only is there no difference in mood between utterances of 'Holmes existed' and 'HOLMES NEVER EXISTED'; both have the same 'force' in Fregean terms, both are assertoric. But we cannot remove the contradiction simply by appeal to a distinction in mode of assertion. If Galileo utters loudly 'The earth does not move' but then *sotto voce* 'But it does move' he has made contradictory assertions (whether they are sincere or not is a different matter) and one cannot get round this by saying one is in 'loud mode', the other in 'whisper mode'.

So we should conclude, in order to remove the inconsistency, that there is a type of ambiguity between 'Holmes existed' in its two modes, fictional and representational, but it is neither a lexical ambiguity of sense or informational content between tokens of constituent words nor a 'syntactic' ambiguity of scope or structure. It is a non-structural ambiguity in the sentence as a whole generated by the fact that the metaphysical contents of the utterances are so different in each case. In the one, the sentence is made true by consonance with Conan Doyle's text, in the other made false by the facts about the non-linguistic world. How could two utterances mean the same when they are made-true or false in such different ways, and in fact have different truth-values on the different readings? The differences in metaphysical content are far wider than those which give the content of 'that was sublime' as uttered by Niamh versus the content as uttered by Orla. Moreover, if Orla utters 'infinitely many primes exist' in the mathematics class while I utter 'no primes EXIST' in the 'metaphysics' room, Calum should not report these utterances as his sister saying that primes exist whilst his father denied it. This is evidence of a difference in cognitive meaning, informational content, for the sentences as wholes, generated by their different metaphysical contents.

This 'metaphysical ambiguity' as I will call it, is not, however, one to excite the attention of the lay person or syntacticians since it emerges only at the level of *philosophical analysis* at the metatheoretical level of investigation into what makes utterances of sentences in certain fairly general types of context true or false.[33]

We can disambiguate such metaphysical ambiguities by devices such as the Horgan/Putnam convention used here of small capitals for clauses in representational mode. The use of small capitals, however, is best thought of as a performative device, akin to lowering one's voice in a conversation, even though no one else can hear, if one thinks (rightly or wrongly) that the topic is a sensitive one. In uttering 'MUONS EXIST' I am signalling that I think my utterance is in representational mode. Of course I may be wrong; if the whole distinction between different modes of assertion and the whole notion of metaphysical content is misconceived, for example, then certainly I will be.[34] If not, then the difference between 'Holmes exists' and 'HOLMES DOES NOT EXIST' is a

---

[33] I say a little more in Chapter 3, §III.2 about the right relationship, as I see it, between philosophy and linguistics.

[34] The reader who starts out highly sceptical of the whole notion will have to engage in some charitably empathetic reading of the text (until illumination dawns!).

difference in the metaphysical content of the two uttered sentences. But this difference could arise purely through a change of context, without any performative signalling.

As remarked in §I, there has sometimes been thought to be a difficulty for projectivists in distinguishing their position from realists whilst still being able to account for mixed inferences (Hale 1993, p. 385). How can the projectivist distinguish her position from the realist about, e.g., aesthetic properties if she agrees with the latter that utterances of 'the sunset is beautiful' are fully assertoric and liable to be true or false? The answer to the dilemma, from the foregoing, should be clear: the distinction is at the level of the metaphysics which emerges in the semantic metatheory. Aesthetic utterances have non-representational truth-makers, ordinary factual discourse has representational ones.

Another level of divergence, alluded to at the end of Chapter 1, §III.1, is between disquotational truth and metaphysical content. To be sure, if we wish inferential patterns involving the standard logical operators to carry forward their validity automatically to 'mixed' reasoning involving both representational and non-representational elements, then we will need 'makes-true' and 'makes-false' to distribute over the logical operators in the same way as 'true' and 'false'; or at any rate for there to be no distinctive notion of 'make-true' for logically complex sentences which can come apart from disquotational truth.[35] But since one thing which pulls metaphysical content apart from informational content is a difference in behaviour in modal, temporal, and propositional attitude contexts, this distributivity can fail in these cases.

Consider 'If sentient beings had never existed, there would still have been beautiful sunsets'. It is quite easy, even for someone who does not believe that such beauty is an objective property of the world, to think of this sentence as true on at least one coherent reading. To get this reading, one has to evaluate the aesthetic consequent with reference to *current* and *actual* aesthetic attitudes, not the attitudes, if any, which may obtain were the antecedent to be realized. What determines whether 'beautiful' applies to sunsets, in the counterfactual situation, is the attitude language users *actually* adopt to sunsets which have the properties they are being supposed to have in the counterfactual case (pretty much the same properties as they have today, let's say, ignoring for current purposes human influences on climate); what attitudes they would have adopted in other scenarios is irrelevant, as is the fact that they would not exist at all, given the truth of the antecedent (cf. Blackburn 1984, pp. 217–19).

But now we have the makings of a divergence between disquotational truth and 'metaphysical' make-true. For disquotational principles and fairly uncontroversial interactions between the truth predicate and grammatical markers for mood yield, from the truth of 'If sentient beings had never existed, there would still have been beautiful sunsets':

---

[35] For logical inference operates at the level of informational content, and the truth-functions logical operators express are disquotational truth functions, *pace* the quasi-non-cognitivist.

If 'there are (tenselessly) no sentient beings' had been true then 'there are beautiful sunsets' would still have been true.

But the projectivist cannot say that if 'there are no sentient beings' had been made-true then 'there are beautiful sunsets' would still have been made-true (a subjunctive whose components have representational metaphysical content); not without abandoning anti-realism.

This failure of 'made-true' to distribute in modal contexts in the same way as 'true' means that the problem of reasoning with mixed sentences which was overcome for inferences involving standard logical operators resurfaces in the case of modal (and temporal and epistemic) 'logic'. The projectivist has to give a distinctive account of modal locutions when applied to sentences with projective metaphysical content. But one does not have to have Quine's hostility to modal notions to empathize with my scare-quoting 'modal logic'. If there is no genuinely logical inference in these cases, if, for example, transitions essentially involving modal terms are regulated by principles involving context-switching,[36] not logical principles, then this problem vanishes.[37] At any rate in the case of interest to us, mathematics (pure and applied), we need not be concerned with any inference other than standard logical inference.

## §IV.  A Map of the Terrain

Face-value hermeneutic fictionalism gives us an example of an anti-realism not just about properties but also about putative objects, 'fictional characters', one which is ontologically reductionist. There is no incoherence in holding to this anti-realism while viewing truth in general as evidence-transcendent—perhaps even fictional truth, if the fact that S follows in the right way from the text, and thus is true, can be evidence-transcendent. We have a reductionist anti-realism which I will call 'ontological anti-realism' but which is combined with metaphysical realism.

This division between two aspects of realism, the ontological and the metaphysical, is fairly commonplace now.[38] But I suggested earlier (Chapter 1, §II.3) that we might effect a compromise or 'combined rules' amalgamation of the two: the ontological realist about φs holds that φs exist but not only this: the sentences of the language we use to pick out φs have metaphysically realist truth-conditions and the assertion of the existence of φs must be in literal, representational mode. One way to proceed would be to fix a minimal level of metaphysical realism, one which any ontological realist about φs must hold pertains to sentences about φs—unrestricted weak fallibilism

---

[36] In a looser sense of 'context' than Cappelen and Lepore's.

[37] One contextualist account of intensional notions, though arguably not the best, is the paratactic. See Davidson (1968/84), McFetridge (1975), Rumfitt (1993), Segal and Speas (1986).

[38] See e.g. Shapiro (2000, ch. 2.2).

re φ discourse perhaps (Chapter 1, §II.2). 'Hard' ontological realism, then, attributes stronger realist conditions to φ-discourse, e.g. unrestricted strong fallibilism.

Reserve 'metaphysical anti-realism' for the Dummettian rejection of metaphysical realism in the sense of evidence-transcendent truth-conditions in a strong fallibilist sense. These stipulations cover metaphysical realism and anti-realism, and ontological realism, simple and 'hard'. Ontological anti-realism (with a weak form of metaphysical realism built in) bifurcates into (i) simple ontological anti-realism about Fs, where one uniformly rejects the existence of Fs, and (ii) reductionist ontological anti-realism, which affirms the existence of Fs but denies that they EXIST. The conflict is resolved by discerning an ambiguity in the two sentences taken as wholes, an ambiguity which is brought out by looking at their very different metaphysical contents. The assertion of 'Mathematical objects do not EXIST' by this sort of ontological anti-realist is in representational mode; its metaphysical content is given, accommodation for obvious contextual elements aside, in the same terms as its informational content, so that what makes it true or false is the nature of mind-independent reality. According to this view, however, assertions of e.g. 'Transcendental numbers exists' outside the Metaphysics Room are non-representational; they are true but their metaphysical contents contain no ontological commitment to numbers or other abstract objects; what makes them true is something other than the character of mind-independent reality. The ontological realist, on the other hand, differs from both the reductive and non-reductive anti-realists by affirming the existence of Fs in representational mode, in the semantic metatheory as well as in the market place or mathematics class; she need not be a hard ontological realist, she may hold that no existential claims are evidence-transcendent in the strong sense.

We now have the materials with which to sketch the philosophical terrain I am interested in. The twin notions of metaphysical and ontological realism give us four quadrants to work with, for any particular area of discourse, say the language of mathematics or physics.[39] The content of the table is relative to a setting of the strength of the metaphysical realism in itself and as part of the setting for ontological realism.

| + MR<br>+ OR | −MR<br>+ OR |
|---|---|
| + MR<br>−OR | −MR<br>−OR |

In the top left we have, for example, traditional mathematical platonists or, for scientific discourse, scientific realists. Mathematical and physical entities EXIST, we have to appeal to them to explain our grasp of mathematical and physical language, and, moreover, the truths and falsehoods of mathematics or of science can be beyond our ken. The bottom right corner is occupied by a fairly radical anti-realist; an example

---

[39] For a similar quadrant cf. Brock and Mares (2007, p. 4).

would be someone who combines Dummettian anti-realism with instrumentalism in science and some form of anti-platonism in mathematics. The top right column is occupied in philosophy of mathematics by, for example, Neil Tennant, who combines Dummettian anti-realism with a homogenous, non-instrumentalist treatment of mathematics and science. Existence claims in either domain are treated the same way, ontologically realist in both cases; no reductive claims are made. The bottom left quadrant is occupied by philosophers of mathematics such as Charles Chihara and Geoffrey Hellman, both of whom take mathematical assertions to have objective truth-values but who wish, in their different ways, to eschew commitment to an actual ontology of infinitely many abstract objects by making substantial appeal to modal notions, taken as primitive.

I can now stake out my space. I will attempt to barge into the bottom left quadrant too, but with a form of ontological anti-realism, and indeed reductionism, about mathematics which makes no substantive appeal to modality at all. On my 'neo-formalist' view, it is coherent to say both that numbers and other mathematical entities exist whilst, in almost the same breath, denying that they EXIST. The denial is an assertion in representational mode, the affirmation in a non-representational mode. Not, however, a projective mode. For although I have spent some considerable time on projectivism, in fact I think projectivism concerning mathematics is utterly untenable.[40] The reason I have gone into it in some detail is because, firstly, it illustrates well the distinction between informational content and metaphysical content which will be crucial to my account of mathematics and secondly because I happen to believe this approach is the right one with regard to simple judgements of taste, humour, and epistemic probability, as it features in Bayesianism for example.[41] For present purposes, however, it is enough that projectivism be *plausible* in at least some of these areas. For then that lends support to the idea that the informational/metaphysical distinction I appeal to really does have a basis in our language, and its application to the mathematical case is not ad hoc. Similarly any plausibility attending hermeneutical fictional anti-realism helps deflect any claim that neo-formalism is ad hoc. Something like this fictional anti-realism, indeed, is more plausibly exported to the mathematical case than projectivism but is still, I will argue, untenable.

The main positive work of the last two chapters, to sum up, has been to try to map out the conceptual space occupied by the bottom left quadrant, where I situate the neo-formalist position which I will advocate, and provide enough of a general framework, the fairly orthodox SCW framework, in philosophy of language in which to develop the view. In this corner of conceptual space, we combine metaphysical realism, acceptance of evidence-transcendent truth, and ontological anti-realism in

---

[40] Blackburn (1993*a*) and Divers and Miller (1999) have attempted to apply projectivist ideas to mathematics. See Weir (1994) for critical comments on Blackburn, and Shapiro (2007, pp. 369–75) for a critique of Divers and Miller.

[41] So on the latter I am in agreement with James Logue (1995). As it happens, I reject any form of projectivism as an account of moral judgements.

mathematics. I will, in what follows, simply assume metaphysical realism (and ontological realism for everyday and scientific discourse) with no more than a few critical comments in passing on metaphysical anti-realism. For the case for ontological anti-realism in mathematics is even stronger if it can be made in the context of a general metaphysical realism. However I do not think there is a formal incompatibility between the ontological anti-realism which I will defend and metaphysical anti-realism. Thus there is a variant of my favoured form of neo-formalism which can also be found in the bottom right quadrant. However, the overall package of metaphysical realism and ontological anti-realism in mathematics is, in my view, considerably more persuasive than the alternatives. It is to the elucidation of neo-formalism's distinctive account of non-representational metaphysical content that I now turn.

# 3

# Neo-formalism

## §I.  An Initial Specification

§*I.1*

The most rudimentary type of formalism in the literature is probably the 'game formalism' ascribed to Thomae and Heine by Frege, and savagely torn apart by him in the *Grundgesetze* II, §§86–137 (Frege 1903/80).[1] The game formalist holds that mathematics is a game played with empty signs.[2] Now it would certainly be stupid to hold that mathematics is an empty manipulation of meaningless symbols. After all, games such as chess are highly complex, meaningful activities and there is a perfectly reasonable sense in which the chess pieces have meaning.

A less stupid form of game formalism, then, would accept that mathematics, like chess, is a meaningful enterprise. Postal chess is perhaps an even better analogue for mathematics from the formalist point of view, the moves in the game themselves being utterances. The game formalist presses the analogy by claiming that utterances of mathematical sentences do not effect assertions which can be true or false any more

---

[1]  For enlightening discussions of formalism see Detlefsen (2005), Dummett (1991*a*, ch. 20), Lavine (1994, ch. 6, §3), Potter (2000, pp. 10–17), Resnik (1980, ch. 2), Shapiro (2000, ch. 6). Michael Potter notes (2004, p. 10) that many find the doctrine of game formalism so stupid they doubt whether Heine and Thomae could really have held the views Frege ascribed to them. Goodman and Quine, however, in their classic text 'Steps towards a Constructive Nominalism' (1947), do seem tempted by something very like game formalism, see especially the conclusion pp. 121–2.

[2]  Shapiro (2000, pp. 142–4) describes Heine and Thomae as espousing 'term formalism', the view that mathematical discourse is contentful, its subject matter being the domain of linguistic characters and symbols; later Thomae is described as a moderate game formalist on pp. 147–8. But there need be no inaccuracy in describing him as both. Shapiro points out that 'both opponents and defenders of formalism sometimes run them [term and game formalism] together' (p. 141) and, as Frege relentlessly points out, Thomae is not a consistent game formalist. Thus, although he calls the signs empty he then goes on to say 'they have no other content . . . than they are assigned by their behaviour with respect to certain rules of combinations' (Frege 1903/1980, p. 163 (see also Resnik 1980, pp. 54–61)). Heine and Thomae I will leave to the scholars. The doctrine I will try to defend is a clear descendant of game formalism as described in texts such as Resnik's, whether this is a straw man view or an historically important one. For later formalists see Curry (1951) and Cohen (1971); see also Giaquinto (2002, p. 210).

than a move in postal chess, posted snail mail or over the internet, constitutes a truth-valued assertion. Since no propositions are expressed, mathematics has no ontology. The expressions which play the syntactic role of names or predicates do not refer to anything, not even to signs. In this way, we avoid all the standard epistemological worries of platonism: over how we can have epistemic contact with the apparently abstract, causally inert realm of numbers, sets, functions, and so on.

Despite the pummelling which game formalism has received we should acknowledge it has some intuitive plausibility. Certain aspects of mathematical practice, both of the tyro and of those somewhat more sophisticated, do resemble game-play. The child learning to carry out the algorithms of decimal arithmetic, or struggling over a long division, the high-school mathematician or the engineer solving an equation using some known formalized heuristic—it is quite plausible to think that all these individuals are manipulating symbols according to formal rules without paying heed to any semantic content the strings of symbols may, or may not, have for them.

The denial that mathematical utterances are standardly used to make truth-value-bearing assertions, however, is grossly counter-intuitive and, as Frege emphasized, renders it a mystery how mathematics can have practical applications. Armed, though, with the distinction between informational content and metaphysical content, we can modify formalism to a version—'neo-formalism'—which is a 'face-value' or 'hermeneutic' (Burgess and Rosen 1997, pp. 6–7) form of mathematical anti-realism. As we write on the board, type out some symbols on the screen, or agitate the ambient air with mathematical sounds, we *do* (generally) make mathematical assertions which are true or false. These mathematical propositions, however, do not *represent* any external reality (not even a syntactic one, *pace* term formalism or Curry's formalism, Curry (1951)). What makes them true or false is not the properties and relations of abstract platonic numbers but the provability or otherwise of certain strings in a formal calculus. (I will say that their metaphysical contents are *formal* rather than representational.) Nonetheless the description of the proof-theoretic facts which make the mathematical assertion true or false belongs to the metaphysical content, *not* the informational content of the mathematical assertion. That a concrete proof can be constructed is what makes the mathematical sentence true, but the proposition that a concrete proof of a given type can be constructed is not part of its informational content since one can (and non-formalists do!) adopt different epistemic attitudes towards the mathematical sentence and sentences which express the metaphysical content. As is so often the case in language, according to the SCW framework, the metaphysical content which sets out what in the World makes utterances of a sentence true or false (perhaps relative to circumstances) does not form part of the informational content, the *Sinn* of the sentence.

Note that neo-formalism, like its game formalist ancestor, differs in crucial respects from Hilbertian formalism. Hilbert's position depends on a (not entirely clear or sharp) distinction between two areas of mathematical language: a finitary region, in which utterances effect truth-valued assertions, and an infinitistic region in which this is not so. Assertions of infinitary theorems are licit if they are instrumentalistically useful with respect to the finitary sector. For this it is required that a conservativeness property holds of them: we cannot prove from finitary premisses X, by going a detour through the infinitary sector, a finitary thesis which does not follow 'all along' from our initial premisses X. Since in many cases the shortest finitary proof will be much longer than the infinitary one, the infinitary language is useful, and will not lead us astray (granted conservativeness). By contrast there is no such asymmetrical bifurcation of language for the game formalist—in the strict version no sentence expresses a truth-valued proposition—nor in neo-formalism. All sentences, finitary or infinitary, express truth-apt propositions.[3]

Now to see how the neo-formalistic advance on game formalism might work consider, first of all, the game analogy itself and our example of postal chess. Although moves in postal chess do not express assertions, we can of course make assertions about those moves. We can say that such and such a move is legitimate, is in accord with the rules; or that such and such a state of play cannot be reached from the current position. These assertions have, I take it, a straightforward representational meaning and are made true or false by the facts about the game. Though one might adopt a platonistic metaphysics towards such facts—actual chess events and pieces are mere instances of the abstract game—or a platonistic construal of the notion of possibility which is used in saying that such and such a move is possible, I take it that there is no great plausibility in such a position.[4] At any rate, a naturalistic, anti-platonist account of the metaphysics of games is surely not nearly so problematic as anti-platonism in mathematics.

Thus far we have no anti-realism. But imagine that, as well as making moves in the game, players also start to make what superficially seem to be assertions out of declarative sentences closely linked to the utterances which form part of the game. As well as posting their move:

5 . . . . Bc3

they say things like 'Black Bishop can move to c3'. Suppose they are disposed to do so when and only when, allowing for explicable error, the move in question is permissible, at that stage of the game. My suggestion is that such utterances express truth-apt assertions whose metaphysical contents are, as it may be, that the move in question (i.e. the related non-assertive linguistic utterance) is legal according to the rules of chess in the current context, namely that stage of the game, Black's fifth move. But there may be grounds for denying that the metaphysical content is part of the sense or informational content of the sentence.

---

[3] For Hilbertian formalism see Detlefsen (1986, 2005), Tait (1981). Abraham Robinson also defended a Hilbert-style formalism, see Robinson (1965, 1969).

[4] For those who do find it plausible, more will be said on the notion of necessity in Chapter 6, §I.5.

For one thing, the utterers may play the game in an unreflective fashion, obeying the rules, and tying their declarative utterances such as 'Black Bishop can move to c3' to situations where they feel the move is legitimate without having an articulate grasp of the rules (though it so happens they unreflectively do follow them) and so without grasping the concept of being a legitimate move according to the rules of chess. This means that if we compare this sentence with a sentence specifying its metaphysical content, the two may behave very differently in complex contexts such as propositional attitude contexts: 'Hamish believes Black Bishop can move to c3' and 'Hamish believes that the rules $R_1, \ldots R_n$ are compatible with Black Bishop moving to c3' may have different truth-values. (We have already seen, Chapter 1, §III.1, Chapter 2, §III, how metaphysical content and literal content can come apart in modal and temporal contexts, in the cases of the demonstratively salient table and the beautiful sunset.)

## §I.2

Now as Frege rightly says, we have to distinguish between the game and the theory of the game.[5] In fact, in our case there are three levels to distinguish. There is the game itself. The moves in the game are tokens, in the postal chess case utterances, which have no truth-evaluable content; call this the *Game* level and the moves in the game *G-level* tokens. The utterances which are keyed to the legitimacy of the moves, utterances such as 'Black Bishop can move to c3', are contentful in the stronger sense of truth-evaluable, or, if one demurs from evaluating tokens for truth, are tokens of types which are contentful and truth-evaluable. Call this truth-evaluable level the *Contentful* level, meaning loaded with semantic, truth-evaluable content, and the utterance tokens and types *C-level*. Finally we move to a metatheory which gives the metaphysical content, distinct from the informational content, of the C-level utterances and gives the proof theory for the G-level. Since we are trying to explain and account for an area of reality here, this discourse will be fully representational (the meta-metatheory will be essentially homophonic, alterations for 'basic indexicality' aside). Call the sentences of the metatheory with its metaphysical implications, the *Metaphysical* level or *M-level*.

What, then, will the metatheory look like? There is, of course, a well-developed *mathematical* theory of chess. Adapted to the present context, it will set out a syntax for the G-level. In this example, as it happens, there will be only finitely many utterance types. It will also set out a syntax for the C-level language. This will include a finite list of atoms, some of the form ⌜p can move to l⌝ where the parameter 'p' is replaced by one of a finite stock of names of pieces, 'l' by a name of a square of the board, as well as other symbols for capture, check, castling, etc. Next we must specify all possible legal games—to do this we characterize the initial position and then lay down clauses which

---

[5] Frege (1903/80, §97, p. 172), where he distinguishes the theory of the game from the game, warns, correctly, against confusing the two levels and says 'that the two modes of treatment agree cannot automatically be assumed'. See also ibid., p. 183.

determine which extensions of any finite sequence of moves/utterances, are legal. Given the rules concerning stalemate, repetition of positions, fifty moves without capture or pawn-moving, etc., there are 'only' finitely many games; but perhaps of the order of $10^{123}$! So in practical terms this characterization will be carried out recursively. Moreover, it is of interest to consider the variant of chess in which those rules are dropped and the number of legal games is infinite.

Now in the M-level metatheory we have to set out a non-representational semantics (and indeed syntax) for the C-language, but of course the language of M-level is itself representational. If we are to eliminate the ontological commitment of platonism, it must itself be free of mathematics; thus it cannot be the mathematical theory of chess. Similarly if neo-formalism is to avoid the problems besetting platonism, the M-theory for mathematical 'games' or calculi and for the C-level of contentful mathematical utterances must be completely free of mathematics and any other commitment to abstract objects, such as syntactic types. It is not, to say the least, obvious how this can be done, even in our little example of postal chess.

I will not directly address the question of how to do this until Chapter 6. In order to given an introductory overview of the position and then reveal in more detail the overall structure of the neo-formalist treatment of mathematical theories, it is best first to work at the level of formal metatheory (FM), later explaining how to replace this with a mathematics-free M-theory in representational mode. By an FM theory I mean metamathematical discussions of proofs and models which, as the name indicates, are themselves branches of mathematics and so, though contentful, have formal metaphysical content and are not asserted in representational mode. Thus in the case of the C-level language for postal chess, such an FM theory can set out an infinite correlation between the sentences of the C language and the corresponding sentences of the G-level formal 'language game'. Truth and falsity are relativised to initial segments of legal (formal) games. A sentence is true, relative to segment $s$, just in case the correlated move is legal, false otherwise.

## §I.3

So much for the illustrative and imaginary example of assertoric discourse keyed to postal chess. What about mathematics? Let us start with a fairly simple example, the decimal arithmetic (DA) familiar from primary school, or rather a formal regimentation thereof. So once again we remain for the moment at the metamathematical level of an FM theory. Where in real-life decimal arithmetic we have tokens of ten distinct digits, an FM theory of the formal language of DA will start from ten abstract digit types. We might as well represent by them by the numbers zero to nine in the obvious order. A simple numerical expression type, then, is a finite sequence of digits in which the first digit is not zero. We also have brackets, the signs for addition and multiplication, and the equality and inequality signs. These can be coded by numbers $>9$; I will name the codes by the usual notations '(', ')', '+', '×', '=' and '$\neq$'.

Numerical expressions are built up recursively from the simple ones in the standard ways. I will represent them in non-Polish form by $(b + c)$, and so on. A sentence is the result of flanking an inequality or equality sign by numerical expressions on either side.

The rules of proof will contain as a subset the basic rules for addition and multiplication. The familiar addition and multiplication tables and algorithms for calculating long addition and multiplication are realizations of these rules. Neo-formalism is neutral as to how these rules are implemented in concrete cases. Arrangements of ink, including drawing tables, pictorial methods,[6] manipulation of abacuses or of calculators, can all constitute tokens of applications of the rules. All can be represented formally, the simplest method would be to add as a rule that every correct equation or inequation of the form:

$$(b + c) = d; \quad (b \times c) = d; \quad (b + c) \neq d; \quad (b \times c) \neq d;$$

may be written down at any stage as a line a proof, where b, c, and d are simple numerical expressions. Though there are infinitely many of these formulae, the basic rules provide an algorithm for checking, of any equation or inequation involving simple expressions, whether it is correct or not. Perform the basic school rule on the complex term on the left. If the result is the same string as the one on the right then the equation is correct, if not, the inequation is correct.

For the non-basic rules we will need reflexivity and substitutivity of identity (Leibniz's Law):

$$(i) \quad t = t \quad = I$$

$$(j) \quad \varphi x/t \quad \text{Given}$$

$$(k) \quad t = u \quad \text{Given}$$

$$(l) \quad \varphi x/u \quad j, k = E$$

where t and u are any numerical expressions. That is, we may write down a self-identity at any line in a proof, and, given any equation or inequation at line $j$ and an equation $t = u$ at line $k$, we may substitute u for some or all occurrences of t in the formula on line $j$ and write down the result at any line $l$ later than both $j$ and $k$.

Associativity and commutativity of addition and multiplication will be enforced by the usual rules, for example associativity of addition by the following (b, c, d, any numerical expressions simple or complex):

$$(b + c) + d = b + (c + d) \quad \text{Assoc.}(+).$$

To these rules we need to add distributivity:

$$b \times (c + d) = (b \times c) + (b \times d) \quad \text{Dis.}$$

---

[6] Thus drawings as in the Greek geometric tradition (cf. Giaquinto 1992), Venn diagrams, diagrammatic modes of proof more generally, cf. Bundy, Green, and Jamnik (1997), Peirce's diagrammatic logic (Peirce 1933), and so on, are perfectly licit from a neo-formalist perspective. See also Giaquinto (1994, p. 795, fn. 6) for some doubts as to whether visual methods can constitute proofs.

The proofs are then the strings of equations/inequations which belong to the inter-section of every set of such strings which is closed under those rules and which contains the results of basic rules. When a sentence S is the last item in a proof we write in the usual way ⊢ S. We could also add, if we wished, a notion of refutation, ⊣ S, with any proof of an equation b = c counting also as a refutation of b ≠ c and any proof of an inequality b ≠ c counting as a refutation of the identity b = c.

This gives us the formal G-level language $L_{GDA}$ and proof system for DA. For the semantic, contentful level, let us first of all consider a 'semi-atomic' C-language $L_{CDA}$ which allows for the expression only of equations and inequalities. The sentences of this language we could take to be simply the sentences of $L_{GDA}$. There is no need for the syntax of the G and C-levels to be different, indeed in actual practice they typically are not. However to keep things clear at the metalevel let us make them completely distinct. In the formalized language the simple numerals will be codings of natural language numerals, e.g. in English 'zero', 'one', 'two', 'eleven', 'one hundred and thirty seven', and so on, coded as numbers in some way, e.g. via ASCII coding.[7] Complex numerals are built up using these together with numerical codings of 'plus' and 'times' (and strictly speaking, special brackets, if we want the G and C languages to be totally distinct). This sets up a direct isomorphism mapping one:one the simple and complex C-level numerals with the simple and complex G-level numerical expres-sions. The sentences of $L_{CDA}$ are the equations and inequations of the form ⌜n is identical with m⌝ or ⌜n is distinct from m⌝ where n and m are numerals, simple or complex, of the C-language. The non-representational semantics is then straightfor-ward. The sentence ⌜n is identical with m⌝ is true (and thus ⌜n is distinct from m⌝ false) just when ⌜$\alpha = \beta$⌝ is provable in DA, where $\alpha$ and $\beta$ are the G-level numeral expressions corresponding to n and m respectively. Similarly the equation is false, and the inequation true, just when ⌜$\alpha \neq \beta$⌝ is provable in DA. The use of two different syntactic systems for the G-level and the C-level makes it clear that there are no vicious explanatory loops; truth for C-level sentences is determined by provability for distinct G-level ones which does not depend in any way on C-level truth. But this remains the case if we use a single syntactic language and distinguish two uses, a G-level versus a C-level one (see further §II.5).

What is it for a speaker to grasp the contentful language $L_{CDA}$ thus described? Clearly the speaker must be competent with the G-level calculus for DA. In addition, a crude grasp of $L_{CDA}$ will require that the speaker assent to an $L_{CDA}$ sentence S, allowing for explicable error, whenever a comprehensible concrete proof of $S_G$, the G-sentence correlated with S by the semantics, is manifest to the speaker. Similarly the speaker will dissent from S whenever a concrete refutation of $S_G$ is manifest to her, allowing for error once more. A fuller grasp will require firstly that the speaker

---

[7] To enable the notation to handle clearly and unambiguously arbitrarily large numbers we could utilize, at least beyond a certain number, say one billion, a place-holder system. Thus 'one four six zero five billion, nine million, thirty-two thousand and sixty-three' is the C-language equivalent of Hindu–Arabic '14,605,009,032,063'.

sincerely assents to S just when she believes that $S_G$ is provable in DA, dissents just when she believes that it is refutable, whether such beliefs are based on acquaintance with actual proofs and refutations or not. These are the 'snapshot' practices associated with decimal arithmetic. Secondly, the speaker must have correctional practices which 'settle' on genuine proof in the DA calculus, at least for relatively simple and comprehensible equations. The speaker may be disposed systematically to make mistakes, to fail to carry over properly in long additions, for example. She may be disposed to answer 115 to the sum 68 + 57 even after carrying out a long addition algorithm (but in the absence of any special coaching). However, if, even after patient explanation of the mistake, she does not agree that the answer is 125 then I think we have to say this person does not have a competent grasp of decimal arithmetic. (However, an inability to grasp what are in fact, given the rules of the calculus, proofs may not constitute failure to grasp the calculus or the language, once the proofs attain a particular level of complexity.)

Full grasp of $L_{CDA}$, then, requires a fairly reflective grasp of the notion of provability in DA. Nonetheless it does not require a *metamathematical* understanding of the notion; the speaker need not, for example, be able to define proofhood—set-theoretically say. Still, given the reflective grasp of provability, why not say that the informational content of $L_{CDA}$ sentences is representational, in particular represents derivability in DA?[8] This will be an error if the speaker's attitudes to intensional embeddings of $L_{CDA}$ sentences differ from those for the corresponding representational sentences, if the speaker would, for example, aver that it would still have been true that nine is equal to three times three even had the calculus DA not existed, even, indeed, if no humans had existed (as, I conjecture, most of us actually would aver). Or if the speaker might give different assent reactions to 'Hamish believes 7 + 5 = 12' and "Hamish believes that '7 + 5 = 12' is provable in the calculus DA", which she might reasonably do, especially if Hamish is not a very reflective user of arithmetic. Similarly no competent speaker will uniformly give the same assent response to 'Hamish believes 7 + 5 = 12' and "Hamish believes that I believe '7 + 5 = 12' is provable in the calculus DA". Hence, though speakers modulate their (snapshot) assent to arithmetic equations to match their beliefs about provability, the informational content for a speaker of a mathematical utterance does not contain any allusion to the beliefs of the speaker.

This shows we cannot equate the informational content aspect of the meaning of S with ⌜$S_G$ is provable⌝. Is this sufficient, however, to deprive S entirely of representationality, that is justify denying that assertions of S are in representational mode? And does it justify interpreting S in the neo-formalist fashion according to which no non-trivial paraphrase[9] or synonym, in general, exists? Even granted that assertions of

---

[8] The correctional abilities, which fix on real derivability rather than believed derivability as the condition on which corrected verdicts settle, show that the metaphysical content is not to be given in terms of what is believed to be derivable but what is actually derivable.

[9] That is, the informational content of 'seven plus five is identical with twelve' will include sentences like 'the sum of seven plus five is identical with twelve', 'seven plus five equals twelve', and so forth, but no

S are not in representational mode, do the above points justify assigning S the metaphysical content $\ulcorner S_G$ is provable$\urcorner$ rather than some other?

As to the first question, if mathematical assertions represent facets of a mind-independent reality, what could it be that they represent? The platonist has an answer: our mathematical sentence S represents the relationships among abstract objects. If S is, for example, 'twelve is distinct from seven plus four', it represents the distinctness of the two abstract denizens of reality eleven and twelve and a relation between the former and two other abstracta. But the neo-formalist, defending a naturalistic perspective on mathematics, denies[10] that there are such objects, and a fortiori, that there are relationships among such objects; hence there is nothing of the right sort for the sentences truly to represent. Other things being equal, the neo-formalist is in a stronger position than the platonist, not having to face the enormous ontological and epistemological difficulties the latter confronts.[11]

The platonist, of course, will argue that *ceteris* is not *paribus* whereas rival anti-realist positions, for example forms of constructivism, will associate a different content with mathematical claims. Thus the defence of neo-formalism will require, on the positive side, showing that the neo-formalist theory can accommodate not only DA but, more generally, standard mathematics (the less can be accommodated, the less attractive the position). Negatively, the neo-formalist case is strengthened by cogent criticisms of rival positions and I will advance some of those in later chapters. (As always in philosophy, no knock-down conclusive proofs or refutations ought, in general, to be expected; rather we have a holistic balancing of strengths and weaknesses across a number of areas.)

The neo-formalist distinction between informational content and metaphysical content answers the problems which Resnik finds with what he calls (1980, p. 61) 'derivation game formalism':

It may be granted that assertions in mathematics can be construed, incorrectly in my opinion, as assertions that certain formulas are provable, and these in turn as claims that certain moves in a game of symbol manipulations are possible. But this shows at most that mathematics is a theory of a game—one that even mathematicians themselves hardly play. (ibid., pp. 64–5)

It is indeed true that mathematicians do not, typically, make assertions about what is provable. There is no reason to think a non-trivial analysis of the meaning

---

sentence which provides philosophical illumination, none which reveals the semantic structure, in the sense of metaphysical content, of the original sentence.

[10]  More cautiously: refuses to assert that.

[11]  If S *represents* something more earthly, for example the existence of concrete proofs, then this would form part of the informational content of S. The metaphysical content of an utterance in representational mode can contain more than is in the informational content, but always incorporates the informational content suitably contextualized; as remarked, it is not plausible that reference to proofs, even formal proofs, and certainly not concrete proofs, is part of the informational content of mathematical sentences (outside of proof theory, of course).

(informational content) of their assertions can be given. But propositions about provability are what ground the truth and falsity of the mathematicians' assertions nonetheless.

## §II. Contentful Language

§*II.1*

Even with this very simple C-language, however, an important question arises. What right do we have to use phrases like 'is identical with' or 'is distinct from' in the language $L_{CDA}$? For they also occur in other sectors of language which are not mathematical, neither of the pure nor of the applied variety. They therefore have autonomous meanings, a linguistic life of their own, independent of the use the neo-formalist claims they are put to in mathematics. What, then, is the relation between the meaning of 'is distinct from' in 'Glasgow is distinct from Edinburgh', a non-mathematical claim,[12] and its meaning in 'nine is distinct from seven'? Many philosophers hold that identity statements are only true when the terms involved refer. For these philosophers, 'Santa Claus is identical with Santa Claus' and 'Vulcan is identical with Vulcan' are not true (and perhaps not false either). Indeed there are philosophers who claim such sentences do not even express propositions, in some interesting sense of 'proposition'. So certainly from this perspective, the use of the term 'is identical with' in, for example, 'nine is identical with three times three', is not innocent. If 'is identical with' works the same way here as it is claimed to do in empirical utterances, this truth commits us to the existence of a referent for 'nine'.

What the neo-formalist has to say is that sentences containing the phrase 'is identical with' which occur in mathematical practice are being used to make formal, not representational assertions. This contrasts with the phrase's non-mathematical use. Even if it has no ontological commitments there, understanding it clearly does not consist in keying its use to the provability of certain strings in formal calculi. As with the case of 'exists' surveyed in the last chapter, we should deny that there is any ambiguity of the type found in standard linguistics, no ordinary lexical ambiguity in particular. The ambiguity is more of a 'contextual' one, pertaining to differences in meaning which hold between whole sentences in which the term occurs. Again the important point is that the metaphysical content differs between the cases and that the contribution of the phrase to what makes-true (or makes-false) mathematical sentence S is purely formal. The G-level rules for $=$ induce at the C-level (given the tight link between assent and dissent to $L_{CDA}$ sentences and belief in the provability or refutability of the corresponding G-level ones) parallel rules for 'is identical with' forcing it to express an equivalence relation subject to the formal principle of

---

[12] Albeit one which inhabitants of both cities hold to be true with a degree of apodeictic certainty equal to that of any mathematical claim.

substitutivity—Leibniz's Law that from $\varphi x/t$ and $t = u$ we can conclude $\varphi x/u$. This is a formal principle to which the expression is subject in its general use.[13] It is not that in the mathematical case the term is, as it were, shorn of any non-formal aspects of its meaning leaving a pared-down meaning which it could bring to bear to any well-formed sentence matrix into which the term could be plugged. Rather, in this formal mode the formal patterns are the only aspect which matter, these patterns ground our use of it.

It is essential, at any rate, to posit shared contributions to the metaphysical content of some C-level terms, in particular logical operators, contributions shared across both representational and formal mode, if we are to explain the applications of mathematics or if we are to reason logically in C-language. For, as Frege emphasized, logical reasoning is contentful, it is more than just the carrying out of transformations in some calculus or other. But for logical reasoning we must expand the language $L_{CDA}$ by adding some logical operators. Suppose we add conjunction, disjunction, and negation, whose formal codes I will represent by the expressions '&', '∨', and '∼', to generate in the usual way a 'molecular' language $L_{CM}$ from the atoms of L (count ⌈n is distinct from m⌉ as an atom for these purposes). Neo-formalism, in contrast with game formalism, holds that the atoms of $L_{CM}$ have truth-values. Hence there is no need to try to find special meanings for the logical operators as they occur in this discourse and certainly no need to give a distinctive explanation of their meaning which ties it to provability in the G-level calculus (cf. the discussion of the defects of 'slow-track' or 'contrastive' projectivism in §I of the last chapter). On the contrary, it is much easier to explain how we can reason from 'mixed' premisses including sentences which contain terms from both $L_{CM}$ and general language, if we assume that the logical operators, just like 'is identical with', share their formal meaning across both sectors. If, as is often claimed, the meanings of the logical operators are *purely* formal[14] then the propositional operators will have a univocal use, both at the informational and metaphysical level, inside and outside $L_{CM}$. Even when they occur in sentences in representational mode, in other words, their contribution is purely formal.

## §II.2

But although it is a mistake to look for new meanings for the C-level operators in the workings of the G-level calculus, what are we to say if the calculus itself contains

---

[13] As the 'Santa Claus' case shows, though some G-level practices may establish that self-identities are C--level theorems, it is a contentious matter whether such sentences are also theorems of empirical language.

[14] The most extreme form of this view holds that the meaning of a logical operator is given by certain inference rules governing it; in order to rule out 'tonk'-like connectives, constraints are placed on the nature of these rules and their interrelations. Some take introduction and elimination rules (or one of this pair) to be central and require that they exhibit an appropriate form of 'harmonious' interaction. See Dummett (1991b, esp. chs. 11–13), Tennant (1987), Prawitz (1975, 1977, 1979), Read (2000), and contra: Weir (1986b), Milne (2004). But this is only one way, a particularly radical way, to fill out the idea that logical operators have a purely formal meaning.

expressions which function like logical operators? Suppose we augment a G-level calculus K by adding sentential operators. Again, to make matters clear, let us suppose the signs are syntactically distinct from the operators of the C-level language $L_{CK}$. There are, let us suppose, two binary sentential operators $\wedge$ and $\oplus$ in the G-language $L_{GK}$, a unary sentence operator $\neg$ and a nullary constant $\mathbf{f}$. Imagine the K-rules for $\wedge$ are 'conjunctive', meaning by this (somewhat vaguely) that they have been used in calculi in which it has seriously been proposed that $\wedge$ be interpreted as conjunction. Similarly the rules for $\oplus$ are disjunctive, those for $\neg$ are negative. For $\mathbf{f}$ we have the rule that A, $\neg$A $\vdash_K \mathbf{f}$. (In systems like DA we can add rules which ensure the interderivability of $\alpha \neq \beta$ and $\neg(\alpha = \beta)$.) How are we to correlate compound sentences of the K system, (e.g. if we augment DA by these sentential operators these will include sentences such as $(7 + 5 = 12) \oplus (7 + 5 = 11)$), with the sentences of the C-level language $L_{CK}$?

Well the *faithful* correlation for a given speaker will be one which maps each sentence S of $L_{GK}$ to a sentence $S^*$ of $L_{CK}$ such that the speaker modulates her sincere assent or dissent to $S^*$ to match her beliefs as to the K-provability or refutability of S (idealizing out correctible errors by the speaker). It may be that a speaker attempts to modulate assent or dissent for the contentful sentence to more than one GK sentence, but if their linguistic behaviour is to be coherent these sentences will have to be proof-theoretically equivalent: each derivable or refutable iff all the others are. For simplicity let us just assume that each CK sentence is the image of exactly one GK sentence, that the faithful correlation is one:one from the GK language into the CK one, in other words.

Call any such mapping* from $L_{GK}$ onto $L_{CK}$ *distributive* iff:

atoms of $L_{GK}$ are mapped to atoms of $L_{CK}$;
$(A \wedge B)^* = A^* \,\&\, B^*$;
$(A \oplus B)^* = A^* \vee B^*$;
$(\neg A)^* = \sim(A^*)$ and finally
$\mathbf{f}^* = \perp$

where $\perp$ is the absurdity constant of $L_{CK}$ (let us assume for simplicity that it has one) and the operators on the right are 'real' conjunction, disjunction, negation and absurdity.

The justification for the first clause is as follows. Speakers' grasp of complex sentences in the contentful language is determined, in part, by knowing how their truth-value is determined by their grammatical structure, and not by a linkage between the sentence as a whole and provability in the underlying calculus. So CK complex sentences should not be the images of GK atoms. Should the injection from GK atoms into CK atoms be a bijection, be onto? Well, there are cases one can imagine in which complex G-level sentences are mapped to contentful CK atoms (see §II.4 below). Still, such a combination of game calculus and contentful language is not going to be one which interests us much in what follows so that at least typically we will have a bijection from GK atoms onto CK atoms, whose truth or falsity is determined by the provability or refutability of its game calculus correlate. In this case, we can say that the contentful language satisfies an *atomicity* condition.

Looking beyond the atoms, say that the metatheoretic semantics for $L_{CK}$ is *global* with respect to a mapping $^*$ iff for *all* sentences A of $L_{GK}$:

$\vdash_K$ A iff $A^*$ is true according to the semantics.

A further condition, call it *global$^-$*, is:

$\dashv_K$ A iff $A^*$ is false according to the semantics.[15]

A semantics which violates either condition is *local*.

Could neo-formalism rest with mere atomicity and eschew 'globalization', the obtaining of the global criteria?[16] This, in effect, is what I argued the canny projectivist ought to do: give projective metaphysical contents for simple projective utterances and then, granting that these typically are used to make truth-valued assertions, let the ordinary truth-functional meanings of the logical operators take the strain of generating complex meanings for compound sentences. Why not take the same stance for the neo-formalist reading of mathematical sentences? There might, indeed, seem good reason to do so when we look at the consequences which follow for a speaker's practice if the faithful correlation from game to contentful level is both distributive and global.

## §II.3

To investigate these consequence, however, we need to know how we are going to interpret the logical constants in $L_{CK}$. The following assumptions, call the system comprising them the *Basic Semantics* (BS), are quite widespread[17]:

A conjunction is true iff both conjuncts are true. It is false if *and only if* at least one conjunct is false.

Dually, a disjunction is false iff both disjuncts are false; it is true if *and only if* at least one disjunct is true.

A negation is true iff the sentence it negates is false.

I read these assumptions as claims (highly plausible ones) about logical notions which do feature in natural languages such as English, though of course the relation between

---

[15] If there is no notion of refutation for the calculus then $\dashv_K$ A is to be identified with $\vdash_K \neg$A.

[16] When there is need to be more specific between the two global conditions I will subdivide this into globalization$^+$ and globalization$^-$.

[17] Intuitionism, in particular the Heyting interpretation of the constants, provides an, at least prima facie, rival approach. Given the use of constants in mixed sentences of applied mathematics, it is hard to see how this can work unless a uniform intuitionistic account of the logical constants in empirical as well as mathematical contexts is given. Dummett, of course, takes this programme very seriously as also does Tennant (1997b). A proper critique of this programme would require far more space than can be given here. Hence I will largely ignore the intuitionist tradition in philosophy of mathematics, arguing against it indirectly and positively, by presenting a distinctive way to link truth to proof in mathematics.

the logical notions and phrases such as 'and', 'but', 'or' (or perhaps the hideous 'and/or'), 'it's not the case that', and the plethora of other negative locutions is a complex one. It is probable that these phrases and others like them express the logical notions only in some, not all, contexts of usage.

The BS assumptions do not impose a classical bivalent semantics on the operators because BS does not impose the requirement that every sentence must be true or false; indeed, as it stands it does not rule out the dialetheist possibility of some sentences being both. The principles parallel Quine's conditions for assent/dissent in his verdict matrices in *Word and Object*, §13 (Quine, 1960) except for the italicized conditionals for conjunction and disjunction. I have italicized these because they are more controversial. The supervaluationist, for example, will not accept that a disjunction is true only if a disjunct is nor that a conjunction is false only if one conjunct is.[18] So much the worse for supervaluationism.

With all that by way of background, we can see that distributivity, the BS, and globalization can easily conflict, if we are quite liberal about what counts as a formal system. For example, we can present relevant logics such as R using an operator which, though interpreted as conjunction, does not satisfy $\wedge$E.[19] That is for some sentences A, B, the derivability $A \wedge B \vdash A$ can fail to hold. Suppose, then, that such an $(A \wedge B)$ is the sole non-logical axiom of our K-calculus whose underlying logic is R. If $*$ is distributive, $(A \wedge B)^* = (A^* \& B^*)$. By globalization[+], $(A^* \& B^*)$ is true since $\vdash_K$ $(A \wedge B)$[20] yet $A^*$ is not true since by hypothesis we do not have $\vdash_K A$, contradicting the very first clause of the Basic Semantics.[21] Or suppose that primality fails for the K-calculus, that is for some disjunction $(A \bigoplus B)$, we have $\vdash_K (A \bigoplus B)$ but neither $\vdash_K$ A nor $\vdash_K$ B. Then by globalization[+] and distributivity, $(A^* \vee B^*)$ is true but neither of the disjuncts are, once more contradicting the Basic Semantics, this time the italicized clause for disjunction.[22]

There are four points at which we can relieve this tension:[23] (i) lay down fairly tight constraints on what counts as a formal system, constraints which go beyond

---

[18] The principles fail, at any rate, for their most important concept of truth—supertruth; most important because it is the one in terms of which logical consequence is defined. Call the variant of the Basic Semantics in which we drop the italicized clauses 'The Minimal Semantics'.

[19] See the account of 'fusion' in Stephen Read (1988, ch. 3), where he defends the idea that the operator he calls fusion is conjunctive but does not respect conjunction elimination.

[20] Here I assume the reflexivity of $\vdash$, namely that $(A \wedge B) \vdash (A \wedge B)$ implemented as the rule 'H', for 'hypothesis', in the proof systems I will use. I am also assuming thinning (for the 'comma' mode of combination of premisses)—if $X \vdash A$ then $X, Y \vdash A$. Hence we cannot have $\vdash A$ else we would have $A \wedge B \vdash A$.

[21] Of course a defender of 'fusion' who also has a fairly deflationary conception of truth must reject this clause. I take that as a reductio of her position. But the only point I need here is that there is a formal calculus with an operator which behaves in many respects like classical conjunction but differs in such a way as to cause trouble for a simple translation into a standard conjunction in the contentful language.

[22] Dually, if we can have $\dashv A \wedge B$ but neither $\dashv A$ nor $\dashv B$ then distributivity and globalization[−] will conflict with the italicized BS clause for conjunction.

mere consistency; (ii) eschew globalization, in favour of mere atomicity, for example; (iii) drop distributivity; (iv) abandon the BS in favour of some weaker constraints on truth, for example the Minimal Semantics (MS).

The latter move is fairly unproblematic granted some pretty uncontentious inference rules for the connectives of the contentful language. First, define truth (relative to a given calculus) for an arbitrary sentence P* simply as provability of P in the calculus, thus ensuring globalization by fiat. Then the minimal semantics are met, as an easy inductive proof shows. Truth and provability, falsehood and refutability coincide for atoms by atomicity. In the case of disjunction, the truth clause is met easily: if a disjunct is true, hence provable, then $\oplus$I and globalization yields the truth of the disjunction. The falsity clause for disjunction is a biconditional. In one direction we have that if both disjuncts A and B are false then by IH, $\vdash \neg$A and $\vdash \neg$B. But we then have $\vdash \neg$(A $\oplus$ B) and thereby, via globalization, the falsity of A $\vee$ B, via the following proof:

| 1 | (1) A $\oplus$ B | H |
| 2 | (2) A | H |
| — | (3) $\neg$A | Given |
| 2 | (4) **f** | 2,3 $\neg$E |
| 5 | (5) B | H |
| — | (6) $\neg$B | Given |
| 5 | (7) **f** | 5,6 $\neg$E |
| 1 | (8) **f** | 1,4,7, $\oplus$E |
| — | (9) $\neg$(A $\oplus$ B) | $\neg$I |

Conversely, if (A $\vee$ B) is false then by globalization$^-$, $\vdash \neg$(A $\oplus$ B). We have $\vdash \neg$A hence, by IH, the falsity of A, via this proof:

| 1 | (1) $\neg$(A $\oplus$ B) | H |
| 2 | (2) A | H |
| 2 | (3) A $\oplus$ B | 2 $\oplus$I |
| 1,2 | (4) **f** | 1,3 $\neg$E |
| 1 | (5) $\neg$A | 4 $\neg$I |

with a symmetrical proof for B. In all these proofs we have used only the GK versions of standard $\vee$I, $\vee$E and the (intuitionistically acceptable) negation rules $\sim$E, or *ex falso quodlibet* and $\sim$I or *reductio ad absurdum*.

Similarly the MS clauses for & can be established if we have just those negation rules plus standard &I and &E. For negation, we argue that if $\sim$A is true then $\vdash \neg$A by

---

[23] The need to resolve tension here shows that Blackburn is right to suggest that one cannot move swiftly from non-factualism about atomic sentences of some language to the conclusion that all sentences, simple and complex, have truth-conditions which are anti-realist or 'non-factual', Blackburn (2006, pp. 249–50), see Chapter 2, §I.

globalization hence by IH, A is false. Similarly if ∼A is false then ⊢ ¬¬A by globalization hence ⊢ A by double negation elimination[24]—hence by IH, A is true.

Thus there are superficial attractions for the neo-formalist in dropping the Basic Semantics in favour of Minimal Semantics. However, I think the attractions are indeed rather superficial. For one thing, in order to avoid the extension of the Frege–Geach objection from projective utterances to applied mathematics, the neo-formalist has to assume that in sentences and inferences involved mixed empirical and mathematical terms, the logical constants have the same meaning. But it is even less clear that supervaluationism is the right account of the meaning of the logical connectives outside formal mathematics than inside it. Hence I will eschew this resolution of the problem for neo-formalism and assume the BS is correct.

The penultimate resolution of the quandary is to drop distributivity. It is easy to do so, as we shall see in the next section. But only if the game calculus language is distinct from the contentful language one. This, however, as the succeeding section §II.5 makes clear, is not the actual case. This identity of the G and C languages also forces globalization on us (§II.6). Hence my final resolution will be to accept that sound mathematical theories should be 'fully prime', that is, satisfy primality and also primality⁻ :

If ⊣A& B then ⊣A or ⊣ B.

I will not return in detail to how this can be effected (or to what we should say where it fails) until Chapter 8.

## §II.4

Firstly, then, failure of distributivity. Formally, there is no problem in specifying such a situation. Simply ensure that *all* G-level sentences are mapped to *atoms* at the contentful C level (thus ensuring that the mapping from the GK atoms is not a bijection onto the C level atoms). One way to do this is to associate sentences of $L_{GK}$ with singular terms of $L_{CK}$ and then, via these, indirectly with sentences. For example, as well as linking $(7 + 5 = 12)$ with 'seven plus five is identical with twelve' we could link it with the singular term

the proposition that seven plus five is identical with twelve

and thence, more circuitously, with the sentence

The proposition that seven plus five is identical with twelve obtains.

Formally, we could use $\lambda$ terms and think of the propositional locution as a 0-place $\lambda$ operator. Thus the term above becomes

$\lambda x$(seven plus five is identical with twelve)

---

[24] OK, I was kidding about the fairly uncontentious rules—the intuitionist rejects double negation elimination. This, indeed, rather than failure of the law of excluded middle, which holds in a wide variety of logics, I take to be the distinctive principle of intuitionism. I am also assuming here some structural principles, though fairly basic ones.

with a vacuous variable $x$. Call such descriptive terms $\lambda$-terms and sentences of the form [$\lambda x$(A) obtains] $\lambda$-sentences. Then if $s$ and $r$ are two K-sentences which are mapped to the $\lambda$-terms $\lambda x$(A) and $\lambda x$(B) respectively then we associate with $(s \wedge r)$ the $\lambda$-term

$\lambda z(z$ is the K-conjunction of $\lambda x$(A) and $\lambda y$(B))

($z$ new to A and B) and map the sentence to

$\lambda z(z$ is the K-conjunction of $\lambda x$(A) and $\lambda y$(B)) obtains

with similar clauses for disjunction and negation. In this way, *even if K is a trivial calculus* in which all K-sentences are provable, the contentful language $L_{CK}$ can express (non-representationally) these facts; all $L_{CK}$ atoms will be true. Thus a speaker could coherently adopt a contentful mathematical system—language plus rules and axioms, standard propositional rules for example—which is grounded in a trivial calculus in which everything is provable. It is just that it would be a very uninteresting system, a sort of night in which all (atomic) cows are black. Moreover such systems do not occur in actual mathematical practice. If they did then the connectives of the G calculus would be different from those of the contentful language and they are not different. It is to the actual 'homophonic' situation that I now turn.

§*II.*5

To have any plausibility at all, neo-formalism will need to accommodate a 'homophonic' (and therefore *ipso facto* distributive) mapping from G-level to C-level. Though for ease and clarity of exposition I have supposed that the G-language and the C-language are completely distinct, this is not what obtains in actual practice. It is not credible to claim that in our actual mathematical practice we work with two systems, one an uninterpreted calculus, the second a distinct one which 'comments on', unreflectively, the first. What is plausible, I maintain, is that competent users of, for example, decimal arithmetic have the capacity to 'bracket' the informational content of arithmetical expressions and calculate with them according to formal rules drilled in to them at school; indeed this capacity is often actualized. Moreover, their arithmetic assertions are coordinated with the results of these calculations or their beliefs as to what these results will be. A similar story can be told for the mechanical application of more complex algorithms used for calculating identities and non-identities in e.g. analysis and thus in generating proofs (which might consist in no more than a string of identities connected by applications of Leibniz's Law). But this means that, syntactically, the G-level language and the C-level language are, in actual life, one and the same. Hence the only reasonable transformation in these cases is a trivial homophonic and thus distributive one. Therefore from now on I will consider only contentful languages distributively grounded on their underlying calculi and in general assume the homophonic case where the G-level and C-level languages are the same (and so only work with one set of propositional operators, $\perp$, $\sim$, $\vee$, and &).

Thus failure of globalization in either form certainly seems a live option given the strong requirements, such as primality, which it, in conjunction with distributivity and the BS, imposes. But since we are assuming that the logical operators of the contentful languages have the same autonomous (formal) meanings they have in language in general, why should this be any problem? Why the emphasis, in previous sections, on globalization? I argued in Chapter 2 that it was a mistake for the projectivist to look for some special projectivist meaning in logical compounds such as 'Beethoven's last string quartets are sublime but "Hoots mon" by Lord Rockingham's XI is not'. There is no need to because the truth-value of this sentence is determined truth-functionally from that of its atomic constituents and it is only at the atomic level that the non-representational link between truth and attitudes occurs. So why is globalization a worry, why not similarly drop globalization in favour of *atomism*? In other words, why not say that in mathematics atomic contentful sentences are true (false) just in case, construed as atomic sentences in a G-level calculus, they are provable (refutable). All other sentences have their truth-values built up in the usual way whether or not, as G-level sentences, they are provable when true, refutable when false.[25]

The reason why we must abandon atomism is basically the same reason as the one which explains why distributivity is *de rigueur*. Since, in the usual cases at any rate, the G-level and C-level languages are the same at the syntactic level this means that the derivability relation in the two languages will be the same. For what is it for &E, say, to be an inference rule of a contentful language such as $L_{CDA}$? It is for me to derive from sentences such as '2 is even & 3 is odd' the conclusion '2 is even' and to do this not because of particular features of the conjunctive premiss but in virtue of a formal rule which applies to any (comprehensible) sentence of the form A&B (whether I am reflectively aware of the rule or not). The meaning of the terms in '2 is even & 3 is odd', other than that of the ampersand, is irrelevant; the meaning of the other terms is bracketed in other words. But this is just what it is for this rule to be a rule of the underlying game calculus DA, since the items which are manipulated and transformed by the formal rules are the same in each case. Similarly, for a formal, purely syntactic, inference pattern (that is an inference rule or axiom) to be one that I implement in $L_{GDA}$ is for me to implement it in $L_{CDA}$ since, syntactically, the two are identical. The same goes for all the rules, including the mathematical rules. So in the usual homophonic case the derivability relation is the same in both languages.

This communal derivability relation is fatal to atomicity indeed to locality, but before looking at this, I will address a further worry. It might seem, given the foregoing, that the very distinction between G-level and C-level is threatened and that the assumption of two distinct syntactic systems is not merely convenient but

---

[25] Or fairly usual way: if our language is quantificational then on this approach a substitutional account of the quantifiers would be needed. It is a contentious matter whether the notion of an 'atomic' sentence makes sense for real sentences of a natural language. For present purposes, a non-atomic sentence is one containing locutions which we would normally paraphrase into formal logic using sentential operators and the quantifiers.

essential for the coherence of the position. For what is it for a sentence to be used in a G-level way? For us to implement formal, syntactic, inference rules with respect to instances including that sentence? If so, then every non-atomic sentence, including highly empirical sentences, will have a G-level use, since all can feature in logical inferences which are purely formal, dependent solely on grammatical form (at least according to an orthodoxy which I follow). Neo-formalism threatens to obliterate the mathematical/empirical dichotomy, but from the opposite direction to Quinean empiricism, as it were: all discourse is mathematical!

That all non-atomic sentences have a G-level formal component, however, is a perfectly plausible consequence of neo-formalism. The 'triviality' of simple logical truths of the empirical language—'if snow is white then snow is white'—fits in well with the idea that we bracket their non-logical content in appreciating their logical truth. The important point is that the terms of such sentences have a life, a meaning and a use, outside of formal calculi, whilst this (the neo-formalist maintains) is not true for mathematical terms and in this the distinction between mathematics and empirical language is maintained.[26]

We still need some explanation of the nature of the difference between using a sentence as part of the G-calculus and using that self-same syntactic string contentfully. It does not have to be the case that a mathematical sentence ever gets actually used in the G-level calculus. Our beliefs as to the string's *provability*, to which our assent or dissent as to its truth is tied, do not require this. But we do have to make sense of what it would mean for it to be used purely formally. Moreover it is implausible to suppose that the G-level/C-level distinction essential to neo-formalism could ever actually obtain for a real language, such as our language of decimal arithmetic, if pure G-level uses of some sentences were never actually implemented.

One of the seminal ideas behind formalism is the idea that purely formal manipulation of symbols is akin to following the rules of games such as chess. But one and the same string of symbols can be used now contentfully and on another occasion, non-contentfully—formally—in some cases literally as part of a game. This can be seen by returning to our original example of postal chess. What makes postal chess a competitive game is that, typically, players are attempting to win and achieve thereby the rewards, financial or purely in terms of prestige, which this brings. (This may not happen in some cases but that should not lead us to deny that postal chess is a game; these cases can be written off as atypical.) If, however, I assert some mathematical claim—that the sum of items bought adds up to a particular figure, or I affirm a consequence of the axiom of choice as a lemma in proving some model-theoretic result—I am not taking part in a game with conventionally determined goals which are to be achieved in each typical play of the game.

---

[26] Not that this is an exclusive dichotomy. The application of mathematics is possible, I will argue in Chapter 5, only because there is a third category, of mixed sentences, which have both an empirical component and a formal component, one that, in contrast with the tautology above, goes beyond pure logic.

The rules and moves of chess, however, can be followed whilst not actually taking part in a game. A teacher, in a chess class or column in a newspaper, might take us through alternative developments of an actual game to show us that a better outcome could have been achieved, or to explain why the player resigned—checkmate was inevitable, against a top player at any rate, no matter what move was made at the given stage. Suppose the teacher had the habit of making assertions 'Checkmate follows', say, in such circumstances. Then these assertions could be interpreted exactly as mathematical assertions are to be interpreted, according to neo-formalism. The utterances are contentful and not part of a game. They are true or false not by dint of representing an external reality, but as keyed to what can or cannot be done in the formal 'calculus' of the game from that stage on. One might attempt to use this as a *reductio ad absurdum* against neo-formalism; if the latter is right, then these kinds of uses of chess are a form of mathematics. But I do not see the consequent here as false and thus a refutation of neo-formalism. Certainly I do not see a sharp distinction between such practices and many mathematical practices.[27]

Conversely, we can turn mathematical practice into a game in a perfectly standard sense of game, in mathematical Olympiads for example. Or more simply, one might set some calculations for children and offer a reward, some sweeties, to the first child to carry them all out correctly. Indeed, school exercises are quite close to games in this sense. In the good old days the reward was not being thrashed for being wrong, now it is mere prestige or avoiding having further homework set. This is a paradigmatic example, then, of G-level use of mathematics.

It is clear, then, that one and the same form of words could literally be used playfully in some cases but not in others, even though there is no sharp distinction between games and non-games and no interesting necessary and sufficient conditions differentiating games from non-games (the term is a family-resemblance term, as the Wittgensteinians say). (It is true, moreover, that there is not a simple dichotomy between contentful uses of mathematics—e.g. when one asserts that the sum of items bought is £5.62—and definite game playing as in school exercises.)

Of course purely formal manipulation of strings goes on even when one is not taking part in a game. Thus another practice I have classed as G-level activity is carrying out formal algorithms with a view to making some genuine assertion. Examples include following through the rules for differentiating products in order to arrive at a result in calculus which is of practical importance in a problem or formalizing an argument and writing it out as a proof in some recognized proof architecture. The reason these are game-level uses is that firstly the strings which are manipulated are not put to any assertoric use and secondly one need pay no attention

---

[27] Perhaps mathematics proper emerged from a pre-mathematical phase in which people started treating moves in calculating games *as if* they were genuine assertions. However neo-formalism holds that mathematical theorems are literally true, not make-believe (*pace* Yablo 1998, 2005); as mathematics emerged, the pretence died out. Saying that mathematical truths are literal may not seem to amount to much, given the difficulty of demarcating the literal from the metaphorical. Some, indeed, reject the distinction. But not me.

to the meanings, if there are any, of the terms other than those aspects of meaning which manifest themselves in the formal rules one is following. Such uses are not 'game-theoretic' in any literal sense, but I think that in a clear enough sense they are not contentful either and so stretching 'game' to include them is legitimate. Certainly they can be classed as moves in a calculus prosecuted with regard only to formal structure. The distinction between G-level and C-level distinction, whilst not completely precise, is sharp enough for the purpose of developing neo-formalism.[28]

It may be countered that the neo-formalist, if motivated by a naturalistic horror of abstract objects, is obliged to give some form of naturalistic specification of what makes a practice of uttering sentence tokens, and manipulating them according to calculi which are analogous to games, a *mathematical* practice.[29] Now no one now thinks that naturalism is committed to the provision of such a specification in the language of hard physical sciences, that one should look for some purely acoustic specification of just which sounds are chemical sounds, for example, or a neural predicate which picks out all and only the brain activity involved in chemical thinking. Or rather, if anyone thinks that it is so committed, that person must surely regard naturalism as absurd. Exactly what naturalism can reasonably amount to, in connection with matters of meaning and cognition, is a difficult question (I make some remarks on this in Weir 2003*b*).

Why, though, should the neo-formalist feel any obligation to attempt some kind of analysis of the notion of mathematicality? We agree fairly well on what counts as mathematical activity, whatever our philosophical views. The neo-formalist is entitled to start from this agreed, if not entirely sharp concept (do chess problems count as mathematics?) and put forward a theory of what our understanding of the utterances antecedently distinguished as mathematical consists in. It would not be classed as a failure if it was unable to deal with some sub-class of the intuitively mathematical, so long as it accounted for most. Moreover, if the account is illuminating then it might post hoc, as it were, offer some help in analysing the notion of 'mathematicality'. Mathematical judgements must, at least typically, show some sensitivity to beliefs about provability and refutability. The latter, in turn, require an ability to carry out or check on formal transformations of symbolic elements, formal not in the sense of set out in a formal logic in an artificial language, but rather as specifiable in terms of non-semantic patterns—grammatical, diagrammatic, or whatever.

Thus we can do justice to the fact that the G-language and the C-language are in actual practice the same; in particular, we do not make different inferences, do not generate a different derivability relation, when switching from G-use to C-use or back again whilst still maintaining the distinction, essential to neo-formalism, between G-calculus and the logic of the contentful language. The worry that the two levels

---

[28] And of course, as we have seen, one and the same string can feature in distinct calculi, its two game level and contentful level uses differing from calculus to calculus.

[29] Thanks to Tim Williamson for raising this point.

collapse has been addressed. It arose in the context of the claim that a single derivability relation for the two levels blocks atomism and enforces globalization. How does that come about, and why is it in turn a worry?

## §II.6

Globalization$^+$, it will be remembered (well perhaps not), is the condition:

$\vdash_K$ A iff A$^*$ is true

where K is the underlying calculus of the language L$_{GK}$.[30] I will write the derivability of the contentful language L$_{CK}$ unsubscripted as $\vdash$. But since the derivability relation $\vdash$ of L$_{CK}$ is extensionally equivalent to $\vdash_K$ and since $^*$ is homophonic, globalization$^+$ gives us $\vdash$ A iff A is true. The right to left direction is a very strong form of completeness, stated not in terms of validity but in terms of truth. Every true mathematical sentence of our molecular calculus is provable. The right to left direction is the soundness one.

Since our semantics is essentially proof-theoretic, since truth is constituted by proof in the calculus, even a form of completeness this strong is not surprising and fairly trivial to prove from atomicity, granted some relatively uncontentious rules are part of the formal system. The proof is inductive. We prove the more general result that if A is true it is provable, if false refutable (which we can take to be the provability of its negation). Atomicity provides the base step:

$\vdash$ A iff A is true; $\vdash \sim$A iff A is false (for atomic A).

For the negative case:

Suppose $\sim$A is true hence A is false. By IH, $\vdash \sim$A.
Suppose $\sim$A is false hence A is true. By IH and $\sim\sim$I, $\vdash \sim\sim$A.

For disjunction:

Suppose A $\vee$ B is true; by the BS, one disjunct is, suppose without loss of generality, A. By IH and $\vee$I, $\vdash$ A $\vee$ B.
Suppose A $\vee$ B is false; by the BS, both disjuncts are so that by IH $\vdash \sim$A and $\vdash \sim$B. The argument given above (§II.3), which uses standard $\vee$E, $\sim$E and $\sim$I, yields $\vdash \sim$(A $\vee$ B).

The case for conjunction is dual, the rules we need (along with standard structural rules) are &I, &E, $\sim$E, and $\sim$I.

---

[30] It is worth perhaps acknowledging again that the neo-formalist cannot rest at this kind of semantic level, the level of formal metatheory FM, but must ultimately press on to a 'metaphysical' non-mathematical M-level treatment (Chapters 6 and 7). The derivability relation $\vdash_K$, for example, is a set of ordered pairs, and so does not actually EXIST, according to the neo-formalist.

So we have one direction, the completeness direction, of globalization[+] indeed globalization. But if the other direction fails, the system is unsound. Here we have, then, the reason why we cannot rest, as the projectivist can, with atomicity but have to go for globalization. One direction is provable, given fairly uncontentious rules in the contentful language, whilst to abandon the other is to abandon soundness, which we must not do.

But though the neo-formalist has to embrace globalization, this has some apparently threatening consequences (in conjunction with the BS), in particular, as we have seen, both forms of primality. Thus if $\vdash$ A $\vee$ B (hence A $\vee$ B is true) we must have either $\vdash$ A or $\vdash$ B (since one or other disjunct is true). More generally, since globalization links truth to proof, provability must distribute over the connectives just as truth does.

This does not happen in classical mathematical theories unless they are negation-complete, a very strong requirement. Soundness then means that neo-formalism either has to embrace only very special classical theories, negation-complete ones, or else be driven towards a logic which can ensure that interesting negation-incomplete theories are 'fully prime' that is respect primality and also primality[−] :

If $\dashv$A & B then $\dashv$A or $\dashv$ B.

However, this will involve a radical revision of logic and thus mathematics, an even more radical revision than intuitionism, indeed. Thus although intuitionistic logic, considered as a theory with no non-logical axioms, is prime and we can give conditions for a more substantive theory, a set of non-logical axioms, to be prime in a framework of intuitionistic logic,[31] intuitionistic logic is not prime[−], since $\vdash$ $\sim$(A& $\sim$A) for any A, including those for which we have neither $\vdash$ A nor $\vdash$ $\sim$A.

Once again we see that merely adopting a relatively deflationary theory of truth together with a general idea for a non-realist semantics does not automatically yield a successful non-realist semantics for particular languages, that there is usually some serious work still to do. How the neo-formalist can have globalization, both forms of primality and the BS, without revisionism will not be fully explained until Chapter 8. For now, we have enough of the nitty-gritty detail of formal interrelations between G-level and C-level in molecular languages, and of the problematic aspects for neo-formalism, to proceed.

# §III. Quantification and Existence

## §III.1

Thus far, however, I have only considered propositional contentful languages. I have left out of account quantification and the enormous step in logic which was taken when Frege and Peirce, in their different ways, saw that in a

---

[31] Cf. Prawitz (1965, Corollary 6, pp. 55–6); see also Gentzen (1969, pp. 105–6).

sentence such as ($1 < 2$ & $2 < 3$) we can discern lots of predicative patterns: ($x < 2$ & $2 < 3$), ($1 < y$ & $2 < 3$), ($1 < y$ & $y < 3$), ($1 < 2$ & $2 < z$), ($x < y$ & $y < 3$), and so on. To these complex predicates, crucially including those with more than one free variable, we can apply one or more quantifiers (perhaps after crystallizing them into unitary predicates by a binding device such as $\lambda$ abstraction—$\lambda x(x < 2$ & $2 < 3)$, $\lambda xy(x < y$ & $y < 3)$ etc.). Can the neo-formalist expand from a molecular language $L_M$ to a quantificational language $L_{QU}$ and explain the role of quantification in mathematics? The theory will be of little use if not.

Certainly the explanation of the role of quantifiers cannot take the same form as for the sentential operators such as conjunction. The neo-formalist cannot allow that, in the contentful mathematical language, 'for all' and 'there are some', have exactly the same, essentially formal, role as in 'empirical language'. As ontological anti-realists and reductionists, neo-formalists hold that 'exist' in mathematical discourse is typically used in a non-representational mode of assertion. As with 'is identical with', there is no ordinary ambiguity between the word in mathematics and in empirical discourse, but the metaphysical content of entire existential assertions in mathematics is determined by formal criteria, by what is provable or refutable. They have formal, non-representational content, at the metaphysical level.

What exactly is the formal meaning of the universal quantifier $\forall$ or the existential quantifier $\exists$ and how do these meanings relate to those of natural language quantifiers such as 'there are'? In a tree-form natural deduction setting the standard rules are

$$\frac{\forall x \varphi x}{\varphi x/t} \qquad \frac{\varphi x/t}{\exists x \varphi x}$$

with $\forall$E on the left and $\exists$I on the right. $\forall$I and $\exists$E are as below, left and right, with a global ban on the occurrence of b on the overall premises on which $\varphi x/b$ in $\forall$I depends and, in $\exists$E, on its occurrence in $\varphi$, C, or any of the other premises on which the sub-proof of C from $\varphi x/b$ depends:

$$\frac{\varphi x/b}{\forall x \varphi x} \qquad \frac{\exists x \varphi x \quad \overset{\overline{\quad}^1}{\varphi x/b}\quad C}{C}\,1$$

But both $\forall$E and $\exists$I are problematic as formal rules for natural language quantifiers. If the logical powers with which the logician endows the existential quantifier are taken to match the ordinary language ⌜there are one or more $\varphi$s⌝[32] this would allow us to

---

[32] Of course the whole business of the relationship between the standard quantifiers of logic and natural language quantifiers is highly contentious, with the Frege/Russell orthodoxy challenged by a host of alternative interpretations, (and the question of whether there is, as free logicians say, a first-order existence predicate—contra Frege and Russell—also a moot one). On the other hand, the standard logical quantifiers have actually worked their way into 'real' mathematical discourse, in the language spoken, or at least written, by mathematicians and logicians. Perhaps some rival interpretation, plural or whatever, of the natural language locutions for which the standard quantifiers are generally proffered as (rough) paraphrase is better. Even if so, I conjecture that the overall approach adopted here—distinguishing representational assertions

conclude that there are one or more winged horses from 'Pegasus is a winged horse' or even more bizarrely, that there are one or more non-existent things from 'Pegasus does not exist'. Some do not find this last inference bizarre! I am not alluding here to Meinongians but to those who think the inferences are valid but untroubling because, in these cases, the premiss is not true. Reference-failure introduces a truth-value gap or some similar pathology. However, even if we accept the highly counter-intuitive claim that 'Pegasus does not exist' is not true, because truth-value-less, the validity of such inferences conflicts with the principle that in a valid inference with one premiss and one conclusion, if the conclusion is false then the premiss is also. This is as firm a principle, I would argue, as the converse principle that if the premiss is true, the conclusion is true (see also Chapter 8, §III).

This motivates the amendment of ∀E and ∃I to:

$$\frac{\forall x \varphi x, \mathrm{E}(t)}{\varphi x/t} \qquad \frac{\varphi x/t, \mathrm{E}(t)}{\exists x \varphi x}$$

where $\mathrm{E}(t)$ represents some way of expressing the claim that t exists (it being a controversial matter just what this expression should amount to). Here I am going along with a widespread, perhaps majority view, among logicians. It is perfectly reasonable to present logic, classical logic in particular, using the simpler quantificational rules, having laid down the background assumptions that the domain is non-empty and all terms refer. For under these assumptions, the logic will never lead one from true premises to untrue conclusion or false conclusion to non-false premiss. Nonetheless, strictly speaking, the 'unfree' ∀E and ∃I rules are not sound, as the fallacious arguments which emerge in empty domain or empty name contexts demonstrate. Hence in a rigorous presentation of logic one should work with the restricted rules.

That being so, if we have three predicates, one first-order and two second-order,[33] which conform to the above two rules in a contentful language $L_{QU}$ (and, in the homophonic case, occurring in the same way in the game-level calculus QU), then the metaphysical content of these predicates, the aspect they add to the truth conditions of sentences of the formal contentful language to which they belong, is just the formal ingredient of the metaphysical content of the existence predicate and the two standard quantifiers in non-mathematical language. However, there is no conflict between $\exists x(x$ is a prime number) and 'NO PRIME NUMBER EXISTS', if both the

---

where quantificational locutions are the dominant operators from formal ones—will be applicable in any such case too. Granted my non-Quinean take on formal quantifiers, I should add that I read 'ontological commitment' as determined by the existential consquences of a theory, where existential sentences are those prefaced by the natural language quantifiers 'there are' and 'there is'.

[33] For we can think of ∃ and ∀ as applying to first-order predicates. One way of realizing this is forming the first-order terms by λ abstraction.

distinction drawn between informational content and metaphysical content, and the application the neo-formalist makes of it, are sound.

## §III.2

Burgess and Rosen, however, have argued (1997) that 'hermeneutic nominalists' (such as the present author) who argue that mathematical discourse, taken at face value and without any reconstrual of its meaning, is not committed to the existence (or in my case EXISTENCE) of a realm of abstract objects should submit their claims about the meanings of mathematical sentences to the linguistic community and defer to their judgement. More generally, these authors powerfully argue the case that nominalism is, at the very least, not obviously correct and that, in particular, the burden of proof is not on the anti-nominalist. Moreover, they mount this attack from the naturalistic perspective which most nominalists adopt. The naturalistic philosopher, they argue, should defer to the scientific community and the scientific community shows no interest in, for example, nominalistic reconstruals of physical theory or in reducing ontological commitment to abstract objects. Furthermore, Burgess and Rosen (ibid., § III.C.2.b) clearly doubt whether the linguistic community will find nominalistically acceptable readings of mathematical discourse plausible.

Now it is certainly the case that philosophers should defer to relevant experts in the scientific community. But there is deferential and there is doormat. They cite (ibid., p. 34) a jocular passage from David Lewis (1991, pp. 58–9) a sort of *nostra culpa* admission of the follies of philosophers. Lewis chides philosophers who question platonistic mathematicians. What right do we have to pass judgement on mathematicians given the major 'results' of our discipline such as the non-existence of the external world or the denial of plurality? This is an example of a doormat attitude to scientists, or in this case mathematicians.

Certainly, a Quinean who holds that philosophy is continuous with science and that the scientific subdisciplines form a network interlinked indirectly to varying degrees cannot consistently forbid philosophers from critically evaluating the findings of fellow scientists in a neighbouring discipline. But even if one rejects, as I would, the Quinean view in favour of a fairly sharp, traditional distinction between 'conceptual' philosophy and 'empirical' science, there is still plenty of room for informed philosophical criticism of scientists, in both the natural and the human sciences.

For one thing, scientific results require interpretation and when scientists interpret them they engage to some degree in philosophy, whether they know it or not, sometimes very bad philosophy. So whilst philosophers should of course take very seriously the views of a great scientist such as Niels Bohr on the interpretation of quantum mechanics, by no means must they accept the Copenhagen interpretation (or interpretations) without question, or leave the issue of the interpretation of quantum mechanics to be resolved by card-carrying physicists alone. They should certainly pay serious attention to the results of the great Belfast physicist J. S. Bell which have been used to argue that hidden-variable quantum mechanical theories are ruled out if his Inequality is borne out by the experimental data, as seems to be the case. But if Bell's reasoning in favour of such incompatibilities[34] includes some philosophically contentious assumptions about causal asymmetries in time together with views of free-will which do not so much reject compatibilism as fail even to register the doctrine on the conceptual map, philosophers are entitled to intervene. Indeed, philosophers with sufficient competence in physics ought to engage in this debate, to educate the physicists, if nothing else. Whilst it is hard to make an objective judgement on this, I would suggest that many of the leading philosophers of physics know a lot more of physics than all, or virtually all, top-flight physicists know of philosophy. Many physicists indeed seem trapped in a grotesquely crude verificationism, with others by contrast in the grip of a rustically simple-minded realism. It is not, I contend, hubristic for the philosophical community to suggest they could learn a lot by a little immersion in the tradition of rigorous reasoning and conceptual analysis which philosophers have developed.

When we turn away from the physical sciences, the doormat attitude is, if anything, even less appropriate. I am sure that Burgess and Rosen would not for a moment say that philosophers must take on trust the view of any group of theorists who merely claim to be scientists, must accept the view of this or that sect of 'creation science' for example. But moving to borderline cases, have philosophers no right to venture any opinions on whether psychoanalysis is a science (or any sort of respectable intellectual endeavour) or not? Or when philosophers such as Searle claim that the very notion of deeply unconscious representational thinking which underlies much of cognitive science, taken literally, is simply incoherent, must they fall into chastened silence as soon as some guy with a white coat, a clipboard, and a doctorate in some area of cognitive science firmly disagrees? To think so is to be not an under-labourer for science but an undertaker to philosophy.

When we turn in particular to linguistics (not, it may be noted, a mature, long-standing science like physics) we move to an area not too far removed from the issues of representationalism et al. in cognitive science, especially as Burgess and Rosen, in their discussion of hermeneutic nominalism, are alluding not to syntactic theory but to semantics. Should philosophers accept uncritically that there is such a thing as a science of meaning, something which is a matter of debate among the linguists themselves? Moreover what is at issue here is not whether there might be worth in the production of translations of natural language sentences into meaningful sentences of a more artificial language. Rather what is at issue is a theoretical account of what constitutes

---

[34] See the account in Huw Price (1994) where it is noted that Bell's philosophical inclinations were strongly realist and he was therefore troubled by the implications his result and realist views had for locality in relativistic physics.

a speaker's understanding of certain areas of language, what it is for a speaker to know the meaning of, for example, various mathematical terms and sentences.

If Burgess and Rosen say we should accept what the experts tell us such understanding consists in, where they can arrive at a consensus, I would perhaps agree subject to the observation that the experts in this area are the philosophers (and there is no consensus!). At any rate, philosophers have long engaged in sophisticated debates on these most complex issues, and have sought to bring the arguments and findings of linguists and psychologists into the debate (with the relevance of these findings and the very possibility of a general systematic account of what it is to understand language being one of the questions at issue, of course). I suggest it is perfectly legitimate for philosophers to take a stance on what mathematical utterances in natural language mean, and in particular on whether, and in what sense, such utterances are committed to the existence of abstract objects. There is no community better placed to address the issue than the community of philosophers of mathematics.

Of course the foregoing can only show that there exists a legitimate intellectual space for a distinctively philosophical contribution, independent of, but informed by, relevant sciences, on the issue of the meaning of mathematical language. It does not show that the neo-formalist view is right. Moreover, Burgess and Rosen might counter-reply that while all science, as it is practised, contains a philosophical element, especially in the interpretation of the meaning and import of scientific results, in the present case we are dealing with a specific 'empirical' question. Do terms such as 'identity' and 'existence' have a different meaning in mathematical discourse than in newspaper reports or history books?

I argued in Chapter 1, §III.2 that the neo-formalist does not (or need not) seek to read an underlying syntactic 'deep structure' or 'logical form', distinct from superficial grammatical structure, into mathematical utterances. When the neo-formalist says that whilst prime numbers exist they do not EXIST, though beer bottles, in fact, do EXIST, this is not to be compared to a (moderate) Meinongian saying that beer bottles exist whilst prime numbers subsist. In the latter case, there already are two phrases of (relatively) ordinary language with two different meanings corresponding to the two terms pressed into service as terms of art, namely 'concrete existence' and 'abstract existence'. Non-linguists can understand the difference in meaning between the two phrases and understand the stipulation of technical senses for 'exist' and 'subsist'.[35] Similarly, if somebody stipulated that 'exast' applies only to vertebrates, 'exist' to all else, we do again have two distinct meanings in a perfectly ordinary sense and linguists can investigate whether in any real language related terms with those meanings occur. But the use of small capitals is a performative notation which signals (if the account of ontological reduction I gave is broadly right) changes in mode of

---

[35] The full Meinongian programme of saying that there are things, including concrete things, which lack Being is a different and much more dodgy and problematic matter. It is not to be explained away as mere terminological eccentricity. The same is true also of Lewis's view that there are non-actual things, for all Lewis's undoubted differences from Meinong.

assertion for a *whole sentence*, signals switches in metaphysical content, not changes in informational content, grammatical mood, or force nor change of meanings for lexical primitives.

We cannot say that 'EXISTS' corresponds to 'exists in mind-independent reality' and 'exists' corresponds to 'when applied to a predicate the resulting sentence is made-true by its formal provability in some underlying system'. The latter is not a phrase of anything like ordinary language and does not provide a synonym. Rather it is a clumsy attempt to gesture at a 'contextual definition' of how 'exists' works in the indefinitely many sentences and utterances of sentences in which it occurs. Such a definition would itself be a garbled version of a metalinguistic account—provided from the perspective of the theorist and not necessarily the object-language speaker—of the non-representational use of the term. The community best placed to judge whether the meta-theoretic account is right, whether there is such a thing as the informational content/metaphysical content distinction, and if so how and where changes in metaphysical content occur, is the community of philosophers, not linguists.

## §III.3

I return finally to the FM-level account of quantificational mathematical languages. Suppose we create a quantificational calculus QD by expanding DA not only with the addition of sentential operators but also the three new predicates, the existence and first- and second-order existential predicates, as above. Since we are considering only 'homophonic' contentful languages, the corresponding C-language, $L_{QD}$, is syntactically identical with the G-level one so we can drop the 'G' and 'C' subscripts. For the logical system we add to the rules of DA the appropriate propositional rules[36] plus the free logic quantificational rules. But to get anywhere interesting with the latter, we need some existential axioms. The obvious course is to add to the rules for DA an axiom E(t) for every numerical expression t. Of course this case illustrates how the retreat from free logic to the ordinary classical ones is highly attractive for pragmatic reasons. However, the need to mark the difference can be seen if we imagine the language expanded by adding a subtraction operator without, at this stage, the corresponding conceptual extension to allow for negative integers or a division operator without the extension to rationals. We might add such rules as:

From $t/u = b/c$ conclude $t \times c = u \times b$ and
From $t - b = u$ conclude $t = b + u$.

We could then retain the existential axioms E(t) for every numerical expression lacking the subtraction and division operators.

---

[36] What exactly these are is, of course, up for dispute; I say more in Chapter 8.

What of the 'non-representational' semantics[37] for the contentful language of a quantificational calculus? If we wish to expand the truth-functional ideas of the Basic Semantics to cover quantification, but in a formalist framework where quantificational sentences do not actually quantify over ANYTHING then a substitutional approach is inevitable:

> Any atom $t = u$ or $E(t)$ is true if it is provable, false if refutable.
>
> The Basic Semantics (at least) for propositional connectives;
>
> $\exists x\varphi x$ is true iff there is some numerical expression $t$ such that $E(t)$ and $\varphi x/t$ are both true;
>
> $\exists x\varphi x$ is false iff for every numerical expression $t$ such that $E(t)$ is true, $\varphi x/t$ is false.

with dual rules for the universal quantifier. This semantics is well-founded—the truth-value of generalizations, for example, is determined by that of sentences of lower complexity, including the atomic $E(t)$ sentences.

On the substitutionalist semantics globalization imposes even greater requirements. We will need strong forms of primality (and, for globalization$^-$, primality$^-$). Specifically, it will need to be the case that there is some term $t$ with $\vdash_{QD} \varphi x/t$ and $\vdash_{QD} E(t)$ whenever it is the case that $\vdash_{QD} \exists x\varphi x$, and similarly there will have to be some $u$ with $\dashv_{QD} \varphi x/u$ and $\vdash_{QD} E(u)$ whenever $\dashv_{QD} \forall x\varphi x$. The first requirement holds for intuitionist theories (with 'unfree' quantifier rules) which meet certain (substantive) constraints, as can be shown via normalization results (see Prawitz 1965, ch. 4, Corollary 7, pp. 56–7) but, just as with the parallel failure of primality$^-$ for $\vdash_I \sim(A\&B)$, the latter will fail intuitionistically. Looking at it from a classical perspective, even if we have negation-completeness the results can easily fail. All we need to do is to provide a standard model-theoretic semantics for a sound classical system with a language in which there are no names. True, this kind of framework is irrelevant for the neo-formalist adopting a substitutional interpretation but, on the other hand, there are strong objections to the idea that substitutional quantification is a way of avoiding ontological commitment to abstract objects: cf. Burgess and Rosen, (1997, §III.A.2.b, pp. 203–4), Kripke (1976).

An alternative non-substitutionalist approach, compatible with retaining the BS for the sentential operators, is to adopt what might be called a *molecular* position. Atoms and generalizations are true (false) just when provable (refutable) in the underlying calculus, with the truth-value of molecular sentences determined truth-functionally by the appropriate truth tables for the dominant sentential operator. Granted the same proof-theoretic strength for the propositional sub-logic we assumed for the proof of globalization in the non-quantificational case above, a simple inductive proof shows globalization$^+$ and globalization$^-$ hold for $L_{QD}$ too. Let us leave, however, the question of globalization versus local semantics, substitutional versus non-substitutional quantification, to one side for now and return to the matter later (Chapter 8, §V*). What we seem to be left with in any case is a quantificational

---

[37] But, at this stage, still formal FM-level semantics. So, once again, an obligation to recast this in purely concrete terms has been generated.

extension of the DA calculus QD where in the contentful language $L_{QD}$ we can prove (pretty trivially) infinitely many pairs of existence theorems of the form Et and $\exists x(x = t)$. All that we need for all these theorems to be true are that QD be sound, that all its axioms be true, and the rules, both logical and mathematical, preserve truth downwards (and falsity upwards). Now, by globalization, truth is simply provability. But we cannot immediately assume that the axioms are all true, that is, that provability in the calculus satisfies the constraints on truth imposed by the Basic Semantics. We need, obviously, to know that no sentence is both provable and refutable. But, furthermore, we require full primeness and that is not a trivial requirement. Nonetheless, as we shall see later, it can be met in this case.

Not only can we prove infinitely many existence theorems in QD; where t and u are distinct simple numerals, we can also prove $t \neq u$. Indeed, the language of QD can express a form of infinity hypothesis:

$$\sim\exists x(x + 1 = 0) \text{ \& } \forall x \exists y(y = x + 1) \text{ \& } \forall x \forall y(x + 1 = y + 1 \rightarrow x = y)$$

which could be added as an axiom. Yet according to neo-formalism, though all these infinitely many distinct numbers exist they do not EXIST. That is, the neo-formalist maintains that while all these existential claims are correct, and hence true, in $L_{QD}$, what grounds their truth is merely the provability of certain uninterpreted strings of symbols, provability according to a system of rules including those which we drum into our children. The C-level arithmetic sentences of $L_{QD}$ do not, therefore, report relations holding among abstract platonic objects, they are innocent of any ontological commitment. We can have our mathematical cake and eat it.

Overall, then, the picture thus far is this. Neo-formalism represents a marked improvement on game and term formalism by dint of its use of the informational content/metaphysical content distinction. Mathematical utterances have sense, they are generally used to make assertions, and are typically true or false. But what makes them true is the existence of proofs or refutations. We distinguish a game-level use of mathematics from its contentful use, and we do this in a third metatheoretic level. If there is to be ontological gain over the platonist, the metatheory must carry no ontological commitment to abstracta. Terms which occur in both mathematical and empirical language carry only their formal meaning over into mathematical language. For sentential operators this may exhaust all their meaning. But this content imposes, given the neo-formalist equation of truth with provability, strong requirements, going beyond consistency, on what mathematical theories are legitimate, according to neo-formalism. Quantificational locutions occur in mathematical language solely with their formal meaning. Existence statements in mathematics have purely formal meta-physical content; they are made true by the appropriate concrete proofs, which may even be one line axioms. We can have essentially all the mathematical existence theorems we like (subject not just to the consistency of the underlying theory, but some other factors too such as primeness) at no ontological cost.

Is this too good to be true? I turn in the next chapter to some basic objections.

# 4

# Objections and Comparisons

In this chapter I will look at some of the more obvious objections to the position I have just developed. I will also, in the starred section §II.5*, look critically at aspects of some alternative philosophies of mathematics which bear on the points raised in these objections, arguing that the neo-formalist position emerges as stronger in the comparison.

## §I. Closure

The metamathematical FM-level theory in which we specified the proof theory and 'syntactic semantics' of quantified decimal arithmetic QD was assumed to be a portion of mathematics, some set theory strong enough to carry out the arithmetization of syntax. With suitable bridge principles and definitions, we can embed QD and its language $L_{CQD}$ in this theory. But the metatheory, thus augmented, is much stronger than the object theory and has a more extensive ontology (read platonistically) of sets as well as numbers (or sets which are not numbers as well as sets which are).

The neo-formalist, therefore, has to provide an account of the metatheory. If the meta-metatheory is even stronger we are off on a regress, and a vicious one at that. For the neo-formalist seeks to give an *explanation* of the nature of mathematical truth and if this explanation in turn uses mathematics, it too requires a neo-formalist explanation. But explanations must come to an end somewhere. We need a 'fixed point' where the progression *closes off*, a mathematical theory T such that the account of the semantics of T utilizes a mathematical theory $T_1 \subseteq T$. Otherwise we will terminate our investigation at a point at which something remains unexplained which was part of the original explanandum.

This 'need for closure' problem is a devastating problem for standard model-theoretic semantics. For models are sets, and so the standard semantics for mathematics, including set theory, is set-theoretic. But formal results related to the ancient Liar paradox, notably Tarski's Undefinability of Truth result (1936/56), seem to show that the semantic closure envisaged in the previous paragraph is impossible.

We cannot give a set-theoretic semantics for a theory which includes the set-theory of the semantics. (Indeed, the result generalizes to any semantics, set-theoretic or not, provided the background logic is strong enough and the language has the resources for expressing the requisite syntactic properties and proving lemmas such as the 'diagonalization' lemma.)

However this problem seems to vanish from a neo-formalist perspective since neo-formalist semantics is largely syntactic, as it were. That is, truth for atoms is defined proof-theoretically and although we have assumed the sentential operators have a truth-functional meaning, in the usual case globalization enforces an equivalence between truth and proof. Truth for the quantifiers is defined either proof-theoretically or substitutionally, so it all winds down to the proof-theoretic basis. Furthermore, the syntactic notions of proof and syntax are, for standard formal languages, highly tractable, mathematically. More precisely, in a standard language with expressions of finite length, it is typically required that wffhood be decidable, likewise the set of axioms, and also that the rules of proof are to be such that the set of pairs $<X,A>$, where X is a finite set of premises and A is derivable from X, is recursively enumerable. That is, proofhood is $\sum_1$, it can be characterized by a wff of the form $\exists x_1, \ldots x_n \varphi(x_1, \ldots x_n)$ where $\varphi(x_1, \ldots x_n)$ is a recursive predicate.[1] Hence we reach a fixed point in our sequence of metatheories very quickly. We can characterize (or 'represent' see ahead §III.2) wffhood and proofhood for $L_{CQD}$ ($=L_{GQD}$) in a fragment of Peano Arithmetic such as the theory Q whose axioms are

$$\forall x\, 0 \neq Sx,$$
$$\forall x \forall y (Sx = Sy \rightarrow x = y).$$
$$\forall x\, x + 0 = x,$$
$$\forall x \forall y (x + Sy = S(x + y)),$$
$$\forall x\, x \times 0 = 0,$$
$$\forall x \forall y (x \times Sy = (x \times y) + x),$$
$$\forall x (x = 0 \lor \exists y\, x = Sy).$$

stated in a language with expressions for zero ('0') successor ('S') and the usual terms for addition and multiplication. Q is capable of representing all $\sum_1$ notions. So now we have reached stability and 'closure', for Q can represent wffhood and proofhood in Q itself. Indeed in Q we can represent the syntax not only of Q but any theory in a

---

[1] Roughly speaking, this says there is a mechanical method for determining whether the predicate applies or not to any given $n$-tuple of natural numbers. Here I am in effect identifying algorithms (or equivalence classes of algorithms) and recursive functions and this presupposes a strengthened form of the Church–Turing Thesis (Kleene 1967, p. 232). Such a strengthening equates those numerical functions whose output, on given input, can be calculated by (idealized) careful human calculators working strictly according to finite instructions to the members of the class of recursive functions, a class specifiable in a number of interestingly different ways.

standard countable language (of any order), thus including much stronger (recursively axiomatizable) theories such as PA and ZFC.

This means, in turn, that the neo-formalist account of mathematics can not only be applied to fragments of arithmetic but to much stronger theories, any mathematical theory T, in fact, which can be formalized in a system whose syntax and proof theory is tractable, for example by being characterizable by a theory whose standard models are isomorphic to a sub-model of the standard model of arithmetic. And that amounts to any interesting mathematical theory, most mathematical logicians would say. So, for example, the Maximum Value Theorem of real analysis which says that

$$\forall f, a, b \ (f \text{ is continuous on } [a, b] \rightarrow \exists x \in [a, b], \forall y \in [a, b], f(y) \leq f(x)).$$

indeed holds but not because there is a real continuum of abstract objects and abstract functions over those objects which has the property ascribed in the theorem. It is true, rather, because a string of symbols (which might be syntactically identical to the above) can be arrived at by playing the game whose rules are the classical rules of deduction,[2] starting from the axioms of real analysis. Similarly the theorem:

$$\forall \alpha \leq \beta, \aleph_\alpha^{\aleph_\beta} = \aleph_{\beta+1}$$

of ZFC+GCH[3] is true, relative to that theoretical system; but not because there exists an infinitely long (how long?) sequence of set-theoretic transfinite numbers, the alephs, satisfying the above generalization. There is no such uncountable realm of abstract sets. Nonetheless, the sentence is true in that system because the above formal string, or one which plays that role, is derivable from the axioms of the theory in question. We need not worry about our epistemological access to these mysterious realms, of unfathomable size, of abstract objects.

## §II. Relativism or Pluralism?

### §II.1

Now the GCH is neither provable nor refutable from the axioms of (first-order) ZFC. Indeed this is true of the special case of the continuum hypothesis—the thesis that $\beth_1$, the cardinality of the real numbers (also the cardinality of the power set of any countably infinite set) has the next biggest infinite cardinality after countable

---

[2] As we saw in the last chapter, since the operator expressions of the contentful language cannot be assigned any old rules we like, if they are to express the connectives which give the sentences the meanings we want, it cannot however be taken for granted that we are entitled to use the rules of classical logic. We will return in Chapter 8 to the question of how much of classical logic can be justified neo-formalistically and how much is needed to generate standard mathematics.

[3] Using the usual acronyms here i.e. ZFC is Zermelo-Fraenkel set theory plus the Axiom of Choice whereas GCH is the generalized continuum hypothesis: $\forall \alpha \ \aleph_\alpha = \beth_\alpha$. For an account of what the series of transfinite numbers represented by the alephs $\aleph_\alpha$ and beths $\beth_\alpha$ are, see any standard set-theoretic text such as the excellent introduction by Enderton (1977) or more advanced texts such as Kunen (1980).

infinity—$\aleph_0$—namely $\aleph_1$. I will call a sentence neither provable nor refutable in theory T *indeterminable* in T.[4] Presumably the neo-formalist has to hold that the GCH is neither determinately true nor determinately false, at least relative to ZFC, so that neo-formalism seems to come out as a strongly revisionist position.

This argument immediately suggests a further objection. The neo-formalist ties truth to provability. But provability with respect to which system of proof? Add the GCH to ZFC and it is provable in a system which Gödel showed is consistent relative to ZFC, thus according to the neo-formalist, true. Add its negation and it is refutable in a system likewise consistent relative to ZFC, as Cohen showed, hence surely false, according to neo-formalism. Which is it? The problem multiplies. Even though we are restricting ourselves to 'homophonic' systems which must be grounded in non-trivial calculi at the G-level and even if we assume a fixed set of background *logical* rules then, on any reasonable set of such rules, there are infinitely many distinct such coherent systems. If we say that a sentence is a mathematical truth if it is provable in some such system, then any sentence which is logically consistent (at least in the sense of not entailing everything, given our fixed set of rules) will have to be admitted as a mathematical truth.

There is a parallel here between neo-formalism and 'deductivism' (also known, in some versions, as 'if-thenism' or 'postulationism').[5] In one of the simplest forms of deductivism it is held that a typical assertion by a mathematician of a sentence S is elliptical for the assertion of a conditional A ⊃ S, with the antecedent a set of axioms (say the finite set of second-order axioms of Peano–Dedekind Arithmetic) and the consequent a sentence syntactically identical with the utterance elliptically asserted but which, on pain of a vicious circle of semantic dependence, is given a different semantic interpretation. Mathematical knowledge, on this view, is not knowledge of an abstract domain of objects, but 'merely' logical knowledge of the implications of certain axiom sets. If we abstract away the particular mathematical content of the axiom set, replacing mathematical constants such as 0, S and + by schematic letters, we get a view quite close to structuralism.[6]

An objection to this type of structuralist position, a troubling one for those who do not think of mathematics as an empirical discipline, is that if no actual structure satisfies the axiom set A and if ⊃ is the material conditional then both A ⊃ S and A ⊃ ∼S are true and so every mathematical falsehood, as well as every mathematical truth, is

---

[4] The usual terminology is 'undecidable' but I will apply decidability to sets of sentences, rather than sentences. A decidable set is one for which there is an algorithm which, applied to any object in the domain, yields a positive result iff that object is in the set. In formalized systems (and assuming Church–Turing, given the usual understanding of 'algorithm'), decidable sets of sentences are those whose codes form a recursive set.

[5] The latter associated with Russell's view in *Principles of Mathematics* (1903, p. 3) though it is not clear whether this view is the target of his famous jibe (1919, p. 71) that 'the method of "postulating" what we want has many advantages; they are the same as the advantages of theft over honest toil'. See also Putnam (1967a/75).

[6] Cf. Shapiro, (1997, ch. 5).

correctly assertible. The coherence of mathematics, for this sort of structuralist, seems to depend not just on logical knowledge (though that is no unproblematic thing itself) but on knowledge that a structure satisfying A exists. One way to get round this is to go modal, and take S to be elliptical for $\Box(A \supset S)$ or $A \rightarrow S$, where $\rightarrow$ is some intensional conditional. But now we have upped the ante ideologically and imported problematic concepts into mathematics, intensional notions which intuitively do not belong there. Moreover, the constraint that we know that a structure satisfying A exists is now replaced by the need to know that A is possible—$\Diamond A$—(indeed that may be built into the fully explicit content, so that S becomes elliptical for $(\Diamond A \,\&\, \Box(A \supset S))$ ). But the claim that we have this knowledge is also problematic.

If the deductivist eschews models and structures it might seem she must then take the sentences which atomic mathematical assertions are said to truncate elliptically to be purely formal uninterpreted strings, and thus neither true nor false. If $\sim S$ is truth-valueless when S is, then $(A \supset S)$ will have the same truth-value on any extensional scheme as $(A \supset \sim S)$ has (no value on the strong Kleene valuation, true on the Lukasiewiczian) and we are back where we were with simple deductivism. So we must amend deductivism to say that the assertion of S is elliptical for truth-apt claims of the form Conseq($|A|$, $|S|$) where $|P|$ names the sentence P. This claim thus asserts that S is a consequence of the axiom A. (Presumably the deductivist will not define 'consequence' either model-theoretically or proof-theoretically as this would seem to involve commitment to mathematical objects, as would appeal to *sets* of axioms.)

Such an amendment to deductivism evidently brings it quite close to neo-formalism. But neo-formalism differs in rejecting the idea that mathematical sentences are elliptical or that the fully explicit informational content of an utterance S is really one of the form Conseq($|A|$, $|S|$). Something a bit like this is part of the metaphysical content attributed by the metatheorist but is not part of the cognitive content of the utterance. Neo-formalism differs also by holding that axioms are true, not uninterpreted strings. Both these differences are great improvements on this form of deductivism. However there are a number of objections to deductivism which might seem to apply to neo-formalism too, see for example (Resnik 1980, pp. 131–6) for a statement of many of these.

## §II.2

Firstly, many mathematical results are accepted without benefit of a fully formalized proof. In fact this understates the case. It is not just that many proofs are accepted in this way—nearly all are, certainly if one excludes computer-generated proofs, and prior to the rise of mathematical logic in the late nineteenth century absolutely all were. Are we to say that mathematics did not exist before Frege? Secondly, mathematicians often believe mathematical theses on evidence less than that provided by a conclusive proof. Many believed Fermat's Last Theorem before Wiles's proof (and correction!) appeared, for example, and most seem to believe the Riemann Hypothesis.

Thirdly, mathematical logicians often remark, of a set of axioms they are interested in and working with, that it is *inadequate* in not fully characterizing the realm or domain the axioms are 'about'. There are truths about the domain which are not consequences of the axioms. But this inadequacy objection cannot make sense on a deductivist or neo-formalist account, since mathematics is not, on these views, about ANYTHING. Whilst the deductivist can assign a given body of mathematical results to a particular theory, that is to some axioms A, it does not make sense to say that there are A-truths, i.e. consequences of A, which are not consequences of A.

A further argument is due to Quine (1936/75). Deductivism has no obvious resources for laying down restrictions on what sentences can play the role of axioms, other than, perhaps, consistency of the total system and other formal criteria such as primeness. Hence knowledge that the velocity of light *c* is a constant is, or can be, a priori logical knowledge of a mathematical truth, namely knowledge that this constancy claim is derivable from the Maxwellian theory of electromagnetism. In fact, since, on this form of deductivism, the axioms are not supposed to be self-evident truths concerning an abstract realm, nor justified nor validated in terms of anything more fundamental, but merely supposed or postulated, there can be no objection to taking any proposition one likes as an axiom. So, to take a random example, the proposition that St Mirren won the Scottish Cup in 1987 can be derived from a suitable axiom set (for example the unit set consisting of that proposition itself). In this way we could come to know a priori, in virtue of our logical knowledge that each sentence entails itself, that the proposition that St Mirren won the cup in that year (or indeed any other non-absurd proposition, true or false) is a mathematical truth. This is absurd.

Now some replies on behalf of neo-formalism. As to the first point concerning mathematics conducted outside a framework of formal languages, one should note that proofhood in 'informal' natural languages is also at least partly formal. Some types of reasoning rest solely on structural properties of the chain of reasoning which are independent of semantic content—grammatical structure for example. It is simply not the case that the only formal structures are those generated by the grammars for the artificial languages of mathematical logic familiar from Frege's time on. It is absurd to suppose that prior to Frege no one had a practice of following inferential patterns which were determined by grammatical structure and that no one ever performed calculations by following through syntactic algorithms. Humans have been proving mathematical theorems since at least the time of Euclid and, as remarked, neo-formalism is neutral as to the precise concrete form proofs must take. Tokens of formal proofs in artificial languages have certainly hitherto been a small fragment of all actually existing proofs.

One might argue that in the case of pictorial or diagrammatic methods of demonstration, so prominent in ancient mathematics, there is no recursive structure whilst such structure is essential to the modern notion of proof. There are no combinatorial operations for building bigger proof-diagrams out of smaller. Now this is not the case in some more recent pictorial forms of proofs, such as Peirce's existential graphs (Peirce 1933) in which such rules are explicitly stated.

Moreover even in more ancient forms of visual proof, it is clear that in many cases, at least, what does the convincing is not the diagram alone but the diagram plus a piece of linguistic reasoning. This is so even in a very visual case such as:

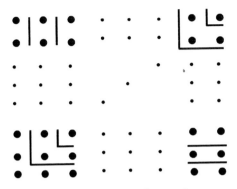

(Figure from Bundy, Jamnik, and Fugard 2005, p. 2383)

where it is natural to say that we can simply and immediately *see* that $n^2 = (1 + 3 + \ldots + (2n{-}1))$. We see this by looking at the L-shaped sub-parts of the grid and seeing that as we add another 'L' we add two more dots than were in the last-added 'L'—for the 'old' bottom left corner 'splits in two' and a new one is added. However, the proof here includes not just the figure but some gloss of the type I have just added in which we have to engage in a little verbal reasoning about the figure.

Thus this sort of case reduces to, or contains as an essential part, mathematical proofs in natural language, or extensions thereof formed by introducing logical notions such as $\forall$; the normal case, in fact. Here, in these 'informal' proofs, I have suggested there may be as much formal grammatical structure as in the regimented logical case. (Of course one also has to acknowledge the very heavy contextual dependence, both syntactic and semantic, of natural languages). Similarly, when one looks at investigations by those in the 'critical reasoning' or so-called 'informal logic' tradition one often finds that in attempting to give a systematic account of reasoning in natural language, they develop structures similar to the structures to be found in formal systems (see e.g. Fisher 1988).

But suppose this is wrong. Suppose neither natural language reasoning nor diagrammatic proof have the recursive structure we are familiar with in modern formal proofs in which all proofs are generated from atomic steps by iterated application of a bunch of purely formal rules. Perhaps a more connectionist model of our ability to appreciate proofs is correct. Competent users divide the space of purported proofs into two disjoint and exhaustive subgroups (perhaps not completely precisely, perhaps with a fuzzy boundary), the genuine proofs and the non-proofs. They do this in somewhat the same way in which connectionist cognitive scientists say humans divide views of faces from particular angles and lighting into those which are faces of known and familiar people (or a particular acquaintance) and those which are not. Whatever exactly that way is. The usual story involves supposing we have a more primitive recognition of a number of basic features, or rather of the magnitude of the observed scene along each of a number of dimensions representing each of the basic characteristics. Hence sensory input can be represented as vectors whose components represent the magnitude on each dimension. The subject divides the points in this space into those within some convex subspace representing her friend's familiar face (or a proof of the displayed sentence, as it may be) and those which do not so belong.

This sort of story raises many complex and controversial issues in philosophy of mind, as well as in empirical psychology. However, if something like this is true, the neo-formalist can simply apply this model to grasp of proofs. A sentence S of contentual language $L_{CK}$ is true just in case the correlated sentence, which may be S itself, is provable in underlying calculus K. If the 'calculus' is specified simply as a sub-region of a multi-dimensional 'proof space' then we can treat the case as formally identical to that in which the calculus consists of a very large number of atomic rules and no recursive rules for generating complex proofs. The reasoners in this language would be rather like those who master a character-based written language in which sound:written transformations are not based on iterable rules, as in syllabic and alphabetic systems but, in the purest case, just learned one by one.

Of course on this picture, there would presumably be only finitely many proofs in K. (Moreover with no logical complexity, there is little or no room for any substantive role for normativity. 'Fallacies' would be akin to misperceiving faces.) So perhaps a more realistic model would involve a mix of 'connectionist' and recursive elements. Our calculus K is defined standardly as the intersection of all the sets inductively generated by some recursive rules from a class of base atomic rules or axioms with the difference that this class contains not just a handful of atomic principles or rules; nor even infinitely many atomic principles with each a mechanically checkable instance of a handful of schemata. Rather the atomic elements of the proof system number thousands or tens of thousands, say, and we do not master them in turn by instantiating from a small number of schemas.

Whether this type of picture is more accurate than the standard recursive picture makes no difference to neo-formalism. The philosophically crucial aspect of neo-formalism is not the stance it takes on the nature of proof, it can be very liberal on that. It is rather the claim that mathematical truth is determined by proofhood with the crucial proviso that the grounding in proof is built into the metaphysical content, not informational content.

Turning to the second point, that mathematicians can be convinced about the truth of mathematical theses in the absence of proof, again there is nothing which conflicts with neo-formalism in this. For the neo-formalist, truth is determined by prov*ability* not by our being acquainted with an actual concrete proof.[7] It may be perfectly

---

[7] A concrete structure which would constitute a proof, its elements suitably interpreted, may lie forever undiscovered. Here I must resubmit the promissory note to be redeemed in later chapters. 'Provable' for now is a notion from metamathematics but if there is to be any ontological gain over platonists, it must ultimately be reduced, at M level, to something non-mathematical and 'concrete'.

reasonable for a mathematician to be convinced that a sentence is provable in the absence of an actual proof. It is true that some mathematicians may claim to believe a mathematical thesis and also believe that it will never be proved in any reasonable sense of proof. In particular, mathematicians who adopt a strongly platonistic philosophy of mathematics may take this stance. But, as with science in general, the philosophical views of those practitioners of the discipline who are reflective enough to adopt a philosophical standpoint are many and varied. It would be wrong to test and find wanting a philosophical theory on the nature of mathematics (or physics) by laying heavy weight on the opinions of a body of practitioners who are not representative of the whole, especially if their views may be distorted by firm adherence to a contrary philosophical position. If the practice of the mass of jobbing mathematicians is at least consonant with the view that mathematical truth equates to provability, though not to 'known to be proven', this, I maintain, suffices to deflect this objection.[8]

## §II.3

The last two objections set out at the beginning of §II.2 are (i) the *inadequacy* objection—mathematicians often feel an axiom set fails to do justice to the domain it is 'about', that is, does not entail all truths about the domain, but according to neo-formalism there is no such domain; (ii) Quine's reductio of postulationism to absurdity, probably the most fundamental of this group of objections. I will deal with Quine's reductio in this section and the inadequacy objection in the next.

Is neo-formalism in the same bind as the postulationist? That is, is the neo-formalist committed to saying that 'J. F. Kennedy was assassinated in 1963' is a mathematical truth, a truth of any system of sentences from which it can be derived, 'J. F. Kennedy was never assassinated' a mathematical truth of another, both these systems equally entitled to be classed as parts of mathematics and on exactly the same terms as arithmetic, analysis, or set theory? That would indeed be absurd. But the neo-formalist cannot avoid this absurdity by saying that mathematical truth is to be characterized in terms of provability, not in any old system, but rather only from special sets of axioms, such as the Peano–Dedekind axioms for arithmetic or ZFC for set theory. For once we abandon mathematical realism, what is so special about these sentences? They do not depict the structure of some realm of abstract entities so why should the consequences of such axioms enjoy any special status or necessity as compared with the consequences of any other set?

It is indeed true that for the neo-formalist, any syntactic string at all—'$3 + 1 = 0$', 'Quadruplicity drinks procrastination', 'Rome is north of Glasgow'—can express a truth of pure mathematics. But only if it is part of an utterance made in formal mode, only if the metaphysical content is formal—linked to provability in an underlying calculus—not representational. In that case, any representational metaphysical content

---

[8] I return to related issues, in connection with set theory in particular, in Chapter 8, §VII.

the string has in other contexts is irrelevant to the question whether the utterance as a whole is made-true or made-false. Indeed, the string can have different formal metaphysical content in different contexts. So '3 + 1 = 0' can be false because the relevant string, itself say, is not provable in one calculus, DA, but true because the relevant string is provable in another, modular arithmetic modulo 4. In this sense the neo-formalist position might seem to be relativist, comparable to the projectivist theory of taste (Chapter 2, §I–III). The string is not true or false absolutely but relative to a formal calculus for a language it belongs to.

However, what makes such projectivism relativistic is the fact that the very same proposition—that haggis is tasty—is true relative to one standpoint (Hamish's) and not relative to another (Nigel's). That is, there is no ambiguity, the sentence 'that haggis is tasty' has the same sense or informational content on both Hamish and Nigel's lips, though the metaphysical contents (and in some cases truth-values) differ. But it is not so clear that '3 + 1 = 0' has the same sense when part of decimal arithmetic as when part of modular arithmetic. Applying Cappelen and Lepore's 'inter-contextual dis-quotation' test, imagine I am asking a number of people who have been performing sums in decimal arithmetic what the answer to a particular equation, say 68 + 57, is. Simultaneously I am on the phone to Hamish, whom I know to be doing sums in arithmetic modulo 12. Would I sincerely report Hamish as saying that 68 + 57 is 5? Would I not rather say that he says that the sum, in arithmetic modulo 12, is 5? In just the same way I would not, if we were all bird watching, report his phone conversation as 'he too says he is looking at cranes', if I know he is in Belfast looking at Ulysses and Samson, the giant shipyard cranes.

This suggests that some sort of reference to an underlying calculus is an ingredient of the sense of at least some mathematical terms. Although, as I have argued,

$$68 + 57 = 125$$

is not synonymous with, does not have the same informational content as,

The string '68 + 57 = 125' is provable in decimal arithmetic

the numerals and the addition sign carry as part of their connotation something like 'numeral of decimal arithmetic', 'addition function of decimal arithmetic'; when, that is, they are functioning as part of that system and not, say, modular arithmetic or as names of sports players in a team, or bus routes.

Thus the neo-formalist position is *pluralist* rather than relativist. The truth-value of '68 + 57 = 125' is not relative to a formal system. Rather, there is a plurality of formal systems[9] and the sentence expresses different senses in each, whilst it is made true (or false) in the context of a given one iff it is provable therein. Similarly 'Rome is north of

---

[9] Difference in systems, I will argue, is to be determined by difference in the derivability relation. Two different proof architectures (or algorithms for determining the truth of atomic sentences, for another example) are different presentations of the same system if exactly the same conclusions are derivable from any given set of premisses.

Glasgow' can be true where its metaphysical content is a formal one, if it is made true iff provable in a calculus K in which, in fact, it is a theorem (by dint of being an axiom perhaps).[10] Here again it seems clear that we have a switch in informational content from the usual 'empirical' meaning of the term, and so pluralism not relativism. So the neo-formalist concedes that the strings 'J. F. Kennedy was assassinated in 1963' and 'Rome is north of Glasgow' can be used to represent pure mathematical truths—but not with their normal literal meaning; and this is pretty much uncontentious. If the calculus which grounds their metaphysical content is in each case a system containing those strings as the only axioms, then they will, of course, be truths of an exceptionally uninteresting system.

What does sameness of informational content, for mathematical sentences, come to then? In Chapter 2, §III, I suggested that expressions such as 'tasty' and 'sublime' have, or can have, the same informational content on different lips even though, perforce, what makes them true (on a projectivist account) will differ. This was on the basis of Cappelen and Lepore's indexicality tests, but I did not (discretion being the better part of valour) offer a positive and comprehensive criterion for sameness of sense. In the mathematical case, I will be a little bolder and proffer a sufficient condition in Chapter 7, §II.4.

## §II.4

This takes us to the inadequacy objection. Take, for example, the formal set of axioms Q. Even if one makes no presumption that an axiom set should be *negation-complete*, that it should prove one of P or $\sim$P, for every sentence of the language P, this axiom set is clearly inadequate as an account of the numbers. For example, one cannot even prove from its axioms the commutativity of addition (though, as remarked, one can prove many important syntactic results from Q, relative to a coding of expressions strings as numbers; see Boolos 1993, p. 49).

Such an estimation of the inadequacy of Q would, I conjecture, be pretty much universally held by number theorists. But how can a neo-formalist make sense of it? THERE IS NO domain of numbers, in mind-independent reality, according to the neo-formalist. THERE ARE NO numbers. Truth, for contentful sentences of mathematics, is grounded in an underlying calculus of rules and perhaps axioms. It is incoherent to hold that there are Q-truths, sentences provable in Q, which Q cannot prove. So how can it make sense to say that there are truths 'about numbers' which a given axiom set cannot capture?

A proper response to this objection will require paying attention to the underlying logical framework of the mathematical theory, which I will address more fully in

---

[10] We would be well advised, however, not to use empirical constants in the purely formal sector of language, for otherwise we will introduce merely terminological contradictions into our applied mathematics. We will have 'Rome is north of Glasgow' true and also 'Rome is not north of Glasgow' true too, with the first token of the sentence having a purely formal explanatory truth-maker, the second representational.

Chapter 8. But we can give an indication of the structure of this response by considering the example of 'Frege Arithmetic', the second-order theory[11] whose sole non-logical axiom is the somewhat honorifically named 'Hume's Principle' (HP)

$$\forall X \forall Y ((nxXx = nxYx) \leftrightarrow X \ 1\text{–}1 \ Y)$$

where $nx\varphi x$ is the numerical operator, read as ⌈the number of $\varphi$s⌉ and $X \ 1\text{–}1 \ Y$ abbreviates the second-order sentence which expresses the existence of a one–one correspondence between the $X$'s and the $Y$'s. George Boolos gave the name 'Frege's theorem' to the result that one can derive in standard second-order logic a theory even stronger than (though equi-consistent with) the usual Peano–Dedekind formulation of second-order arithmetic from HP (relative to standard bridge principles defining the notions of the one theory in terms of the other).[12]

Neo-logicists (or 'neo-Fregeans') such as Crispin Wright and Bob Hale hold that HP is analytic or meaning-constitutive or an implicit definition of our concept of number.[13] A somewhat weaker position is the claim that 'Finite Hume' (FH), in which the quantifiers are restricted to finite properties, is analytic.[14] Certainly, grasp of a one: one correspondence between ensembles of objects and tokens of numerals is one of the most primitive aspects of mathematics one learns. One might actually argue from this that it is not HP which is fundamental but an ordering principle of the form:

$$\forall R \forall S ((oxyRxy = oxySxy) \leftrightarrow R \approx S)$$

where $oxyRxy$ reads ⌈the order-type of the relation $Rxy$⌉ and $R \approx S$ is the second-order sentence which expresses the existence of an *order-preserving* one:one correspondence between the relation $R$ and the relation $S$. For when the child counts out the number of apples in the bowl as five she does not give the number as the size of the set $\{3, 5, 4, 1, 2\}$ but takes the numerals in ascending order and pairs them off with the

---

[11] See Shapiro (1991) for an account of standard second-order logic which I take to include Axiom Schemata of Comprehension for predicate formulae of any adicity.

[12] Crispin Wright's *Frege's Theory of Numbers as Objects* (1983) contains a detailed sketch of 'Frege's Theorem' and this book was the major impetus in the revival of Fregean approaches to mathematics. Boolos introduced the term 'Frege's theorem' in 'The Standard of Equality of Numbers' (1990/98, p. 209); see also Crispin Wright (1997/2001, p. 273). On the strength of the Fregean system, see Richard Heck (1996). Burgess, Hazen and Hodes also noted the consistency of the system (Heck 1997, fn. 12). Wright notes (1997/2001, p. 273 fn. 4) that Charles Parsons first pointed out in 1964 that HP yields second-order arithmetic. Frege cites the principle in the *Grundlagen*, §63 with the reference to Hume's *Treatise of Human Nature*, Book I, part iii, Section I owing to Baumann (1868).

[13] Hale and Wright (2001a). Neil Tennant has developed a rather different, constructivistic version of neo-logicism within an intuitionist-cum-relevantist logical framework. Tennant too argues for the analyticity of arithmetic but takes inference rules involving zero and successor rather than the HP axiom as his foundational basis. See Tennant (1987, 1997a, and 1997b). A further variation on the theme of neo-logicism is to be found in Linsky and Zalta (2006).

[14] Heck (1997). Finitude can be defined in a number of different ways, equivalent only with certain further assumptions such as the axiom of choice. Heck (1997, pp. 590–1) uses a definition from Frege which is equivalent to 'is equinumerous with a natural number' (which Frege defines without presupposing 'finite'). An alternative is 'Dedekind finite', true of properties for which there is no one:one function mapping from the extension of the property to a proper subset of the extension.

apples, temporally ordered (this first one, this second one, and so on) taking the last numeral as the ordinal index of the ensemble.[15] But though in one sense the child is more sophisticated than our Humean Fregean, in another she is less so in that young children do not grasp the basic principle of transitivity of one:one correspondence, order-preserving or not. It is only later in development that children grasp that if the apples in one bowl can be paired with the numerals from 1 to 5 in that order and the oranges in this other bowl paired with the apples then the number of oranges is also five (cf. Butterworth 1999, ch. 3). Perhaps what the young child grasps is a purely empirical first-order predicate which we might represent by $\text{Num}(\varphi, x)$ where $\varphi$ is a predicate and the substitutions for $x$ which render it true are names of numerals in some system the child understands, e.g. in Hindu–Arabic notation. The metaphysical content of $\text{Num}(x$ is an apple in the bowl, '5') is that it is true just in case there is a one:one order-preserving map from the apples to the Hindu–Arabic numerals[16] for one to five in the usual order. It may be, indeed, that the same metaphysical content applies to 'there are five apples in the bowl' as the 'the number of apples in the bowl is five'. The idea that English speakers grasp e.g. 'there are 589 students in the first year class' as shorthand for a giant quantification of the form

$$\exists x_1, \ldots \exists x_{589}((\text{Student-in-class } x_1 \ldots \text{Student-in-class } x_{589} \ \&$$
$$(x_1 \neq x_1 \ \& \ x_1 \neq x_2 \text{ etc. })\&$$
$$\forall y(\text{Student-in-class } y \rightarrow y = x_1 \text{ etc.}))$$

is implausible. Perhaps the metaphysical content of such a sentence is essentially the same as $\text{Num}(x$ is student in the class, '589'). Child and adult alike may grasp this numbering notion without grasp of second-order logic or of functions or mappings in general, the grasp manifest in their (fallible) ability to detect (at least for small numbers) when the pairing can and when it cannot be effected. When such a predicate applies, the result is an empirical, a posteriori truth.

Can we say, though, that for mature speakers of natural languages such as English, something in the region of HP is analytic? Something a bit more sophisticated than grasp of the empirical Num predicate perhaps, but certainly less sophisticated than full second-order HP, so only 'in the region'. For even if one views second-order logic as somehow implicit in ordinary language, which is doubtful, it is obviously nonsense to suppose that the principle is known to the average English speaker, far less that it plays a role in her mathematical calculations and judgements.[17] But consider the schematic inference rules (RHP) which permit us to conclude:

[15] Unrestricted, the ordering principle is inconsistent in second-order classical logic, as the Burali–Forti paradox shows.

[16] Which we might think of as mereological fusions of concrete tokens or something similar: more will be said on this in Chapter 6.

[17] Of course the neo-Fregean does not suppose that HP does play this role for the ordinary speaker. Their route to knowledge of arithmetic via HP is supposed to be a rational reconstruction, but this means they owe us an account of how the mathematical knowledge of all those who have never even entertained HP (which

the number of φs = the number of ψs

given the premiss:

there is a one:one correspondence between the φs and the ψs

and vice versa with the roles of premiss and conclusion reversed. Grasp of the notion of one:one correspondence does not, arguably, require grasp of second-order quantification.[18] Restrict the RHP rule to simple, comprehensible instances of φ and ψ at least; perhaps further.[19] It is plausible that grasp of such a rule is required for a competence with the concept of cardinal number. Someone who cannot grasp that the number of knives is the same as the number of forks on the table, when seeing that they can be paired off one:one, just does not grasp the concept of number.

Of course some are sceptical of the very notion of analyticity[20] but granted that some mathematical principles or inference rules are built into the mathematical language of competent language speakers we can sketch one possible answer to the problem of inadequacy, for arithmetic at least. An arithmetical axiom set such as Q is inadequate not because it fails to capture important truths concerning an objective domain of abstract numbers. Rather, it is inadequate as a formalism for capturing all the truths which flow from our everyday concept of (natural) number. For, the argument will go, our everyday concept of number is at least partly constituted by stronger principles such as HP (or RHP) principles which are analytic of number. Any set of axioms which does not prove theorems derivable from HP is inadequate.[21]

However, can we really say that HP (or even FH or RHP) is partly constitutive of our everyday concept of number, given that we have allowed that the Woman on the Auchenshuggle Omnibus may have no glimmer of second-order logic, nor be able to apply correctly even the schematic rule stated in terms of a primitive notion of correspondence beyond some rather simple instances? We may attempt to deflect at least the second point by appeal to the idea of a legitimate idealization of our practice. We might claim that arbitrary instances of RHP (which will license arbitrary instances of commutativity under suitable definitions of addition) form part of a legitimate idealization of actual practice. The notion of what is a legitimate idealization of

will include a great many great mathematicians of the past) is acquired. A philosophy of mathematics which is at a loss to account for this is clearly inadequate.

[18] Or one might replace the premiss with ⌈there are just as many φs as ψs⌉. Dummett discusses the Frege ⟨ Husserl debate concerning the equivalence of this with the existence of a one:one correspondence between the φs and ψs, and whether the phrases are synonymous in Dummett (1991a, pp. 148–54).

[19] Richard Heck argues for the restriction to Finite Hume, but I doubt whether there is this restriction in our ordinary practice. It only needs a very little mathematical ability to conclude that the number of even numbers is the same as the number of odd numbers (cf. MacBride 2000). Crispin Wright (1999/2001, pp. 12–14) has argued for restrictions on substituends to sortal concepts and perhaps more narrowly to 'definite' properties.

[20] Against which see Weir (2005a, pp. 463–4) and Chapter 5, §III.

[21] We have to add, though, that we are allowed bridging definitions of the constants of the axiom system in Fregean Arithmetic, so questions may be raised as to what is legitimate and what not in bridging principles.

practice is an extremely difficult, and important, issue in philosophy of mathematics which I return to in Chapter 6.

But even, allowing that generalizing the practice of conforming to comprehensible instances of RHP is legitimate, it is not obvious that Hume's Principle or variants thereof are central to our grasp of arithmetic. It might be said that what is essential to grasp of arithmetic by adults who are not innumerate is not HP, FH, RHP, nor even mathematically interesting restrictions thereof, but the standard algorithms for decimal arithmetic (at least in the modern Western world). Brian Butterworth (1999, pp. 178–80) presents a tragic but intriguing case. 'Monsieur Van' suffered from neurodegenerative disease yet had impressive abilities in decimal arithmetic—picking out which were squares from sets of numbers represented decimally such as $\{839, 841, 4096, 4099\}$. However he was hopeless on even primitive applications of HP-like principles. For example, he could tell there were the same number of cubes and discs when ten of each were lined up with the distance between cubes equal to and equal to the distance between discs, but thought there were more cubes than discs when the distances between the cubes were lengthened.

Of course, one should not place too much emphasis on atypical individuals. But such cases add weight to the sense that it is the school algorithms for decimal arithmetic which are constitutive of everyday practice in pure arithmetic, whilst HP and analogues are more important for practical applications. It is the numerical operator featuring in HP which enables us to form concepts such as 'the number of knives' and introduce principles relating these terms to decimal numerals.

The issue of the relative importance, in legitimate idealizations of our arithmetic practice, of HP-type systems versus formalizations of the algorithms for addition and multiplication is largely independent of the issue of inadequacy. So long as there is a concept such as 'number' which we grasp through our immersion in a practice which is governed by certain, perhaps implicit, rules or principles, so long as this obtains there is scope for axiom systems proposed as formalizations of that practice to fall short. Thus if the schematic rule

$$a + b = b + a$$

is drilled into a whole community as one they must accept with respect to '$+$', then Q, as an axiom system governing a set of primitives including '$+$' taken to have its sense given by that everyday practice, clearly is inadequate. We know that the above commutativity rule is not a derived rule of the Q theory, hence there is a clear sense in which Q is inadequate, one which does not require platonistic acceptance of a mind-independent domain of numbers which arithmetic theories, systems, and axiom sets try to capture.

This non-platonistic notion of inadequacy generalizes from the language of arithmetic to the language of any set of mathematical primitives which are not stipulated into existence by a fixed and definite axiom set but around which a practice grows up and develops, a practice which may, unlike arithmetic, be restricted to a small group such as professional mathematicians. (Actually this can happen to a set of primitives stipulated to be characterized by an axiom set, since the stipulators cannot control what future mathematicians will do with their theories.) In many cases the question as to what are the principles governing the informal pre-axiomatic practice of the community may be an even more tricky one than with arithmetic; set theory is a case in point and I will return to this in Chapter 8, §VII.

## §II.5*

In this section I turn defence into attack and argue that neo-formalism is in better shape than platonism with respect to the topics discussed above and others closely related. Some knowledge of the relevant literature is presupposed here.

I start with a number of problems which face mathematical platonists, the threat from Gaius Julius Caesar, for one. Frege, whom I take to be a platonist, assumed that Julius Caesar $\neq$ five but struggled to explain how we can know this. Perhaps it might seem there is no need to struggle hard, that it is obvious that five cannot be a transient, long dead, flesh and blood human animal (but would dualists have to worry over whether the number five could be Caesar's immortal soul!). However the platonist needs to give us some general explanation of why the categories of numbers and of concrete objects are (and presumably must be) exclusive, as well as an epistemological account of how we know this.[22] Anyway, even if that can be done, Benacerraf (1965) provided more testing examples from among the platonic domain of abstract objects. Is the number two the same or different from the set $\{\{\emptyset\}\}$, a set which 'plays the role' of two in Zermelo's development of arithmetic inside ZF set theory? Is the empty set $\emptyset$ in ZF set theory the same as the empty set in Boolos's set theory based on his principle New V (Boolos, 1989/98):

$$\forall X \forall Y (\{x : Xx\} = \{x : Yx\} \leftrightarrow$$
$$((\text{Big}(X) \,\&\, \text{Big}(Y)) \vee \forall x(Xx \leftrightarrow Yx)))$$

where a property is Big iff there is a function from it onto the universe? The platonist may adopt some form of indeterminacy of reference or relativity of ontology principle and simply live with the absence of any fact of the matter in these identity claims. But from the perspective of a fairly traditional form of platonism, this is a species of revolutionary defeatism.

Boolos's principle is a special case of a more general class of abstraction principles which I have called 'distraction' principles (see Weir, 2003a) because they are dis-

---

[22] Of course insofar as one has any truck with a notion like Frege's notion of sense, one will hold that the sense of 'Julius Caesar' and the sense of 'five' are very different. But so is the sense of 'dull headache' and that of any term from neurophysiology. Yet one cannot move straight away from this to the conclusion that the referents must differ. For a more optimistic appraisal of neo-Fregean prospects for resolving the Caesar problem see Hale and Wright (2001b, pp. 335–96).

junctivized versions of Frege's ill-fated (according to the conventional story) Basic Law V. The schematic disjunctivized version is

$$\forall X \forall Y (\{x : Xx\} = \{x : Yx\} \leftrightarrow$$
$$((\text{Bad}(X) \ \& \ \text{Bad}(Y)) \lor \forall x (Xx \leftrightarrow Yx)))$$

different instantiations for 'Bad' yielding different principles. The most interesting cases are those in which Badness is a second-order property of properties for which equinumerosity is a congruence. Examples include:

finite; infinite; being at least (or exactly) of size $\aleph_n$; or $\theta_n$, where $\theta_n$ is the $n$th-inaccessible cardinal for finite $n$.[23]

Given a suitable background theory (such as ZFC or a distraction principle of similar power to that theory) one can show that there are infinitely many such distractions, each consistent and indeed conservative (meaning, roughly, that adding the principle, suitably restricted, to any theory does not induce new consequences in the language of the original theory) but with any pair taken together inconsistent. This is the 'embarrassment of riches' problem.[24]

This problem can be generalized to a second problem for platonists, in addition to the Julius Caesar/Benacerraf problem. Which is the correct set theory: ZFC, NBG, New V, Kelly-Morse, Quine's NF, Church's, or Mitchell's theories with universal sets? One might hold that there are a plurality of different set-like entities, just as there are commutative groups and non-commutative groups or different types of number—natural, rationals, reals, and so on (Stewart Shapiro suggested this response to me). The different theories each have a different subject matter, dealing with different subdomains of the domain of set-like entities.

This is a reasonable point to make with respect to some theory pairs, for example, a theory which deals with well-founded sets compared to one which can handle ill-founded ones. But in this type of case, we can often conjoin the theories together, with appropriate restrictions on their quantifiers to the appropriate subdomain. The resultant joint theory is (at least we hope) a consistent account of a single mathematical reality. But, as noted, when we turn to New V and the infinitely many other distraction principles one finds consistent pairs which are incompatible with one another, which impose different sizes on the overall universe. We can get round this by restricting the first and second-order quantifiers of theory T which forces a universe of size $\alpha$ to a subdomain of that of $T^*$ which forces a universe of larger

---

[23] The first few inaccessibles are the smallest of the large infinite cardinal numbers, in the weird terminology of the set theorists. See Enderton (1977, p. 254), or Kunen (1980, p. 34), or, for the definition, Chapter 8, §V*.

[24] See Weir (2003a). 'Taking them together' need not mean specifying two different principles as holding of the set operation represented by the brackets $\{x: \varphi x\}$. Because distractions can impose constraints on the size of the universe, two such principles even taken as determining different notions of set, notated as $\{x: \varphi x\}$ and $[x: \varphi x]$ perhaps, can be inconsistent.

size $\kappa$. Even so, we can still, with a little bit of artificiality (Heck 1992), get inconsistent principles, e.g. if $Bad_T$ is ⌜exactly size $a$ & P⌝ and $Bad_{T^*}$ is ⌜exactly size $\kappa$ & $\sim$P⌝. One could restore consistency either by maintaining that principles which, to human tastes, are artificial cannot (as a matter of necessity?) accurately depict the objective universe or else by adopting an outright metaphysical relativism. There is, according to this relativism, no single all-encompassing mathematical domain so that the conflicting principles are both true in equally real, but not fully commensurable, universes. Neither response fits in well with traditional platonism.

The negation-incompleteness of theories such as (first-order) ZFC raises a third difficult question: are indeterminables, such as the general continuum hypothesis GCH, true or not? Although a realist of a sceptical bent might dismiss the epistemological worries, prepared to accept that we might never know the answers in these cases, a 'scientific realist' might find it harder to stomach the idea that there is a determinate answer in each case, though this answer might be forever beyond our ken. For, as remarked in Chapter 1, scientific realism is usually presented as a 'have one's cake and eat it' position, combining the 'mind-independence' of reality, whatever exactly that is, with the optimistic view that it is reasonable, in some objective sense, to think that human cognitive methods will take us closer to the truth.

Neo-formalism enables us to avoid all the above problems. Turning firstly to the Caesar/Benacerraf problem, we note that there are formal calculi in which the syntactic string '$2 = \{\{\emptyset\}\}$' is provable, others in which it is refutable, still others in which it is neither provable nor refutable. These are different but equally legitimate mathematical systems, in the first of which the claim is true, in the second it is false, and in the third it is neither determinately true nor determinately false. The metaphysical content of '$2 = \{\{\emptyset\}\}$' changes as we move from system to system (since the formal truth-makers, the axioms, and inference rules change), so it is no surprise that the truth-value changes. And if, as suggested above in the case of modular arithmetic, the informational content of the sentence changes too as we situate it with respect to different set theories, we do not even have to see this as a case of relativism. Rather the sentence expresses different propositions in each case; there is a plurality of set theories in which the syntactic string expresses different things, each of which can sit side by side in peaceful coexistence. There is no question, for the neo-formalist, of one of the sentences corresponding correctly to an external reality, the others not.

In the Julius Caesar case, the neo-formalist can say much the same thing. However, in the theory in which it is true that Julius Caesar equals the number five, 'Julius Caesar' has only its formal meaning in common with its use in empirical language (perhaps little more than that it functions as a singular term). There is no identification of the real Julius Caesar with an abstract object. Of course, since there are some sentences which, relative to a given framework providing by an underlying calculus, are neither determinately true nor false, the law of excluded middle (LEM) cannot hold in full generality. This clearly has implications for the logic governing contentful use of mathematical language, and raises worries that the viewpoint will be implausibly revisionary; implications I turn to in Chapter 8.

The second problem is what, if anything, is the right set theory, a metaphysical problem, though, as usual, one with an epistemological follow up—if there is a correct one, how can we know what it is? But since for the neo-formalist THERE ARE NO mind-independent domains of mathematical objects (far less a unique and absolute all-encompassing one) there is no problem. There is no need to worry which, among pairwise inconsistent set theories, is the true one. All the set theories considered above are true, if consistent, true in the contexts of their own proper systems.[25] (One will not, of course, combine inconsistent principles into the one system.) Again there is reason to hold that different notions of 'set' are in play in the differing systems since the set-theoretic constants, be it the membership predicate '∈' or the term-forming operation $\{x: \varphi x\}$, get their (formal) metaphysical content by reference to different systems of rules and axioms and it is arguable that this determination of truth-value by underlying system does impinge in a very general way on the informational content of the set theoretic terms, much as it does with '+' and its relation to different types of arithmetic.

The same line can be taken with the third problem of indeterminables. The general continuum hypothesis (GCH) is true in the system ZFC+GCH, false in ZFC+∼GCH and neither determinately true nor false relative to the system ZFC itself. Likewise for the large cardinal axioms over whose adoption set theorists sometimes debate: are there inaccessibles, hyper-inaccessibles, Mahlo cardinals, indescribable cardinals, compact cardinals, and so on? Should we accept the existence of measurable cardinals, or the axiom of projective determinacy?[26]

The neo-formalist adopts a position of non-interference in such debates. So long as there are no good grounds for believing an axiom system has formal properties which debar it (in conjunction with the Basic Semantics) from being truth-apt, inconsistency most obviously, the question of whether to adopt it or not is entirely a matter for the specialists in question, the set-theorists. What counts is their judgements about mathematical interest and elegance, fruitfulness in other areas, and so forth.

Not that the neo-formalist is a doormat. For one thing, inconsistency, as remarked in the previous chapter, is not the only formal property needed for truth-aptness, primality is another. This then raises some question marks over the higher flights of set theory, which will be addressed in Chapter 8. Secondly, though some 'technicians' may simply carry out the calculations and heuristics with no thought for what it all means, in general mathematicians will reflect on and interpret their work and develop, with greater or less degrees of sophistication, a philosophy of mathematics. Platonistic mathematicians, therefore, might move beyond adopting or eschewing this or that

---

[25] Here the neo-formalist position, ironically, bears comparison with the 'full-blooded Platonism' entertained by Balaguer (1998) since on this view 'consistency entails existence'—any consistent system is bound to encapsulate a body of mathematical truths; this position was also held by Hilbert.

[26] For some discussion see Maddy (1988a, 1988b), Potter (2004, pp. 231–3, 275–80).

axiom system, to believing, and seeking to persuade others, that their favoured system is a true description of an external reality, and conflicting systems absolutely and objectively false. To these mathematicians, the neo-formalist says: 'get unreal'! THERE IS NO such reality. You are dealing with a free creation of humans, though one which transcends the ability of any of us to grasp as a whole and which, like many such creations (common law, languages, economies) is autonomous of the intentions and designs of any single human or coordinated group of humans.

What, though, of the hunch many set theorists have that, for example, the axiom of constructibility is false and probably the GCH too? It does not seem as if only those in the grip of the philosophical theory of mathematical platonism feel the force of such conjectures, yet how can the neo-formalist explain this? Well, in some cases at least we can put this down to the hostility such mathematicians feel to extending the set theories they have been comfortable working in by adding constructibility or GCH. This hostility is not inexplicable except on the assumption that they have some mysterious awareness of a realm of acausal non-spatio-temporal particulars. On the contrary, postulation of the latter as the proper subject matter of mathematics renders it a mystery how any reliable knowledge of mathematics could ever arise. Rather we might simply conjecture that a substantial body of mathematicians, at any rate, find that to extend the set theories they are currently happy working with by adding these axioms, of constructibility or the GHC, yields results not to their mathematical taste. Constructibility, for example, may be too restrictive for them; their mathematical imagination is simply cramped too much if they have to work inside that system.

## §III.   Incompleteness

### §III.1

I now turn to a much more difficult problem for neo-formalism, that raised by the argument of Gödel's awesome first incompleteness theorem. For example, one version of Gödel's argument shows that the fragment of formal arithmetic Q, and any stronger theory T *whose theorems are recursively enumerable*, is negation-incomplete. More exactly, if T is $\omega$-consistent then there are 'indeterminable' sentences $\varphi$ such that neither $T \vdash \varphi$ nor $T \vdash \sim\varphi$.[27] The neo-formalist will have to say in such a case that indeterminable sentences are indeterminate, neither determinately true (since not provable) nor determinately false (since not refutable) in that system. Why, though, is this a problem for the formalist?

The problem arises because in many cases we have strong intuitions that one or other of the indeterminable sentences is true. To see this we need look at the Gödelian example in a little more detail, detail which will, additionally, provide us with some

---

[27] An $\omega$-consistent arithmetic theory T is one such that if $T \vdash \varphi t$ for all canonical numerals $t$ (see ahead) then it is not the case that $T \vdash \exists x \sim \varphi x$.

concepts and tools we will need in later discussion. Thus in our informal FM metatheory we discuss a formal object language, for example, the language of first-order arithmetic which in turn is used to express a syntactic theory for a target language (which may be the same as the object language); Gödel's techniques provide the tools we need here.

## §III.2

We start from a formal regimentation of informal and intuitive ideas we have about syntax. In the formal regimentation we develop a syntax for simple formal languages, normally generating the language from atoms with a context-free phrase structure grammar or something similar. We start by supposing we have a set of simple symbol types, objects about whose nature we care not one whit (except that they must turn out to be distinct from all the complex entities); we then construct a theory of how the more complex entities, most importantly sentences and proofs, are constructed from them. We might use set theory to do this, but alternatively we could use second-order logic. Thus we divide our array of symbols into pairwise disjoint sets (or assume there are mutually exclusive properties covering the whole range of simple symbols) and stipulate that atomic sentences are strings consisting of a monadic predicate followed by a singular term, or dyadic predicate followed by a singular term, then a singular term (same or different), and so on. We assume operations for generating more complex strings from simpler—negating a string, universally quantifying a string, and so forth—and then define the wffs as the intersection of all sets which have all the atoms as a subset and are closed under the compound-forming operations. Or, if we eschew set theory we might use some characterization such as:

$$\text{Wff } x \leftrightarrow \forall F[(\forall y(\text{Atom } y \rightarrow Fy) \ \& \ \forall z, w((Fz \ \& \ \text{Neg}(w, z)) \rightarrow Fw)) \rightarrow Fx]$$

but adding clauses for the other operations such as conjunction, universal quantification, and so on. Similarly we give an inductive characterization of which strings or arrangements of sentences count as proofs in the language, more specifically proofs of a given conclusion from given premises.

We then 'mathematize' our syntax and proof theory by mapping the symbols onto mathematical objects. In Gödel's case, we map the primitive symbols into a proper subset of the set of natural numbers, leaving infinitely many numbers spare; this is possible if our language is only countable infinite. If we set up our syntactic theory set-theoretically, the mapping $m$ immediately gives us a wholly mathematical theory of syntax and proof in which syntactic properties, such as being a universal generalization with one free variable, are shadowed by purely mathematical sets. In this case, the shadow of the syntactic property is the set of all *sequences* (the mathematical surrogate for strings) $<n_1, \ldots, n_k>$ of numerical codes of simple symbols such that the string $<\hat{m}^{-1}(n_1)\ \hat{\ }, \ldots, \ \hat{m}^{-1}(n_k)>$, the concatenation of all the primitive symbols which are the respective inverse images, is a universal generalization with one free variable.

Now since we are entirely indifferent as to the nature of the primitive symbols of our formal language, and since these are usually construed as abstract types, there seems no reason why we cannot simply take them to be natural numbers. And then the whole mapping from syntax into mathematics might seem pointless. Our original formal theory of syntax just *is* a branch of set theory, or impure set theory if we take the numbers to be distinct from sets. However, unless we can show some isomorphism between arithmetic structures and syntactic structures, *independently* characterized in a way which links them to intuitive syntactic notions, as a formalization of those notions for example, then the arithmetic predicates have no syntactic, proof-theoretic import at all, and their introduction becomes pointless.[28]

For Gödel's purposes, it was important to show that, whether or not one starts from numbers as the simplest syntactic types, *all* the relevant syntactic entities, including wffs and proofs, can be construed not just mathematically but in particular as numbers. Thus using the unique prime factorization theorem, the fundamental theorem of arithmetic, Gödel showed that each finite string of symbol types (or codes of symbol types if one wishes) can itself be coded as a single number. Not only that, but we can, in algorithmic fashion, recover the component terms of the string from its numerical code. That is to say, there are recursive[29] functions $f_j(x,y)$ such that $f_j(n,m) = 1$ iff $n$ codes the $j$th component of the string (if any) encoded by $m$, 0 otherwise (if $m$ encodes no string or $n$ is not the $j$th component). Similarly Gödel showed how our fundamental syntactic operations, negating, forming generalizations, and so forth can be represented by recursive functions and was able to prove that the set of codes of wffs, under his (or any similar) coding of expression strings, is a recursive set (for a standard countable language). It is a decidable matter whether a number belongs to this set or not. Proofs, which Gödel took to be finite strings of sentences, can similarly be coded by single numbers. He then showed that under his formalization of the proof theory of *Principia Mathematica*, the set of theorems is recursively enumerable. Roughly speaking, a computer could be programmed to churn out all and only the theorems one at a time. Moreover theoremhood is *representable*, that is, there is a predicate (actually there are infinitely many such) 'Bew' such that:

If $n$ codes a proof $\pi$, $m$ a sentence A and $\pi$ is a proof of A, then $\vdash$ Bew($S^n0$, $S^m0$).
If it is not the case that $n$ codes a proof $\pi$, $m$ a sentence A with $\pi$ a proof of A, then $\vdash \sim$Bew($S^n0$, $S^m0$).

(Here '$S^n0$' is a parameter representing a string of $n$ occurrences of 'S' followed by one of '0', a 'canonical numeral'. Under the usual interpretation it stands for the number $n$.[30]) This follows from the more general representability of all recursive relations, that

---

[28] See Boolos (1993, pp. 33ff.).
[29] Primitive recursive, if the various different sets of simple symbols—constants, variables, and so forth—are recursive. See Mendelson (1979, ch. 3.4).
[30] And here, in the metatheory, '$n$' is also a parameter, for which we substitute names for numbers.

is for any such relation R there is a predicate P such that if R holds between $n$ and $m$ then ⊢ P(S$^n$0,S$^m$) and if R does not hold between those numbers then ⊢ ∼P(S$^n$0,S$^m$), together with the fact, which Gödel painstakingly demonstrated, that for the PM system under study the proof relation between a number coding a string of sentences (premises) and a code for a sentence is itself recursive.

Gödel's techniques can be applied not only to Russell and Whitehead's *Principia Mathematica* theory but to any theory in a countable language whose syntax is representable in arithmetic in the above fashion and whose set of codes of theorems is recursively enumerable—thus to formalizations of all the main theories of standard mathematics, PA, ZFC, formalizations of real analysis, general topology, the theory of tensor spaces and so on—and where our background mathematical theory is a fragment of arithmetic at least as strong as Q. It is this which makes his arithmetization of formal syntax so important.

A crucial lemma in modern presentations of the Gödelian argument is the *diagonalization lemma*. Let us use the notation of a vertical line '|' followed by an expression $e$ followed by another vertical line '|' as a metalinguistic singular term standing for a numeral of the form S$^k$0 in the object language of arithmetic.[31] If the expression $e$ is a metalinguistic name of an expression string $s$ of the syntactic system which we have arithmetized—the *target system*—then $k$ is the Gödel code of $s$. Similarly if the expression $e$ is a metalinguistic free variable whose range in the intended interpretation is some syntactic subcategory of the syntactic system, for example the wffs of the target language, then '|ˆ$e$ˆ|' is a metalinguistic free variable whose range in the intended interpretation is the set of canonical names of members of that category—in our example the set of names of wffs. For every assignment of a string with Gödel code $k$ to $e$, '|ˆ$e$ˆ|' is S$^k$0.

I will employ, from now on, standard notation for metalinguistic free variables and, as is customary, treat the metalanguage as multi-sorted. Thus in the context of syntactic and proof-theoretic discussions, italicized Roman letters, generally from the end of the alphabet '$x$', '$y$', and so on, possibly subscripted, are metalinguistic variables whose range is the set of object language variables (but also, where context dictates, variables over tokens and expression strings in general). Unitalicized Roman letters from 'b' on are variables ranging over object language individual constants, upper-case Roman letters range over object language wffs (but with F and G, possibly subscripted, reserved for predicate constants), and Greek letters range over object language predicate expressions except that the first few letters of the Greek alphabet are additionally used for special sorts, as determined in context. (Often metalinguistic variables will be used parametrically, that is, treated as temporary names of objects in a given context, often left unspecified.) Further sorts will be introduced as occasion demands and the usual names of object language logical operators and special signs,

---

[31] Later we will generalize this so that '|ˆ$e$ˆ|' names not a numeral but a canonical singular term of a set-theoretic object language system. This is a singular term which denotes, in the intended interpretation of the object language, the set-theoretic object which codes the string named (in that interpretation) by the expression embedded in the vertical lines.

such as identity and membership signs are employed. Concatenation is represented simply by adjacency.[32]

Now let the target language be the same as the object language and suppose the latter has the resources (a zero constant, signs for successor, multiplication and addition) to express an arithmetic theory T at least as strong as Q. If $\varphi$ is any one-place open formula of arithmetic then one form of the diagonalization lemma is that there is a sentence D of arithmetic such that

$$Q \vdash D \leftrightarrow \varphi|D|.$$

So in particular, there is a sentence G such that:

$$Q \vdash G \leftrightarrow \sim \exists x \mathrm{Bew}(x, |G|).$$

Bearing in mind our coding, and the shadowing of syntax by arithmetic, we can say loosely that G 'says of itself'[33] that it is not provable.

Gödel, in his first Incompleteness Theorem (1931) shows that if Q[34] is consistent, G is not provable and if it is $\omega$-consistent, $\sim$G is not provable. Rosser strengthened Gödel's result by applying diagonalization to get a sentence R:

$$Q \vdash R \leftrightarrow \forall x(\mathrm{Bew}(x, |R|) \to \exists y \leq x\, \mathrm{Bew}(y, |\sim R|)).$$

If Q is consistent, this sentence R is undecidable, we have neither $Q \vdash R$ nor $Q \vdash \sim R$.

The problem for formalists is that once we read Gödel and Rosser's proofs we will come to believe that both the Gödel sentence G and the Gödel–Rosser sentence R must be true, providing we believe that arithmetical sentences have determinate truth-values and that Q is true of the natural numbers. We can argue thus: if we grasp Gödel's proof and the idea behind arithmetization of syntax via coding, then we see that since G, provably equivalent in Q to $\sim \exists x \mathrm{Bew}(x, |G|)$, is not provable, it is true. For that it is not provable is what it 'says', under the coding. Similarly R 'says' that for any $n$, if $n$ codes a proof of R then there is a proof, of no higher code, of its negation. If

---

[32] An exception occurs in clauses of the form: for any open sentence $\varphi(x_1, \ldots, x_n)$. Such clauses are best interpreted as multiple quantifications along the lines of: ⌐ for any open sentence $\varphi$ and for any variables $x_1$, $\ldots$, $x_n$ free in $\varphi$ … ¬. From time to time the metalinguistic variables of the various sorts will occur not in complex names of mentioned object language sentences but *used*, not mentioned, in 'Loglish' sentences which are asserted, denied, or considered in the metalanguage. (The term is due, I believe, to Richard Jeffrey, see Burgess and Rosen (1997, p. 67).) But it should be clear enough in context when a sentence is 'on active service', rather than merely being mentioned. For one thing, Loglish sentences in use will usually be a mixture of logical symbols and English expressions.

[33] Very loosely; for elucidations and qualifications see Giaquinto (2002), Potter (2004), and especially Milne (2007). He notes (p. 194) that this way of diagonalizing, using 'fixed point' theorems, is not Gödel's original way and that one can create Gödel sentences which are false in the standard model, if one represents derivability in a false extension of Q. The neo-formalist cannot object to this necessary qualification to the above argument that the notions of 'true in the standard model' or 'Q is true of the natural numbers' are to be rejected. For though neo-formalists believe that numbers do not EXIST, we do believe numbers and standard interpretations exist.

[34] Actually he shows this for a formulation of the simple theory of types, but the argument can be reworked to apply to Q.

we believe Q is consistent and grasp the Gödel–Rosser proof we must believe that no number is the code of a proof of R, thus $\sim$Bew$(x, |R|)$ is true of every natural number hence

$$\forall x(\text{Bew}(x, |R|) \;\rightarrow\; \exists y \leq x, \text{Bew}(y, |\sim R|))$$

is trivially true, hence, we conclude by elementary logic, R is true. Or, eschewing talk of what our Gödel sentence 'says' we can argue: if we believe Q is true, it is consistent and so no number $k$ codes a proof of G (else we have $\vdash$ G and also $\vdash$ Bew$(S^k0, |G|)$, whence by $\exists$I and the diagonalization lemma, $\vdash \sim$G). Hence by representability we have $\vdash \sim$Bew$(S^n0, |G|)$ for every $n$, so that $\forall x \sim$Bew$(x, |G|)$, i.e. $\sim \exists x$Bew$(x, |G|)$, and therefore G, is true in the standard model.

One might respond that G and R are rather odd sentences. On the usual sort of codings they would be too long to be graspable unabbreviated and even a super-being who could grasp them would likely see nothing of mathematical interest in them unless she knew the coding. In what sense, then, can we believe them or hold any propositional attitudes towards them? Does it even make sense to think of them as true or false? We never could assert them as we can assert, say, the fundamental theorem of arithmetic; 'G' and 'R' stand for esoteric mathematical objects, not real sentences.

Here we confront the issue of idealization in mathematics. The formal language PA and its sentences such as G and R are clearly idealizations of real arithmetical language and we can see the model theory for PA as an idealized theory of truth for that language, likewise the proof theory an idealization of the notion of provability in 'real arithmetic'. Hence if idealized truth and idealized proof fail to match up, that is bad news for formalism.

This argument cannot be properly evaluated without getting clear on what idealization can legitimately amount to, but at the very least we have a prima facie problem for neo-formalism. Moreover, there are 'mathematical examples', such as Goodstein's theorem; these are sentences with independent interest to mathematicians other than mathematical logicians (undoubtedly an odd breed), which can be shown to be undecidable in Peano arithmetic. (See Potter 2004, pp. 216–17; Kirby and Paris 1982). Although unprovable in Peano arithmetic, we can show that Goodstein's theorem is true in a standard set-theoretic model of arithmetic.[35] This seems to give those who accept the set theory, in particular who accept it shows that the $\omega$ model is a good model for the language of arithmetic, compelling grounds for believing that Goodstein's theorem, as expressed in the language of arithmetic, is true. Once again we have sentences we believe to be true but know to be unprovable, a seemingly fatal problem for formalism. To refuse to believe in the truth of such sentences or in sentences such as (leaving aside the worries about idealization) G and R, would render formalists liable to the charge of mathematical incompetence whilst to believe them

---

[35] The domain of the model is the set-theoretic ordinal $\omega$ ('$\omega$' on active service), the constant 0 of the language of Goodstein's theorem is assigned the empty set $\emptyset$, and so on.

true seems to land them straight in contradiction, affirming both that some mathematical truths are unprovable and that all such truths are provable.

How do we, though, 'see' the truth of G and R? As sketched above, we see it by following an argument, an argument which can in fact be formalized in a stronger set-theoretic setting;[36] similarly a set-theoretic argument shows us that Goodstein's theorem is true. Since we can prove G and R and Goodstein's theorem in set theory, the problem for the formalist vanishes, it would seem. More bluntly, we can simply add G or R or any undecidable sentence to our axioms to yield a strengthened system in which each such sentence is trivially provable, and thus true, according to the formalist.

But this response is too quick. For one thing, mathematical truth for the formalist as for anyone else depends, like all truth, on the meaning of the terms in the sentence; but for the formalist one key aspect of meaning is metaphysical content and this in turn is determined by the rules of proof and axioms which give the true mathematical sentence its meaning. Moreover it was suggested that many, at least, mathematical terms contain a reference to the system which determines the metaphysical content of sentences they belong to as part of their informational content. That is, in any utterance containing the term, the sense of the utterance picks out the system which determines the metaphysical content of the utterance. Such terms, however, can be ambiguous, picking out different systems—standard arithmetic versus arithmetic modulo 4, ZFC + GCH set theory versus ZFC + ∼GCH, and so on—on different occasions of utterance. This contextuality of truth to system is what causes the problem for the neo-formalist.

It is certainly the case that any undecided sentence U will be true$_S$ for the neo-formalist, for some S which bestows meaning on U, if only one with U as its sole non-logical axiom. But the belief that G or R or Goodstein's theorem are true, as expressed in the language of arithmetic, not set theory, is a belief that they are true of the *numbers*. It is true that the formalist cannot put things quite like that, at least whilst in representational mode, since the neo-formalist does not believe that NUMBERS EXIST. However I argued that formalists could capture much of the intuition that sentence A is true of numbers by recasting it as the claim that A is provable in a formal system which captures our intuitive notion of numbers, perhaps which is meaning-constitutive or analytic of it. The system of decimal arithmetic is one such formal system, the axiomatic theory of Peano-Dedekind arithmetic, especially the second-order version PA², another. A further candidate, as we have seen, is Hume's Principle or some related principle such as Finite Hume.

If, then, I was right to suggest (above §II.3) that a mathematical string expresses different propositions in the context of different systems, these systems generating different metaphysical contents (different in the sense of generating different deriva-

---

[36] Or by expanding arithmetic by the addition of a truth predicate which can feature in the induction scheme.

bility relations), then the utterances of G, R, and Goodstein's theorem which we prove true in a strengthened system express distinct propositions, according to neo-formalism, from the propositions those utterances express in the original system of arithmetic. Can we then say that these set-theoretic propositions are determinate but the arithmetic propositions are not? The problem is that grasping the set-theoretic truth of the set-theoretic analogues (for instance) one 'sees' right away that the sentences are true in the 'intended' arithmetic structure, which is isomorphic to the set-theoretic one. But formalism seems incapable of doing justice to this. How can formalism even talk of the structures which make the sentences true?

The problem for the formalist thus remains. Our intuition that G, R, and Goodstein's theorem are true of numbers is to be recast as the thesis that these sentences are provable in the formal systems constitutive of these notions. But this is false, granted the Gödelian constraints on provability. In particular, for every Gödelian system in which the theorems are recursively enumerable there is a G or R sentence which is unprovable in the system. No matter how we strengthen our system, adding Gödel sentences as axioms, moving up to set theory or whatever, so long as the theorems of the augmented system are still recursively enumerable, there will always be new G and R sentences undecidable in the new system. The formalist seems to be playing a game of catch-up in which at every stage she is the loser.

Similar problems, it has to be said, beset any philosophy of mathematics which ties truth to proof, for instance various forms of constructivism such as intuitionism. One response intuitionists have made is to hold that the notion of proof is not a formal notion. By this they do not mean that proofhood is dependent on contextual factors, or is inherently vague or ambiguous. In Dummett's version, at any rate, the idea is that the predicate 'is a theorem' is *indefinitely extensible*. This is a notion Dummett takes from Russell. An indefinitely extensible concept is one expressed by a predicate φ such that given any *set* S all of whose members instantiate φ, one can construct an instance of φ which does not belong to S.[37] Dummett then goes on to differentiate definite and indefinite (presumably indefinitely extensible) totalities. The set of proofs of a mathematics is, he claims, an indefinite totality. I have criticized the Dummettian notion of an indefinite totality on the grounds that it amounts to nothing less than that of a naïve set and thus, since Russell's paradox goes through in intuitionistic as well as classical logic, the whole idea is incoherent (Weir 1998a, §III.i; 1998b, §10). If this is right, this line offers no resolution of the incompleteness problem. It thus remains an important issue for neo-formalism to address. I will advance a different resolution to the problem of incompleteness in Chapter 7, §II.

Another promissory note, then, has been issued. Leaving this aside, where have we got to? The argument of this chapter has been that neo-formalism is immune to various objections which cripple related anti-platonist positions such as deductivism

---

[37] Cf. Dummett (1991a, p. 317, esp. fn. 5). See also Dummett (1963b/78, pp. 194–7), (1981a, pp. 532–3), (1993, pp. 441–3, 454–5).

and has better answers to a whole range of problems which afflict the more alien positions, such as platonism in its various guises. However, the problem of the incompleteness of intuitively determinate mathematical systems, such as that of arithmetic, remains to be addressed. But before I do so, I turn to another formidable problem for neo-formalism—explaining how mathematics can be applied to the empirical world to yield empirical truths, if mathematics itself answers to nothing in reality independent of ourselves and our linguistic practices.

# 5

# Applying Mathematics

## §I. Conservativeness

*§.I.1*

One of Frege's most forceful complaints against formalism is its alleged inability to explain the applicability of mathematics. The latter, Frege points out, is an enormously important fact about mathematics:

> it is applicability alone which elevates arithmetic from a game to the rank of a science. (Frege 1903/1980, p. 167, §91)

This objection has far less force against neo-formalism, which not only rejects the idea that mathematical utterances are meaningless but also holds them to be, typically, true or false. Nonetheless, the neo-formalist is under an obligation to provide an account of the applicability of mathematics. This account must not only cover simple situations such as the classic computation, via simple arithmetic, that the number of pieces of fruit on the table is twelve, given that there are five apples in one bowl and seven oranges in the only other bowl but also the much more sophisticated uses of mathematics in the physical sciences. The naming or indexing of physical magnitudes, force strengths, and so forth, by real and complex numbers, vectors and tensors, geometrical objects and other mathematical entities, and then the use of these representations of physical entities to yield predictions about physical reality must also be explained—and without supposing that mathematical entities EXIST. A proper answer to this question would require a separate treatise on the philosophy of science. In this section, I will restrict myself to the basics of a neo-formalist treatment of applied mathematics of a simple nature, sketching how an extension to more complex applications might go in §III.

Let us start with simple arithmetical applications. Suppose L is some purely empirical language, let us suppose it has the logical resources of first-order logic with identity, and for the moment let us assume a classical logical framework for it. We then expand L to L* first by adding a new one-place predicate N$x$ (in the intended interpretation to be read as ⌜$x$ is a number⌝), the numerical operator $nx\varphi x$, read informally as ⌜the number of $\varphi$s⌝,[1] and the addition and multiplication signs $+$ and $\times$. We define 0 by $nx(x \neq x)$ and $n{+}1$ by $nx(x = 0 \lor \ldots \lor x = n)$. Any sentence of $L^*$ which contains no non-logical constants of L and whose quantifiers are restricted to N (i.e. which takes the form $\forall x(Nx \to \ldots)$ or $\exists x(Nx \ \& \ldots))$ is a pure (i.e. purely mathematical) sentence. Any sentence of L is an empirical sentence (thus including, somewhat awkwardly, the logical truths of L). Sentences which are neither pure nor empirical are mixed. Thus '$nx(x$ is an apple in the bowl$) = 5$' is a mixed sentence (if we imagine L to contain that English predicate).

Now the metaphysical contents of empirical sentences are representational. In general, these sentences are made-true or made-false by the way the mind-independent physical world is (except for the logical truths and falsehoods, though of course Quineans would dispute this). For the pure sentences, we take over the rules of quantified decimal arithmetic applied to the simple numerals now definitionally equated with numerical terms. A pure sentence provable by these rules plus logic is made-true, refutable made-false. In each case the 'truth-maker' is the existence of a structure which could be interpreted as a proof (or refutation) of the sentence.[2] The sentence, however, does not represent the obtaining or not of provability or refutability; it has formal, non-representational metaphysical content. But what of the metaphysical contents of the mixed sentences?

To determine truth-values for those we need *Bridge Principles*. For example, let, as usual, $\exists_0 x\varphi x$ abbreviate $\sim\exists x\varphi x$ and $\exists_{n+1} z\varphi z$ abbreviate $\exists z(\varphi z \ \& \ \exists_n y(\varphi y \ \& \ y \neq z))$ with $z$ new in $\varphi$. Then as bridge principles we add

$$\frac{\exists_0 x\varphi x}{nx(\varphi x) = 0} \qquad \frac{\exists_1 z\varphi z}{nx(\varphi x) = 1} \quad \ldots \quad \frac{\exists_n z\varphi z}{nx(\varphi x) = n}$$

The double line indicates that the rule allows us to derive the bottom formula from the top and also allows us to derive the top formula from the bottom. We will also need further bridge principles connecting addition and multiplication to our empirical language, for example:

$$\frac{\sim\exists x(\varphi x \ \& \ \psi x); \ nx\varphi x = n; \ nx\psi x = m}{nx(\varphi x \lor \psi x) = n + m}$$

where $\varphi$ and $\psi$ are any one-place open sentences of the mixed empirical/mathematical language and $n$ and $m$ any two numerical terms. Similarly for the application of multiplication we need a rule of the form:

---

[1] In a detailed treatment we would consider $L^*$ to be the union of a sequence of languages $L_i$ with $L_0$ containing no occurrences of the numerical operator and $L_{n+1}$ having among its simple terms all results of applying the operator to open sentences of $L_n$. Note that, though we have the numerical operator, we do not have second-order quantification into predicates embedded inside the operator.

[2] A further government health warning that we are still at the formal FM level, the level of the existence of proofs rather than the EXISTENCE OF CONCRETE PROOFS.

$$\frac{nx\varphi x = n;\ \forall x(\varphi x \rightarrow ny(Rxy)) = m);\ \text{Func}^{-1}(R)}{ny(\exists x(\varphi x\ \&\ Rxy)) = n \times m}$$

where Func⁻¹(R) abbreviates:

$$\forall x \forall y \forall z((Rxz\ \&\ Ryz) \rightarrow x = y).$$

How can we use these rules to make an empirical application of the pure calculus of decimal arithmetic? Imagine I have the following problem. I am confronted, visually, by a matrix m each cell of which is a pattern of dots. I can count the rows and columns of the matrix; perhaps indeed I can 'subitize' the matrix and see that it is a five by five matrix. Moreover, visual inspection leads me to think that the pattern of dots is the same in each case. I cannot be sure, but an overall glance, reliably as it turns out, leads me to believe that all the cells of dot patterns take the following form.

So the non-mathematical facts (E) before me are:

$\exists_5 x(\text{Row } x),\ \forall y(\text{Row } y \rightarrow \exists_5 x(y \text{ contains pattern } x)),$
Func-¹($\lambda yx$(row $y$ contains pattern $x$)),
$\forall y(\text{Pattern } y \rightarrow \exists_5 x(y \text{ contains dot } x)),$
Func-¹($\lambda yx$(pattern $y$ contains dot $x$).

Now, let AA be the applied arithmetic calculus whose rules are the bridge principles set out above plus the rules of quantified decimal arithmetic. I can deduce, using AA and the empirical facts, firstly that $nx(x$ is a row) = 5, next that for each row r, $nx(x$ is a pattern in r) = 5, and that therefore given the functionality—the fact that no pattern is on more than one row—that $nx(x$ is a pattern) = 5 × 5, which decimal arithmetic tells me equals 25. I also deduce that for each pattern p, $nx(x$ is in p) = 5 and from the fact that no dot is in more than one pattern that $nx(x$ is a dot) = 5 × 25, which I calculate to be 125. Finally I deduce that $\exists_{125}x(x$ is a dot in m), saving myself the tedious effort of counting out each dot in turn, a process probably more liable to error than my reasoning above.[3]

The sentence $\exists_{125}x(x$ is a dot in m) is an empirical truth, made true by the arrangement of dots on the page. But what about the mixed sentence $nx(x$ is a dot in m) = 125, which I can deduce using AA? It is presumably true, but what makes it true?

---

[3] Of course, if I had to write out the unabbreviated form of $\exists_{125}x(x$ is in m) this would undo all the savings and I would certainly make a mistake in writing out the formula. As remarked, it is implausible to suppose 'there are 125 dots' in natural language really has the semantic structure given by the usual logical paraphrase. A more realistic account of the above sort of reasoning would perhaps equate $nx\varphi x = 125$ with the 'empirical' Num($\varphi x$, '125') of the last chapter. The reasoning still gives us a faster and more reliable way of calculating how many dots are in the matrix than counting them out, the 'canonical' way of establishing that Num($x$ is a dot in the matrix, '125').

Not the rules of the pure calculus AA; it is not a theorem of this calculus. But neither can it represent some feature of the empirical world since THERE IS NO number one hundred and twenty five, or so I have claimed. The neo-formalist answer has to be that its truth is a joint product of two factors: representational truth, in this case the truth $\exists_{125}x(x$ is in m) and non-representational, formal truth, truth which is determined by provability in a calculus, in this case calculus AA. The sentence $nx(x$ is in m) $= 125$ is true (relative to calculus AA) because it is entailed by a combination of true empirical sentences and the rules and axioms (including the bridge principles) of the calculus AA. If we have naturalistic scruples about using the notion of 'entailment' in giving metaphysical content, we can say that what makes it true is provability in the calculus AAE which results by adding to AA the empirical truths E above. The metaphysical content of a mixed sentence S, in other words, relative to a calculus K, is that it is made-true iff there is a derivation of S in K plus some empirical truths, made-false iff there is a derivation of ~S in K likewise augmented with some empirical truths.

As for the bridge principles themselves, or, since we have expressed them in rule form, their associated biconditionals such as:

$$\exists_2 x(\varphi x) \leftrightarrow nx(\varphi x) = 2$$

what makes them true or false? Despite the fact that these are mixed sentences, their truth or falsity is determined in exactly the same fashion as for pure principles such as $7 + 5 = 12$. That is, they are made-true or made-false, relative to a given calculus, just when provable or refutable in that calculus. Since the biconditional $\exists_2 x(\varphi x) \leftrightarrow nx(\varphi x) = 2$ follows using very elementary logic from the corresponding bridge rule, its truth is pretty much immediate. Indeed, we could just as well have used the above biconditional as the bridge rule, and then its truth would be determined simply by its being an axiom. The truth of bridge principles, in other words, arises essentially by a process of stipulation or postulation. The difference between a bridge principle and a common-or-garden mixed sentence is simply that the former is taken to be axiomatic in (or an analytic rule of) the applied calculus in question. The mixed theorems which follow from bridge principles plus empirical assumptions will, in general, owe their truth to two sources, formal/mathematical and empirical. The metaphysical content for a mixed sentence is that there is a proof of it from the formal rules and axioms plus empirical, representational truths and only sometimes is the latter clause redundant.

What of ordinary empirical phrases such as 'is an apple' as they occur in mixed sentences, including bridge principles made true by stipulation as axioms? The metaphysical content of an entire sentence such as:

$nx(x$ is an apple) $= 2 \rightarrow nx(x$ is an apple) is even

is purely formal and non-representational (its truth depends on no empirical truth). But it seems implausible to say that 'apple' as it occurs in such a sentence has a different informational content. Certainly 'the number of apples in the bowl $= 2$' strikes the mind very differently from 'the number of ajookabiddles $= 2$'.

But the situation for the mixed sentences is not really all that much different from logical truths. The phenomenology of reading ⌜if $x$ is an apple, then it is an apple⌝, is very different from that if reading ⌜if $x$ is an ajookabiddle then $x$ is an ajookabiddle⌝ because we cannot just forget or discard the informational content of 'apple' whereas 'ajooka-biddle' has no informational content. But on an anti-Quinean view of logic, what makes-true the apple sentence is not something representational, some general logical fact in the world; it is made-true purely by virtue of the meaning of the conditional, in the traditional phrase. Where a term has a pre-existing sense or informational content, there is in cases like 'the number of apples in the bowl = 2' at the very least no reason to suppose that 'apples' has switched to a *distinct* informational content. The case is not comparable to switches in the sense of '+' between ordinary and modular arithmetic. Of course we could, and indeed do, use ordinary everyday predicates in a distinct purely formal mathematical way —'field', 'ring', 'filter', 'hull'—the list, not quite endless, is large. Here, as with '+' we can indeed say it is part of their informational content which role they are playing, and it would be a pun to say that there were two rings Senga thought about today, her eternity ring and the ring of integers.

As for other terms in mixed sentences, sentential operators arguably have the same purely formal content in all sentences. What of terms such as the identity symbol and quantificational expressions in sentences such as

$$nx(\text{Apple-in-bowl } x \lor (\text{10} < x < \text{15})) = 9$$
$$\exists_6 x(\text{Apple-in-bowl } x \lor (\text{Even } x \text{ \& Prime } x))?$$

The sentences as a whole have a mixed representational plus formal/mathematical content. What of the informational content of the quantifier or identity sign? Just as there is no reason to suppose a lexical ambiguity when we move between their use in empirical contexts and those in purely formal contexts, so too there is no standard sort of ambiguity here, no change in any aspect of meaning which is relatively transparent to any competent user and can be made manifest by provision of phrase-for-phrase distinct synonyms in distinct contexts.

## §I.2

Turning back from informational to metaphysical content, the fact that bridge principles owe their truth merely to being postulated as axioms raises an obvious worry. We can, if the neo-formalist is right, postulate what we like in pure mathematics (though the results may not provide a very interesting or rich structure). But surely we cannot be so free in the case of the mixed sentences we stipulate to be bridge principles of applied mathematics, not if we hope to use it to arrive at empirical truths. For instance, if we swap around the bridge principles dealing with $\exists_0 x$ and $\exists_1 x$ to get

$$\exists_0 x(\varphi x) \leftrightarrow nx(\varphi x) = 1$$
$$\exists_1 x(\varphi x) \leftrightarrow nx(\varphi x) = 0$$

whilst leaving all other rules the same, disaster, indeed inconsistency, will ensue (since we can prove in decimal arithmetic $0 \neq 1$, and similar inequalities).

In order to be justified in utilizing a mixed calculus such as AA in empirical applications, we need a *conservative extension* result, a result which applies to our empirical language L and is thus, itself, an example of applied mathematics. We need to know that if we derive some results in the empirical language L from true empirical premisses in L, but via some applications of mathematics embodied in a calculus such as AA, then the empirical results we have arrived at in this indirect manner will also be true. But how can we establish that the conservative extension result is true, for a particular calculus?

The obvious route is via some model theory, the best-known approach to semantics and one which is carried out using the background framework of set theory. There is no need for the neo-formalist to adopt an exclusivist attitude here, perhaps other frameworks will serve as well but I will work with the familiar set-theoretic apparatus. So we expand $L^*$ to $L^{**}$ by adding the conceptual resources needed for an *impure*, applied set theory such as ZFCU, ZFC plus 'urelements', where urelements are non-set-theoretic atoms. Thus we need to add a membership predicate $\in$ and perhaps also set brackets $\{\ \}$ together with a predicate $Ux$ whose intended meaning is that $x$ is an urelement ('empirical' item or number). The quantifiers in the axioms are general. That is, in rules such as $\exists I$ and $\forall E$ we can generalize on, or instantiate to, singular terms which are either purely set-theoretic, such as $\emptyset$ (that is $\{x: x \neq x\}$), or mixed, such as {The Morning Star}, or wholly non-set theoretic, for example empirical terms. In axiom schemes such as the subsets scheme:

$$\forall x \exists y \forall z (z \in y \leftrightarrow (z \in x \ \& \ \varphi z))$$

($y$ not in $\varphi$), the formula $\varphi$ may be pure, mixed or empirical. It is also usual to add an axiom stating that the atoms form a set:

$$\exists x \forall y (y \in x \leftrightarrow Uy).$$

Of the axioms of ZFCU, only extensionality:

$$\forall x \forall y ((\sim Ux \ \& \ \sim Uy) \rightarrow \forall z ((z \in x \leftrightarrow z \in y) \rightarrow x = y))$$

is restricted to sets (allowing a little bit of slack in the non-official formulation of the double restriction $\sim Ux \ \& \ \sim Uy$) so all the other axioms are formally speaking mixed sentences and thus bridge principles. Just like the bridge principles of AA, they are made true purely by their postulation as axioms. With ZFCU as background we can derive from empirical facts E (such as the existence of the Morning Star and its identity with the Evening Star) truths which owe their truth jointly to statements of empirical fact and their interaction with formal calculi, for instance {The Morning Star} = {The Evening Star}.

The most important truths for our current purposes are the 'mixed' truths of model theory. For in ZFCU we can develop the theory of semantic models and in particular define the notion of the satisfaction of an open sentence in a model M relative to an assignment $\sigma$ to free variables. Among the models of L which we can show in ZFCU exists, is a model H (the 'homophonic model') which assigns to each closed term $|t|$ of L the 'empirical' individual t. That is to say, the interpretation function is the set of all pairs $<|t|, t>$. Likewise H assigns to each name of a primitive $n$-place predicate $|F(x_1, \ldots x_n)|$ as its interpretation the set

$$\{\langle x_1, \ldots x_n \rangle : F(x_1, \ldots x_n)\}.$$

For every sentence $\varphi(x_1, \ldots x_n)$ of the sub-language L of $L^{**}$ we can prove in ZFCU the Tarskian biconditional:

$$\text{Sats}(|\varphi(x_1, \ldots x_n)|, H, \sigma) \leftrightarrow \varphi(\sigma(x_1), \ldots \sigma(x_n))$$

'Sats' being our defined satisfaction predicate. Truth, as usual, is satisfaction by all assignments.

In the particular case of our decimal arithmetic calculus AA, we can also prove in ZFCU that a *conservativeness* property holds for AA, that is we have a conservative extension result of the form:

If P and all members of theory T are sentences of the empirical sub-language L and $T' \vdash_{AAT'} P'$ then if all of T are true in model M, so is P.

Here $'$ is the restriction operation which restricts all sentences of L to the non-numbers $\sim Nx$ (these restricted sentences are sentences of $L^*$ of course) and $AAT'$ is the result of adding to the calculus AA the axioms of T thus restricted.

The theorem shows that decimal arithmetic plus the bridge rules never takes us from true empirical sentences to untrue ones (and as we have seen, often takes us from truth to truth by a shorter route than if we had not taken a detour through applied mathematics). For suppose T is a conjunction of our true empirical sentences and let H be the 'homophonic model' as above. If we assume each member of T (or assume its 'truth' in a disquotational sense of 'true') then by the Tarskian result we can prove that each is true in H. If we have $T' \vdash_{AAT'}$ P', then by the conservative extension result P is true in H, i.e. P is true.

What makes this theorem a mixed theorem is that it generalizes over models including those whose domains are impure sets, such as H whose domain includes actually existing entities such as you and me, the Andromeda Galaxy, Julius Caesar, the ink patterns on this page and so forth.[4] We can see this most clearly if we use modular arithmetic mod 12 instead of ordinary decimal arithmetic as the pure part of our calculus (call it MA) but keep the same bridge principles. Now we can prove in ZFCU the existence of an actual counterexample to conservativeness in numerous ways, by making it true that there are seven oranges in the one bowl and five apples in the other and drawing the false conclusion that, as the number of pieces of fruit in the bowl is zero, there is no fruit in the bowl.[5]

---

[4] So I take 'actually existent' to be tenseless.

[5] In fact, there is no model of this system, since we can prove from $\exists_7 x(x < 7)$ and $\exists_5 x(6 < x < 12)$ that $\sim \exists x(x < 7 \lor 6 < x < 12)$ which contradicts a theorem of the system (assuming that we have as axioms E$n$, for all numerals $n$).

The conservative extension result for AA gives us, I claim, everything we need from the application of mathematics. Of course we have proved this result for the 'mixed' calculus AA by using a stronger system—ZFCU—which is also mixed. We will not be able to prove the Tarskian biconditionals for the sub-language L, for example, unless we are able to instantiate in axioms such as the pair set axiom:

$$\forall z \forall w \exists x \forall y \, (y \in x \leftrightarrow (y = z \lor y = w))$$

to yield mixed sentences like

$$\forall x \forall y \, (y \in x \leftrightarrow y = (\mathrm{n}x(x \neq x) \lor y = \text{The Morning Star}))^6$$

and, in a free logic setting, this instantiation requires the further assumptions that $E(\mathrm{n}x(x \neq x))$ and E(The Morning Star) (E the existence predicate). If this application of set theory itself to a mixed subject matter—the model theory of empirical languages—is unsound then the guarantee it gives us that the application of decimal arithmetic to empirical matters is sound will be worthless. So what right do we have to assume that the conservative extension result holds for *impure* models, models such as the homophonic H whose domain contains real individuals such as patterns and dots or planets? For the model theory we are using, or rather its fundamental assumptions namely ZFCU plus various existence assumptions, form not a branch of pure mathematics, but rather of applied mathematics.[7] Is not the assumption that the ZFCU result validates decimal arithmetic question-begging? It assumes, does it not, what has to be proved, that mathematics, including ZFCU, can be applied to empirical matters soundly, without leading us from empirical truth to untruth? Indeed it assumes the soundness of a stronger theory, ZFCU, in attempting to validate the soundness of decimal arithmetic.

There is circularity here but of a familiar type. For we can, of course, strengthen ZFCU, with stronger (impure) axioms, such as stronger axioms of infinity, an axiom of inaccessibles for example, and in this stronger theory prove a conservative extension result for ZFCU itself, from which it follows that the conservative extension theorem for decimal arithmetic provable in ZFCU is in turn true. If anyone asks how we know that this stronger theory conservatively extends ZFCU we can move to a yet stronger theory still. The hierarchical regress which ensues is the familiar one in semantics. If neo-formalists take this regressive tack, they are in no worse shape than (almost) everyone else.

Not that to be in the same boat as everyone else is something to be satisfied with in this regard, for this boat is not busily repairing itself at sea but a wreck plunging to the bottom of the ocean. Or so, at any rate, I have argued elsewhere (Weir 1998b) adding my support to the critical assault launched by Graham Priest on the conventional

---

[6] Certainly this will be the case if the syntactic part of the model theory uses numbers to code for expressions and strings. If we use sets, we will need instances of pair sets pairing sets and urelements in order to prove the existence of assignments.

[7] Thanks to Stewart Shapiro for emphasizing the need to answer this point.

hierarchical standpoint (Priest 1987). Note the difference between, on the one hand, proving in e.g. ZF that if ZF is consistent then a stronger theory, such as ZFC is, and, on the other, proving in a stronger theory such as ZFC plus the axiom of inaccessibles that ZFC is consistent or has a model or conservatively extends any theory stated in a non-set-theoretic sublanguage and so forth. The former sort of result carries epistemic punch but of what worth is the latter? It is not a case of epistemological bootstrapping. It is more like getting a giant to lift you up by your bootstraps with the catch that the giant does this by first getting a supergiant to hold his own bootstraps in preparation for pulling both himself and yourself up. The supergiant in turn does this by getting a super-duper-giant to hold the supergiant's bootstraps in preparation for . . . (and then follow the dreaded dots).

   If the boat of formal semantics is a submerged wreck, why has this epistemological disaster been tolerated? The answer is clear. It is because it has been thought that various limitative results, such as Gödel's second incompleteness theorem and Tarski's theorem on the undefinability of truth, leave us with no alternative. A semantically closed theory, a theory T which can prove that a model for T exists and so prove that it itself is consistent, is generally believed to be an impossibility. The dialetheist Graham Priest agrees but since he thinks that some impossibilities are also possible this has not prevented him from developing a semantically closed naïve set theory. I side with the orthodox here in rejecting Priest's claim that there are true contradictions (though I think—Weir 2004b—that Priest's dialetheist position is worthy of serious consideration, particularly the criticisms of the conventional approach to semantic closure). I depart from orthodoxy in holding that, in the light of the epistemological catastrophe noted above, we should investigate the possibility of a *consistent* (impure) naïve set theory NST from within which semantic closure should be achieved. In particular, the aim will be to secure, though the use of NST, a vantage point from which we can prove that it itself has a model and that subtheories such as the application of decimal arithmetic in the calculus AA, or ZFCU, conservatively extend any empirical body of data to which they apply. This would be a genuinely bootstrapping position. As such it would not give us Cartesian certainty that results such as conservative extension truly hold, but it is a mistake to look for such certainty even in mathematics.

   Now it is evident that a consistent naïve set theory requires a framework of non-classical logic. I outline a restricted version of the logic I think is 'the correct logic', thus the right one for mathematics, including naïve set theory, in Chapter 8. But the development of the naïve theory in this framework is too large a tangent to pursue here. For now I will rest content with the claim that neo-formalism, in having to prove conservativeness results for given mathematical theories from within stronger theories, is in no worse a position that any other extant theory (dialetheism aside). The conservativeness results it (fallibly) can avail itself of suffice to explain the applicability of mathematics. An ontology of abstract objects, mysteriously connected to ourselves and our physical world, is neither necessary nor explanatorily useful in accounting for applied mathematics.

## §II.*   Comparison with Fictionalism

Assigning a fundamental role to conservativeness in explaining the application of mathematics is a key feature of Hartry Field's fictionalism, and I have followed his lead fairly closely (cf. his aardvark and bug example in Field 1980, pp. 20–3). Clearly there are strong similarities between neo-formalist and fictionalist approaches, since both deny that THERE ARE numbers in objective reality (or at any rate, deny that mathematics makes no sense unless numbers exist mind-independently). There, are, however, some differences between the two approaches and in this section I highlight both similarities and differences and argue that the neo-formalist position is superior.

As well as giving an account of simple arithmetic applications to aardvarks and bugs, Field goes on to show how, given the right conservativeness result,[8] one can account for considerably more complicated applications of mathematics. He demonstrates this in particular for a formalization of Newtonian gravitational theory involving substantial use of calculus. The neo-formalist should go where the fictionalist goes. Indeed arguably not just formalists but everyone bar heavy-duty platonists should go down Field's road of 'concretizing' physics. Field's 'heavy-duty platonist' (1989, p. 185) concludes from the fact that the magnitude of the electrical charge on the electron has tremendous impact on the nature of the physical world that therefore $1.602 \times 10^{-19}$, the number which (roughly) measures the value of this magnitude in coulombs, is also an enormously important causal agent. Field is right in arguing to the contrary that we should distinguish sharply between physical magnitudes, properties, or regions on the one hand and the mathematical entities which might be used to index the physical entities and relations on the other.

Field's 'lightweight' strategy is to look for a (maximal) group G of mathematical transformations under which a standardly formulated set of physical equations is invariant—the result of applying a transformation in G to any solution is also a solution. Next, formulate a non-mathematical theory which gives the *intrinsic* content of the theory in the following sense. One can prove a representation theorem which shows the existence of a homomorphic mapping from any model of the intrinsic theory into a mathematical structure (in which we can interpret the language in which we formulate the physical equations), a mapping furthermore which is unique up to transformation by any operation in the group G.

The homomorphism need not be one:one and need not be onto the whole mathematical domain. Thus in the case of temperature Field considers a function into a connected subset of the reals (because two regions may have the same temperature and not all reals may correspond to an actual temperature (Field 1980, pp. 56–7)). Idealization presents us with another case in which we may wish to consider functions which map into but not onto a domain. 'Idealization' in science seems to cover a

---

[8] Field's result differs from the conservativeness result I have presented but the differences are not important for present purposes.

number of distinct phenomena. One way it can occur is when one sets mathematical parameters to values which one knows have no correlate in the actual world. One sets a scalar representing friction to zero perhaps, elasticity to a value, one, say, corresponding to perfect elasticity. The pragmatic motive here is that one hopes the resulting theory will still prove approximately true, and the move greatly simplifies the mathematics. Another procedure which is often called 'idealization' is to ignore deliberately a variety of factors which one nonetheless knows are causally relevant because they introduce too much complexity. Again the hope is that the more manageable theorizing or calculations which are thereby enabled yield approximately true results. But a converse process also goes under the heading of idealization. I will call it *injective* idealization. As a schematic example, suppose one thought that space-time was really finite, a finite matrix of atomic cells let us say. Even so, one might still wish to use a four-dimensional Riemannian manifold to represent it because of the convenience of using analytical techniques such as differentiation and integration in accounting for mechanical and dynamical phenomena.[9] We shall return to a somewhat similar sort of injective idealization in connection with proof theory later.

Field's 'nominalism' goes beyond rejection of abstract objects to include a component which is nominalistic in the medieval sense.[10] Although he does not rule out an ontology of properties *tout court*, at least in a sense of property set out by Putnam, he prefers not to take such a route, making do with an ontology of spacetime regions. I think this is a mistake, regardless of the philosophy of pure mathematics one adopts. It is true that some have thought of properties as being a type of abstract object. Perhaps this position is sometimes arrived at by confusing properties with the senses or meanings of predicate expressions. The latter are indeed objects, but to identify properties with senses (and hence think they are abstract *objects*) is to confuse two different categories. Physical properties, like the property of sphericality or the property of having mass, are as physicalistically respectable as physical objects, or so I would argue. Indeed, *pace* Quine, I think it very difficult to conceive of one type of entity existing without the other. Far from physical properties being causal danglers, our epistemic contact with them inexplicable, it is hard to explain causation itself except in terms of relations between properties, or similar entities. It is a property of the moon which causes the tides and it is a property of that pizza, its roundness, which causes there to arise in me the property of seeing it as round.

At any rate, from the perspective of the realist concerning properties, the business of concretizing physics is a little easier than it is for Field, who to some extent is fighting with one hand tied behind his back. Thus if one seeks to explain the invariant non-mathematical content of a theory which posits a range of magnitudes represented by

---

[9] For a real example see Cartwright (1983, p. 115).

[10] This ambiguity is the reason for the scare quotes on 'nominalism'. As remarked in Chapter 1, perhaps 'concretism' is a better term for the modern rejection (or at least suspicion) of *objects* which lack in any clear sense spatio-temporal location. There is no conceptual connection between the two doctrines, between the claim that all particulars are concrete and the claim that there are no non-particulars.

real numbers, I see no objection in principle to simply positing, as part of one's non-mathematical content, the existence of a Dedekind-complete ordered field of magnitudes in reality (in the most straightforward case, positing also higher-order properties, relations, and functions to correspond to addition, multiplication, the less than relation, etc.). More generally, granted a set of physical laws invariant under a class of transformations, we can try to recover an intrinsic structure from it.[11] Take the domain of a particular structure which satisfies the laws as exemplar and add to it all properties and relations which are invariant under given transformations. Thus if special relativity were our example, with rest mass represented by non-negative real numbers, then the less than relation over those reals would be such an invariant relation. The intrinsic content can then be thought of as given by a structure isomorphic to this representative exemplar but a structure whose individuals are urelements (thinking of these cross-categorially as including, in addition to particulars, properties and relations and perhaps higher-order properties and relations).

This is the easier part of the task of finding an intrinsic non-mathematical content, however. The difficult part comes in finding a physically plausible realization of this intrinsic structure. If this can be done, the task of concretizing is over. If the prospects for finding a plausible physical intrinsic structure look bleak, the neo-formalist has the alternative of treating that particular physical theory instrumentalistically.[12] Indeed, this strategy, of looking for plausible intrinsic structure where possible, should be adopted by everyone, granted that Field is right about the unattractiveness of heavy-duty platonism. The conclusion I draw is that neo-formalism has, at the least, no more problems in explicating the application of mathematics than any other position (and that being a realist about properties makes it easier to explain applicability).

Though I think everyone, including the neo-formalist, should take a very similar route to Field's, there are some differences between neo-formalism and fictionalism which relate to differences in the approach to mathematics in general. For Field, the standard results of mathematics are either false or trivially true (cf. Field 1989, p. 94 fn. 16). In particular, a generalization of the form $\forall x(Mx \rightarrow p)$, where $Mx$ restricts the domain of quantification to some purported range of abstract objects—numbers, sets or whatever—is trivially true, one of the form $\exists x(Mx \ \& \ p)$ always false. The conservative extension result I used in the previous section is of the form $\forall x \forall y((Fx \ \& \ Gy) \rightarrow p)$

[11] Here, as always, I take the theorems of pure mathematics as true. As a neo-formalist I am entitled to this, but the Fieldian fictionalist is not. Moreover, I also am entitled, as the last section argued, to the results of applied mathematics, for example to the existence of structures with physical objects as constituent elements. More exactly, the neo-formalist is entitled to assume the truth of consequences of an applied theory wherever there is reason to assume the purely empirical premises assumed in the application are empirically true and where a conservative extension result is provable for the applied mathematical component.

[12] This does not commit one, of course, to a general instrumentalism. Thus I see no problem in being a realist about microbiology or cosmology, or the ordinary everyday world, past, present, and future, but an instrumentalist about quantum mechanics. Since, for the realist, physical reality is independent of our minds, cognitive structures, and investigative techniques, it may well be that some aspects of it, the structure which underwrites the regularities so accurately plotted in quantum mechanics, for example, are ineluctably unfathomable by us.

where Fx says '$x$ is a set of sentences' and G$y$ says '$y$ is a sentence' and where $p$ is of the form:

$$x' \vdash_{\text{AAT}'} y' \rightarrow x \models y.$$

Sentences and sets of sentences being abstract objects, this is trivially true, according to fictionalism. But by the same token so is the sentence $\forall x \forall y((Fx \& Gy) \rightarrow p')$ where $p'$ is

$$x' \vdash_{\text{AAT}'} y' \rightarrow \sim(x \models y)$$

Let us call this the *radical extension* result. Even if one does not require good explanations to be true, how can it be the case that the conservative extension result, interpreted in fictionalist fashion, explains why adding mathematics to a physical theory will never lead to new consequences expressible in the old language? For the equally true (for the fictionalist) radical extension result tells us that anything one can prove using maths, suitably restricted, does *not* follow from the old theory.

So what entitles Field to use the conservative extension result in the way he does? Field's strategy is to dispense with model-theory (and also proof theory, since it too has an abstract ontology) in favour of the use of modal logic in the metatheory, for example in enabling us to express a modal correlate of the conservative extension result. The consistency of a sentence A is represented by $\Diamond$A, where $\Diamond$ is to be interpreted as some form of primitive logical possibility, semantic consequence $\Gamma \models$ A by

$\square$(if every instance of one of the $\Gamma$ is true, so is A) (Field 1989, p. 102)

and conservativeness and other properties reinterpreted accordingly.

This strategy has come in for some criticism. How does Field know that the conservativeness claims, reinterpreted modally, are true? A platonist, of course, has no Cartesian certainty that a given theory T is consistent, that there exists no derivation of absurdity from T. Field argues that the fictionalist is in no worse epistemological shape than the platonist, for whom conservativeness results tell us about an abstract realm of atemporal causally inert entities. Indeed he thinks the modal belief is in better epistemic shape than the platonistic set-theoretic one. It is hard to evaluate this since Field's modal notions are taken to be primitive. Certainly he admits himself that he has 'no clear account of modal epistemology' (1989, p. 140 fn. 15). Since $\Diamond$T cannot be glossed as 'there is a model of T' or 'there is no derivation of $\bot$ from T' it is hard to tell whether it is reasonable to hold that such consistency beliefs are themselves reasonably held, or not. We are owed an epistemology of primitive modality, just as the platonist owes us an epistemology of abstract objects. But if the chief complaint against the platonist is that she has no coherent epistemology, that she cannot explain how she could know or justifiably believe what she asserts, why abandon platonism, with its simple homogenous semantics and intuitive plausibility, for a variant account which is also unable to account for its own epistemology? Note that no such problems attend neo-formalism. The conservative extension results for particular calculi like decimal arithmetic or ZFC are truths of applied mathematics. We know them to be true by grasping presented proofs of them from axioms or basic rules which include some empirical assumptions, for example that a physical world exists, assumptions which we have reason to believe.

Could the fictionalist get round these problems by a slight softening of the denial that mathematics is non-trivially true? Field admits that it is perfectly reasonable to say that the claim that Oliver Twist lived in Glasgow is incorrect, the claim that he lived in London correct. Field has also defended a deflationary approach to truth. If fictional discourse is suited to the application of deflationary truth,[13] then, since it is correct to say that Twist lived in London, given the correctness of the T-schema and some reasonable principles about the distributivity of correctness over operators, it is correct to say the sentence 'Oliver Twist lived in London' is true. Since it is correct to say he did not live in Glasgow, so correct to say the negation of 'Twist lived in Glasgow' is true, we might express this by saying it is correct to say it is false he lived in Glasgow, that one can assert it is false he lived there. Field is prepared to concede the truth-valuedness, in this deflationary sense, of mathematics (1989, pp. 2–3), thus blurring, it would seem, the distinction between fictionalism and neo-formalism. For Field, the sense in which '2 + 2 = 4' is true is comparable to that in which 'Oliver Twist lived in London' is true. The latter is true according to a well-known story, the former 'is true according to *standard mathematics*' (ibid., p. 3).

But for the neo-formalist, the truth of a mathematical claim is emphatically not to be identified with its being held true by the mathematical authorities. The authorities could hold until the end of time a thesis to be true on the basis of a mistaken belief that there exist proofs of it, when in fact it is refutable (but never refuted).[14] Moreover, only a small fragment of mathematical claims will come out as true, namely those sentences explicitly pronounced as proven by the mathematical community.

Of course the import of any assimilation of mathematics to fictional truths depends on one's account of fictional truth. Suppose one holds that the metaphysical content of a sentence concerning a fictional character, such as 'Oliver Twist lived in London', is that it is made-true if derivable from some admissible formulation of sentences from the text, made-false if its negation is derivable. This is a simplified version of the 'hermeneutic' face-value anti-realism about fiction of Chapter 2, §II (one which fails to allow for inconsistent texts and the flexibility we normally allow interpreters in

---

[13] But as remarked (Chapter 2, §I) there will often be substantive constraints, going beyond mere surface syntactic ones, declarative mood etc., to be met before an entire sublanguage, including complex sentences, is suitable for application of deflationary truth.

[14] Mathematical history abounds with faulty proofs of non-theorems by eminent mathematicians (there is hope for us all!), such as refutations of the Axiom of Choice, for example. And of course there have been faulty proofs of theses which turned out eventually to be theorems. There were over 1,000 faulty proofs of Fermat's Last Theorem between 1908 and 1912 (see the entry for Fermat's Last Theorem in O'Connor and Robertson's (E-resource) excellent MacTutor history of mathematics). Indeed, Andrew Wiles's initial proof was also faulty.

drawing out 'fictional truth' from texts). In any such face-value anti-realism, the informational content of a Twist sentence is not to be identified with its metaphysical content; perhaps no non-trivial analysis is possible. If mathematical truth is to be assimilated to fictional truth as characterized on the above theory of fiction then the objections of the last paragraph fail. But now we do not have a clear-cut case, as it were, of the blurring of the distinction between fictionalism and neo-formalism. This is much more like an abandonment of fictionalism for neo-formalism, together with an extension of the formalist approach to embrace fiction; and with it an obligation to meet the objections and difficulties which face neo-formalism.

For the reasons given above, to do with simple inconsistency and the like, it is clearly better not to generalize neo-formalism in this way to fictional discourse but rather to stick to the subtler idea that fictional truth is determined by the 'hermeneutic' equilibrium which would, counterfactually, be reached by seasoned interpreters trying to fill out and make sense of a work (or works) of fiction. Works of 'faction', could, however, be treated in a way somewhat analogous to the neo-formalist account of applied mathematics. The role of the wholly empirical axioms will be taken by empirical truths relevant to claims in the semi-factual piece. As bridge principles, we might include ascriptions of a predicate $A(t)$ for any terms which, in the given context, actually denote. In the hermeneutic set-up, the readers imagine a story in which some of the individuals have a special A-ness property (actuality) which plays no other role in the imaginary world, and there can be truths in that story about relations between A-individuals and others.

Nor need we play the hermeneutic game just with one text. Experienced readers could play games in which they mix subparts of different texts (or different texts plus a selection of empirical truths) and see whether any coherent story emerges. I suggest tentatively that the results of such processes are what determines the metaphysical content (but of course not the informational content) of the problematic sorts of cases for non-Meinongians alluded to by Parsons (Chapter 2, §II). Of course the truths which emerge will be relative to very specific circumstances, specific texts, and specific audiences, and there will be a great deal of indeterminacy—very often no determinate truth or falsity at all will be generated.

## §III. Theoretical Language

I end this chapter with some programmatic remarks on the project (or projects) of giving a theoretical account of theoretical language, an account which can give a satisfactory explanation of the role of applied mathematics in our grasp of theory. I will consider two contrasting approaches to the task. By no means do I believe these are the only two options available. I have chosen to look at these two because one of them I believe to be the right one whilst the other seems to me the best representative of a very widespread viewpoint, roughly speaking that of the thoroughgoing empiricist. I will argue that the defects of the thoroughgoing empiricist position help reveal by contrast the advantages of neo-formalism as a philosophy of mathematics.

This non-formalist position I will call the *holistic empiricist* one, and its most noted proponent I take, with some qualifications, to be Quine. One important element of the holistic empiricist view is the discernment of a fairly sharp dichotomy between theoretical and observational sentences. To be sure, interpreting Quine, that arch-enemy of sharp dichotomies, in this way is contentious. Many view him as a radical semantic holist who thinks of the theory/observation distinction as a matter of degree. The matter is clouded because Quine defines 'observation sentence' in a number of different ways at different times, or sometimes even at the same time, namely 1960, in *Word and Object*. There he presents us with two completely different notions of observation sentence: one in terms of social consensus (1960, p. 43), the other, on the very next page, characterized by direct keying to stimulation (ibid., p. 44). Later his views oscillated, though generally settling on the latter as the more fundamental, at least for the single speaker.[15]

Quine does indeed in some places (e.g. 1960, p. 43; 1975, p. 324) speak of observationality coming in degrees and indeed it does, if one is working with the social consensus distinction; for there are degrees of consensus. But the direct keying definition is the one I wish to utilize for the position I am marking out as holistic empiricist. Quine also notes the fallibility of observational sentences. Certainly 'experimental predictions', in the everyday sense, are fallible (and often highly theoretical in nature), but these are not observation sentences in what I think is the most fundamental sense for Quine. Quine assumed that our first entry into language can only be explained if there are sentences whose meaning is solely determined by exposure to stimulation, not at all by grasp of other sentences. Even if no sentence of our mature language has a purely observational meaning, I do not think the Quinean can view these atomistic meanings as ladders to be thrown away. They are more like geological layers on which the mature understanding rests and depends. At any rate, whether this is accurate as a matter of interpretation of the historical Quine, I stipulate that the holistic empiricist view includes the idea that we cannot understand any sentence unless we understand some sentences whose meaning is atomistic, that is, they can be grasped without understanding any other sentence.[16] This meaning, moreover, is in some substantive sense experiential, 'directly keyed to stimulation', in Quine's phrase.

---

[15] Quine (1975, p. 316) and also (1992, p. 43), where he combines the two views when considering observationality for a community.

[16] So this holism shares at least this aspect of the Dummettian idea (1976, p. 79) of a molecularistic account of language understanding mooted in Chapter 2, §II. It differs in failing to discern any molecular structure in the non-observational, non-atomistic realm. Rather, beyond the atomic level we have a 'seamless woof' of interconnected sentences, or, less charitably, a night in which all semantic cows are black.

A second ingredient of the holist empiricist picture is the verificationist claim that any two sentences which share empirical content are synonymous. 'Empirical content' is, of course, a complex notion which can be explicated in many ways (Quine's stimulus meaning account being, as he later more or less concedes, an unsuccessful one). However this is done, I take it to be an essential part of any explication that empirical content is the only meaning which observation sentences have.

But the holistic empiricist does not claim that all sentences are observational. The third aspect of holistic empiricism is a semantic holism *restricted*, however, to the theoretical sector of language. Theoretical sentences are syntactically complex (at least in their underlying structure, perhaps after unpacking definitional abbreviations) with complex logical interconnections one with the other, and, indirectly, with observation sentences. However, the only illuminating explication of the notion of synonymy available to the verificationist is sameness of empirical content. This holds between two sentences $s$ and $r$ just when exactly the same experiences confirm the one as confirm the other and disconfirm the one as disconfirm the other. The holism kicks in with the rejection of what Quine calls 'the dogma of reduction' (1951/53). This is the Quine/Duhem thesis that no theoretical sentence has any empirical consequences on its own. More moderately and plausibly, the typical theoretical sentence has no empirical consequences on its own, though atypical sentences, for instance the conjunction of the axioms of a 'total system', do. A total system includes theory plus auxiliary hypotheses plus boundary conditions. This epistemic holism combined with verificationism leads to the conclusion that synonymy is an empty notion as applied to typical theoretical sentences, that is those lacking empirical content. One can say that each such sentence is synonymous with all other typical sentences, trivially identical in their empty confirmatory and disconfirmation conditions. But this comes to much the same thing as saying no such sentence is synonymous with any other. Only total theories (including auxiliary hypotheses and boundary conditions) have meaning.

For a concrete example, take Newtonian mechanics. Let N be the conjunction of Newton's three laws of motion plus his inverse square gravity law. N has no empirical content, it entails no empirical hypotheses independently of further auxiliary hypotheses and boundary conditions. Neither does its negation ~N. Without further hypotheses we have no predictions as to which objects are violating the laws. So both have the same (null) empirical content, hence, according to the holistic empiricist, the same meaning. Thus, without need of any appeal to a thesis of underdetermination of evidence by the totality of empirical data,[17] we vindicate Quine's indeterminacy thesis in its most interesting and radical form:

---

[17] On the face of it, a highly realist, sceptical view and thus one which the verificationist Quine came increasingly to question and qualify. For a detailed discussion of various versions of underdetermination in Quine see Lars Bergström (1993), (2004). For the direct argument to indeterminacy, without recourse to underdetermination, see Quine (1969, pp. 80–1), though the argument is already pre-figured in section V of 'Two Dogmas' (Quine 1951/53). The point is made by Føllesdal, (1973, pp. 290–1) and endorsed, as I read him, by Quine (1986, pp. 155–6).

countless native sentences admitting no independent check . . . may be expected to receive radically unlike and incompatible renderings under the two systems. (1960, p. 72)

We have two synonymous sentences which we can see directly are incompatible, since one is the negation of the other. Both theories being expressed in the same 'home' language, the negation sign here is correctly interpreted, homophonically, as negation; the contradiction is not merely terminological.

But now we seem to be driven to a contradiction in the metatheory. If two sentences mean the same then, in any given context, they will have the same truth-conditions and truth-value. But according to the indeterminacy thesis there will be synonymous sentences which have 'incompatible renderings', opposite truth-values: N and ~N directly illustrate this. To avoid contradiction the holist empiricist is driven to a radical relativity concerning truth. Theoretical sentences are not true or false absolutely, as observation sentences are, but only relative to a background system (theory plus auxiliary hypotheses plus boundary conditions). If we call a total system S empirically adequate if it is compatible with the totality PO of true pegged observation sentences—observation sentences pegged to a specific time and place—then we can say that a theoretical sentence T is true relative to system S if S is empirically adequate and entails T, false if S is empirically adequate and entails ~T. If T has null empirical content, then it is true relative to PO $\cup$ T and false relative to PO $\cup$ ~T.[18]

Thus holistic empiricism, though it can be motivated by a recoil from the reductionist empiricism of the operationalists, entails a form of instrumentalism. In particular, there is the same asymmetrical treatment of observational sentences compared to theoretical. The former are determinate in meaning, absolute in truth-value. Theoretical sentences, by contrast, are indeterminate in meaning and their truth-value, in general, relative. Both meaning and truth-value for theoretical sentences derive from the meaning and truth-value of observation sentences. To be sure, instrumentalists were suspicious of the notion of truth prior to Tarski's work on truth definitions. Post Tarski, instrumentalists, as always prepared to affirm the findings of science—electrons exist—were now also able in good conscience to affirm that 'electrons exist' is true. The difference between truth-phobic instrumentalists and truth-loving post-Tarskian instrumentalists is a fairly minor one.

Are there—were there—any holistic empiricists? Quine, I claim, comes near to being one but does not completely fit the bill. For one thing, it is essential to the coherence of the above version of holism that there are logical interconnections between theoretical sentences, connections which are, for the most part anyway, determinate. These may not encompass the full panoply of links traceable using standard classical logic but there is no coherent development of the holist view which does not allow a status close to that of analyticity (but perhaps better applied

---

[18]  Quine shied away from relativism about truth, as opposed to relativism about reference; but his position is not coherent without it. I have argued (in Weir, 2006b, where I note that more than the simple appeal to relativity is needed to preserve consistency).

to rules rather than to sentences) to at least some simple rules. Rejecting the analyticity of all logical rules dissolves away the links which connect sentences in the holistic network.[19] However, Quine (who tends to focus far too much on logical statements rather than on inference rules[20]) notoriously rejects the analyticity of even simple principles of logic such as &E or ∨I. At least the early Quine does, although there is a partial softening of his views later (1974, pp. 78ff.). Note, though, that the Quinean could admit the analyticity of simple inference rules whilst still maintaining that the bulk of logic—and all of mathematics—is non-analytic, that the analytic principles fail to yield the law of excluded middle (LEM) for example. This still leaves us with a radical empiricist account of scientific (and mathematical) theory.

If Quine does not quite fit the bill, perhaps there are no real holistic empiricists. Even so, it is worth setting out the doctrine because it represents a consistent and clear development of a perspective on philosophy of language held, perhaps not fully explicitly, by a great many philosophers, particularly those influenced strongly by Quine. These are philosophers who take a naturalistic approach to explaining language, especially the language of natural science, who think that the empiricist link between theory and sensory stimulation is essential to any such naturalistic approach but who reject operationalism and extreme forms of positivistic empiricism. This leads them to a combination of holism and verificationism and *holistic empiricism*, as characterized, represents a clear and consistent version of this combination. But if the above argument is right, this view leads straight to a relativistic instrumentalism. If one wishes to avoid such a philosophical dead-end (to put it somewhat less than neutrally) one will also have to eschew, I will argue, Quinean platonism and Fieldian fictionalism. Before developing this point, I will first pit against this holistic empiricist picture a rival view which I think is superior.

This anti-holist 'molecular' position (cf. Chapter 2, §II) discerns far more structure than just the two levels of (i) observational atoms, (ii) the rest. Rather, there is a well-founded hierarchy of linguistic and conceptual complexity, more complex, more theoretical concepts presupposing grasp of less complex ones down to a base of observational ones. For a programmatic illustration of the idea applied to mathematics in the sciences consider the following story.[21] Imagine we grasp a four-place predicate $xy\text{Cong}zw$ which we apply to observable rods and rulers (or ruler-like segments of surfaces) and whose meaning is that the ruler whose two end slices are $x$ and $y$ is congruent with that whose end slices are $zw$. We might manifest our grasp of this purely empirical predicate by, among other things, transporting rulers and laying them end to end against a ruler-like surface segment before issuing in a judgment as to the

---

[19] Criticisms along these lines have been voiced by, among others, Dummett (1981a, p. 596), Wright (1986), Shapiro (2000b), Tennant (2003, p. 692).

[20] He is 'theorem-fixated' as Neil Tennant has nicely described it (1997b, p. 4); see also Shapiro (2000b, pp. 336–7) and Priest (1979).

[21] A retelling of the story in Weir (1991), which reviewed Field's *Realism, Mathematics and Modality* (Field 1989).

applicability of the term. (How closely our grasp of such highly empirical predicates is tied to such verificatory behaviour is, of course, a highly controversial matter.) As well as simple judgements that one segment is, or is not, congruent with another we will be able to grasp such ideas as that there is a strip $t$ between the endpoints $zw$ of a segment such that $xy$ is congruent with $zt$ and with $tw$. To this end we need to grasp another predicate Bet $xyz$ as holding just when the region $y$ is strictly between regions $x$ and $z$. This level of empirical science goes beyond the Quinean observational level but since no mathematics is involved I will call it the *pure empirical* level.

Now imagine that we also have an *independent* grasp of basic arithmetic. We might then be taught that ⌜$zw$ is 2 times the length of $xy$⌝ is assertible in exactly the same situations as ⌜there is a strip $t$ between the endpoints $zw$ such that $xy$ is congruent with $zt$ and with $tw$⌝. And so on for three times, four times the length, and for many other small finite numbers. A slightly more complex formula yields a non-mathematical equivalent of ⌜$zw$ is 2/3 times the length of $xy$⌝ and so on for many fractional expressions. Similarly we might be taught to assert that the length of rod $xy$ is less than that of $xz$ whenever we assert that Bet $xyz$. If, in our system, **tu** is a standard unit, like the old Parisian standard metre, then for many rational values $n$, ⌜$zw$ is $n$ times the length of **tu**⌝, which we might gloss as ⌜the length of $zw$ is $n$ units⌝, will be in effect analytically equivalent with an expression which language users utterly innocent of arithmetic can produce.

It may seem that something conceptually new has been introduced by this stage in the story, for we have introduced a function term 'the length of $x$' which purports to refer to a physical magnitude. However, I see no reason to think there has been conceptual expansion. Our pre-mathematical users of *Cong* and *Bet* perceived certain lengths, shapes, and other such qualities, and thus were able to name them. *Pace* the (medieval) nominalist, human knowledge of the existence of objects depends on properties and magnitudes of these kinds causally interacting with properties of our sensory systems to give us knowledge of the existence of these properties (and thereby of their instantiation by certain objects); this is so, whether or not we have terms for them and even if we know no mathematics. Or so I urged above, §II*.

Conceptual expansion occurs, rather, when our applied mathematics breaks free from its initial contexts where it is always eliminable in favour of purely empirical expressions. Our grasp of arithmetic gives us the ability to assert or entertain sentences—the length of $zw$ is $10^{11}$ times the length of **tu**; the length of $zw$ is less than $10^{-11}$ times the length of **tu**—which have no co-assertible equivalent in our non-mathematical language, with its purely empirical notions of congruence and betweenness. Whereas the initial batch of mathematical sentences can all be cashed out in purely empirical terms so that we can view them as merely florid embellishments on purely empirical claims, the new sentences are not thus eliminable and 'the length of' has now taken on a more complex meaning. Even if we take it as still mapping objects to physical magnitudes, it can now interact with mathematical terms and operators in identities such as ⌜the length of $xy$ is $10^{11}$, in **tu** units⌝ and ⌜the length of $zw$ is $10^{11}$ times the length of $zw$⌝ in which we apply the operation of multiplication, platonistically thought of as only applying to numbers, to it.

What of the metaphysical content of a mixed sentence such as ⌜the length of $zw$ is $10^{11}$ times the length of **tu**⌝ or ⌜the length of $xy = 10^{11}$, in **tu** units⌝? These sentences do not have representational content. The length of $xy$ EXISTS and $10^{11}$ does not, so we do not have a case where both terms refer to the same mind-independent entity. These mixed sentences are made-true iff they are derivable from the rules of the underlying calculus—the theory of the rationals, say, axiomatized by the axioms for a field—together with firstly some bridge principles and secondly a body of *empirical* truths. But there is no requirement that these empirical truths be, in the current terminology, *purely* empirical; in fact for any moderately theoretical claim they will not be purely empirical. The empirical truths will be those we can get by Field's process of 'de-mathematicizing' physics and isolating the 'intrinsic structure' (§II* above). In the present case, consider the *physical* relation which holds between any two rods or rulers when the first is $10^{11}$ times the size of the second. Abbreviate this by $R(x, y)$. Then R $(zw, $ **tu**$)$ is the representational part of the metaphysical content of ⌜the length of $zw$ is $10^{11}$ times the length of **tu**⌝. $R(zw, $ **tu**$)$ is not purely empirical. I reject the reductionist idea that we can analyse away theoretical statements into the purely empirical plus some mathematics, pure and applied.

To complete the metaphysical content, we need a bridge principle, true by dint of being stipulated as an axiom. In this case a 'representation' axiom of the form

$$\forall x \forall y (R(x, y) \to \text{length}(x) = 10^{11} \times \text{length}(y))$$

will do the job and once again this sentence does not, ironically, have representational metaphysical content. It is made-true, in the applied calculus, purely by stipulation.

It may be objected that there is no way we can 'get at' the intrinsic, wholly physical, relation R except via mathematical notions such as being $10^{11}$ the length of something. Exactly. It does not follow from the fact that we can only get at the relation via mathematical concepts that the relation itself is not purely physical. This makes the point that mathematics is *conceptually indispensable*. We cannot pick out objects and relations which fall outside our normal pre-scientific experience of everyday things going about their (natural) lawful occasions, not without the help of mathematics.

Now, in specifying the metaphysical content which makes-true the theoretical claim, we use similarly theoretical language (as also in the applied mathematics of any conservative extension result for the system). This is the anti-reductionism. But it means that the specification of metaphysical content, at least as sketched above, is very far from giving a full account of how we can designate objects, properties and relations which transcend the everyday and purely empirical. Even leaving aside Quinean worries about inscrutability of reference, these make-true conditions do not explain how a suitably conservative applied mathematics manages to secure determinate reference to the 'new' theoretical objects and properties in the first place.

Agreed. Developing a realist theory, including a theory of reference, for a particular area of discourse is a substantive task, a task in philosophy of language combined with, and applied to, the philosophy of the area of discourse in question: cosmology, microbiology, quantum physics, or whatever.[22] A full theory should be seen as a type of naturalized epistemology—'naturalized semantics'—in which the knowledge we are trying to account for is the very specialized knowledge we have when we grasp the meanings of linguistics terms. As in naturalized epistemology generally, we are at liberty to bring to bear in our attempt to explain what it is we know, and how we know it, any aspect of our overall theory of the world, from physics, biology, psychology, mathematics, that seems to help. As with naturalized epistemology, the task, as we have seen, is far from trivial and different philosophies of mathematics may differ in how well, or badly, they accomplish it.

It may be thought that a crucial element in a satisfactory naturalistic explanation of theoretical reference is Lewis's structuralist model of the meaning of theoretical terms using the technique of Ramsey sentences (Lewis 1970/83). But, as Lewis makes clear, this will not enable us to enlarge our conceptual reach from the ordinary macroscopic world to the domains of the very small or the very large.[23] As he points out, introducing theoretical terms in his way, by implicit definition, does not increase the expressive power of the new language $L_T$ compared to the old language $L_O$. More exactly, if we expand the old language $L_O$ by introduction of new terms $t_1, \ldots t_n$ via a theory $H(t_1, \ldots t_n)$ and the introduction is successful, then though each of the $t_i$ will have a referent in the new language $L_T$, the referent of each term will not only be a member of the domain of quantification of the old domain of $L_O$, but there will be a formula of $L_O$ which uniquely specifies each referent.

Lewis lays down as a condition for successful introduction of the new terms that there is (in the actual world) a *unique* sequence of items which satisfies $H(x_1, \ldots x_n)$. He acknowledges that one might think to weaken this to the 'Carnapian' requirement, that there merely be at least one satisfier of the 'Ramsey matrix', $H(x_1, \ldots x_n)$ (pp. 83, 89). But in that case, what determines the referents of theoretical terms? The most obvious approach is to use something like Hilbert's epsilon terms. The referent of the $i+1$th term is an *arbitrary* satisfier of the appropriate 'slot' in the matrix:

$$(\exists y_1, ..., \exists y_i, \exists y_{i+2}, ..., \exists y_n)H(y_1, ..., y_n)).$$

yielding:

$$t_{i+1} = \varepsilon y_{i+1}[(\exists y_1, ..., \exists y_i, \exists y_{i+2}, ..., \exists y_n)H(y_1, ..., y_n)).]$$

---

[22] Moreover, it may be that in some domains no theory attributing grasp to speakers of theoretical reference is right because there is no reference to external objects and properties to explain. As remarked above, instrumentalism might be right for some particular types of discourse (intentional ascriptions to present-day computers and robots, for example) though false in general.

[23] Though Lewis (1970/83) considers a theory T in an expansion of a language O, he is at pains to emphasize that 'O' stands for the 'old' terms, not the 'observational' terms.

But though the epsilon operator is a perfectly respectable device to incorporate in a mathematical system (from a formalist point of view anyway), no naturalistic theory can appeal solely to its resources to explain determinate reference. Only an appeal to magic could explain how 'an arbitrary cat' in English could refer to Lucy the cat, rather than some other cat (cf. Weir 2001, p. 292). Lewis's reluctance to go down this route is well-founded.

The moral I draw is that before Lewisian methods can get to work to enable us to single out succinctly particular objects or properties, we must already have expanded our conceptual resources from simpler, purely empirical ones, in such a way that we have concepts which uniquely apply to the entities in question. And a prior grasp of mathematics is an essential element of this expansion.

This point is fatal to any attempt to combine the holistic empiricist account of theoretical language with realism. The whole strategy depends on our having an *independent* grasp of arithmetic, or more generally mathematics, that is an independent understanding of the sentences of these disciplines as meaningful and truth-valued and which are then meshed with purely empirical sentences to generate the sentences (including bridge principles) of empirical theories. No speaker can be accorded such grasp unless she has some significant, albeit fallible, ability to differentiate *correct* from incorrect mathematical sentences, at least of the more basic sort. Indeed, there must be a distinction between correct and incorrect sentences if the mathematical system forms a language at all, independently graspable or not. Granted that, and the applicability of a disquotational notion of truth, we are committed to the existence of a body of truths grasp of which is independent of our understanding of scientific theory. The latter, indeed, presupposes it. Grasp of the highly theoretical sector of language T presupposes grasp of a purely empirical sector and also grasp of a fragment M of mathematics (I take these as necessary but not sufficient conditions for theoretical understanding).

According to the holist empiricist, grasp of mathematics and a pure empirical level is not prior to and a condition of grasp and scientific terms; they are all (atomic observational sentences excepted) grasped together, not separately. We master the terms by grasping some axiom system which mixes together the less theoretical with the more theoretical—set theory, quantification theory, 'empirical' hypothesis (granted also an understanding of some basic analytic logic). This holist empiricism is incompatible, however, with scientific realism.

Scientific realists, then, should reject any account of mathematics which does not take mathematical language to be independent of empirical language, and mathematical truth to be determined independently of scientific truth. Both the Quinean platonist picture *and* Field's fictionalism fail to respect this autonomy of mathematics. For Field, mathematics is both *ontologically dispensable* (the rejection of heavy-duty platonism) and *deductively dispensable* (model theory and proof theory replaced by modal logic) in science. There is no need to think of mathematical theorems as (non-trivially) true, their truth determined independently of the nature of the physical world. But more fundamental than the question of how we *justify* our theories is the question of how we even manage to *grasp* the concepts they express. Field still has to give us a naturalistic explanation of how we manage to grasp the meanings of theoretical terms which refer to items far removed from those we are acquainted with through our normal perceptual abilities; and he has to do this without appeal to an independent grasp of mathematics. Direct noetic intuition will not do. If it works for the meaning of 'muon' why can it not work for the referent of 'prime number' or 'elliptic curve'? Holistic empiricism, for the reasons I have given above, is incompatible with scientific realism. I conclude that the fictionalist cannot provide a realist and naturalistic account of scientific theorizing and the role in it of mathematics. Mathematics is *conceptually indispensable* in science, even if ontologically or (more dubiously) proof-theoretically dispensable.

(Similarly, modal constructivists who wish to combine their view with a rejection of instrumentalism in science have to show that we can grasp the modal notions they take as primitive[24] independently not only of our grasp of mathematics (including proof theory and 'applied proof theory') but of our understanding of theoretical science. As Shapiro has argued (1997, pp. 237–8), it is not easy to see how someone innocent of mathematics and theoretical science could understand not only that it is possible to build a hut in the back garden, but also that an $\omega$ sequence is possible or that it is possible to build wff tokens of arbitrarily high finite complexity.)

There are, of course, other varieties of platonism than Quinean holist ones, but deep problems arise for any brand which takes it that mathematical sentences are made true or false, absolutely, by a world of abstract objects and properties (Chapter 4, §II. 5*). Platonism fails the stability test imposed by naturalistic epistemology on a theory T, namely that the conjunction of T (here mathematics interpreted as about abstract objects) with the thesis that we know T be not merely consistent but plausible. Even granting for the sake of argument that a realm of abstract mathematical objects exists, we have little idea how we could understand words and phrases as referring to, or true or false of, those terms. Perhaps we will come to a better understanding of how a grasp of terms for abstract objects is possible. Perhaps we will never understand how we understand mathematics platonistically construed. This could be a matter which is simply beyond our ken though we do nonetheless grasp mathematics thus construed. I submit, however, that, as things stand, platonism is far less plausible an account of mathematics than neo-formalism.

For our grasp of mathematics obviously has some connection with our capacities to interact with concrete tokens, to produce them and respond to them in certain ways. One way in which we rate people as competent, or incompetent, in a branch of mathematics is by gauging the sensitivity of their mathematical judgements to presentations of concrete proofs or refutations, in whatever shape these take in that particular branch. We allow that one competent in decimal arithmetic may on

---

[24] Including (highly problematically) actuality operators and cross-world predications, see Burgess and Rosen (1997, pp. 143–5) and Hellman (2005, pp. 551–60).

occasion fail to carry forward in doing long multiplication, for example. But someone who can never recognize anything we would call a demonstration or refutation of an arithmetical equation (beyond simple addition and multiplication tables say) would undoubtedly be classed as not grasping ordinary decimal arithmetic. Someone who performs well on this score would—other things being equal. Likewise, an analyst or algebraist who continually proffers flawed non-proofs in examinations will fail to pass muster as a mathematician. More generally, in many areas of mathematics competent mathematicians modulate their judgements as to whether a thesis is true so as to coincide with their belief that a proof of the result could be found, and manifest, when the occasion arises, competence in discriminating genuine from faulty proofs or disproofs. All this counts strongly in favour of the neo-formalist explanation of what grasp of mathematics consists in.[25]

Overall, then, the claim is that neo-formalism is able to explain the applicability of mathematics in much the same way as the fictionalist whilst also denying that MATHEMATICAL ENTITIES EXIST. Since, however, neo-formalism holds the key conservativeness results to be truths, it is internally much more coherent than fictionalism. It also provides a vastly superior account of applications to those of fictionalism and to the platonist view of mathematics as a delineation of the interrelationships of abstract objects in an inert world utterly divorced from the physical world we inhabit.


## §IV. Promises, Promises

For the past three chapters I have been operating at the FM-level, the level of formal metatheory, with the occasional foray into representational mode as in the mathematical entities EXIST claim, denied in the last paragraph. It is time to redeem the pledge to show how one can rework all the specifications of metaphysical content in terms of concrete proof tokens rather than in terms of NON-EXISTENT proofs.

---

[25] Not that it counts solely in favour of neo-formalism, of course, since intuitionists, for example, will also adduce such points in favour of their own position.

# 6

# Proof Set in Concrete

## §I. Tokenism

*§1.1*

Our first step towards a non-destructive 'nominalism'[1] is to specify that the basic ontology of the neo-formalist meta-theory consists of concrete tokens. These I take to be physical objects or events. I think of events in general as certain rather vaguely specified regions of spacetime, not qualitatively distinct from physical 'bodies'.[2] But any broadly physicalistic account of physical bodies and events should be compatible with the concretist syntax to be developed. The precise nature of the tokens is not all that important philosophically. They can be shapes physically realized as ink marks or burnt toner, as chalk marks, as coloured patterns on computer screens or in some other way. They can be bursts of sound, diagrams containing geometric patterns, arrangements of dimples in computer disks, chains of polymers in a biotechnological realization of language, or whatever. For simplicity I will usually think of them as traditional ink markings of shapes and suppose that for a particular speaker S, we have identified a stock of atomic or basic tokens which occur in the corpus of her linguistic history. The key notion in all cases, however, is that of *equiformity*. Even in the case of ink shapes, this is a highly complex notion.

Let us start from the notion of two tokens being perceptually indistinguishable.[3] It is usual to assume that this is an equivalence relation (though a particularly interesting form of the Sorites paradox, involving chains of physically different items in which pairwise adjacent ones are indistinguishable, casts doubt on this). The platonist would

---

[1] I scare-quote 'nominalism' for the reasons given in Chapter 5, §II*, where 'concretism' was suggested as a less misleading title.

[2] Given that they will be relatively bounded wholes with fairly continuous change across time, one who is happy with a four-dimensionalist ontology could view them as spacetime 'worms'. But there is no commitment to that ontology in neo-formalism per se.

[3] This too, a complex notion. In the case of spoken language, one complication is the dependence of phonemic type on the context of the preceding and succeeding sounds. See for example the 'Wickelphones' of Wickelgren (1969) and McClelland and Rumelhart (1986).

then quickly move to a consideration of perceptual linguistic types; for those of a set-theoretic bent, these might be construed as the equivalence classes of the tokens under the relation. The neo-formalist is, of course, permitted to talk of these types too, just as she can talk of the charge in coulombs of the electron. Nonetheless she must hold that in objective reality, in this case objective psychological reality, THERE IS NO such thing as a perceptual type, not of that 'type' anyway, since THERE ARE NO classes. But nor do types EXIST, as non-mathematical, non-concrete objects. The neo-formalist seeks to avoid all metaphysical commitment to such non-concrete, and epistemologically problematic, things. In particular, when working in the metatheory M which seeks to give a non-platonistic account of the metaphysical content of mathematical utterances it is imperative that the neo-formalist eschews talk of abstract objects.

There is a ready substitute: the mereological fusion of all tokens perceptually indistinguishable from a given one. Call this the perceptual tipe of token $t$.[4] Even if indistinguishability is not determinately an equivalence relation, the notion of tipe, though subject to a degree of vagueness, will suffice for our purposes so long as it is not typically indeterminate which tipe a token belongs to.

Should the concretist be so ready to embrace this substitute, however? A critic may urge that there is no gain in swapping a set-theoretic metatheory for this alternative, but also ontologically far from neutral, metatheory which just happens to have the different primitive $\ulcorner x$ is part of $y\urcorner$ (or, equivalently in the usual presentations, $\ulcorner x$ overlaps $y\urcorner$). Indeed David Lewis (1991) proffered an alternative development of set theory using mereology, plural quantification and (crucially) the singleton function (or many such functions, on structuralist versions of this position) which takes objects to their unit sets. So is the anti-platonist jumping from the frying pan into the fire, in embracing mereology, even though eschewing the singleton function?

I think not. For one thing, the neo-formalist should insist that the mereological primitives are not schematic, capable of platonistic interpretation, but are to be interpreted concretely. The table leg is part of the table and it is in that sense (whatever exactly it is) that the neo-formalist uses $\ulcorner x$ is part of $y\urcorner$. On any reasonable reading of 'concretely part of', it is clear that the expression satisfies the minimal axioms usually posited as part of mereology, namely that the relation is transitive, reflexive, and anti-symmetric.

So far, so modest. But mereology only gets interesting when we expand to include further axioms. Prominent candidates include an extensionality, or unique decomposition, principle for mereological entities: t = u only if every part of t is part of u and vice versa. More importantly, a principle of *universal (or unrestricted) composition*, which we can express as a schema holding for any instantiation for φ:

$$\exists x \varphi x \rightarrow \exists x \forall y (yOx \leftrightarrow \exists z(\varphi z \,\&\, yOz))$$

---

[4] I will use italic variables to range over tokens, bold over tipes.

with $Oxy$ reading ⌜$x$ overlaps $y$⌝. This assures us that if there are $\varphi$s, there is a fusion of all the $\varphi$s, this being, on the concrete interpretation assumed here, the object which straddles all and only those regions of spacetime occupied by a $\varphi$, however scattered and discrete they may be.

How much of this can the neo-formalist accept? Clearly, as an anti-platonist, she cannot go along with Lewis and accept unit sets and the 'mysterious' singleton relation. But is it reasonable to accept universal composition? Without it or something like it, the mereology threatens to be too weak to provide us with our tipes. But, as Burgess and Rosen (1997, p. 156) note, it is controversial whether universal composition is nominalistically acceptable.

On the plus side, if one accepts the supersubstantivalist thesis that material objects and (arbitrary) regions of spacetime are one and the same, then this gives us universal composition and a rich ontology of mereological objects. And this is surely still a physicalistic position. It may even be finitistic, if there are only finitely many spacetime regions. Even if spacetime is a continuum, in the classical sense, this of itself does not bring with it platonism. As Field argued (1980), though to a largely sceptical audience, the objection to platonism should not be on the score of the cardinality of the domain, but on account of the abstractness of the objects. Actually, the important objection is epistemological, and if the epistemology of a physical continuum is as dodgy as that of the mathematical one then the sceptics have a point. However, even on the realist picture of theoretical science sketched in the last chapter (in which our ability to conceptualize theoretical domains which go beyond, or well inside, the world of everyday macroscopic things depends on an independent grasp of mathematics), it is still open to the neo-formalist to quantify over spacetime regions, large and small, however many there are, in the anti-representationalist metatheory for mathematical language. What matters for ontological reduction is that there is no quantification over abstracta; that grasp of the concepts involved in the propositions of the metatheory presupposes grasp of mathematical language is irrelevant, if no abstract objects belong to the extensions of the concepts.

Supersubstantivalism, however, is far from obviously correct. Some object because they differentiate objects from their location, perhaps impressed by the argument that objects could have occupied different locations. If one accepts the Kripkean notion of rigid designators then this argument no longer looks like an obvious modal fallacy. Others reject universal composition simply because they find it hard to swallow the idea that, given some arbitrary unconnected objects—my left toe, the crater Copernicus on the moon 100,000 years ago, a supernova taking place in another galaxy a million years hence, THERE IS another object in reality which is the fusion of them all (cf. Simons 2006). It is not hard to see why this is found counter-intuitive; one does not have to take the extreme position that only mereological atoms exist to baulk at this. On the other hand we should beware of thinking that only what is salient to humans EXISTS.

Now neo-formalists do not need the full strength of universal composition for their purposes, in particular in order for there to be an object, the tipe, which contains each of a given plurality of linguistic tokens as its proper parts, and nothing which does not overlap one of these. It would be enough to have fusion restricted to linguistic tokens; but that would be a very ad hoc and implausible stance to take. There may be non-arbitrary restrictions of composition, though, which give us all the tipes we need. Nor need tipes be construed as fusions. For the non-nominalist, mereological objects are not the fundamental, or only fundamental, constituents of physical reality. Various other candidates have been suggested—tropes, states of affairs, events as structured entities, but most plausibly, I would argue, properties and relations. Of course if properties are viewed 'platonistically', as abstract entities, then the neo-formalist will wish to avoid them like the plague. But a more 'Aristotelian' notion of property, as a recurrent pattern in the physical world, say, is a perfectly respectable thing for an upstanding naturalist to believe in. Given such a notion of property, and sufficiently many of them, syntactic tipes can be identified with such properties, with the recurrent patterns of equiform tokens.

The key point, however, is that the neo-formalist metatheory can be carried out with a very parsimonious ontology, since, as will be seen, there is no need to posit more than a finite number of tipes; this should defuse any suspicion that a platonistic ontology is being smuggled in through the back door. If all else fails, the neo-formalist can identify a syntactic tipe with a particular token; for simple symbols, the tipe can be ostensively presented as a sort of standard metre of the syntactic world. For a token to belong to a tipe is simply for it to be equiform with the standard token which is the tipe. If tipes can be thus identified with 'representative tokens', then it will be argued below that all we need in addition is that either fusions, or something playing a similar role to fusions, of relatively contiguous and causally connected objects or events exist. Since we are massive collocations of relatively contiguous, causally connected entities, this does not seem too bold an assumption.

We cannot, however, identify linguistic tipes with perceptual tipes, even leaving aside the complications caused by the context-dependence of phonemes. Two tokens which are perceptually very different can be tokens of the same tipe. This is very clear if we use different media such as oral language versus written language, but even in printed written language the point is obvious by dint of different fonts, different font sizes, different colour, and so on.

The problem of characterizing linguistic tipes on the basis of perceptual tipes is solved if we use semantic criteria. Token $x$ is not equiform with token $y$ (they belong to distinct grammatical tipes) just in case substitution of a token perceptually indistinguishable from $y$ in place of $x$ in the utterance in which $x$ occurred would have changed that utterance's meaning (cf. Quine 1953a, p. 50); otherwise they are equiform. How large a subsuming string of tokens has to be to count as the 'utterance' which $x$ belongs to is vague but not harmfully so. We can let it be as wide as we want consonant with it being meaningful to talk of sameness of meaning between token utterances.

One might object, however, that there is a vicious circularity involved in defining equiformity in semantic terms. One of the first things one learns in theoretical semantical studies is the sharp distinction between syntax and semantics, a sharp distinction which makes the theorems which connect the two domains, such as soundness and completeness theorems, non-trivial and important. When a semantic theory invokes relations of reference and satisfaction between names and complex predicates, on the one hand, and the items in the formal models on the other, it is assumed that the syntactic entities are expression strings specifiable independently of their meaning. There would seem to be a vicious circularity in the semantics otherwise. Certainly in the well-founded set theories which are normally used in formal semantics it is not possible that a name also be a function from itself to its referent. More generally, results for formal languages such as unique readability—the absence of scope ambiguities—are usually secured by locating the symbols at the bottom of a hierarchy, well below the semantic entities which have higher rank.

However, the semantic element imported into the characterization of equiformity introduces no threat of vicious circularity or incoherence. The basic elements of our concrete syntax, the tokens, are physical—patches of ink, bursts of sound—and thus eminently well-founded, in the set-theoretical sense. They stand in a multitude of physical relations one with another and can be partitioned into numerous different groupings. So long as we can characterize a notion of synonymy which holds between tokens (or perceptual tipes) and which does not presuppose grasp of the concept of a grammatical tipe then our analysis of the latter notion is non-circular. One way to do this is to work for these purposes with a primitive pre-theoretical notion of synonymy. We can do this without assuming this notion cannot be bettered, without being sceptics about the idea of a scientific account of synonymy. Or, rather than work with a full-blown notion of synonymy, Quine also suggests (1970, p. 16) as a criterion for distinctness of tokens (in his case for two sounds to belong to distinct phonemes) that

it is sufficient to find an utterance that commands the speaker's assent before the one sound is substituted for the other and commands his dissent after.

Call this criterion one of strong semantic discriminability. For weak discriminability we require only that the reactions differ, where the three possible reactions are assent, dissent, and agnosticism. 'Commands assent' is presumably a dispositional or counterfactual notion, the idea being one would assent to the one utterance and dissent to the other, if presented with them. Grammatical tipes I will define in terms of weak semantic discriminability.

Thus 'cat' and '*cat*' are tokens of the same grammatical tipe for me at a given time if I would not even weakly discriminate them semantically. At that time, there is no comprehensible written utterance containing a token indistinguishable from 'cat' such that I would give a different epistemic response to an utterance perceptually identical except that 'cat' is substituted for '*cat*'. Perhaps we have to require that 'cat' be a single isolated token surrounded by white space. 'Hyper-intensional' contexts, such as quotation contexts, however, play havoc with any such criterion. If I substitute a token of 'cat' for one of '*cat*' in

The following token—'*cat*'—is in italic font.

I will generate a sentence I disbelieve from one I believe. So such contexts have to be excluded from the criterion; it is hard to see that any questions are begged by doing so.

The criterion applies to terms of all categories. Thus at a given time $t$ I may use '~' and '¬' interchangeably as negation signs in some mathematical calculus I am employing. Were you to confront me with two tokens $u$ and $u'$, differing only that some parts perceptually indistinguishable from '~' are replaced by parts indistinguishable from '¬' or vice versa, my reactions would be the same, or at least there would not be assent in one case, dissent in the other.

What, though, of the evident possibility that at a later time $t'$ I might work with a calculus which allows for proof-theoretically distinct forms of negation—Boolean negation versus De Morgan in a relevant logic perhaps, and use different shapes to express the different negations?[5] Interchange may then fail. Suppose $u$ is a token biconditional of the form $[v \leftrightarrow v]$ and $u'$ differs only in that all the occurrences of tipe ~ in the second $v$ are changed to occurrences of tipe ¬. I may well then assent to $u$ but not to $u'$.

This raises a worry for the counterfactual criterion. For might it not be the case that had I been confronted at time $t$ with utterances containing not only tokens of tipes ~ and ¬ but also distinctive vocabulary from the relevantist calculus, I would have switched to using that calculus? The counterfactual criterion might, in other words, distinguish perceptually distinct tokens because they might have been used, will in future be used, perhaps, to express distinct notions even though in a particular given context they differ no more in their use than one occurrence of the letter 'a' does (in normal use) from another 'a' in a different font size.[6]

Perhaps it is sufficient, in the criterion for grammatical tipehood, to specify that the utterances to which one is exposed (in the counterfactual scenario) contain only tokens of perceptual tipes each of whose parts occurs in the speaker S's linguistic

---

[5] Cf. Meyer (1974), Anderson, Belnap and Dunn (1992, pp. 490–2). One has to be careful when trying to employ two different negations simultaneously: fairly standard structural rules will collapse the two. See J. H. Harris (1982). See also Tim Williamson, (1987/8) especially pp. 111–12, footnote 3 and the references therein.

[6] Perceptually indistinguishable tokens can, of course, have different meanings, different information content, as we have seen: the token '$3 + 1 = 0$' is false in ordinary arithmetic, but if I now specify I am using modular arithmetic mod 4 the indistinguishable token '$3 + 1 = 0$' is true. But we cannot work with both arithmetics simultaneously, and indistinguishable tokens would generate the same responses at a given time so long as we exclude, from the counterfactual range, the triggering of a different calculus as in the case of the move to relevantist negations.

corpus around the time in question. If S is engaged at that time in a particular calculus this would block the triggering into action of the rules of a different calculus by the presentation, in the counterfactual scenario, of distinctive tokens of that calculus. So let us settle on the idea that two tokens are equiform at a given time for a speaker just in case the speaker is not disposed, at the time, to discriminate them semantically, not even weakly.

## §1.2

If we wish to give a grammar for our speaker S, at a given time, we must do more than identify the linguistic tipes in use by the speaker at the time. We have to discern syntactic complexity. First of all, how do we identify atomic tokens? We can start from the idea of having a semantically significant proper part. Suppose token $t$ has a proper part $p$ such that there is another token $u$ which is strongly semantically discriminable from $p$. That is, there are tokens $s$ and $r$ which differ only in that a token of $p$'s perceptual tipe $\mathbf{p}$ occurs in $s$ just where a token of $\mathbf{u}$ occurs in $r$ and the speaker assents to $s$ and dissents from $r$ or vice versa. Then the token of $\mathbf{p}$ plays a meaningful role in $s$ since the latter gains assent or dissent, not baffled agnosticism, and the $\mathbf{p}$ token makes a difference as we see from the opposite verdict for $r$. In this case, $t$ has $p$ as a semantically significant part. We might then be tempted to say that where there is no such part $p$ then $t$ is an atomic token.

In natural languages, however, this will not work because many strings which are semantically primitive contain subparts which are semantically significant, only not in that string. Thus the token of 'rabbit' in the fairly Quinean

There goes a rabbit

is, intuitively, atomic. Yet it (considering the written, not spoken, form) contains substrings which are semantically significant in their own right, for example 'rabbi' and 'bit' and 'it' and 'i'. Moreover we can replace them with other significant strings *salva congruitate*, if not for 'bit' and 'i', then (at least if we allow proper names of states) for 'rabbi', yielding

There goes a goat.

We might call words like 'rabbit' *segmented atomics*, as opposed to fully atomic strings. They are a very common feature of natural language where many intuitively semantically primitive words, even quite small ones like 'bit', 'it', and 'at', are segmented atomics.[7] The intuition that nonetheless 'rabbit' in the above sentence is atomic surely rests on the perception that our grasp of the meanings of 'rabbi' and 'bit' play no part in our grasp of the meaning of 'rabbit'. Perhaps we can rest content with this—there is no

---

[7] Of course the notion of a 'word' itself is not a simple one, in the written language it is partly a printer's artefact, cf. Quine (1960, p. 13).

semantically significant substring $t$ grasp of which is necessary to grasp $u$—as an account of the atomicity of $t$ in $u$, without seeking to find any more behaviouristic criterion. We might say an atomic string has no 'active' semantically significant substring. On a molecularistic picture of language understanding (Chapter 2, §II) this is fairly straightforward. If $t$ is a semantically significant part of $u$ yet one could fail to grasp its independent meaning (fail to grasp the meaning of 'rabbi' say) yet still grasp $u$ ('rabbit'), then $t$ is not a counterexample to the atomicity of $u$.

Nonetheless I will restrict attention to languages in which the simpler definition of atomicity—no semantically significant substring—works in the sense that in any token with a semantically significant substring, the substring is active, it 'does work' in the token itself; grasp of its meaning as it occurs in other strings is essential to grasp of the token. Indeed I will assume further that no two distinct atomic tokens mereologically overlap.

Even if no real language, written or spoken, is actually of this type, there could have been such a language. We could create such a language, or rather create a specialist fragment of sublanguage which obeyed those restrictions, systems as complex as full natural languages not being the sort of thing humans can create. Indeed we have done so, to the extent that we have been able to put into use formal languages. If, then, we can give a completely concretist account of mathematics for such a language, that would on its own strike a major blow against platonism. We could, moreover, apply the techniques below to more usual languages with segmented atomics by imagining related languages in which the segmented atomics have letters (or phonemes) replaced with sufficiently many substitutes new to the language (or are assigned fresh words with no significant sub-parts) in order to make them fully atomic. After having defined physicalistically the grammar for this language we can read this syntax back into the real language by replacing the new signs by those for which they were substituted. (It may be, of course, that as a result in some cases a segmented atomic tipe is syntactically ambiguous, with both its atomic reading, and its reading as syntactically complex, being legitimate in the sense that some, but not all, of the time, the semantically significant parts do semantic work inside the tipe.)

What, then, of the metaphysics of syntactic complexity, most simply the notion of the concatenation of two atomic tokens $a$ and $a'$? We could take the concatenation to consist simply in the fusion of the two tokens, if, that is, we think any two tokens have a fusion. Even leaving aside the worry that this mereological principle is false, if we wish to link language to speakers' practice then a fusion of, in the written case, two inscriptions which are vast distances apart in space and time is of little relevance. Moreover it saves on work we will have to do later if we can impose some order, if $a$ concatenated with $a'$ need not be the same as $a'$ concatenated with $a$. Fusions of the two tokens will do the job, if we can use time as an 'extraneous order' (Burgess, Hazen and Lewis 1991). Or perhaps we should admit into our ontology 'processes' as structured entities, ordered by time (relativity theory raises questions here of course), their constituents being events which follow on one another in a linked manner (though the link need not be a simple causal succession). Perhaps in perceiving change this is what we perceive—processes in which events follow on one after the other. Processes in this sense will do perfect duty as complex linguistic tokens, the constituents being the events of uttering phonemes or writing substrings. If one rejects the existence of processes, or of fusions of events linked in the successive fashion one finds in e.g. a piece of spoken dialogue or a musical phrase then it is hard to see a principled place to stop before ending up with the 'mereological nihilist' position that THERE ARE NO complex objects—no tables, chairs, molecules, people, stars. I decline to go down that road.[8]

Let us stipulate, then, that atomic token $a$ is 'immediately concatenated' with $a'$ iff they are relatively contiguous in space and time (we do not need to get too precise about this), $a'$ comes into existence later than $a$,[9] and there is no other atomic token later than $a$ which occurs no later than, and no further away from $a$, than $a'$. I have suggested that there are a number of ontological options regarding the nature of the entity which is the concatenate of two tokens thus immediately concatenated: fusions, properties, relations, processes. Rather than mention each every time, I will plump for fusion, assuming that fusions of linked segments (two or more) of speech or writing exist; the account could be rewritten in terms of the other ontologies, readily so in the case of processes.

Define, then, the immediate concatenation of $a$ followed by $a'$—write this as—$a\,\hat{}\,a'$ by

$\iota x(x$ is the fusion of $a$ and $a'$ & $a$ is immediately concatenated with $a')$

where $\iota x \varphi x$ is the definite description operator [the $x$ such that $\varphi x$]. Hence if neither $\ulcorner a \urcorner$ nor $\ulcorner a' \urcorner$ refer, or if they are not contiguous, or if there is another atom interposed between them no further from $a$, or if $a'$ is not later than $a$, then the definite description does not refer. Similarly

$a\,\hat{}\,a'\,\hat{}\,a''$ is

$\iota x(x$ is the fusion of $a$, $a'$ and $a''$ and $a$ is immediately concatenated with $a'$ and $a'$ with $a'')$

---

[8] The nihilist may hope to reinstate ordinary everyday objects (at least inanimate ones) as 'constructions' from mereological atoms but the prospects of an anti-platonist nihilist achieving this are slim indeed, for want of scaffolding with which to carry out the constructing.

[9] This is the normal situation in spoken language, of course. For written language, too, it is fairly typical for ink splodges to be written down across the page in temporal sequence, in the spatial direction dictated by the tradition of the linguistic culture of the writer. Goodman and Quine, in 'Steps Towards a Constructive Nominalism' (1947), try to make do with basic mereology, as far as possible. However, they characterize their predicate $Cxyz$—$x$ is the concatenate of $y$ and $z$—by '$x$ and $y$ and $z$ are composed of whole characters of the language, in normal orientation to one another, . . . and the inscription $x$ consists of $y$ *followed by* $z$' (1947, p. 112, my italics) and depend implicitly on a notion of order among the parts of inscriptions in, for instance, specifying what inscriptions count as axioms.

and the notion can be generalized in the obvious fashion to concatenations of four or more tokens.

We start to built up complexity in syntax with the notion of an expression string token (EST). This is a (finite) fusion $f$ of atomic tokens such that for each such atomic $a$ in $f$ there is either one atomic token $x$ in $f$ with $a\,\hat{}\,x$ or one atomic $y$ in $f$ with $y\,\hat{}\,a$. By the definition of immediate concatenation there cannot be two distinct tokens succeeding or preceding $a$ and by the finiteness of $f$ there will be exactly one atom $b$ with no predecessor $x$ such that $x\,\hat{}\,b$ is part of $f$ ($b$ is the initial atom of $f$) and exactly one atom (the end atom) $c$ such that there is no successor $y$ with $c\,\hat{}\,y$ part of $f$. We can extend the notion of concatenation to talk of the concatenation $e\,\hat{}\,e'$ of two ESTs $e$ and $e'$. This only exists where the end atom of $e$ immediately concatenates with the initial atom of $e'$; where this is the case, $e\,\hat{}\,e'$ is the EST which is the fusion of $e$ and $e'$.

## §1.3

It is the business of the grammarian to distinguish the well-formed formulae from the ill-formed ones. Our concretist grammarian will interpret this as the task of distinguishing well-formed ESTs and tipes thereof from the ill-formed ones. To set about her task, she must look for complexity-forming operations in the corpus of ESTs uttered by her subject S. The grammarian might then draw up such rules as:

> given any two expression tokens A and B which are not too large, ($\hat{}\,$A$\,\hat{}\,$&$\,\hat{}\,$B$\,\hat{}\,$) is a conjunctive token;
> given an expression token A which is not too large, ($\hat{}\,\forall\,\hat{}\,x\,\hat{}\,$)$\,\hat{}\,$A is a universal generalization token;[10]

and so on, leaving the boundaries of 'not too large' vague. More generally the grammarian will discern in the subject's speech, complexity-generating operations yielding larger token strings—call these strings *complexes*. In this example the conjunctive and universal generalization tokens are the complexes; call the subparts which occur as A and B do above the *constituents* of the corresponding complex. Constituents are immediate parts of a large token which is built up from them using iterative operations. These add to the input constituents a token of the same tipe in each case, the result ordered in the same way each time. A *compound* EST is a complex such that every part which is a constituent of a complex is itself a complex or an atom. The *wff tokens* are then just the atoms and the compounds.

So the notion of a wff token is relative to a specification of complexity-generating operations as being part of the speaker's language. But what makes a bunch of such operations, in effect rules for building bigger strings out of smaller,[11] a correct grammar

---

[10] And so on through a list of different variable tipes; or perhaps the grammarian will have some iterative clause for generating indefinitely many variables.

[11] These rules, or rather the absence of applications of them, are what we appeal to, at least some of the time, when we say that a segmented atomic token is really a semantic primitive.

for speaker S, a correct division into wffs and non-wffs? The grammarian will not feel that she has failed in her task unless every actual utterance in the community she is studying comes out as grammatical, on her criteria. For we know that in linguistic output, as elsewhere, performance often falls short of competence. If we ask what is the difference between a speaker's utterance being genuinely ungrammatical and it being a perfectly grammatical token of a language or calculus different from the one to which this particular grammarian's rules apply, this is a metaphysical question concerning the nature of grammatical correctness; it is not an epistemological question about how we might detect it. However, philosophers of a broadly anti-realist or instrumentalistic bent will give an epistemic answer to the metaphysical question. If the grammatical theory in its confrontation with the facts of actual utterance comes out optimally well on some ranking of a particular group of epistemic virtues such as simplicity, coverage of the data—whilst allowing for normal levels of error—and so on, then that, according to these anti-realists, is what it is for the grammar to describe correctly the syntactic rules of the language. If, by contrast, one has a realist approach to psychological phenomena such as language use and grasp, one will not be satisfied by this. One will hold that there are structures of some sort in the minds or brains of the speakers to which the grammar must do justice (and to which it may be that an 'empirically adequate one' could fail to do justice).[12] The realist position is unsatisfactory unless one can sketch some sort of account of the nature of these structures. My programmatic suggestion, as one who falls into the realist camp, would be that grammatical correctness resides in correctional dispositions (these being, in humans, neural structures), dispositions to withdraw and amend utterances (often when reacting to peer pressure); but this is too large a topic to tackle here. I assume nonetheless that there is a (fairly) determinate distinction between grammatical and ungrammatical tokens.

Thus far we have the notion of a wff token. In order to define a wff tipe (or just wff from now on) we need the notion of two ESTs $x$ and $y$ being the same length: $x \approx y$. We can define this as the existence of a relation which is 1:1 functional between the atomic tokens in $x$ and the atomic tokens in $y$ i.e.

$$\exists R(\forall z(A(z, x) \rightarrow \exists! w(R(z, w) \, \& \, A(w, y))) \, \& $$
$$\forall z(A(z, y) \rightarrow \exists! w(R(z, w) \, \& \, A\,(w, x))))$$

where $A(z,x)$ reads as $\ulcorner z$ is an atomic token in $x \urcorner$.

This definition appeals to quantification over relations but there is nothing wrong with that if one is not a (medieval-style) nominalist. Nor is there anything ontologically extravagant (or epistemologically dodgy) about assuming that physical properties and relations, instantiated by physical objects, exist; certainly if one does not assume the

---

[12] I assume here without argument that Kripkenstein scepticism about rule-following is false, but this is not to say that no argument is needed, that this scepticism can simply be ignored.

axiom of comprehension, that is if one does not assume that any arbitrary predicate designates a relation. Still, if only a rather meagre and austere array of physicalistically acceptable properties and relations exist, might that not mean that two ESTs, perhaps spatio-temporally and causally rather unconnected, come out as being of different lengths because no 'natural' relation one:one maps them, even though intuitively they both are the same size, both contain 42 atomic tokens say?

The simplest way to get round this problem is, of course, to posit a fairly lavish ontology of physical properties and relations;[13] alternatively one can take the notion ⌜there are just as many $X$s as $Y$s⌝, as primitive. Thirdly, granted our assumption that no two atomic tokens overlap, we can use Goodman and Quine's method for translation ⌜there are more atomic tokens in $x$ as in $y$⌝,[14] from which we can define the relation of there being the same number in each. However, this method assumes a fairly liberal mereology admitting spatio-temporally scattered objects, though of course if one accepts universal composition then this will be unproblematic.

Fourthly, at the cost of long-windedness but minimizing on ontological burdens, one can utilize a highly disjunctive definition: $x \approx y$ iff

$$[\exists_1 z(A(z,x)) \ \& \ \exists_1 x(A(z,y))]\vee[\exists_2 z(A(z,x)) \ \& \ \exists_2 z(A(z,y))]\vee...$$
$$...[\exists_{zillion} z(A(z,x)) \ \& \ \exists_{zillion} z(A(z,y))].$$

where the ⌜exactly $n$ $x$s are $\varphi$s⌝ quantifiers $\exists_n x \varphi x$ are defined in the usual way. The long-winded method, however, will only work if the metatheorist has greater syntactic stamina than the speakers of the object language under investigation.

To get to a notion of equiformity between ESTs, we appeal to the easily defined (assuming a modest amount of mereology again) notions of initial string, end string, initial token and end token of ESTs. Thus $x$ is an initial string of $y$ iff

$x$ is an EST which is part of $y$ and there is no atom $w$ in $y$–$x$ (the mereological complement of $x$ inside $y$) and atom $z$ in $x$ such that $w \hat{\ } z$ exists.

There is a parallel definition for end string. Given this, $x$ is an end (initial) token of $y$ if $x$ is an end (initial) string and also an atomic token. Two ESTs $x$ and $y$ are then said to be equiform just in case $x \approx y$ and for every initial string $z$ of $x$ there is an initial string $w$ of $y$ of the same length such that the end tokens of $z$ and $w$ are equiform (this definition does not presuppose the notion of wffhood). A wff tipe (or just wff) is then just the fusion of all wff tokens equiform with some given token. If fusions of equiform wff tokens, which after all may be highly scattered and disconnected, do not in general

---

[13] If one assumes infinitely many such, then one can use this ontology as a foundation for an infinitistic mathematics; in a particularly neat fashion, at least for those fond of the theory of types, if one believes also that there are higher-order properties. But why should a naturalist believe there are infinitely many properties and relations? Certainly, there could be no a priori guarantee of this (any more than of the truth of Russell's axiom of infinity) and so this view, like Russell's compromised logicism, fails to accommodate the non-empirical nature of mathematics.

[14] Goodman and Quine (1947, pp. 110–11, 114).

exist, we can employ the idea of representatives and suppose that a specific token is taken to play the role of the tipe; ⌜x belongs to tipe y⌝ is then redefined as ⌜x is equiform with y⌝.[15]

We can check that this definition of wffhood is acceptable by replacing it by a parallel abstract one in which expression strings are sequences of symbols, these being abstract types, and in which atoms, complexes, and constituents are defined in the same way as in the mereological case except that the mereological 'part of' is replaced by its set-theoretic equivalent.[16] Call the result a definition of a wff* in terms of the parallel notions of complex*, constituent*, and atoms*: every constituent* of a wff* is a complex* or an atom*. The functions paralleling the complexity generating operations generate, it can be assumed, set-theoretic entities of higher rank than their constituents and wffs* turn out to be well-founded set-theoretic entities (even if our set theory lacks an axiom of foundation) with the atomic tipes urelements, so that we can define the degree of complexity* of a wff*. We wish to compare this abstract idealization of our notion of wff with the usual definition of well-formed formula and see whether these definitions pick out the same class of abstract entities. Let us use 'formulae' for the abstract strings defined in the usual way, i.e. as the intersection of all the inductive sets, these being the sets which have the atoms, stipulated to be exactly the set of atoms*, as a subset and which are closed under the complexity-forming operations. An induction on wff* complexity shows us that every wff* is a formula[17] whilst likewise in the other direction an induction on formulae complexity demonstrates that all formulae are wff*s. (This checking, of course, is not part of the purely 'concrete' metatheory MT for our language, but a piece of applied mathematics.)

The above technique for defining wffs will work for any standard formal language which our speaker S could master, including quantificational languages, second-order languages, modal languages, etc., and in cases where the complexity-forming operations apply not only at the level of sentences but also in the formation of complex categories of name or predicate.

## §1.4

Moreover, exactly the same technique we used for defining wffs can be used for defining proofs. Although, as remarked in the previous two chapters, concrete proof systems come in many shapes and sizes, including geometric diagrams, for simplicity let us restrict attention to the case where proof tokens are wff-like—concatenations of primitive tokens which include some new symbols specific to the proof-theoretic

---

[15] Since we assume there are only finitely many tokens, on which more below, no appeal to the axiom of choice is needed here.

[16] What exactly the set-theoretic counterpart of ⌜x is a grammatical part of y⌝ will be is actually quite complicated and depends on how we define complex (abstract) expressions (and how we define sequences set-theoretically).

[17] It is crucial here, and also for such results as unique readability, that no proper part of an atom is an atom hence the atoms* really are atomic.

architecture. These will include a 'line-break' symbol separating off one line of the proof token from the wff token which constitutes the next line. In sequent-style systems the lines will not be single wffs but lists of wffs separated by an additional and non-iterable proof-theoretic symbol, often represented by a single turnstile '⊦', to the left of which occur the antecedents of the sequent, to the right the succeedents (only one, in the case of single conclusion logics). Complexes in the proof-theoretic case are defined in the same general fashion as complex wffs. Thus if there is a conjunction introduction rule in the calculus, then an &I complex might be defined, in a (non-sequent) calculus by:

$\forall x \forall y (x \, \hat{} \, y$ is an &I complex iff $y$ is a token of the form '$(' \, \hat{} \, z \, \hat{} \, \& \, \hat{} \, w \, \hat{} \, )$', for some $z$, $w$ such that both are equiform with constituents of $x$ (i.e. earlier lines of $x$).[18]

A compound proof is a complex each constituent of which is itself either a complex or an atomic proof. A proof token is either an atomic proof or a compound proof. Proofs, that is proof tipes, are then defined from proof tokens by the same technique, matching ends of initial segments of equal length for equiformity, as for wff tipes. The definition is relative to a stock of iterable operations found in the practice of the mathematicians in question. So our characterization of concrete proof takes the form ⌜$x$ is a concrete proof of $y$ relative to basic rules R⌝, $x$ and $y$ ranging over proof and sentence tipes and R over concrete examples of inferential practice.[19] I therefore claim that this definition of concrete proof is fully naturalistically acceptable.

I have assumed that the notion of proof is a formal one even in 'informal reasoning', even for diagrammatic proofs and even if most historical proofs systems have contained a large repertoire of atomic rules grasped in connectionist fashion. Correctness is determined by syntactic structure. However, at this point a distinction is often made between on the one hand 'canonical proofs'—these might be fully explicit proofs which a computerized proof checker programmed to test for proofhood in a formal system would pass—and, on the other, something a bit slacker—demonstrations, proof sketches, and the like. When one looks in mathematical texts, it is almost always the latter one will find, for these carry the epistemic punch of convincing one of theorems. Proofs which are too long and detailed to be absorbed cannot persuade.

Clearly this is a very important distinction in mathematical practice but it is not an entirely sharp one[20] and not, I think, of great philosophical importance. If a 'proof sketch' is unambiguous then in a sense the full proof is already present in the sketch,

---

[18] Generalization to sequent calculus rules is straightforward. I will consider only linear proof systems, for simplicity, but the transformation of tree-form systems, such as Gentzen–Prawitz natural deduction, into sequent systems is fairly direct.

[19] Though deciding which bits of practice are in conformity with the rules the speaker is following, and which are mistakes and therefore not part of R is, as we have seen, a complex matter; figuring out what would make such a decision objectively correct is even more complex.

[20] One can, to be sure, give precise definitions of particular formal proof systems and call proofs in such systems 'canonical' for that system.

not in its primary form but encoded somehow in the context and the ways of interpreting that context which the knowledgeable reader has imbibed in her mathematical education. The most clear-cut cases of proof sketches which are not canonical proofs are cases where one leaves particular cases, say in an inductive proof, as 'exercises for the reader'. Here (where it is not a bluff by someone who does not know how to finish the proof!) we have in effect a sort of promissory note or bet—that a competent mathematician could come up with the proof of the subcase after reflection on the methods of proof in the cases which have been proven. (Often the mathematician will simply be saving space in a book or article and the full proof will be in a drawer or on a hard disk, but there is no distinction in the publicly available material between this case and the promissory one.)

The difference between a proof sketch and a full proof blurs when we can think of the proof sketch as an abbreviation. For abbreviation, or one important species of it at any rate, can be thought of as the extension of the equiformity relation; this type of abbreviation occurs equally for singular terms, predicates, sentences, and proofs. Thus, in the case of singular terms, if a mathematician writes:

$$\text{Let } \omega =_{\text{df.}} \{x : \forall \gamma ((\varnothing \in \gamma \ \& \ \forall z (z \in \gamma \rightarrow (z \cup \{z\}) \in \gamma)) \rightarrow x \in \gamma)\}$$

we can read this as an instruction to take any token $t$ involving '$\omega$' as equiform with various related tokens involving

$$\{x : \forall \gamma ((\varnothing \in \gamma \ \& \ \forall z (z \in \gamma \rightarrow (z \cup \{z\}) \in \gamma)) \rightarrow x \in \gamma)\}.$$

wherever '$\omega$' occurs in $t$. Thus the token '$\varnothing \in \omega$' is equiform with the token

$$\varnothing \in \{x : \forall \gamma ((\varnothing \in \gamma \ \& \ \forall z (z \in \gamma \rightarrow (z \cup \{z\}) \in \gamma)) \rightarrow x \in \gamma)\}$$

although perceptually it does not look very similar (but then neither is '$\omega$' very similar to the sound a competent speaker will make when pronouncing the letter).

This notion of abbreviation by *stretched equiformity* can be extended beyond definitional abbreviation of names or predicates. For instance, consider speakers who have already mastered decimal arithmetic, indeed its expansion to include exponentiation. We might then introduce a definitional convention:

$$\sim \{n\} : p$$

where, in tokens which instantiate the rule, $n$ is replaced by a token of some canonical numerical term and $p$ by a token of a sentence of our original language. The convention is that it is to be considered equiform with an EST consisting of a token equiform with the substituend for $p$ preceded by $a$ occurrences of the negation sign, $a$ being the referent of the numerical term. (There is no inconsistency in a neo-formalist using such conventions, since the neo-formalist accepts the meaningfulness and truth of the usual mathematics.) We could then iterate the convention to allow $p$ to be replaced by tokens from the expanded language. On this convention $\sim \{6\} : \varnothing \in \varnothing$ is equiform with ~ ~ ~ ~ ~ ~ $\emptyset$ $\in$ $\emptyset$. Some abbreviatory tokens, however, may be equiform with no tokens in the original language e.g. ~$\{10^{180}\}$:$\emptyset$ $\in$ $\emptyset$.

Having expanded the notion of equiformity, we should similarly expand the notion of tipe so that e.g. ~ ~ ~ ~ a=b and ~$\{4\}$: a = b are parts of the same tipe. But it is not obvious how this might be done, given that equiform strings now can have different numbers of atomic tokens, that abbreviations can occur as subparts of utterances, and so on. I will postpone discussion of this until the next chapter. For the time being, then, tipes are defined without reference to abbreviation and ~ ~ ~ ~ a=b and ~$\{4\}$: a = b, though equiform in a stretched sense, are tokens of different tipes.

## §1.5

These complexities lead us on to a very evident problem with the concretizing of proof and the interrelations between wffs (wff tipes), wff*'s and formulae, likewise proofs (proof tipes) and abstract proof types. The formulae, we noted, are just the wffs* but certainly the wffs cannot be matched to the wffs*/formulae because there are only a finite number of wffs. The wffs and proofs are fusions (or something playing a similar role) of tokens uttered by our imagined speaker S or, more generally, a community C of speakers. The total corpus of any real community's output, however, is finite. So there can be only finitely many wffs and proofs. This brings with it some very odd syntactic results. Two wffs might exist but their conjunction not exist. A negation ~$p$ might exist but its negatee $p$ might not exist as an independently uttered token. Indeed a negation introduced by our abbreviatory convention above could exist though very many of its subformulae might not.

The obvious way to get round this is to appeal to some notion of possible existence of wffs and proof, to the possible construction of tokens of wffs and proofs. Some modal element is inevitable in neo-formalism anyway, as I have defined it, since truth is not tied to the EXISTENCE of a proof. Given that proofs are concrete, this would be hopelessly restrictive (even if one counts proof sketches as equivalent for these purposes to canonical proofs) if the proofs have to be deliberately constructed and grasped. Truth is tied rather to prov*ability*; we can think of this as the possibility of constructing the requisite proof structures or, better I think (see below), as the possibility of mathematicians coming to interpret structures which actually EXIST or WILL EXIST as proofs, with parts of the structure being equiform with existing atomic tokens, other elements equiform with the constructions which build more complex syntactic entities from simpler.

Now modality has played a crucial role in a number of anti-platonistic philosophies of mathematics, in particular those of a constructivistic flavour, for example the earlier work of Charles Chihara (1973) and Philip Kitcher (1984). It also features in modern forms of intuitionism inspired by Michael Dummett (1973/78, 1991*a*), for instance in the constructivist neo-logicism of Neil Tennant (1978, 1997*a*, 1997*b*), at least if one thinks of the intuitionist reading of the logical constants as inherently modal (cf. Weir

1986*c*). Less constructivistically, examples can be found in some early work of Hilary Putnam (1967*a*/1975), in Geoffrey Hellman's modal structuralism (1989), and, as we have seen, in Hartry Field's fictionalism. The importation of modal elements has also attracted some critical comments or warnings, including one from Field himself—he rejects the use of a specifically mathematical notion of possibility (Field 1989, pp. 38–9). Certainly, if saying that the construction of a (token of) a giant sentence, numeral, or proof is a 'mathematical possibility' is to say no more than that the abstract type exists, this gets us nowhere.

There are minimally unproblematic uses of possibility, however. For example, if I say that a hut could be constructed in the back garden then this, in many contexts, will express a clear truth (especially if there is no implication that it is I who will be doing the constructing). Most, if not all, of the philosophers mentioned in the previous paragraph depend on far from minimal uses of modality. Hellman, for example, presupposes that it is true, and known to be true, that the existence of infinite structures such as $\omega$ structures is possible.[21] Both the metaphysical and epistemological claims are far stronger than the neo-formalist claim that humans, as they actually are and with their actual limitations, could construct proofs of the same sort of size and complexity as those they actually have constructed. The appeal to 'in principle possibilities' or 'ideal beings' found in philosophers such as Kitcher and Tennant will be criticized in §§II.2 and II.3.

The notion that one could have built a hut in the garden, or written a proof of the irrationality of $\sqrt{2}$ on the board is minimally unproblematic, but of course not totally so. A modal realist will interpret this truth as consisting in the existence of a non-actual possible world in which a hut is constructed in my back garden (or a counterpart thereof). Our everyday modal knowledge, for the modal realist, depends on our knowledge of how things stand across a vast array of worlds which are not causally or spatio-temporally connected to us here on earth. And you thought platonism had epistemological problems?

So much the worse for modal realism, a naturalist should say, not so much the worse for ordinary uses of modality. There is, I think, widespread agreement that a non-modal realist reading of 'a hut could be built in the garden' is philosophically much less problematic than a platonistic reading of 'there exist infinitely many numbers (or abstract types)'. One traditional analysis of the quotidian possibility of the hut construction type is in terms of causal law plus background conditions. 'A hut could be built in the garden' is true just in case 'a hut is built in the garden' is consistent with the set of true natural laws (whatever they might be), perhaps augmented by an inventory of particular facts relating to the earth and its history including some fairly detailed descriptions of human society and its constructional abilities, huts, my garden,

---

[21] Here is a context in which I am using '$\omega$' not as the name of a symbol but as on active service naming a mathematical object, cf. Chapter 4, §III.2, footnote 35. (Since no such objects as the symbol type '$\omega$' nor the ordinal $\omega$ EXIST the last sentence is in formal, not representational mode.)

and so on.[22] Such analyses were common in the logical empiricist tradition and fit in well with that tradition's accounts of scientific law and explanation. The eclipse of this tradition has led to a corresponding decline in the standing of those analyses. However, for present purposes, it does not matter much what sort of analysis, if any, of quotidian possibility is given, so long as we take it to be objective enough to be naturalistically respectable and so long as it does not bring with it commitment to abstract objects. Certainly, outside highly theoretical physics, it is hard (even for the Quinean) to imagine doing science without quotidian modality. Is it unscientific to say that necessarily salt dissolves in water? On the other hand, a projectivist such as Blackburn is tempted by projectivist accounts of necessity. Suppose such a person is right? Would that not debar the neo-formalist from using modal notions in giving the metaphysical content of mathematical utterances?

The explanatory account in the M-theory of what it is for us to grasp mathematics is, indeed, supposed to delineate features of the world, not project internal attitudes. But according to neo-formalism, if I say that the velocity of light is $2.99792458 \times 10^8$ metres per second, that too says something about the world, even though it makes reference to an object, 299 million, 792 thousand, four hundred and fifty eight, which DOES NOT EXIST. It is, according to the account of the last chapter, a mixed mode assertion, neither fully representational nor fully formal, made-true by a combination of empirical and formal truths. Similarly it is possible to admit some sort of Humean, projective element into the metaphysical content of modal claims without holding it is wholly non-representational. It would be absurd, indeed, to say that 'necessarily salt dissolves in water' and 'had you boiled the water, it would have been sterile' and so forth are usually uttered in non-representational mode.

The essential (as it were) thing for the neo-formalist is that there is nothing mathematical in the metaphysical content of modal claims, at least not those needed in giving the metaphysical content of mathematical utterances. Sentences which give the metaphysical content of mathematics must not themselves entail the existence of mathematical or other abstract objects. I do not see this as an especially difficult condition to meet (for quotidian uses of modality). True, the traditional analysis might read commitment to abstract objects into the metaphysical content of modal statements by dint of its appeal to sentences and consistency among sentences. Thus, if the neo-formalist is to accept any such analysis, sentences must be construed as tokens or tipes and consistency construed in some more primitive fashion than model-theoretically or proof-theoretically. But I will take it that it is legitimate for the neo-formalist to say things like: 'this concrete structure could have been interpreted as a universal generalization wff token'.

A worry may still remain over the objects of these supposedly harmless constructional possibilities. Exactly what is it that is capable of construction, when one says it is possible to build a hut, or a concrete proof of a sentence token? Are we not committed

---

[22] But, if determinism is true, not so detailed as to decide the issue of whether a hut is built or not.

to 'mere' possibilia, abstract entities every bit as ontologically and epistemologically dubious as the platonist's numbers? We can avoid such shady entities, at least in the mathematical case, by another application of the idea of extending equiformity. The world contains plenty of highly complex structures, for example very complex molecular chains such as DNA molecules. In saying that—though there is no actual proof of S—a proof could be constructed, we need not worry that we are committing ourselves to the existence of a non-actual entity, not even a rearrangement of existing objects. Rather, we simply claim it is possible that we interpret elements of existing structures, long polymer chains of monomers say, as equiform with expression strings in wffs and proofs; certain types of molecular bond representing concatenation, for example. Technological advance has already pressed into service new structures which function, at least suitably probed by technological devices, as proofs: dimples in CD disks for example.

Now, at last, I can redeem the pledge of the Introduction and Chapter 3. A token of a sentence such as the Bolzano–Weierstrass Theorem (BW) is made-true, relative to system S (tokens of the axioms of analysis say, together with classical logic) iff

THERE EXISTS a structure $x$ such that $x$ is a concrete proof of the token of BW relative to basic rules R, where R are the principles of system S.

Similarly it is made-false if THERE EXISTS a concrete structure which is a concrete refutation, that is a proof of ~BW. The small capital 'THERE EXISTS', it will be remembered, signals that the claim is being uttered in a representational mode of assertion, and is itself true or false according as the physical world supplies the requisite structure. The existence of a concrete proof is to be interpreted in a minimally modal fashion. We may never actually deliberately construct and grasp one but the token will be true if there is a structure which, by extending the equiformity relation, we could grasp as a concrete proof. So, more fully, the clause should read something like:

THERE EXISTS a structure $x$ such that (i) $x$ is a concrete proof of the token of BW relative to basic rules R, where R are the principles of system S or (ii) $x$ would be such a concrete proof if those who employ the calculus were to extend the equiformity relation to include the elements of the structure as tokens of various tipes of the system, and were to understand a particular physical relation among items in the structure as concatenation.

These sentences setting out the metaphysical content of BW do not, it is to be emphasized, give the informational content. They are not synonymous with it in any intuitive sense of synonymy, nor in the sense of sharing literal or informational content. The metaphysical content specifying concrete proof tokens belongs to the Circumstance part of the SCW triad relating utterances to the world. As with so many utterances, it does not form part of the *Sinn* or sense, the informational content which is relatively transparent to speakers. Competent speakers may not be reflectively aware of the metaphysical content of BW, or if so, may not modulate their responses to BW embedded in other contexts, such as modal or indirect contexts, as they would to parallel embedding of the specification of metaphysical content; just as is the case with the metaphysical content of indexical utterances, or projective utterances. As in the latter case, there is ontological reduction. In the W(orld) part of the triad, there is nothing corresponding to the ontological contents of the informational content of the sentence, no infinite sequences, no limit points, and yet the sentence is true.

I claim that the overwhelming majority of utterances by competent mathematicians, sophisticated or just with basic abilities, will be made-true or made-false by the existence of concrete structures as described above. Indeed, when we are talking of competent mathematicians working to the best of their abilities and not at the limits of their competence, the vast bulk of their assertions will be made-true. Think of the lay person making some simple calculations in financial cases. Think of the assertions in the calculus textbook on your bookcase, of the theorems which are taught to students in psychology, economics, engineering, physics and mathematics classrooms in universities the world over. Think of the theorems stated in articles in mathematical journals, many of which contain realizations of the concrete proofs (or at least proof sketches) to back up the assertion.[23] Typically, the mathematician's assertions are closely tied to the EXISTENCE of concrete proofs and disproofs, and where the mathematician has not checked an already constructed structure, she believes that such concrete proofs could be constructed.

But problems remain. For one thing, in the Bolzano–Weierstrass example, we need the use of classical logic. But is the neo-formalist entitled to this logic? We noted that, given the homophonic relation between game calculus and contentful language, the mere fact that one could use classical rules in an uninterpreted calculus does not establish the legitimacy of classical logic in the contentful domain. The problem becomes more pressing when we consider the issue of incompleteness, left to one side at the end of Chapter 4.

Suppose, instead of using the example of the Bolzano–Weierstrass theorem I had considered the continuum-hypothesis (CH). If system S is first-order ZFC then THERE WILL BE neither concrete proof nor refutation, because the sentence is independent of the axioms; there is no proof nor refutation in the formal system. One response here is simply to abandon bivalence for the sentence in that framework. It is neither determinately true nor determinately false. But we saw in the case of the Gödel and Rosser sentences G and R that there will always be formally undecidable sentences which we intuitively think of as true. Moreover, even if a sentence is formally decidable (according to our FM level formal proof theory) what right do we have, in every case, to suppose that it is concretely provable or concretely refutable?

---

[23] At least think of those sentences claimed to be theorems in well-read articles in prestigious journals where more than just the author and the referee have read the article. There the chances of a purported proof being faulty are low, but of course not in general zero.

Certainly the range of sentences which are concretely provable can go far beyond the range of sentences for which concrete proofs actually have, or will be, deliberately written down or physically realized in some other sense. But how far can this extension go? And what about the sentences themselves? Can we think of the existence of a sentence as requiring merely that a physical structure with the internal complexity and structure required in order to mirror the syntactic structure of the sentence exists, even if it (a vast interstellar dust cloud say) never could feasibly get used as a sentence? Field raises the possibility of treating unwritten derivations as 'derivation-shaped regions of space' (1980, p. 46), though he does not find such a view in the least attractive. Goodman and Quine decline to assume that such regions of spacetime are infinite in number (1947, p. 106). Should the neo-formalist, however, go down this road?

## §1.6

A distinction which Neil Tennant makes is relevant here. Tennant talks of 'aspectual recognition' and of our competence in parsing sentences or grasping proofs as 'factoriz-able' (1997b, § 5.5, pp. 152 ff.) He imagines (crediting the idea to Jon Cogburn) speakers

> presented with a non-surveyable proof—(or disproof)—token: one that is too long for them actually to complete their check of it as a proof (or disproof). Nevertheless, there is still a *factorizable* way that they could exercise their recognitional capacities with respect to it, . . . The factorizable way is to direct their attention to various aspects of the token, and to ask them whether those aspects are locally in order. (ibid., p. 153)

We must, that is, have the competence to check any 'aspect' of the proof for correctness, even if we cannot check all aspects because we would be dead (or the universe would have suffered a heat death) long before any such complete check had finished.

I think he is right that there is no need to require more than aspectual checking. The idea, which resembles Descartes' distinction between intuition and deduction in the third section of the *Regulae*,[24] is an important one. Tennant's point goes further than the Cartesian one, though. Not only would it be far too restrictive to maintain that one only understands sentences and proofs which one can digest in one single glance, as it were. It is too restrictive to think that one must be always able to check, by a process which may take some time, an entire sentence or proof for correctness by appealing to one's memory that earlier sections or parts have been duly 'ticked off' as in accord with the syntactic rules.

The requirement, therefore, is that on some suitable understanding of 'aspect', it must be the case that *for any aspect* of the sentence or proof, it is possible for us to check whether it is syntactically or proof-theoretically correct. (What we do not require is the variant condition, where the universal quantifier is inside the scope of the modal operator: it is possible that we can check that *every aspect* is syntactically or proof-

---

[24] René Descartes (1628/1911); see Anthony Kenny (1968, pp. 175–6).

theoretically correct.) Consider, for example, our grasp of the syntax of a sentence, our ability to parse it and discern its grammatical structure. Suppose Rebecca speaks a standard propositional language with a simple context-free phrase-structure grammar and suppose that it is determinate for us, if not Rebecca, with respect to strings of length $\leq l$ whether they are well-formed or not. Suppose further that, for every sentential operator in expression strings of no more than that length, Rebecca is able to process, perhaps using some auxiliary devices, the strings and come up with diagrams such as:

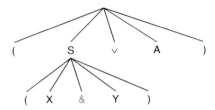

Here the operator which Rebecca is checking on is the ampersand. The letters are dummy letters, the expression strings which they stand for may well be enormous. Rebecca's checking procedure or device determines that the ampersand in question is the main connective of a substring S, with conjuncts X and Y, if, that is, X and Y are themselves well-formed; this has not been checked. S itself is a substring of a local section which, so long as S and the string which occurs in place A are well-formed, is a disjunction.

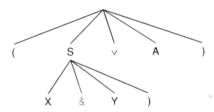

Alternatively Rebecca may discover that the local terrain around the particular occurrence of ampersand which has been focused on is as above. This gives her once again *conditional* assurance that the formula is ill-formed. If X is a wff (and not for example a wff prefixed by a left parenthesis) then the overall string is not a formula. There may even be more categorical evidence of ill-formedness. If Rebecca can verify that the local context for the ampersand is as below:

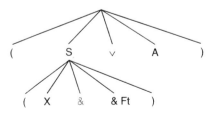

then Rebecca has also verified that the whole string is not a wff since an inductive proof shows that two ampersands never occur adjacently in a standard propositional language.[25] Though the evidence is stronger here, it is still of course fallible. Rebecca's checking routines will be fallible as will be the operations of any machine she uses. If, for example, sentence tokens are strings of DNA molecules then she might use something like a gene-splicing machine to enable her to determine local correctness. If the machine works well on small strings which Rebecca can independently check, it might be entirely reasonable to rely on it when applied to strings which are far too long to check in one 'cogitizing' Gestalt perception. The result can yield partial assurance that a string is grammatical even though it is so long that Rebecca could not even verify its correctness, as a wff or proof token, stage by stage over a period of time ('could not' here expressing the humdrum notion of causal possibility).

But though we can in this way extend the size of sentence tokens and proof tokens which can be classed as part of *our* language, there will still be finite upper limits on the size of tokens which we can be said to grasp and process, at least if 'can' is our relatively uncontentious, everyday notion of causal possibility. For one thing, there may be an upper limit on the size of the structures we have imagined ourselves utilizing as tokens. Perhaps the universe is finite in the large and small, a gigantic but finite matrix of atomic spacetime cells. Or, if tokens are taken to be massive physical objects or events, perhaps there is an upper limit on their size built into physical law, or at least on the parameters which govern our entire universe, beyond which one cannot go on pain of reversing field asymmetries and annihilating all matter. It would be uncomfortable for naturalists who wished to do justice to the idea that mathematics is a priori and not empirical to have to rely on the falsity of empirical claims such as those above concerning the fundamental geometry of the universe, or the value of basic physical parameters in order for their account of mathematics to get off the ground.

But even leaving these considerations aside and supposing that arbitrarily large structures (or sentence and derivation-shaped regions of spacetime) exist, beyond a certain vague limit we will reach structures which we cannot process and parse, even in the Tennantian 'factorizable' way. (I continue to read possibility as humdrum causal possibility.) Once the structure becomes big enough then it will cease to be possible for us to penetrate inside it to arbitrary 'depths' and single out arbitrary operators checking their local context for correctness. The local context, for one thing, may be enormous. An occurrence of '&', say, may have as immediate constituents gigantic substrings, so large that no machine which we could build (and assure ourselves of its reliability) could scan the structure to find a schematic truncated tree of the above type. So not only will it not be possible for us to check all aspects, but there will be some aspects we cannot check because we cannot 'get at them'. This is clear where the

---

[25] Such inductive proofs are available to the neo-formalist who takes the theorems generated by such truths to be true. We do not have here an illicit use of ontologically committed mathematics in the M theory. This point will be dealt with in more detail in Chapter 7, §I.

possibility in question is still a fairly unproblematic everyday notion. It can be wider than 'possible with current technology'. But suppose there really are giant structures with $10^{80}$ parts. It is not plausible to say that we flesh and blood humans could so manipulate the structure that we could extract the information about arbitrarily large substrings in a form which could presented to us for checking.

To get a sense of 'possibility' here in which we could do such a thing, in which it is possible for us to 'interrogate' substrings of any size in arbitrarily large structures, we need not only to relax very specific particular details about current conditions and technological developments for the human race, in our explication of the relevant notion of possibility. We would also need to excise quite general facts about the universe as a whole, perhaps drop various physical laws, and utilize a notion of possibility which equates to compatibility merely with logical law or perhaps logical law and some very general structural physical principles concerning the universe.

If a naturalist cannot appeal to such a notion of possibility, the conclusion which has to be drawn is that not only are there only a limited finite number of sentence utterances and concrete proofs in the actual corpus of human mathematical history past, present, and, presumably, future. There are only a limited finite number of wffs and proofs which *could* be produced, in any naturalistically acceptable notion of 'could'. It might seem as if there could be indefinitely many primitive symbol tokens and thus indefinitely many languages generated from among these. But there is presumably a finite limit to the number of perceptible tokens we can discriminate. Anyway, the more important point is that for a fixed finite set of primitive symbols there is a finite upper limit on the size of sentence and proof tokens we could manipulate and thus which can count as part of the language built on those symbols. So at any time, our language is finite. Moreover if, as seems reasonable, there are only finitely many semantic primitives which could be expressed by our syntactic primitives, then there can only be finitely many propositions overall which we could ever understand.

The conclusion the naturalistic philosopher is driven to, if this line of argument is sound, is that human languages, both in their syntax and their semantics, are finite. This conclusion is diametrically opposed to Chomsky's assessment of the matter. For him, human language, even if we consider its syntactic and phonological elements alone, is an infinite system of structures, a system resident in every normal human mind (cf. Chomsky (1980, pp. 220–2, 224, 240); the plurality of human languages, for Chomsky, is a fairly superficial matter of the differential fixing of linguistic parameters in different communities). Only a finite portion ever emerges in the capacities of humans to produce linguistic utterances, an even more meagre, and often corrupted and error-strewn, fragment emerging in actual output. But these are just the finite tips of an infinite linguistic iceberg in the mind.

Now whatever the instrumental merits of Chomskyan theory in explaining and predicting grammatical output, and our reflective intuitions on grammar, naturalists should not take seriously, under a realist interpretation, this talk of infinite structures and grasp of infinitely many sentences. Although the idea of the mind as infinite cannot be ruled out a priori—after all, even on a mind:brain identity theory this could be true if the brain is an analogue device—the whole idea is hopelessly implausible. There is no evidence in favour of it. The systematicity of language and, more especially its productivity, i.e. our ability to understand novel utterances, these two features have never manifested themselves in abilities to understand sentence tokens with $10^{900}$ or more significant parts, and never will. Everything we know about our brains, our biology, and our natural powers tells against it, just as these natural facts tell against us having direct, quasi-perceptual intuition of an infinity of abstract particulars.[26]

## §II.  The Spectre of Strict Finitism

*§II.1*

A naturalist approach to syntax and proof seems to have driven us towards very finitistic conclusions. This is unsurprising, surely. What else can one expect from a conception of proof as concrete tokens, manipulated and digested by finite humans? But may this not represent a *reductio ad absurdum* of naturalism in mathematics? For the spectre of 'strict finitism' makes a ghoulish appearance here.

I scare-quote 'strict finitism' because it is not entirely clear (as is the way with 'isms') what doctrine this is, not clear indeed if there is a single coherent doctrine which goes with the phrase. It has been associated with some interpretations by Kreisel of posthumously published work of Wittgenstein on mathematics (Kreisel 1959). The badge has also been claimed by Yessenin-Volpin (Yessenin-Volpin 1961). If the strict finitist claim is that there are only finitely many mathematical objects, natural numbers say, then this seems to be a mathematical claim. If so, I think we should adopt the blunt approach of saying it is not only false, but necessarily false. For Yessenin-Volpin, the idea seems to be to connect the notion of Dedekind infinity with that of the indefinite extendibility of series with vague final cut-off points, series with which we seem to be acquainted in everyday finite experience, such as the series of heart beats in one's childhood. But it is not clear that such vague indefiniteness ought to be seen as finite.[27]

---

[26] The Chomskyan might object that this whole argument rests on a crude reading of what is 'natural' or 'physical', categories which have changed as physics has changed: compare billiard ball atoms with gluons or quantum fields (cf. Chomsky 1980, pp. 5–6). I do not agree, however, that the category of the 'physical' is utterly open-ended or empty, nor that we can make no reasonable restrictions on what form a future physics might take. But the debate is too large to take up here. The fact, if fact it is, that attribution of an ability to grasp infinitely many distinct propositions, or infinitely many distinct proofs, is ruled out by our current scientific understanding of the way humans work is sufficient for us to rule out of current linguistic and philosophical theory the idea that human languages are infinite structures.

[27] Wright remarks that it is only from a non-strict finitist point of view that the strict finitist can be straightforwardly seen as stressing the finitude of human capacities, (1982/93, p. 107 fn. 2). Perhaps we need to make a leap of faith from orthodoxy onto a strict finitist standpoint in order to see it as coherent. I decline to make the leap!

The limitless series of transfinite alephs, for example, might also be thought of as having this vague and indefinite quality.

At any rate, my use of the term 'strict finitism' will be strictly negative, as a foil to certain positive doctrines, or as a challenge they have to meet.[28] (For a very full discussion of strict finitism, which deals also with many of the issues touched on in this section, see Wright 1982/93.) The term is used in something like this fashion by Michael Dummett to mount a challenge to the anti-realist position in metaphysics which he himself has sympathetically developed ('Wang's Paradox', Dummett 1975/78, pp. 248–68). Dummett's 'realist' defends the idea that we can explain how we understand determinately true or false propositions which, *for us*, are evidence-transcendent by appeal to the verifiability of these humanly unverifiable propositions for beings with god-like powers. The obvious riposte is to ask what possible relevance appeal to such beings could have in explaining *our* grasp of *our* language.[29] Tennant makes a similar point. Attacking those who would try to argue for the determinacy of questions undecidable by current methods by appeal to possible future extensions of those methods, he says:

the extensions are being invoked to justify the Gödelian realist's claim that our extensions with their *present* meanings, are bivalent *now*. But are not the *present* meanings of our sentences exhaustively determined by all the principles that *at present* govern them? (Tennant (1997*b*, p. 234), italics in original)

Thus the problem Dummett poses for the anti-realist is that of finding a stable position between that of his (straw man) realist and the strict finitist. For the strict finitist can ask what relevance to the explanation of *our* grasp of *our* languages are the imagined powers of beings who have verificatory abilities which, if not god-like, are far more powerful and extensive than our own?

Good question. Why is the answer not simply that there is indeed no relevance at all, that the strict finitist is right? What is so bad about strict finitism if it means accepting the conclusion of the last section? We grasp only finitely many propositions and proofs, with an upper limit on the complexity of the propositions and proofs we can grasp. It is unintelligible to suppose that there are any others, any propositions or proofs inherently ungraspable by humans. The platonist will say that we have missed out infinitely many more complex propositions and (in the case of mathematical language) infinitely many proofs and disproofs. But, by hypothesis, they will not be able to present the naturalist with any examples of these supposed ungraspable propositions which the naturalistic philosophy of mathematics cannot accommodate. Why not say to the platonist that we have no more reason to worry about accommo-

---

[28] For a very different finitistic approach to mathematics, strict in the sense of rigorous and sophisticated, see Lavine (1994) and the critical comments in Weir (1996).

[29] It is hard to think of any 'real' realist unwise enough to take the very unpromising line of defence suggested by Dummett.

dating these alleged entities than the physicist has to accommodate the notorious angels dancing on the head of pins in the legendary medieval debate?[30]

The reason is this. There are concrete, eminently graspable, tokens of mathematical sentences for which there could never be a concrete proof or disproof. Moreover among these 'concrete indeterminables' as I will call them, are tokens of sentences in mathematical sub-languages which are negation-complete and decidable in both the intuitive sense—there is an algorithm which determines their truth value—and the formal sense—the set of codes of theorems of the sublanguage is a recursive set. Indeed we can produce concrete proofs of the formal decidability. An example is $\Delta_0$ arithmetic, that is the fragment of the language of first-order Peano arithmetic (PA) in which all quantifiers are bounded, that is all universal quantifiers occur in contexts $\forall x(x < S^m 0 \to \ldots)$ and all existential quantifiers occur in contexts of the form $\exists x(x < S^n 0 \ \& \ \ldots)$. There are algorithms which transform each such sentence into an equivalent (in PA) conjunctive (or disjunctive) normal form, the atoms being atomic sentences of arithmetic. Since the latter are decidable so are the former (Mendelson 1979, pp. 130–1). A simple example of $\Delta_0$ claims are claims of primality, for we can see that the $\Delta_0$ formula

$$n > 1 \ \& \ {\sim}\exists x \exists y(x < n \ \& \ y < n \ \& \ x \times y = n)$$

expresses the claim that $n$ is prime. It says that no two smaller numbers multiply together to yield $n$ (one and zero being excluded by definition, avoiding complications and qualifications in many important theorems although complicating Goldbach's conjecture).

As Tennant puts it, there are sentences which

would admit only of verifications that were too long to be recognized as such. And this could happen even for sentences that themselves were relatively short and surveyable such as the claim that

$$\left(2^{2^{2^{2^{2^{2^2}}}}} + 1\right) \text{ is prime.}$$

(Tennant 1997$b$, p.152).

For another example consider the calculation of the Goodstein sequence. Even for numbers as small as 51, this takes an unfeasible number of steps (Potter 2004, pp. 212–15). For a third example, Boolos in 'A Curious Inference' (Boolos 1987/98) sets down a valid argument of first-order logic in only sixty or so symbols but then shows that we could never write down a derivation in a first-order system.

---

[30] Legendary and indeed, it would seem, NON-EXISTENT, the product of an, evidently very successful, late eighteenth-century anti-scholastic slur (there does seem to have been a mention, in a medieval mystical text, of angels on the point of a needle, but no debate). See Stephen Clark (1993, pp. 221–2) and George Mcdonald Ross (1985).

The number of symbols in any derivation of the conclusion from the premisses (in a fairly standard natural deduction system, that of Benson Mates) will include at least this many:

$$2^{\langle 64K \rangle} = 2^{2^{2^{2}}} \text{ i.e.} 2^{(2^{(2^{(\cdot^{(2^2)\ldots))}})})}$$

symbols. $2^{\langle 64K \rangle}$, in other words, is used as a shorthand abbreviation for an exponential stack of 64K, 65,536, '2's. This is a stupendous number much bigger than Tennant's number of one more than an exponential stack of six '2's. Boolos counsels us not to confuse $2^{\langle 64K \rangle}$ with the 'minuscule', by comparison, $2^{64K}$. (This pathetic tiddler cannot even muster 20,000 digits in its decimal expression.) The scope of the exponentiation operator in a stack such as $3^{3^3} = 3^{(3^3)} = 3^{27} = 7,625,597,484,987$, is different from that in $(3^3)^3 = 27^3 = 19,683$ and this scope difference is what makes for the awesome gulf between $2^{\langle 64K \rangle}$ and $2^{64K}$.

The number $2^{\langle 64K \rangle}$ utterly dwarfs not only Tennant's number but also 'Skewes' number' $e^{e^{e^{79}}}$—approximately $10^{10^{10^{34}}}$—which Boolos tells us has been called 'the largest number found in science' (Boolos 1987/98, p. 377)[31] not to mention the piddling figure of $10^{87}$ which has been given as an estimate of the number of elementary particles in the observable universe. To say that we could produce a derivation of the conclusion of Boolos's Curious Inference from its premisses is to appeal to a notion of possibility utterly removed from any naturalistic one, if indeed there is any coherent notion of possibility here at all.[32] Of course we could read ⌈it is possible that there is a derivation of C from X⌉ as elliptical for the mathematical claim that there exists the abstract structure which satisfies the conditions for being a proof of the abstract correlate of C from the correlates of X. But then saying that 'it is possible for us to produce a proof of the Curious Inference' would yield absolutely no explanation at all of how we grasp the proof, but merely assert that it exists.

It is true that alterations to the proof theory, the addition of new axioms or inference rules, a move to a higher-order logic, can drastically reduce the size of the shortest proof of a given theorem. This is the phenomenon of 'speedup' (Gödel 1936). For example, we could just add Boolos's curious inference as a basic inference step to our logic and make the move in one fell swoop. Since the conclusion is derivable from the premisses in first-order logic, adding the inference as a basic rule

---

[31] Perhaps an allusion to a comment of G. H. Hardy's to the effect that it was the largest number of any use in mathematics. This number, strictly the 'first Skewes number', was calculated by Samuel Skewes in 1933 for use in the theory of prime numbers in connection with Gauss's estimate of their frequency of occurrence but is now of largely historical interest.

[32] It is no use to say that it is 'logically possible' for us to produce a proof, where this means that the claim that we have done so cannot be reduced to absurdity using rules or axioms for the logical operators alone. One cannot go from [X does A] is logically possible to [X can do A] except, perhaps, in the case of omnipotent beings. Even the coherence of that case has been challenged, but since we are not omnipotent, the powers and capacities of such beings are of no relevance to the explanation of how beings like us have the capacity to grasp mathematical language and proofs.

does not alter the derivability relation so that there is no question, even from a neo-formalist point of view, of there being a change of subject. How do we know the inference is valid in first-order logic? Certainly not, we have seen, by producing a first-order derivation. We do so because a comprehensibly short demonstration of the conclusion from the premises is available if we expand the logic to second-order logic (Boolos 1987/98). If the conclusion was not derivable in first-order logic then by first-order completeness there is a counter-example model. But any counter-example model to a first-order argument immediately generates a second-order counter-example.

Similarly we can show, in set theory, that there is a finite (abstract) proof yielding a calculation of the Goodstein sequence for any input pair of numbers (though of course Goodstein's theorem, that the sequence always terminates in 0, is indeterminable in first-order arithmetic, as remarked in Chapter 3). So in some cases we can produce metatheoretic proofs in one system of the metamathematical claim that a given derivation exists in another system, and this can motivate us to add that derivation, reworked as an inference rule, to the rules of the second system thus enabling us to provide a concrete proof. None of this alters the fact that, however much we speed up the proof theory, or even extend it to generate new theorems (but in that case thereby changing the meaning of some terms, if the argument of Chapter 4, §II.3 is right), there will still be concrete indeterminables left over or new ones created in the new system. In the nature of the case, this fact is not susceptible of formal demonstration but the speed-up results make it overwhelmingly plausible. For instance, it follows from Gödel's results that for any number $k$ there are infinitely many sentences A which are theorems of both first- and second-order logic and are such that the shortest first-order proof of A is $k$ times the length of the shortest second-order proof; this phenomenon generalizes to higher-order logics.

Neo-formalism ties truth to proof, with the metaphysical content of mathematical utterances given in terms of concrete provability. Since there will always be concrete indeterminables, neo-formalism seems to entail the indeterminacy, the lack of determinate truth or falsity, of vast swathes of very elementary mathematics including readily graspable sentences of $\Delta_0$ such as large primality claims and many equations of the form $f((n_1, \ldots, n_i) = g(m_1, \ldots, m_j)$ where $f$ and $g$ are recursive functions and the $n_i$ and $m_j$ are standard numerals of the form $S^k 0$. Since the indeterminable is neither provable nor refutable, granted that truth and falsity are globally linked to proof and refutation, the sentence is indeterminate, is neither determinately true nor determinately false. But a philosophy of mathematics which is committed to the indeterminacy of such sentences is not going to sell well among jobbing mathematicians. And for good reason. Such a position is hopeless. If this is strict finitism and naturalism is driven to it, so much the worse for naturalism in the philosophy of mathematics.

## §II.2

Perhaps, then, we should rethink the claim that a naturalistic philosopher of mathematics should have no truck with notions of possibility beyond everyday notions of what is practically possible. This has been the response of some philosophers of mathematics who have appealed to a more powerful notion of 'in principle' possibility. A related notion is that of appeal to the capacities of an 'idealized' human being. In fact this seems to be essentially the same idea. Thus while it is not possible in an ordinary sense ('practical' or 'feasible' in Tennant's terminology, 1997*b*) for me to decide the truth value of a concrete indeterminable, e.g. a primality claim for a number 'so gargantuan that Eratosthenes' sieve, as a matter of physical law, could never reach it before the Big Crunch' (Tennant 1997*b*, pp. 145–6), nevertheless it is 'in principle possible' that I figure out whether, for example, $(2^{2^{2^{2^{2}}}} + 1)$ is prime or not. Or—and this seems to be the same basic idea—an idealized version of myself could do it. This move to in-principle possibility and ideal beings is very widespread among constructivistic philosophers of mathematics in the sense of philosophers with revisionist tendencies in logic, the intuitionists being a prime example. But it is not only to be found among them (and of course the idea of 'construction' is to be found very widely in mathematics and philosophy of mathematics).

For example, Philip Kitcher developed a philosophy of mathematics one of whose key ideas is that our grasp of mathematics is constituted by the collecting and correlating operations of an ideal being. Indeed these operations seem to be the subject matter of mathematics for Kitcher (1984, pp. 109, 115–17, 134, 146–7). Kit Fine, too, provides an intriguing and original technical foundation for mathematics in the form of 'procedural postulates' which are non-truth-valued sentences akin to instructions in a computer language (Fine 2005, for a critique see Weir 2006*a*). Truth, even for the simplest sentences of arithmetic such as $7 + 5 = 12$, is grounded in the infinitely iterated execution of the procedures which thereby generate structures such as that of the natural number system. To carry out these iterated executions, Fine enlists the help of a 'genie', who thus seems essential to the philosophical cogency of his position as a contribution to the epistemology and ontology of mathematics. I think we can assume this genie is an 'idealized being' and that Fine does not believe that genies exist in the same sense or way that he believes dogs do.[33] This appeal to idealization, then, is a very

---

[33] Many platonist philosophers of mathematics seem to concede that the epistemology of our grasp of large numbers and structures is a mystery to be met with a cheery wave of the hands. An exception is the platonistic structuralist Stewart Shapiro who makes two suggestions (1997, pp. 116–18) as to how to extend a pattern-recognition epistemology beyond small finite structures. Both his ideas, however, seem to me to beg the question if what we are trying to explain is what our grasp of mathematical concepts consists in and how we acquire them.

common move (see also Chihara 1990, p. 46). For short, I will call those who make the move, IPP idealists, 'IPP' standing for 'In Principle Possible'.[34]

Now in trying to understand the IPP claim that it is 'in principle possible' for me to find out the truth-value of concrete indeterminables, I find myself interpreting it in a non-homophonic fashion, along the lines of:

> It is not in the least possible at all but I really, really regret this and wish it was possible. For that infernal impossibility refutes my philosophy of mathematics.

Similarly, to say *s* is provable because a non-existent being can prove it—is this not just saying that it is not provable at all but in a way which hides this unpleasant fact from reflective self-consciousness? Is IPP idealism based not just on a mistake but massive self-delusion? Or am I being unfair? Well, it is difficult to extract a decent account of ideal beings from the constructivists. When faced with challenges to the notions of in-principle possibility and ideal beings, some IPP idealists re-route us to a call centre run by Ideal Beings Inc. where we are put on indefinitely extensible hold, (listening to Ideal Vivaldi's Mod-4 Seasons on a loop).

An honourable exception is Neil Tennant. He devotes an entire chapter (Chapter 5) of his *Taming of the True* (1997b) to trying to meet this challenge.[35] Tennant argues that the type of abilities a being would need to be able to work with $2^{\langle 64K\rangle}$-long derivations are essentially all of a piece, the 'same kind of thing', as the abilities we flesh-and-blood humans manifest when we work with actual concrete proofs of practically manageable size. He says, in connection with 'huge numbers' which might take longer than the life of the solar system to compute:

> no conceptual leap is involved when we try to conceive what kind of fact it would be that such a huge number were prime. It would be *the same sort of fact, essentially*, as the fact that 17 is prime. It is just that it would take much longer to establish it as a fact, that is all. (Tennant 1997b, p. 145; my italics)

Now 'same sort' is a notoriously tricky notion, witness the metaphysical debates surrounding the concept of natural kinds. There are lots of salient mathematical divisions relevant to the consideration of our mathematical capabilities. Inside the realm of the decidable, for example, there are divisions between P-decidable (polynomial time decidable) questions, NP (non-deterministic polynomial time) decidables (widely thought to be a larger class), and so on. Then there is the division between the decidable problems as a whole and the undecidable. There is the division between the finite and the infinite, at the level of models or structures as well as at the level of

---

[34] A similar, and similarly problematic, appeal to ideal mathematicians is made by Lucas and Penrose in their attempt to use results from recursive function theory to draw conclusions about the material basis, or otherwise, of the human mind. For a critique, see Shapiro (1998, 2003). See also Frege on infinite series construed as a potential infinity by his formalist opponent (or punchbag anyway) Thomae: 'Does the possibility [of unending expansion] exist? For an almighty God, yes; for a human being, no' (Frege 1903/1980, §125, p. 200 and the salutary remarks of §126).

[35] Tennant takes it as a desideratum of any explanation of 'ideal being' or 'in principle possible' that it does not validate the law of excluded middle for arithmetic (1997b, pp. 144–5). Hence his account cannot be used to give a non-question-begging defence of the intuitionistic critique of classical logic.

numbers, and, within infinite domains, between the countable and the uncountable, the accessible and the inaccessible, and so on. Do these divisions correspond to different 'sorts of facts' or not?

Rather than delve further into this rather nebulous question it is perhaps more important to ask what sense of 'would' Tennant is employing when he says it would take much longer to establish facts which require, for example, $2^{\langle 64K \rangle}$ many steps than it takes us to make calculations in real life. After all, it may well not so much take longer to do as be causally impossible in the sense that it is incompatible with causal law that a temporal sequence that long, or a physical structure the length of the proof itself, exists. This seems an epistemic possibility for reasons scouted at the end of the last section. Perhaps time is grainy, finite, and discrete, with fewer 'chronons', atoms of time, than the number of steps which would be required in the shortest proof. Perhaps for a structure of elementary particles to reach the same size as the number of symbols in the proof it would have to exceed upper bounds imposed by the geometry of the universe or the amount of mass/energy it could contain. Even if this is not the case, the existence of structures as large as the proofs in question may well be incompatible with true physical law in combination with some very basic non-nomic truths about the actual universe we live in, about its temporal length, the number of elementary particles it contains, and so on.[36] As remarked, it does not sit well with a conception of mathematics as a priori or necessary to rest the coherence of the idea that we can grasp mathematics on the physical possibility, in the wide sense above, of the existence of arbitrarily large finite structures.

Moreover, even if there are giant structures which could serve as sentences or proofs appropriately interpreted by some being or other, (infinite beings in a wider universe of which ours is a mere fragment, perhaps), still we can press the question: What relevance are they to the explanation of *our* grasp of mathematics? As we have seen when discussing factorizability, that a $2^{\langle 64K \rangle}$-long structure exists does not show that a human[37] has the power to 'parse' it, interact with it in such a way as to discern an arbitrary node in its structure, carry out phrase-structure tree analyses of arbitrarily deeply embedded subformulae, for example. What would it mean for a human to have such a non-natural power?

---

[36] Thanks to Crispin Wright for emphasizing to me the potential importance of this distinction between compatibility with general law, and (roughly) law plus boundary conditions.

[37] Including humans aided by machines. I grant that computer technology increases the range and size of structures which we can reliably check for grammatical correctness, proofhood, and so on. I take it that we can rely on machines when we know the general principles according to which they work, have written at least the outline sketch of the software or verification programs for the software, and so on. But such advances in technology will always increase the range of wffs and proofs we can check by a finite bounded amount, leaving, to put it platonistically, an infinity of wffs and proofs untouched. To think we might arrive at machines whose pronouncements can furnish us with knowledge of the provability or otherwise of arbitrary wffs (even among those we can grasp) is to substitute a superstitious faith in oracles for a scientific appraisal of the potentialities of human technology.

Tennant, in support of his notion that it is in principle possible for humans to answer any formally decidable question, appeals to various fantastic scenarios in which we are invited to

conceive of there being no limit to the degree of miniaturization that could be effected (Tennant 1997b, p. 146)

or imagine a

superendowed human subject with much more neuronal circuitry in his head. (ibid.)

If we are to conceive of miniaturized humans with enough neurons and with enough time, via perhaps a 'simple linear compression of the time-line' (ibid.), to work out questions which take a stack of $2^{\langle 64K \rangle}$-many $2^{\langle 64K \rangle}$s to answer, we are conceiving of possibilities which amount to little more than logical possibilities and, as remarked (footnote 32) this is useless in accounting for the capacities and powers of non-omnipotent beings. As Crispin Wright puts it (1982/93, p. 124):[38]

If it really is to be *we*, creatures of bone and blood, of whom it is to make sense to hypothesize arbitrarily large, though finite, increases in capacity, the hypothesis simultaneously has to be of radical alterations in our present conception of physical and biochemical law.... Is it evident, then, that we really do understand, quite independently of prevailing physical theory, what it would be to undergo such increases in capacity?

The counterfactuals appealed to here—'If I had $2^{\langle 64K \rangle}$ neurons then I could calculate whether or not $\left(2^{2^{2^{2^{2^{2}}}}} + 1\right)$ is prime'—are almost certainly empty (and if not, there is no reason to believe them true rather than false). Even if the antecedent is compatible with physical law, it is almost certainly incompatible with the non-nomic facts about humans and their history in terms of which such counterfactuals make non-trivial sense. To use (but here I hold my nose) the framework of possible worlds, by the time one gets 'out' to the set of worlds in which the antecedent is true and yet in which actual causal law obtains, there is no reason to suppose the consequent is true in every or even most such worlds. So many basic facts about our world fail to obtain in these worlds that almost anything not incompatible with causal law itself could ensue. These counterfactuals are comparable with that favourite of the Glaswegian street-philosopher: 'if your grannie had four wheels, she'd be a double-decker bus'.

We could just as sensibly say that had I $2^{\langle 64K \rangle}$ neurons I could correctly and instantly answer any mathematical conjecture put to me, or annihilate every galaxy outside our own with a click of my fingers. What relevance to our actual capacities as competent understanders and users of mathematical language do the 'capacities' of these ideal beings—characters out of superhero comics—have? I cited earlier Tennant's argument against Gödelian realists' citing future principles of verification to ground present meanings:

---

[38] See also Kripke (1982, p. 27).

the extensions are being invoked to justify the Gödelian realist's claim that our extensions with their *present* meanings, are bivalent *now*. But are not the *present* meanings of our sentences exhaustively determined by all the principles that *at present* govern them? (Tennant 1997*b*, p. 234)

Indeed, and the same point applies against citing superheroes' verificatory abilities to underwrite human meanings.

In particular, how can someone who is trying to give a *naturalistic* account of mathematics appeal to fantastic figures with magical powers, in explaining our grasp of mathematics? It as if a biologist were to try to explain the development of life on earth by appeal to interventions by undetectable aliens from the planet Zorg who intercede in ways unknown and perhaps unknowable to us. Alas, there are some biologists who make similar appeals, the proponents of 'intelligent design', but the overwhelming majority of scientists eschew recourse to any such conjectures in scientific investigation. I suggest that 'in principle possibility' and 'ideal beings' should be similarly excised from naturalistic accounts of our grasp of mathematics.

## §II.3

It may be said in reply that the appeal to 'in principle possible' powers is not a resort to magic and a regression to pre-scientific thinking but rather exemplifies a feature central to all science: idealization. The IPP idealists acknowledge that the ideal beings they appeal to do not exist (Kitcher 1984, pp. 110, 134). But many reject the idea that a false hypothesis (here the existence of superhumans) can have no explanatory power, most notably perhaps Nancy Cartwright (1983).[39] What physicists call 'phenomenological laws', relatively detailed descriptive regularities applicable only to very specific domains, can be true, or true to a high approximation; but, she claims, they have no explanatory value. The fundamental laws of classic theories, the equations of Newtonian dynamics, Maxwell's electromagnetic theory, general relativity theory, and so on, *are* explanatory but are also false, it is claimed. So might it not be the case that the false assumption of the existence of ideal beings with supernatural powers can explain how *we* have the capacity to understand mathematical sentences and proofs longer than the number of elementary particles in the actual observed universe?

There is, however, an enormous difference between appealing, on the one hand, to beings with supernatural powers to explain an aspect of human psychology, namely our grasp of mathematics, and, on the other, idealization as it occurs in science. One of the simplest of the many ways idealization occurs in science is the 'frictionless plane' case discussed in Chapter 5, §II*. We have some experimental data, and some equations. We can solve the equations, or solve them more easily, if we set some parameters in the equations to values we know to be false. When we do so we can get results which approximate satisfactorily to the data we have collected for a number of

---

[39] See also Cartwright (1999) and Laymon (1985).

cases and we might then feel confident in extrapolating into the future on the basis of the false parameters, subject to some approximation bounds. How exactly we should interpret these equations is a matter of controversy. We can interpret them in a purely instrumentalistic fashion. The procedure enables us, perhaps, to predict to an acceptable degree of approximation future data values but nonetheless, it may be said, the equations should not be thought of as true. Or one might hold that the mathematical structures which render the equations true, given the false values of parameters, are in some sense close to, though not isomorphic with, real physical structures which give rise to the experimentally detected data.[40] This might be the case in an 'injective idealization' of the sort mentioned in the last chapter where a gross but 'messy' structure is represented abstractly by a much more fine-grained but mathematically tractable one.

However, consider the supernaturalist account given by Tennant of how human languages contain infinitely many sentences with more expressions than neutrinos in the observed universe, or of how there are formally decidable sentences provable only by dint of proofs with a similar number of steps. Such an account is nothing like an idealization in the above sense. What is the equivalent of the data to be accommodated? The actual history of mathematical utterances? What are the equations which the supernaturalist brings to bear to explain or predict those utterances? What equivalent is there to the idea of setting parameters to false but convenient values? There are no such equivalences. No philosopher of mathematics is in the business of trying to predict or understand why particular utterances were or will be made. Nobody says: if we set the number of neurons in the human brain to $\aleph_0$ and plug that into this or that system of equations we will get a reasonable retrodiction, relative to boundary conditions, of why these utterances were made, or prediction that these proofs will appear in the future.

Perhaps this absurd comparison arises because I have looked at schematic accounts of idealization in the physical sciences. Idealization also occurs in economics and the subject matter of economics: the complex structure of patterns of human economic activity and its products bears an interesting resemblance to the human manifestation of mathematics as crystallized in records of proofs and results. In both cases we have complex products of human cooperative activity which transcend, and are autonomous of, the deliberate designs and intentions of the individual producers. One type of idealization in economics, however, seems ominously similar in general structure to the examples of idealization in physics which have proved fruitless in illuminating mathematical ontology and epistemology. Introductory textbooks contain simple examples. Take, for example, the Cobb–Douglas equations, relating output $Q$, labour $L$ and capital $K$:

---

[40] Cartwright, as noted, demurs, where the equations are part of a fundamental theory. See Cartwright (1983, Introduction and Essay Six).

$$Q = kL^{\alpha}K^{\beta}$$

for constant $k$, $\alpha$, $\beta$. Marginal productivity theory, under assumptions of perfect competition and profit maximization, tells us that factors are hired until marginal products, $\frac{\partial Q}{\partial L}$ for labour and $\frac{\partial Q}{\partial K}$ for capital, equal their costs, wages $w$ and rent $r$ respectively. Aggregate returns to factors are

$$W = \frac{\partial Q}{\partial L}L \text{ and } R = \frac{\partial Q}{\partial K}K$$

and differentiating we get

$$\frac{\partial Q}{\partial L} = \alpha k L^{\alpha-1}K^{\beta} = \alpha\frac{Q}{L} \text{ and likewise } \frac{\partial Q}{\partial K} = \beta\frac{Q}{K}$$

so that the ratio of aggregate wages to rent is $\frac{\alpha}{\beta}$, a constant.

We can see in this textbook example how particular applications of mathematics in economics will often be more controversial than in physics. As well as attempting to estimate how good an approximation one should expect results to be in the real world, where the idealized assumptions fail to hold,[41] economics brings with it political implications and thereby accusations that the idealized assumptions mask ideological biases designed, for example, to justify preservation of traditional divisions of wealth and resources between workers and capitalists. But that aside, if we had some empirical data which suggested that the Cobb–Douglas functions were roughly right and that the share of labour and capital remains fixed regardless of the quantities of labour and capital employed (as has been claimed)[42] and furthermore if the labour and capital markets are thought to be fairly competitive then one might use the above idealized mathematical models to explain the data and to extrapolate the data into the future. There seems nothing qualitatively different from the physical case: application of mathematical equations, true of simplified models, to empirical data to predict future data and perhaps explain (if one thinks real structures crudely match the mathematical structures underlying the equations) the given data. Supernaturalist accounts of idealized parsing of giant sentences and provability of sentences which have no concrete proofs bear no relation at all to such idealizations.

This may be to look at the wrong aspects of the economic modelling. I have focussed on the use of mathematics in some forms of idealization but, though the case we are interested in involves mathematics (or our grasp of mathematics) in the explanandum, the supernaturalists do not employ mathematical models in their

---

[41] Even in the physical case, this approximation procedure often cannot be reduced to the pure mathematics of discarding negligible terms or, more complexly, subsumed under mathematical approximation theory; see Cartwright (1983, pp. 114–15).

[42] Here, of course, there is the implicit assumption that one can quantify in a homogeneous fashion 'labour' and 'capital' according to single scales, enormously controversial assumptions called into question by the literature on joint products and the like.

explanans. A better point of comparison, then, is the *ideal economic agent*, with perfect information, transitive preference relations, and (but here mathematics does re-enter!) continuous, everywhere differentiable, utility functions. A related ideal agent even more closely analogous to our idealized mathematician is the idealized believer/chooser of Bayesian decision theory, armed not only with a utility or preference function but also a belief function conforming to the Kolmogorov axioms. This figure is not only an idealized chooser but also an idealized believer who assigns the same degree of belief to any two logically equivalent first-order propositions even though there is no general decision procedure for logical equivalence in first-order predicate calculus.

This last case, however, is far too close to our problematic case of the idealized mathematician, raising essentially the same problems. But do the ideal agents of economic theory shed illuminating light? The economic theorist who employs such models to explain, for example, my shopping behaviour with respect to choosing bottles of Old Speckled Hen beer not only makes various 'rationality' assumptions such as transitivity of preference but also embodies palpably false assumptions in ascribing to me a utility function. That is, she not only assumes that if I prefer a 750ml bottle of Old Speckled Hen to a 500ml one and prefer the latter to a bar of chocolate (as if I wouldn't), I will prefer the larger bottle to the chocolate. She also assumes that there are continuum-many options for me to bear preference relations to and that it is possible for the structure of my preference relations to have the structure of the continuum too. That is, I can choose between 750ml, 749.9ml, 749.99ml bottles and so on through all real numbered sizes of bottle. It is also assumed to be possible for me to have preferences of different ordinal grades for each of the continuum-many variants in my shopping basket. But no economic theorist thinks that there really are these continuum-many options in reality, nor that I as an agent have this finely differentiated a preference structure.

Now supernaturalists in philosophy of mathematics such as Kitcher do not believe that *we* can, in any ordinary sense of 'can', produce proofs with more steps than elementary particles in the observed universe just as the economic theorist does not believe in continuum-many different sized bottles of beer. Is the idealized mathematician, then, to be compared to the economists' ideal agents? No. In holding that *there are* sentences of $\Delta_0$ arithmetic which could not be proved or disproved in less than $10^{87}$ steps but which *are actually* provable or else actually refutable, IPP idealists owe us an explanation of what this actual but extraordinary sense of 'provable' is. Merely to appeal to the analogy with the ideal economic agent does not give us an answer. From a neo-formalist point of view, the mere claim, in non-representational mode, that the sentences *are* provable or refutable is simply a reiteration of a mathematical fact. We need to know in what sense THERE ARE proofs or refutations. If the IPP idealist rejects the distinction among modes of assertion in favour of a unitary approach, then the question simply is: how can it be that there are these proofs? In what sense are they proofs unless we can grasp them? And in what sense can we grasp proofs of this length, supposing they exist?

Idealization as in the economic model provides no basis for a supernaturalist answer in philosophy of mathematics. The economic theorist takes mathematics for granted and applies it to build mathematical models of economic behaviour. For vividness and pedagogic effect some of the items in the mathematical models are designated 'ideal agents' or 'baskets of commodities' but it is not supposed they really are agents or commodities. They are mathematical entities. The theorist then attempts to draw conclusions about real agents and commodities in the real world—predictions of future data perhaps, or maybe conclusions about the existence of certain types of causally relevant structures. But it would be utter superstition, albeit a delightful one, to hold that inference to the best explanation from the fruitful application of the mathematical models of classical pure economic theory (granting for the sake of argument that they can be fruitfully applied) leads us to acknowledge the existence of continuum-many different-sized transcendental bottles of beer and a transcendental self which can discriminate in its preferences between them all. To be sure, economic theorists who are platonists in mathematics will hold that the mathematical structures are real. However, even they will undoubtedly hold that the ideal agents and ideal baskets of products are not real, being mere figures of speech.[43]

For heavy-duty platonism is at least as unappealing in economics as in physics. It is not numbers and functions which cause more or fewer people to be out of work, but decisions and actions by large numbers of people (or perhaps more holistic properties of fusions or aggregates of people, if methodological individualism is false). So in the economic case we have *three* levels: on top, the purely figurative level of the 'ideal agents', then the mathematical models, and finally the base, the real, causally active properties and relations in the social world. Moreover, our theories of the bottom two levels are supposed to explain 'data'. This term can be taken at two levels, firstly to refer to economic statistics at the second level, and secondly to refer to the particular facts[44] which these statistics attempt to represent, facts grounded in, or constituted by, actual events of buying and selling things at the base. A realist in economics will hold that the structure of an optimally good mathematical model is approximately isomorphic, in some coherent sense, to the causally active pattern of relations in the social world and that no other model, at least none that is tractable enough to be of any use to us, approximates any better to it.

If the IPP idealist's appeal to ideal mathematicians is to conform to this scientific pattern then we should see the same tripartite structure of figurative superstructure, mathematical modelling in the middle, and non-mathematical base. The ideal mathematician calculating primality for $2^{\langle 64K \rangle} + 1$ using Eratosthenes' sieve will be conceded to be a mere figure of speech and give way to something mathematical: the sieve method of dividing the numbers up to the largest integer $\leq (2^{\langle 64K \rangle} + 1)^{\frac{1}{2}}$ by 2, 3, 5 . . . as

---

[43] Yablo (1998 and 2005) would assimilate the two cases, wrongly I claimed in Chapter 3, §II.5.

[44] Or particular properties and relations among particular objects, on a non-factualist metaphysics.

an abstract algorithm, a computer program say. But it is not (unless one is a crazed Pythagorean!) mathematical structures which understand other mathematical structures; it is we who do so. So at the base level, the IPP idealist must make it plausible that the structures of the mathematical model, say an abstract specification of a theorem-proving program, are the best approximating match to the real structures at work in human minds when engaged in mathematical thought.

But this is preposterous. It would be like saying that the theory that there are $\aleph_0$ neurons in each of our brains is a good approximation to the real facts. We can easily state a better approximation, namely that there are around $10^{11}$. Similarly the theory that there are $\aleph_0$ sentences in our language of mathematics, $\aleph_0$ proofs in our logical system, and $\aleph_0$ refutations is not a good approximation to the real psychological structures which underlie our parsing of sentences and checking of proofs. That there are fewer than $10^{87}$ sentences, proofs, and disproofs is a much better approximation.

Let us grant, in the spirit of naturalized epistemology, that arbitrarily large structures exist. The explananda include such things as: how can some of these structures be sentences or proofs in *our* mathematics; how could it be that a concretely graspable but concretely undecidable sentence of $\Delta_0$ arithmetic is either provable or refutable in *our* language and proof system? The metaphor of the ideal mathematician does not explain any of these mathematical phenomena, just as the continuum-many beer bottles do not explain economic behaviour. Mere mention of abstract algorithms does not help either, any more than Molière's infamous dormitive power helps explain the sleep-inducing properties of opium. For it is our very ability to grasp and represent items (such as these algorithms) from a supposedly abstract world which is at issue. Ultimately, explanation could only lie in the neural structures of the brain and the causal powers and abilities these embody just as the explanation for changes in employment can only lie in the enormous, but finite, pattern of actual economic interactions by flesh-and-blood humans. But the neural structures of human brains do not endow humans with the ability to carry out Eratosthenes' sieve method up to such numbers as $2^{\langle 64\mathrm{K}\rangle}+1$. Nor are there any mathematical 'data', real events, or objects (what could these be: particular mathematical utterances or presentations of proofs?) represented mathematically in statistics and which are to be predicted or explained in the way that economic data encapsulating real events are supposed to be explained by economic theory.

The IPP idealist model of idealization, therefore, does not correspond at all to the way idealization occurs in the sciences. There is no hierarchy of figurative language cashed out in terms of mathematical models presumed, with some plausibility, to model real structures in the physical or social world. The idealist, rather, turns the first two upside down and drops the third element, the fundamentally explanatory one, out entirely. With respect to the top two levels, instead of taking mathematics for granted as the economic theorist does and treating the ideal agent as a fictional *façon de parler*, the supernaturalist is trying to explicate our grasp of abstract mathematics on the basis of ideal mathematical agents. Thus the epithet 'supernaturalist' is justified for such idealism: a pantheon of magical quasi-deities plays the role which real physical and social entities and forces play in real science. Naturalists should have no truck with such supernaturalism. IPP idealism is not an option for a naturalistic account of the epistemology of mathematics.

# 7

# Idealization Naturalized

## §I. Idealization

### §I.1

Chapter 4, §III left unresolved the problem of incompleteness. If truth is grounded in proof then surely we cannot affirm bivalence for the sentences undecided by incomplete theories such as standard arithmetic, ZFC, and so forth. Yet this is highly counter-intuitive, particularly in the case of arithmetic where, for at least some of the undecidables, we seem to have strong reason to believe not only that they have a truth-value but also that we know what it is. The considerations of the last chapter, however, leave us in even worse shape. Truth is grounded in *concrete* proof for the neo-formalist. This seems to mean that indeterminacy of truth-value strikes much deeper than just at those utterances which can be shown to be deductively independent of (for example) one's favoured arithmetical axioms. It looks as if the neo-formalist, indeed any naturalist in mathematics, must bite the bullet and become a strict finitist.

If that is too much to stomach, should the naturalist not then accept that mathematics is naturalistically inexplicable, by current lights anyway, a glaring anomaly right at the heart of naturalism? Or is there a genuinely naturalistic way to use idealization in order to avoid strict finitistic indeterminacy permeating down into $\Delta_0$ arithmetic? How can there be, if genuine idealization in science takes mathematics for granted, takes models as real, albeit abstract, *mathematical* entities and the anthropomorphized ideal agents and powers as mere *façons de parler*?

This problem of escaping the clutches of the strict finitist by appeal to idealizations is a very difficult one for a fictionalist who denies that mathematics is true. There are no functions from concrete tokens into mathematical structures, formal languages, and so forth, according to the fictionalist. Moreover, it is hard to see how the positing of mathematical structures in idealizing our syntactic and proof-checking abilities can have any of the virtues other than truth which are alluded to by Field. It does not, for example, shorten inference from concrete physical theory to concrete physical prediction. However, the neo-formalist is committed to the truth of the theorems of mathematics (though, as we have seen, precluded from appealing to a mathematical ontology in the M-theory of mathematics) and can, I argued, account for the truth of theorems of applied mathematics; hence neo-formalism does not suffer from this problem.

Before considering naturalistically acceptable ways to idealize mathematical language and reasoning, consider first of all the related case of the investigation of the grammar of real languages. Psychologists or neurologists might be interested in this from the perspective of studying aphasias. To do this they will look at the actual corpus of concrete utterances made by a subject or group of subjects. They will look, for example, to differences in linguistic output before and after a subject has suffered some brain trauma in order to figure out which areas of the brain are responsible for which aspects of language use. More recently, and less tragically, they will use brain imaging techniques to delve more deeply into the neurology of language production, again paying close attention to actual performance.

The grammarian of a particular natural language or sublanguage, however, has much less interest in the actual recorded details of speakers' output than the neurologist. Of course she must have some interest in it, if her study is to be of English rather than Finnish (how detailed an interest being a matter of some contention between Chomskyans and more corpus-oriented linguists). But if we consider, as in the last chapter, a grammar for a fairly simple, readily formalizable sub-language such as the language of decimal arithmetic, what the grammarian will do[1] is assemble a lexicon then set down rules for constructing atomic sentences and finally specify recursive rules for generating more complex sentences from simpler. If the grammarian were to approach her task in a formal and rigorous fashion, she might inductively specify the set of wffs of the language as the intersection of a set of inductive sets, these being those supersets of the set of atoms which are closed under the sentence-forming operations. She would employ some applied set theory, in other words.

What makes the exercise one in applied rather than pure mathematics is that the formal structure must mirror the structure of actual practice, in particular the language community's practice of emitting token utterances of atoms or in uttering complex strings built up from already mastered parts. But 'mirror' here does not mean that the structures are isomorphic. As noted in the last chapter, §I.3, the grammarian is not in the least perturbed by the fact that only a tiny fragment of the formal structure is, or indeed could be, found in the utterances of the community, expressions strings less than some quite low, finite bound. (Or, if the bound is quite high, a fragment which is very gappy—for many lengths under the bound, only some, or none at all, of the strings of a given length occurring.) Moreover if someone in the community under investigation utters strings of the form

$$A \lor B \ \& \ C$$

or

$$(A \lor (B \ \& \ C)$$

---

[1] At least the grammarian of 'surface structure'.

the grammarian will not necessarily scrap her rules for forming disjunctions and conjunctions, rules such as:

If $\varphi$ and $\psi$ are sentences, so is $(\varphi \vee \psi)$ and $(\varphi \ \& \ \psi)$.

She may well conclude, however, that the subject is either not a speaker of the language in question or has made a mistake.[2]

In grammar, in other words, there is an important normative aspect or at least, to engage in some nested normativity, there ought to be a normative element, even if current fashion is to eschew prescription for description. There is, that is to say, a tendency for some to think of grammatical norms as merely statistical; that locutions which are accepted by most are thereby correct. This is a mistake, at least insofar as there is a practice of deference to authorities among the language users. Non-prescriptive studies are the domain of the psychologist and neurologist but to prescribe that there should be no prescriptive grammar (in the non-statistical sense), to insist that the grammarian should not attempt to mould or constrain the language she is studying, is to confuse the grammarian's role with that of psychologist and neurologist.

## §1.2

What exactly is the grammarian's role then, if it is neither to engage in pure mathematics nor in purely empirical psychology but rather some sort of mixture, including in the mix some normative elements? We can see the grammarian as, at least in part, engaged in a type of injective idealization of the sort outlined in Chapter 5, §II*. The grammarian could use, for example, set theory with urelements to demonstrate the existence of a mapping $h$ from tipes whose tokens occur among the actual output of speakers of the concrete language (call this CL) into (but clearly not onto) a set-theoretic structure of the kind familiar from formal syntax, a formal language FL. For a concrete language CL used to express a rather formalized presentation of decimal arithmetic the mapping $h_0$ from tipes of atomic tokens onto numbers might go like this:

| | | | | | |
|---|---|---|---|---|---|
| "0" | $\Rightarrow$ | 0 | "=" | $\Rightarrow$ | 14 |
| "1" | $\Rightarrow$ | 1 | "$\sim$" | $\Rightarrow$ | 15 |
| ... | $\Rightarrow$ | ... | "$\vee$" | $\Rightarrow$ | 16 |
| "9" | $\Rightarrow$ | 9 | "&" | $\Rightarrow$ | 17 |
| "(" | $\Rightarrow$ | 10 | "$\forall$" | $\Rightarrow$ | 18 |
| ")" | $\Rightarrow$ | 11 | "$\exists$" | $\Rightarrow$ | 19 |
| "+" | $\Rightarrow$ | 12 | "$x$" | $\Rightarrow$ | 20 |
| "$\times$" | $\Rightarrow$ | 13 | "/" | $\Rightarrow$ | 21. |

---

[2] Assuming, in the first case, that brackets are used to express scope and that there are no conventions for scope binding precedence manifest in linguistic practice.

Here "o" is the tipe of the token displayed inside the quotation marks. On the mereological reading of 'tipe', this is the fusion of all tokens equiform with the symbol inside the marks; on the representative reading, it is a particular token in a particular printing of the page. In a set theory with urelements such as ZFCU[3] we can thus form the set $S_0$ of all atomic tipes.

The neo-formalist, of course, denies that the mapping $h_0$ EXISTS. However, it is a truth of applied mathematics that it exists. What makes-true this claim are firstly the axioms and rules of ZFCU together with the background logic (the axioms including bridge principles); these give the non-representational ingredient of the metaphysical content of the existence claim. The second source of truth for the existence claim is provided by the representational empirical truths, such as that the tipe "o" EXISTS.

I note, in passing, that there is no need for the mathematical analogue of the tipe to be a finite mathematical object, not unless one has some general mathematical objection (as, for example, the intuitionists have) to the existence of infinitary mathematical objects. If one has no such objection, as of course neo-formalism does not (unless infinitary mathematics is inconsistent) then one can just as readily map the tokens to transfinite ordinals or to infinite sequences:

$$h_0("0") = <0, 0, \ldots >, h_0("1") = <1, 1, \ldots >,$$

and so on. In the case of our standard formalization of first-order decimal arithmetic, of course, there is no necessity that a formal system which the range of the idealization map be infinitary.

Now for each EST, I assume that it is a determinate matter how many atomic tokens there are in that concatenation of tokens.[4] (More than one token equiform with a given token can occur in an EST of course.) This number gives us the length of the EST. Though we cannot appeal to numbers in the M-theory representational account of language grasp and informational and metaphysical content, we can in injective idealization, an aspect of applied mathematics.

Thus for each natural number $n$ we can define (again by the comprehension principle, the axiom of separation, in ZFCU) the set $T_n$ of all tipes of tokens of length $n$ (though for most $i$, $T_i$ will be the empty set). For each tipe $s$ in $T_n$, define $h_n(s)$ to be the $n$-ary sequence $\langle h_0(s_1), h_0(s_2) \ldots h_0(s_n) \rangle$ where $s_i$ is the tipe of the $i$th token, in temporal order, of any EST in $s$.[5] We define our injective idealization $h$ as the union of all the $h_i$, $i \in \omega$. This is a function since the ranges of any non-empty $h_i$, $h_j$, $i \neq j$ are

---

[3] Though this is much more powerful than we need here. ZU would be sufficient so long as we have a large enough set of urelements; the set of all physical objects in our galaxy would certainly do the trick.

[4] Since I reject epistemicism (for which see Williamson 1994) this is a false assumption. But I do not think it leads us too far astray. It is a legitimate simplification of the type which occurs often in science. One ignores certain elements which, though undoubtedly present, generate great, perhaps insuperable, complexities in any attempt to incorporate them into theories; though they make a difference they do not, one hopes, make too much difference. See for example, Cartwright (1983).

[5] So in fact we define a function on the natural numbers, which yields, for each $n$, a set which is in fact a function from $T_n$ onto a set of $n$-long sequences.

pairwise disjoint; its domain is all the atomic tipes plus all the tipes of non-atomic ESTs. Thus in this idealization, expression strings are sequences of numbers and we can then go on to give the usual inductive separation of formal strings into the grammatical wffs and the ungrammatical sequences of abstract symbols.

The notion of tipe, remember, takes no account of stretched equiformity abbreviation. The two tokens '∼∼∼∼∼John is bald' and '∼{4}: John is bald' are tokens of different tipes, though the latter is an abbreviation of the former. However, if definitional abbreviation in CL conforms to the usual constraints on definition then we can partition FL into equivalence classes of strings under the relation ⌜$x$ and $y$ are definitionally equivalent⌝. For instance, if our only form of abbreviation consists in expanding languages one term at a time by adding an individual constant which is to be equiform with a (possibly complex) singular term of the old language, then definitional equivalence is easily defined. Indeed, if our syntax is arithmetized then the relation is a recursive one. Say that A and B are immediate definitional equivalents if B results from A by replacement of a simple singular term b in A by the singular term c which b abbreviates, at one or more occurrence; we also add b = c to the axioms of the logical basis. The relation of definitional equivalence is then the ancestral, in Frege's sense, of immediate definitional equivalence.[6] This idea easily generalizes to abbreviation of $n$-place open sentences by $n$-place predicate constants, where we add universally quantified biconditionals to the axiomatic basis, rather than identities.

Things are slightly more complicated with some of the other abbreviatory devices we have considered, for example abbreviation of iterated applications of sentential operators such as a string of negation signs (the same idea can easily be applied to two-place operators such as conjunction and disjunction, if we use Polish notation). The example given was the notation $\sim\{n\}$: A, for $\alpha$ occurrences of tilde followed by sentence A, $\alpha$ being the referent of a standard numeric expression $n$. Formally we can think of this in terms of the recursive generation of a countable sequence of new one-place sentential operators, $\sim\{2\}$:A, $\sim\{3\}$:A and so on, and then the expansion of a base language $FL_0$, through a sequence $FL_i$, with $FL_{n+1}$, generated from $FL_n$ by the addition of the $n$th operator. With FL the union of the $F_i$, we say that for A, B ∈ FL, if B results from A by the replacement of one or more occurrences of the subformula $\sim\{b\}$: A by a string of $\alpha$ tildes followed by A, where a is the number represented by $b$ in some fixed background system of arithmetic, then A and B are immediate definitional equivalents. The addition to our formal logical basis is straightforward: we add rules allowing us to derive A from B, or B from A, where they are definitional equivalents in this sense.

---

[6] The base class is the set of all pairs ⟨A, A⟩, A a sentence of the language. A class X is inductive, relative to this notion of definitional equivalence, if it is a superset of the base class and it is closed under immediate definitional equivalence. That is, if ⟨A, B⟩ belongs to X and C is an immediate definitional equivalent of A, then ⟨C, B⟩ and ⟨B, C⟩ belong to X. The ancestral of the relation (taken as a class) is just the intersection of all the inductive classes.

Using this partition of a formal language FL under definitional equivalence we can then define a wider notion of tipe for the concrete language CL. (Rather than introduce new terminology, I will let 'tipe' represent the wider notion from now on, unless the use is marked explicitly as expressing the original narrow notion of tipe.) Two tipes $t$ and $u$ are equiform in the wider sense iff $h(t)$ and $h(u)$ are definitional equivalents. A tipe, in the new wider sense, is then the mereological fusion (or the representative instance) of all tokens equiform, in the wider sense, with a given token. Moreover, if the length of the formal string $h(t)$ is less than that of $h(u)$ then we can say that $h(t)$ is an abbreviation of $h(u)$. Notice that the wide notion of tipe could not be defined without use of mathematics. In the simplest cases of immediate definitional equivalence we could give a purely concrete account: if one EST is of the form $e^\wedge b^\wedge f$ and the other $e^\wedge c^\wedge f$, where b is a singular term token abbreviating token c then they are immediate equivalents. But cases where more than one term in the token is an abbreviation cannot be handled in this way. At best we could go through cases of two substitutions, three substitutions, and so on, until we got fed up. Once we turn to iterated abbreviatory conventions such as $\sim\{n\}$:A, we need recursive structure. Without mathematics, we can generalize over concrete languages CL and concrete proof systems only in a fairly restrictive sense; we cannot go too far beyond the completely unabbreviated systems. So this is one important function and value in injective idealization from concrete languages into formal.

Now if the concrete language or language fragment CL in question has no forms of abbreviation then there will be quite a low upper bound $k$ beyond which each $T_j$, $j > k$ is empty. The break will be rather 'jaggy' in the sense that if $k$ is the least such bound then there will be many $k$-long abstract sequences in the formal abstract counterpart FL of CL which do not have an inverse image under $h$ in $T_k$. For speakers may find it easier to parse and process some sentences of a given length compared to others with a different grammatical structure or containing different atomic parts.

A similar phenomenon holds for singular terms. Suppose, for instance, that CL can express decimal arithmetic augmented with an exponentiation operator, adding a primitive term 'E' to the list of arguments to $h_o$ in the notation ( . . . E __). Palpably, CL has readily graspable concrete tokens whose tipe is mapped by the expanded version of $h$ to the abstract string type

$$h[ \text{ '}(10 \ E(10 \ E \ (10 \ E \ 34)))\text{'}]$$

Equally clearly, not all the $10^{10^{10^{34}}}$ types which are the abstract numerals standing for numbers less than this number, the decimal approximation to Skewes's number, have concrete tipes as inverse images under $h$. Our idealization is 'injective' not 'bijective' and this means that the numerals of CL are not 'downward closed'. By 'downward closure' I mean that if THERE IS an actually existing tipe which is the numeral of a number $n$, then for every $m < n$ THERE IS an actually existing tipe which is a numeral of $m$. The language CL is 'patchy', in other words. The expression strings of FL which are 'realized' by having concrete images under the partial function $h^{-1}$ do not form a syntactically natural set. It is true that we cannot say that there is a number greater than which no number can be named by a numerical token of a tipe which we can grasp. We cannot lay an upper bound on the possible referents of terms such as 'the number of neutrinos currently in existence' or ⌐the number of solutions to equation E⌐. But we know that there could be no language or notational system we could grasp in which more than a finite number of numbers are named by comprehensible singular terms (cf. Dummett 1975/8, pp. 249–50).

Furthermore, if we introduce abbreviations for logical operators of the form outlined above—$\sim\{10^{100}+1\}$: $0=1$ and so forth—we will find a corresponding failure of syntactic downwards closure. THERE WILL BE negations which are realized by concrete tokens even though some embedded subformulae are not. Likewise there will be failure of ordinary closure. For example, THERE WILL EXIST SOME TOKENS A and B such that NO TOKEN conjunction whose conjuncts are equiform with A and with B respectively EXISTS. These failures show how essential the wide notion of tipe is in a naturalistic account of mathematics. Without it we have no way of systematically expanding our concrete languages to include tipes such as that of $2^{\langle 64K\rangle}=2^{2^{2^{2^2}}}$, where, as before, there are 64K '2's in the exponential tower. This is not the definitional equivalent of some term of CL whose internal structure is fully explicit, and which unpacks that complexity residing in $2^{\langle 64K\rangle}$ from which the inferential links of sentences containing it flow. For there are no unabbreviated companion tipes to which terms like that can stand in relations of definitional equivalence. Such tipes are 'stranded' in the patchily realized FL in the sense that there are huge gaps below the unabbreviated abstract correlate of the term before we get down to numeral tipes which are concretely realized.

## §1.3

I have talked freely here of homomorphisms such as $h$ which map from concrete tipes to abstract types, that is whose range is a system of abstract objects. As remarked there is no inconsistency in a neo-formalist doing this so long as she does not use the theory (or any other theory which entails the existence of abstract objects) in the metatheoretic account of the metaphysical content of the contentful languages of mathematics. But what is the point of it all? This type of idealization certainly does not possess the instrumentalistic virtues stressed by Field, of inference-shorting and such like. No one thinks, moreover, that formal grammar will prove useful in predicting what the future utterances of the language speakers will be.

Logicians investigating the syntax of language ask questions such as: 'Do the sentences satisfy a unique readability requirement?', or 'Does the syntax permit ambiguities of scope?'. They ask proof-theoretic questions such 'As is every proof normalizable?'.[7] When they interpret the systems semantically, they ask questions

---

[7] For a classic study of normalization in natural deduction proofs see Prawitz (1965).

about expressive power, and relate semantics to syntax by trying to discover whether soundness or completeness theorems hold. In asking all these questions, they are only very indirectly interested in the properties of tokens of the expressions of the language.

Suppose, for example, that I want to prove, of a given concrete language CL, that there are no scope ambiguities and thereby show that it is possible to define a unique truth-assignment, via the truth-functional meaning of the logical operators, for the language, given an assignment of truth-values or extensions to the atomic formulae. What we need to show, first of all, is that the complex wffs are *freely generated* from the atoms. That is, the syntactic operations such as the formation of conjunctions or universal quantifications are one:one operations—taking each tipe or pair of tipes to a unique tipe—whose ranges are pairwise disjoint and disjoint also from the set of atomic formulae. But in the case of a concrete language, the function can only be partial, at best, since for some pairs or lists of lengthy tipes there will be no conjunction of the tipes, nor universal quantification on some open sentence tipes. Either no structure large enough to do duty as the conjunction or generalization EXISTS or, if any does, we cannot parse it and test for syntactic correctness arbitrary 'joints' in its articulated grammatical structure.[8] But we need fully defined functions for the standard techniques for defining languages and proving things about them.[9]

Moreover, since the set of wff tipes and proof tipes in the concrete language is not defined inductively, one cannot prove results by induction over the complexity-forming operations, the usual means of proving metatheoretic results. True we could try arithmetical induction over the index in the sets $T_i$ defined as above, yielding the set of narrow wff tipes of each particular length. But if the concrete language uses abbreviation then many wffs or singular terms will not have the appropriate constituents as parts, so that no attempt to prove syntactic results by induction on the length of wffs will work. That is, with respect to the set of abstract wffs of a formal language FL

---

[8] Assuming the falsity of epistemicism, there will be a Sorites sequence of larger and larger wffs, each slightly less comprehensible than the other. One might argue, therefore, that there is a vague function taking each open sentence tipe to its universal generalization and so on. Cf. Dummett (1975/78, pp. 258–9). I think this idea should be resisted. There is this much truth in supervaluationism: it is false that I have ten trillion televisions in my house, even though the spatial boundaries of the (admittedly far too many) televisions which I do have are vague and permit perhaps that many precisifications. Similarly it is false to say that for each comprehensible wff, there is a larger comprehensible wff.

[9] Consider a simple formal language L generated in the usual inductive fashion from one atom P by the negation operation of adding tildes. Select a sentence (or sentences) to be tagged as merely 'virtual'. Then there is a partial function neg* which is like negation except it is undefined on virtual sentences as arguments. We could redefine closure for a set X as closure*; this is to mean that X contains ~A wherever (i) it contains A and (ii) neg* is defined on A. We could then go on to try to generate the language as the intersection of all the inductive* sets, the closed* sets containing the atom P. But suppose ~P is the only virtual sentence so ~~P is not, is 'real'. The set M = {P, ~P} is inductive in the new sense, it is inductive*. The set of atoms {P} is a subset and if $x$ belongs to M and neg*($x$) is defined, (i.e. if $x$ = P) then neg*($x$) belongs to M too. M is clearly a subset of any inductive* set. Hence the 'real' wffs ~~P,~~~P ... do not belong to the language as defined: we cannot 'reach' them with our definition. We could run a similar argument with the first virtual wff ~~ ... ~P, for any number of iterations of tilde, so the real wffs run out later on in the formula. Hence the usual techniques, which are used in proving results such as free generation, cannot reach out to all the sentences we want them to, it cannot reach all the 'real' wffs.

with abbreviation, we can define grammatical constituents of abbreviations to include all the constituents of the unabbreviated equivalent, constituents which may even be longer, as formal strings, than the abbreviation itself. But though a token of '$\sim[\mathbf{10}^{100}+\mathbf{1}]$ $\mathbf{0}=\mathbf{1}$' EXISTS, this being a token of length 14 (counting a white space as an atomic token) there might BE NO token equiform with '$\sim[\mathbf{10}^{100}]$ $\mathbf{0}=\mathbf{1}$'. (Of course I have just wrecked that example, as is the way with explicit instantiations of the uninstantiable, but clearly there will be many other constituents in the above sense of the abstract type $h($'$\sim[\mathbf{10}^{100}+\mathbf{1}]$ $\mathbf{0}=\mathbf{1}$'$)$ such that NO concrete inverse image EXISTS.) So we cannot prove free generation for wffs in $T_{i+1}$, here $T_{14}$, by assuming it holds for $T_n$, $n \leq i$, cf. footnote 9. Indeed we have seen that we cannot even define the wide notion of tipe we need for languages utilizing abbreviation without the application of mathematics in formal syntax.

None of these worries trouble the grammarians, nor should they. Syntactic theorists prove their results as exercises in applied mathematics, as results about the formal language FL. They can, however, work back to the concrete language, inverting the homomorphism from CL to FL, where the inversion exists, to draw conclusions about concrete tipes and tokens. For example, they might draw the conclusion that any actual concrete token of CL will have the same number of right as left brackets, or will be decomposable in a unique way corresponding to the phrase-structure tree of its formal image, or will have a unique truth-value on any assignment to atoms and so forth. Of course many actual ESTs enunciated as complete self-standing utterances by our speaker S of CL will not have a balanced number of left and right brackets or will not have unique phrase structure trees; but these must then be classed as ill-formed. Indeed, here we have one role for idealization, one which applies to the grammarians of real languages we considered earlier. By using mathematics to analyse structure, it might prove much easier to detect ill-formedness in a concrete string which violates the rules of grammar tacitly followed by speakers than if we had no recourse to mathematics, even though these rules can be stated non-mathematically. This will be particularly the case when the structures are large (for graspable structures), for these are precisely the situations when mathematics is essential in practical terms. Thus computerized proof checkers, products of applied mathematics, will detect near instantaneously the ill-formedness of pseudo-wffs or incorrectness of pseudo-proofs where unaided humans might never have managed to do so.[10]

---

[10] The concrete language might, in fact, not be entirely independent of the idealized theoretical representation of it in the way in which physical reality, according to the scientific realist, is independent of physical theory. For if, as I averred above, some grammatical norms reside in speakers' deference to authorities, personal or institutionalized in dictionaries, websites, and the like, and if those authorities themselves resort to theory and idealization, as they will inevitably do if they wish to have a systematic overview of the language, then the linguistic practice which forms the corpus of CL utterances, the data which ground the correctness of grammars for CL, will in turn be different from what would have resulted had theorists not constructed formal grammars. There will be feed-back from the idealization of the practice into the practice itself, undermining the whole project of descriptive grammar.

If we turn, then, from grammar to our main topic, the formalization of mathematics, what are the instrumental virtues of formalization? There are a number of reasons why mathematical logicians engage in formalization. One is for the sheer fun of it. Not everyone's idea of fun, true; *chacun à son goût*. It may be thought, moreover, that, considered as mathematical structures, there is no interest in proof theory and syntax. After all, in the usual cases, the structures in question are isomorphic with structures which can be formed on the domain of natural numbers. But Gödel's beautiful results, and further developments in proof theory since, show that this is wrong. Even if one considers the entities of formal syntax to be numbers, viewing the respective properties of numbers through the lens of syntax yields interesting mathematics.

A second reason for formalization and idealization is epistemic, as an aid to the discovery of theorems. Of course this is not the case for simple theorems such as Kant's beloved $7 + 5 = 12$. A full proof of this from the Peano–Dedekind axioms in a standard logical system would add not a whit to our 'moral certainty' about this theorem since we are as certain as we can be of this in mathematics. But as the programme for increased rigour in nineteenth-century mathematics showed, formalization is useful for results of greater mathematical difficulty. Indeed, this use for formalization was one of Frege's key aims in developing his *Begriffsschrift* (Frege 1879). After formalizing key concepts used in intuitive proofs, we can often spot errors in the proofs, for example, in the 'proofs' that all continuous functions are everywhere differentiable.[11] True, even for results which we are less sure of than we are of $7 + 5 = 12$, long formalized proofs of results might add nothing to our confidence, if constructed by hand, as it were. We might be fairly sure, in fact, that somewhere in the proof there is a mistake, if only a typo. But formalization enables computerized construction and checking of formal proofs where there is less likelihood of error than in the human case, and so in this way can increase our stock of mathematical knowledge. Of course, none of this can yield Cartesian certainty. Even if one has run a verification program on the theorem-finding or theorem-checking program and it passes the test, there may be an error because of a bug in the verification program or because of a hardware fault.[12]

Another important fruit of formalization is conceptual innovation. Locutions and concepts developed in the formalization feed back into ordinary less formal practice (a different type of feedback, then, from the correction of ill-formedness in an existing linguistic practice). We can see this in 'real' mathematical proofs which, as remarked, are often written in a 'Loglish' mixture of ordinary English and technical notation. Conceptual innovation is not a mere matter of using a new symbol. Thus merely substituting an upside down 'A' for occurrences of 'all', 'every', or 'any' does not constitute conceptual innovation. As remarked in Chapter 3, §III.1, the real innovation which Frege and Peirce separately introduced was the idea of applying multiple

---

[11] This is, it is true, a controversial example since one might hold that the geometric result which intuition reveals is not, in fact, the analytic thesis about functions over the reals which analysis showed to be false. A neo-formalist will agree that the geometric and analytic results have different meanings if the analytic derivability relation differs from the geometric.

[12] On computer-generated proof see the contributions in Bundy (2005).

quantifiers to complex predicates conceived as patterns generated from sentences by removing one or more occurrences of a given singular term (an idea that is perhaps most perspicuously represented in $\lambda$ notation).

Such locutions then find their way into contentful reasoning in Loglish which is an expansion of English, not a mere notational variant, as the medieval difficulties with *suppositio* show. Prior to the innovations of the late nineteenth century, it was impossible to represent certain valid inferences in a general way because the forms which feature in inferences like $\forall$E or $\exists$I, forms such as

$$\forall y(\text{only if } (\forall z \in y, z \in x) \text{ then } y \in x) \text{ and } \varphi x$$

were not adequately represented. Similarly, a complex singular term such as

$$\{w : \forall x((\forall y(y \in x \rightarrow (\forall z \in y \rightarrow z \in x)) \& \varphi x) \rightarrow w \in x)\}$$

was simply not conceivable in pre-Fregean German, English, or other natural language.

One last reason for formalization should be mentioned, one which is at least as important as any other. Formalization is essential for proving general results about the overall proof-theoretic or semantic structure of a language, results such as soundness, completeness, normalization, and so forth. We have already seen this with respect to such properties as lack of scope ambiguity and uniqueness of truth-value assignment. Indeed, even the characterization of the concrete language itself needs partly mathematical concepts, such as the wide notion of tipe, if the language has features such as abbreviation (as all useful languages do). In the same way, without formal idealization how could we show that every tipe which is a genuine derivation in our system CL, past, present, or future, is an entailment, its premisses entailing its conclusion? Not by looking at each one in turn. And anyway we would want to know that this would be true of any derivation tipe we might have produced, and we cannot inspect these non-existent entities (merely looking at complex structures which might have been used to express this or that proposition will not help). Similarly, we do not check each tipe which is an argument, with premisses, inference marker, and conclusion, and show one by one for each case that there is or could be a derivation of its conclusion from its premisses.

## §I.4

How, then, do we achieve generality? We cannot utilize recursive substructure in the tipes of derivations or sentences, because there is none. The class of tipes is not defined as the intersection of suitably defined inductive classes. We could partition proof tokens by length, as with wff tokens above; $D_i$ is defined, in other words, as the set of all derivations of length $i$. But for the same reason as before, arithmetical induction will not enable us to prove our results. The operations which generate larger proofs from smaller are not, taken concretely, genuine, fully defined functional operations at all since, for some number, there are proof tokens of that length but none any longer. In like fashion, if we use abbreviation in proofs in ways such as this:

1   (1) $\sim\{2^{2001}\}$: $a = b$      H
1   (2) $\sim\{2^{2001} - 2\}$: $a = b$      1 DNE
     ... $2^{2000}$-1 *steps of DNE*
1   $(2^{1000}+1)$ $a = b$        $2^{1000}$ DNE

(here 'DNE' is double negation elimination) then there will be proof tokens which lack the requisite sub-proofs.[13] The metatheorist of course proves these results as results about the formal language FL. Again, we can treat this as applied mathematics and read the results back into CL via the partially defined inverse function $h^{-1}$ in order to draw conclusions about concrete proof and argument tipes and tokens.

The crucial point in all this is that each of these uses of idealization is one which the neo-formalist is perfectly entitled to use. The neo-formalist does not deny the truth of the theorems of pure mathematics. The neo-formalist's maxim has to be that if one believes a concrete proof of a sentence EXISTS, or COULD BE CONSTRUCTED, one should affirm that sentence, if one believes A CONCRETE REFUTATION EXISTS or COULD EXIST one should deny it.[14] Similarly the neo-formalist affirms the truth of theses of applied mathematics where she believes (i) that THERE IS a concrete proof that the appropriate conservative extension result obtains for the system in question, (ii) that the relevant empirical claims hold (e.g. the existence of the concrete tokens on which the homo-morphism $h_o$ is based), and (iii) that concrete proofs of those theses from the empirical truths plus the pure axioms of the system and any bridge principles EXIST or COULD EXIST in an everyday sense of 'could'. But just as THERE ARE concrete proofs (more exactly proof tokens) of the infinity of the natural numbers (quite short ones in many systems, as short as one line) so too THERE ARE *concrete* proofs, or at least proof sketches, of the existence of *infinite syntactic systems*, such as standard formal languages (proofs from the axioms of standard set theories, for instance; just look in a standard logic text). Moreover, THERE ARE concrete proofs of various formal facts about these systems, such as their soundness, completeness, primality, normalizability results, decidability results, such as the decidability of the $\Delta_o$ fragment of arithmetic. Hence in the formal idealization of $\Delta_o$, every $\Delta_o$ sentence is either provable or refutable.

But how does that resolve our problem about the concrete indeterminability of, as it may be, '$(2^{2^{2^{2^2}}} + 1)$ is prime'? *If* the instance of LEM with this sentence as a disjunct is a 'concrete theorem' of the system then a concrete proof EXISTS that

[13] Note that this is not a proof sketch but a token of a full canonical proof, albeit a token which makes use of abbreviation just as a token of the complete sentence ($1 \in \omega$) does.

[14] The antecedent conditions here are sufficient, not necessary. As we have seen, one might affirm a theorem of first-order logic on the basis of a concrete second-order proof that an abstract first-order derivation exists. Note, however, that there is no analogue of Hilbertian finitism here. There need BE NO concrete proof that for every derivation of concretely instantiated conclusions from concretely realizable premises which we can (concretely) prove exists as an abstract type, a concrete realization of that derivation will also EXIST. In fact, we know that is false, see Chapter 6, §II.1.

$(2^{2^{2^{2^{2^2}}}} + 1)$ is, or is not, prime. Granted Tarskian disquotational truth-rules for each disjunct and fairly weak logic, we also have a concrete proof that it is either true that that number is prime or untrue. But of course these are very big ifs. We have an intricate loop here. For the neo-formalist, truth is grounded in provability, which is determined in turn by the logic and axioms, whose soundness is determined by alethic considerations such as determinacy of truth, taking us back where we started. But we can cut through the knot by observing, as remarked earlier (Chapter 3, §II.6) that, at least for a language which is not wholly representational and is such that bivalence fails, classical logic is not sound. So surely we are not entitled to help ourselves to the instance of LEM with this primality claim as a disjunct, for it is neither determinately true nor determinately false. The requisite make-true *and* make-false conditions both fail.

Thus given the neo-formalist link between truth and proof *it would seem* that the affirmation of excluded middle, and the application of classical reasoning more generally, to indeterminable sentences is unsound. Proof-theoretic indeterminables are semantic indeterminates so that affirmation of excluded middle is affirmation of a non-truth (the Basic Semantics is not supervaluational). To be sure THERE IS, or COULD EXIST, a concrete proof that the $h$ image S of a concretely indeterminable $\Delta_0$ sentence tipe satisfies a $\sum_1$ formula (Bew $x$ ∨ Bew neg $x$) which we can interpret (via some arithmetization of syntax) as meaning 'provable or refutable'; here 'Bew' is the provability predicate, representing proof in some classical formulation of arithmetic and 'neg' a term expressing the function which takes (codes of) sentences to (the codes of) their negations. But this does not in the least imply that THERE IS either a concrete proof of the sentence itself nor that THERE IS a concrete refutation. A neo-formalist who takes the formal decidability of $\Delta_0$ as justification for affirming the law of excluding middle for '$(2^{2^{2^{2^{2^2}}}} + 1)$ is prime' or for affirming '$(2^{2^{2^{2^{2^2}}}} + 1)$ is prime is either true or untrue' cannot get round the fact that she is violating globalization. She is affirming the truth of a disjunction, hence, under the standard semantics, one or other disjunct must be true; yet neither is concretely provable.

Indeed. Moreover, I conceded (Chapter 3, §II) that a local form of neo-formalism is untenable. If we are to give the logical operators of the contentful language their normal meaning then the standard semantics must apply. Thus truth must distribute over the connectives in the usual way whilst the syntactic identity of the G-language and C-language, and consequent conflation of derivability in the calculus with entailment in the contentful language, enforces globalization. Provability must distribute over the operators in the same way as truth, refutability as falsity. However, here we have no refutation of neo-formalism because soundness and globalization must apply *at the level of the formal language FL* in the same way that all systematic grammatical and semantic questions must be directed at the formal idealization. That is, it is enough for neo-formalism that, in a *legitimate* idealization FL of the concrete language CL, formal provability coincides with truth, as defined for the formal language, and distributes over the logical operators in the same way that formal truth does. And this is, indeed, the case for $\Delta_0$ arithmetic (given our standard semantics): a formalized version of globalization holds for (and is concretely provable for) $\Delta_0$:

For all sentences $P \in \Delta_0$, $\vdash P$ iff $P$ is true, $\vdash \sim P$ iff $P$ is false

where we define truth and falsity inductively and truth and falsity for atoms is simply identified with provability (from a suitable set of axioms, such as Q) and refutability (provability of the negation). Quantifiers can be interpreted substitutionally, the standard numerals being the substitution class.

Similarly we can demonstrate the soundness of our actual practice, by providing (concrete) proofs of soundness for the abstract language FL, with respect to abstract notions of proof and formal notions of truth.[15] Indeed, there is no other way to prove soundness, as we have seen.

It has been conceded that if we employ classical logic for the $\Delta_0$ fragment, globalization will be violated at the concrete level. We have seen that there will BE sentence tipes $(P \vee \sim P)$ such that neither $P$ nor $\sim P$ is concretely provable. But $(P \vee \sim P)$ is concretely provable, now we have helped ourselves to classical logic, and so made-true. By the Basic Semantics, one disjunct is; suppose without loss of generality it is $P$. Then we get a failure of the instance of globalization:

P is concretely provable iff P is true.

If we reject excluded middle even for $\Delta_0$ arithmetic, we may as well give up on serious mathematics. But the violations of globalization at the level of the concrete language CL—which we know is a finite, patchy, and imperfect correlate of the idealization FL—matter not one iota more than the violations of grammatical rules and principles, such as conjunction-formation and free generation, at the concrete level. The fact that a couple of giant sentences may lack a conjunction does not show that the rule for forming conjunctions is wrong. There is no reason to conclude this as long as the rule is a legitimate idealization of grammatical practice. Similarly, the EXISTENCE of concrete indeterminables should not inhibit reasoners from applying excluded middle to them so long as THERE IS *a concrete proof* that, in a *legitimate* idealization, the image of the indeterminable is decidable in the formal sense. There is no affirmation of an untrue sentence because the notions of truth and proof which guide us in our norms of inference are *theoretical* notions. They are defined and apply in the first instance to the formal language FL, and only indirectly apply to concrete tokens. So long as the link between truth and there EXISTING a concrete proof is typically the case in actual practice (just as typically, for any two sentences we utter we could grasp their conjunction), the idealization will be a legitimate one. And I argued (Chapter 6, §I.5)

---

[15] Appeal to formal notions of truth is perfectly licit even from a deflationist perspective. In the latter case, a desideratum on the formal definition will be that it sustains what one takes to be the inferential content of the deflationistic picture: 'naïve' introduction and elimination rules for a truth predicate, or the provability of each instance of the Tarskian T-schema, and nothing more.

that in the overwhelming majority of actual mathematical utterances, this link between truth and concrete proof does obtain.

One can make this point, so crucial to the viability of neo-formalism, another way by distinguishing between a *fundamental* and an *idealized* sector of our actual or potential (in the weak, quotidian sense) concrete output (this distinction is not the Hilbertian distinction between finite and ideal mathematics). Concrete tokens and tipes of sentences belong to the fundamental sector just in case THERE EXIST concrete proofs or disproofs of them (whether utterers are aware of this or not), that is structures which we could 'digest' and which, on interpreting the components suitably and in accord with the practices governing our use of mathematical terms, would count as proofs or disproofs. A token expresses a fundamental mathematical truth, in particular, if a concrete proof of it EXISTS.

Sentence tokens and tipes belong to the idealized sector, by contrast, if

(a) they do not belong to the fundamental sector but there is an optimal idealization, an applied theory T, which asserts the existence of a function $\mu$ with certain good-making properties and according to which $\mu$ maps from the token or tipe onto some type $\tau$ in a formal system.

The good-making properties will include such things as closure under syntactic operations for forming more complex expressions, primeness (and primeness) of the derivability relation, together with soundness and completeness theorems for the system into whose wffs the tokens are injectively mapped.

(b) The sublanguage to which $\tau$ belongs is decidable, either $\vdash$ A or $\vdash \sim$A for every A in the sublanguage.

The claim then is that it is entirely legitimate to assert any instance of LEM taken from the idealized, as well as the fundamental, sector, even if THERE COULD BE NO concrete proof nor disproof graspable by us of either disjunct.

Why is this legitimate? The crucial point is that *the applied theory T must be a fundamental truth*. THERE MUST BE a concrete proof (or at least proof sketch) of T. Only then is the idealization legitimate; only then can it play a role in governing our inferential practice, in particular in deciding which instances of LEM are acceptable. The formal proof theory $\Pi$ which proves, for example, that $\Delta_0$ arithmetic is negation-complete is not made true by any segment of mind-independent reality. But there is, or could be, a concrete token proof of an utterance of the $\Pi$-thesis that $\Delta_0$ arithmetic is negation-complete. This justifies us in using it to justify, in turn, LEM for the concrete tokens of $\Delta_0$ arithmetic for the very same sort of reason as the grammarian is justified in holding that unique readability holds of the language, namely that it holds of the formal idealization. General, systematic properties hold of concrete languages if they hold of their legitimate idealizations; indeed it is only coherent to apply them to concrete languages indirectly via their application to the FL idealization.

Note also that this perspective on the role of the formal language FL resolves the worries we had over the neo-formalist semantics for quantification (Chapter 3, §III). Should we define it substitutionally or adopt a more molecular approach? Semantics applies directly to the formal language, not the concrete one, and FL gives us the resources to adopt either approach. In particular, if one adopts the substitutional approach then the fact that there ARE not enough concrete singular terms to instantiate true existential or false universal theorems is no objection. Nor does the substitutional interpretation when adopted in an idealized formalization mean that the neo-formalist is ontologically committed to abstract objects, namely the expression types in the substitution classes. For this quantification over expression types occurs only in the idealization, not in the metatheory which sets out metaphysical content.[16]

Now clearly the notion of a legitimate idealization is central to this whole picture and has been invoked a number of times already. What counts as a legitimate idealization? We need not assume that the concept is precise or admits of a simple analysis in terms of necessary and sufficient conditions, but if it is to be reasonable to suppose it marks out a fairly determinate and objective notion, we need to say something about its conditions of application. In the case of a grammatical rule, one necessary criterion for legitimacy will be that the rule applies perfectly well to the *typical* concrete sentences one deals with in practice. Another criterion is that no alternative fits practice (considered reflectively, corrected for performance errors, and so forth) better. Any revision tailored more closely to practice would, for example, result in a set of rules so restricted as to be useless for the purposes idealization serves to fulfil. For instance, laying down strict upper bounds on wff size would itself block the free generation theorem, whilst with vague boundaries on wff length, the use of classical logic in the proof of the theorems becomes suspect.[17] A necessary condition in the proof-theoretic case will be that the (concrete) globalization condition is satisfied for the typical token which one deals with in actual mathematical practice and we have seen that this is the case. Mathematicians tend to assert mathematical sentences only when they believe them to be provable. This tendency is not universal of course and the neo-formalist position is the stronger if it can explain the deviations from this linkage. Some of the atypical violations can be down to practical limitations of the sort to which Tennant alludes. The reason for the non-existence of a wff or proof of the requisite type is that there are no structures we can manipulate which are large enough to contain such a wff or proof. Just as the rules of grammatical well-formedness are not threatened by the existence of concrete (abbreviated) wffs which lack concrete

---

[16] As regards the stronger forms of proof-theoretic primality needed to ensure globalization in quantified languages, probably the easiest approach is to treat quantifications as regular infinitary conjunctions and disjunctions in a language for which primality holds. This issue will be tackled in Chapter 8.

[17] This is not a conclusive objection, more of a challenge (at least to non-epistemicists). If one works with notions of wff, truth, and proof assumed to be vague or indeterminate then one must attempt to be explicit about the logic used in the metatheory and indicate in sufficient detail that the relevant proofs, e.g. of soundness, still go through.

constituents, so too it is no threat to completeness, for example, that a particular argument, e.g. Boolos' 'Curious Inference', lacks a concrete proof in its own 'proper system'. Not so long as we can explain this as due to practical limitations and not to a failure of completeness at the formal level.

Not all violations of the link between 'asserted by the mathematical community' and 'believed by that community to be true' arise from practical limitations, though. Others arise because of error or ignorance on the part of the mathematical community with respect to the existence of concrete proofs or disproofs. But there are also cases where mathematicians affirm theses but refuse to assert that they must be provable even though they are guilty of no false or incomplete beliefs regarding provability. This will be the case for mathematicians who adopt a highly realist attitude to a theory which is known to be negation-incomplete. I will return to this case in Chapter 8, §VII, but the general response has already been outlined (Chapter 4, §II.2): we should not abandon our account of mathematics simply because the practice of those mathematicians who reject that philosophical position has been distorted by their philosophical views.

A further type of case arises from the prevalence of probabilistic reasoning and judgement in mathematics. Mathematicians often have degrees of belief in mathematical theses which are neither degree 1 nor degree 0, a classic problem for any probability theory which accepts the standard Kolmogorov axioms. If the degree is close to 1, however, they may do something which looks like affirming a conjecture without proof, purely on the basis of probabilistic considerations. Goldbach's conjecture and the Riemann hypothesis concerning the zeros of the zeta function are often cited here. As yet, there ARE NO proofs nor ANY counterexample but they are both widely believed. Statistical data concerning the number of confirming instances plays a role though clearly no simple frequency considerations can work for universal generalizations with infinitely many instances. Analogical reasoning is often held to play a part here,[18] reasoning which looks similar to non-deductive reasoning in the physical sciences.

None of this is a problem for the neo-formalist so long as mathematicians modulate their belief in the probability that mathematical hypothesis $H$ is true so that it matches their belief in the probability that a proof of $H$ exists. If considerations other than the existence of a proof function equally well as probabilistic indicators that a proof exists on the one hand and as indicators that the sentence is true on the other, all is in accord with neo-formalism.[19] Now clearly not all mathematicians believe that it is highly

---

[18] See Corfield (2001).

[19] Why should *any* considerations, other than proofs, function as indicators of truth for mathematical conjectures, if neo-formalism is right? For if neo-formalism is right then mathematics does not delineate a mind-independent realm, as independent as the microphysical world, or the cosmos as a whole, a realm for which the data can be thought to give substantial, but fallible, clues. This is a tricky question for a neo-formalist who is not a subjective personalist in probability theory; trickier, perhaps, than the same question applied to a non-subjectivist platonist. Were I a non-personalist regarding probability I would argue that nonetheless the advantages of the neo-formalist position still greatly outweigh those of the platonist. As a

probable that a proof of $H$ (from the relevant axiom system) exists whenever they believe that $H$ is highly probable. But once again, if the exception cases mostly arise where the mathematician is influenced by a platonistic philosophy of mathematics, then the case is no different from the non-probabilistic case, to be addressed by the neo-formalist in the same way.

The danger of strict finitism is one faced by all thoroughgoing and consistent ontological naturalists. A proper view of the role of idealization in syntax and semantics, however, shows that strict finitism is a paper tiger. The resolution of the problem of idealization is, in slogan form, idealize the language, not the speakers. That is, we idealize the finite corpus which is the concrete language CL by mapping into a formal language. We do not seek to explain our grasp of mathematics by appealing to supernatural beings alleged to be idealized versions of ourselves. The proper view on idealization is not attainable from the supernaturalist perspectives of many other, allegedly naturalistic, forms of anti-platonism, but is on the neo-formalist framework.[20]

# §II.  The Spectre of Finitism

*§II.1*

Thus we have clawed our way out of the abyss of strict finitism. But we must remember where we were when we plunged down into it. We had set to one side—Chapter 4, §III—the problem of Gödelian negation-incompleteness, the existence of sentences of formal arithmetic which are neither formally provable nor refutable, to look at the problem of the applicability of mathematics, and then turned to the definition of a physicalistically acceptable notion of proof. Having restored, as it were, law, order, and determinacy to $\Delta_0$ and similar decidable fragments of arithmetic, we are still faced with the formal indeterminability of the Gödel and Rosser sentences,

---

personalist 'intersubjectivist' rather than 'subjectivist' about probability—cf. the non-subjectivist forms of projectivism of Chapter 2—I would appeal to social and psychological factors, to the moulding of the degrees of belief and dynamics of belief change of trained mathematicians by their inculcation into the practices of the mathematical community, in order to explain the intersubjective consensus which often exists with respect to probabilistic judgements, even in mathematics. Sherif's autokinetic effect experiment (Muzafer Sherif 1935) famously shows how group psychological factors can lead to a consensus which has no basis in objective reality.

[20] Not from a fictionalist perspective, because for the fictionalist the applied mathematics of the idealization is not true. Modal forms of naturalism face problems too. There are the general problems modal treatments face. If, in mapping from an actual magnitude—the length of a rod, the length, in a different sense, of a tipe—to a number we have to switch to 'non-actual possible worlds', then how do we exclude worlds in which the rod is longer or shorter, the tipe is longer or shorter? See Burgess and Rosen (1997, §II. B.2–3, pp. 121–45), Field (1989, pp. 252–6). Moreover, if the modal construal of the claim that a homomorphism from CL into FL requires that in some possible world the full system FL EXISTS, then further problems ensue whether one treats the non-actual formal language as a system of abstract objects or of concrete objects (how could we, with something like our actual powers, have grasped this system in the counterfactual circumstances, for example?).

Goodstein's theorem and indefinitely many other sentences which intuitively seem to have perfectly determinate truth-values, namely, true.

We cannot wriggle our way out of this by adding piecemeal, as axioms, those sentences we reckon are true but cannot prove in our existing formal system, because there will always be other intuitively true sentences left still undecided if the set of theorems is recursively enumerable. This clause is, however, important. Often Gödel's limitative theorems are stated very inaccurately, even in textbooks. 'Gödel showed there are unprovable arithmetical truths' or words to that effect are often used to explain his first incompleteness theorem. Even at an informal level one can do much better than that. 'Gödel showed that, if proofhood is mechanically checkable, there are sentences neither provable nor disprovable'; or something along those lines. More formally yet, if an arithmetic theory T with $Q \subseteq T$ is $\omega$-consistent and T's theorems are recursively enumerable, then there are indeterminable sentences of the theory, neither provable nor refutable. If one drops the requirement that theoremhood is recursively enumerable Gödel's results no longer apply. With one bound our hero is free.

Yet there is near unanimity that this is not an escape route from Gödel's results because the requirement that theoremhood be recursively enumerable is viewed as an essential constraint on any formal system which has an entitlement to be classed as a system of *proof*. The reason usually given for this orthodox position is the *epistemic* nature of the concept of proof. Indeed often a stronger requirement than the recursive enumerability of the theorems is laid down. Michael Potter talks of the 'obviously essential requirement that . . . proofs be mechanically checkable' (1993, pp. 190–1). Neil Tennant puts it this way:

Membership in the set of axioms has to be decidable because we need to be able effectively to tell, when giving proofs, whether each of the premisses used in any proof is indeed among the permissible axioms . . . .Proofs have to convince. To do so, they must be finite. (Tennant (2000, p. 269))

Such is the orthodox view: proof-theoretic finitism.[21] Proofs must be finite objects with axiomaticity and proofhood mechanically decidable. But as Gregory Moore has pointed out (Moore 1980, 1988 see also Shapiro, 1991, ch. 7) it was not ever thus.[22]

[21] Finitism in this sense differs from Hilbertian finitism, an instrumentalistic view of mathematics (Chapter 2, §I.1). Neo-formalism is not finitism of this sort. There is no finitary/ideal distinction. All mathematics is contentful though the truth-values of all mathematical sentences rest on provability in the relevant uninterpreted 'game' or calculus.

[22] One reason for the 'triumph' of first-order logic over the higher-order and infinitistic systems in which modern logic first emerged might be Gödel's 1930 completeness theorem for first-order logic which showed that a reasonable system of rules is adequate for the natural semantics for first-order systems (Gödel 1930). But, as Zermelo in effect urged, why should adequacy vis à vis *that* semantics not tell *against* first-order logical systems, given the manifest expressive limitations of first-order semantics as witnessed by e.g. the Löwenheim–Skolem theorems. And as Boolos remarks in a different context (Boolos 1975), we could argue on those lines even more strongly in favour of propositional logic as 'the' logic. Perhaps the triumph owes more to the grip of finitism (and perhaps verificationism) among leading figures in proof theory of that period than

Finitism in proof theory represents a sharp turn away from the position of a great many of the early pioneers of modern logic—Peirce, Schröder, Löwenheim, the early Hilbert, for example—a turn which was strongly resisted by Zermelo, in his reactions to the Gödelian incompleteness theorems. For Zermelo, the first theorem did not show the existence of undecidable sentences of arithmetic, but the weakness of Gödel's methods of proofs. There then emerged a 'samizdat' tradition of infinitary logic, with the early pioneers Ramsey, Carnap,[23] and Rosser followed by Scott, Tarski, Karp, and others. But orthodoxy has it that such systems are of 'merely technical' interest because no one can actually grasp an infinitely long formula. Infinitary proofs are of no epistemic value, it is usually said.

A little thought should show that the orthodox position is a very strange one indeed. It is maintained that the 'Gödelian' notion of proof is the epistemically important one, even though all but an insignificant finite fragment of Gödelian proofs, that is abstract proofs which meet the standard requirements of recursive enumerability, have far more steps in them than Skewes's number, not to mention the estimated number of elementary particles in the universe. What possible epistemic value do such abstract proofs have? Even if there are concrete structures of the requisite size, what epistemic role could they play? How are we in the least better off epistemically when faced with a proof, wff, or task with $10^{10^{10^{34}}}$ steps as compared to one with $\epsilon_0$ steps?[24] Imagine a crackpot bursts into your class and threatens to blow your head off if you do not count to Skewes's number, without gaps, in the next 30 seconds. Your colleague standing next to you remarks: 'look on the bright side, she could have asked you to count to $\epsilon_0$'. Perhaps you would appreciate the dry humour; perhaps not.

There is absolutely no epistemic distinction between (almost all) Gödelian and infinitary proofs. What convinces us in all cases are small finite structures, mostly proof sketches; it is they which play the epistemic role. All the rest is idealization. There is no reason, furthermore, to restrict the range of the idealizing homomorphism from finite concrete tokens to be finite mathematical objects unless one already rejects the infinite in mathematics.[25] There is, of course, no such reason for rejection from a neo-formalist

to the philosophical and logical merits of first-order, finitistic, formulations of theories, for these merits seem rarely to have been argued for explicitly (cf. Shapiro 1991, p. 181). And of course the most important figure in proof theory was Gödel, see footnote 25.

[23] Once Carnap became aware of Tarski's sanitized notion of truth he was happy to work with a semantic notion of consequence but at the time of *Logical Syntax of Language* (Carnap 1934/7) consequence was identified with proof-theoretic derivability and his reaction to Gödel's results was to appeal to infinitary notions of logic.

[24] $\epsilon_0$ is the first 'epsilon number', the least fixed point of the function $\omega^x$. It is the limit of $\omega$, $\omega^\omega$, $\omega^{\omega^\omega}$, and so on.

[25] Which of course Gödel did not, which makes his proof-theoretic finitism more puzzling. Martin Davis (2005) suggests that Gödel's views changed significantly over time, though he appears in his later writings not to have realized this. In particular, whilst around the time of his incompleteness results he was rather anti-platonist and sympathetic to Hilbert's finitism, later on he became markedly more platonistic and unsympathetic. But by then, I suggest, given the justifiable prestige owing to the discoverer of those great theorems, the finitist damage had been done and a baseless prejudice against infinitary proof theory had taken root.

perspective. For there is this similarity with Hilbert's position: consistency is sufficient for existence. If a consistent contentful mathematical system has as one of its theorems that φs exist, then such objects do exist in the non-representational sense which all mathematical existence theorems have. So from a neo-formalist perspective, there is no bar on infinitistic mathematics, including not only infinitistic model theory but also infinitistic formal proof theory.

## §II.2

There is, on the other side, a certain stability in an intuitionistic constructivist such as Tennant rejecting infinitely long wffs and proofs as determinate objects of mathematical investigation since he denies there are domains containing pluralities of distinct and distinguishable infinite mathematical structures. For the position to be persuasive there would need, of course, to be independent grounds for rejecting the infinite and, like most contemporary theorists, I certainly find no such basis in Brouwer's subjectivist ontology of alleged private mental data. Nor am I convinced by vaguely behaviouristic appeals to 'inferential practice', with Wittgenstein the usual inspiration, as a basis for constructivism. For it is hard to see how this leads to constructivism unless one takes the faulty view of the role of idealization in systematic syntax and semantical studies which I have criticized. In this case, however, it leads, as we have seen, to a crippling form of strict finitism, if carried through thoroughly. Proper consideration of idealization, on the other hand, yields no non-question-begging bar to infinitary methods.

Indeed, though there is a certain stability in a constructivist rejecting the (definite) infinite in proof theory as elsewhere (and a corresponding instability in the orthodox combination of finitistic proof theory and infinitistic semantics and model theory), a mismatch emerges when we reflect again on Tennant's own supernaturalistic interpretation of idealization. Tennant wishes to withhold determinacy from theses which are 'undecidable' in an intuitionistic or constructivistic sense, though he wishes to maintain that decidability can extend all the way through $\Delta_0$ arithmetic to include concrete indeterminables. But if one is allowed to appeal to fantastic supernatural figures who can carry out tasks with arbitrarily large finite numbers of sub-stages why not appeal to supernatural figures who can carry out 'supertasks',[26] such as completing infinitely many steps in a finite time by dint of the usual converging sequences, first step in ½ a second, next in a further $1/(2^2)$ seconds, $n+1$th step $1/(2^{n+1})$ seconds after the $n$th, and so on? If $\varphi x$ is decidable for each number, then both $\forall x \varphi x$ and $\exists x \varphi x$ can be decided by our 'supertasker'. This process can be iterated up the recursive hierarchy of $\Delta_i$ sentences by iterating supertasks to create super-super tasks. If we extend the convergent sequence process as far as $\omega^2$, which we can do since there is a one:one

---

[26] Or appeal to a 'supertime' in which ideal humans carry out inaccessibly many operations. Philip Kitcher is prepared to countenance such 'idealizations' of our actual practice, Kitcher (1984, pp. 146–7).

order-preserving map from it into any real interval (**a, b**) then we can settle all arithmetic questions.[27]

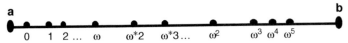

Indeed Mark Hogarth (1994) has shown how, in certain types of relativistic spacetime (not necessarily physically plausible ones) there may be no physical impossibility in the existence of a 'supertasker'. In these spacetimes all of an infinitely long curve can be bounded before and after by points $p$ and $q$ finitely far apart. Firing, along the curve, a Turing Machine which is set to signal iff it finds a counterexample to Goldbach's conjecture, one can find out the answer a finite time later, at $q$. This type of procedure can be iterated in more complex spaces in such a way as to decide all arithmetic questions.

Naturalists would be in rather desperate straits if they had to rely on such possibilities to secure a satisfactory account of mathematics. In fact, even if we countenance such possibilities we still cannot escape supernaturalism: the intrepid mathematician or Turing Machine blasted off down the infinite curve in order to verify or falsify the Goldbach conjecture or other indeterminable would, in general, have to acquire supernatural powers of manipulation and memory in order to check the (arbitrarily large) finite subtasks. Infinite time is not enough, one needs the memory resources and calculating powers to make use of it and I argued in the last chapter that no human or similar being could expand memory and the ability to parse sentences and proofs to any finite degree, not in any naturalistically acceptable sense of 'could'.

Naturalists should vacate all these unstable positions[28]—for example, Tennant's appeal to a supernatural agent limited in ad hoc ways to suit prior intuitionist preconceptions, the orthodox rejection of finitism in model theory but not proof theory, and so on—for an integrated and coherent acceptance of the infinite in mathematics. After all, from a neo-formalist point of view, in embracing the transfinite we do not embrace a mind-independent ontology of infinite abstract objects, just concrete token proofs of wffs which make infinitary existential claims. Among these concrete proofs are the proofs of the existence of homomorphisms from very small finite tokens to infinite objects.

## §II.3

For example, there is a mapping which assigns to the abbreviatory tipe '($\sim\{10^{50}\}$: $1{=}1$)' the sequence $\langle \alpha_i, 1, 14, 1\rangle$, $i \in 10^{50}$ with $\forall i$, $\alpha_i =$ fifteen, our code for the tilde, one our code for the numeral '1' and fourteen our code for the identity sign. The tipe of the twelve-long token '$\sim\{10^{50}\}$: $1{=}1$' is mapped to this $10^{50}{+}3$ long abstract object even though in reality THERE ARE NO unabbreviated tokens $10^{50}{+}3$ long which we can

---

[27] $\pi_1$ and $\Sigma_1$ sentences, as we have seen, can be settled by stage $\omega$, molecular combinations of these can be settled after $\omega.k$ steps, for finite $k$, $\pi_2$ and $\Sigma_2$ sentences by stage $\omega.2$, and so on.

[28] Here I am in agreement with Wright (1982/93), at least to the extent of endorsing his scepticism about the existence of a middle position between strict finitism and non-constructivistic mathematics.

cognitively digest (and no abstract objects!). By the same token (but not using the same token!), we can easily demonstrate the existence of functions which map the tipe of concrete token '$\&[t_i{=}t_i]_{i\in\omega}$' to an infinite sequence, say $<17, \alpha_i, 14, \alpha_i>$, $i \in \omega$ with $\forall i$, $\alpha_i = 2i + 24$. We might want to do this in a formalization of an infinitary language in which, once again, fourteen codes for the identity sign, seventeen for ampersand, but we also wish to have infinitely many individual constants in the formalization, coded by the even numbers greater than twenty-two. All tokens of the tipe of the displayed token, then, are tokens of an infinitary conjunction which conjoins the self-identity claims for each individual constant.

We can prove in weak (applied) set theories that such objects as the above sequence $[\langle 17, \alpha_i, 14, \alpha_i\rangle, \alpha_i = 2i + 22, i \in \omega]$ exist. Moreover tokens such as '$\&[t_i{=}t_i]_{i\in\omega}$' are every bit as REAL as tokens such as '$t_1{=}t_1$', '$10^{10^{10^{34}}}$' or '$(\sim\{10^{50}\}{:}\,1{=}1)$'. Like the latter, '$\&[t_i{=}t_i]_{i\in\omega}$' is an abbreviation in the sense that it is shorter[29] than the mathematical object it is mapped to under a homomorphism $h$ which assigns one basic mathematical object (in our case these are finite numbers) to each atomic tipe. But this does not impugn the determinacy of the mapping. Given our specification of the homomorphism $h$ it is as determinate a mathematical fact as any other that '$\&[t_i{=}t_i]_{i\in\omega}$' maps to $\langle 17, \alpha_i, 14, \alpha_i\rangle$, $i \in \omega$, with $\forall i$, $\alpha_i = 2i + 24$ rather than with $\forall i < 10^{87}$, $\alpha_i = 2i + 24$ and $\forall i \geq 10^{87}$, $\alpha_i = 3i$.[30] No practical notation dispenses with abbreviation, and only a prejudice against the infinite in mathematics could ground a refusal to allow abbreviations for infinitary formal objects. Like the stacked Cartesian notation for Skewes's number, the introduction of tokens of infinitary wffs ensures that the language is 'patchy', that most of the abstract wffs will not be represented by tokens. But this is nothing new, it is an inevitable part of the relation between formal and concrete language.

It is important to note that '$\&[t_i{=}t_i]_{i\in\omega}$' is not a token of a finite *schematic* wff. Its tipe is mapped to an infinite string of representatives of atomic tipes, none of which play the role of schematic letters and not to a finite string which includes expressions whose role is schematic.

As well as infinitary wffs we can also introduce infinite proofs. Of course no infinitely long token EXISTS but then we have already seen a token equiform with this one:

| 1 | (1) $\sim\{2^{2001}\}$: $a = b$ | H |
|---|---|---|
| 1 | (2) $\sim\{2^{2001} -2\}$: $a = b$ | 1 DNE |
|   | $\ldots 2^{1000}-1$ steps of DNE |   |
| 1 | $(2^{1000})\ a = b$ | $2^{1000}-1$ DNE. |

---

[29] 'Shorter' does not have a physical meaning here, since the mathematical objects do not have physical lengths—for one thing, they do not EXIST! Rather, the number which gives the length of the token, under the definition we gave of its 'empirical' length$_e$, is smaller than the number which is the length$_m$ of the sequence under the mathematical definition of length.

[30] I am assuming without argument that Kripkenstein scepticism and radical Putnam/Davidson ontological relativity (for which see Weir 2006b) is false. Even so, this leaves open the possibility of more limited forms of indeterminacy, and one might think that the idea that a term of our language can pick out uniquely a function whose range is an infinite class of abstract objects—or even a function whose range is finite but extremely large, is an obvious target for scepticism. This might well be so for a platonist, but for a neo-formalist, determinacy is secured by bare stipulation alone.

Those two tokens of the DNE proof ARE tokens of a full canonical proof tipe whose length is considerably shorter than the mathematical object which formalizes them in a standard idealizing homomorphism. Similarly:

—  (1) $\sim$Bew(0, $|G|$)        Given.

   $\ldots\ \ldots\ \ldots$

—  ($n$) $\sim$Bew($n$, $|G|$)        Given.

   $\ldots\ \ldots\ \ldots$

—  ($\omega$) $\forall x(\sim$Bew($x$, $|G|$))    $n \in \omega$; $\omega$ rule.

IS a concrete token of an infinite proof, in a suitable arithmetical system, of the Gödel sentence G: $\forall x(\sim$Bew($x$, $|G|$)) of an ordinary Gödel system[31] in a stronger system in which we have added an '$\omega$-rule'. One sequent form of the $\omega$-rule is this:

If we have proofs of the sequents $X_n : \varphi x/S^n 0$ for every natural number $n$, then we can conclude $\underset{i\in\omega}{\bigcup} X_i : \forall x\varphi x$

Note that the above (description of a) token of a proof of the Gödel sentence is not a token of a proof schema just as '$\&[\mathbf{t}_i=\mathbf{t}_i]_{i\in\omega}$' is not a token of a wff schema. Nor is it a proof sketch. There is no promissory note or wager that competent mathematicians will be able to fill in the other stages of the proof. All the stages are there in the formal proof. Given the appropriate explanation of the $\omega$-rule, we have all the details we need to 'construct' the infinitary object which is the formal proof, just as we had in the case of the proof with $2^{1000}-1$ applications of DNE.

A sceptic might say that the token of the infinitary proof does not contain all the details we need. In the case of the $\omega$-rule, how do we know that there are indeed infinitely many genuine proofs, one for each instance $\varphi x/S^n 0$? To this we could respond by producing a concrete proof of $\varphi x/0$ and then a concrete demonstration that any proof of $\varphi x/S^n 0$ can be extended to a proof of $\varphi x/S^{n+1} 0$ thus showing concretely but inductively that all the premiss sequents do indeed exist. (If this induction over proof-theoretic properties is to be digestible, it will in fact probably be carried out in set theory or something of similar power.) The sceptic may retort that what does the work here is the (finitary) inductive proof. Even if the infinitary rule is not one each application of which can be 'encoded' in arithmetic or implemented in a programming language, as in a recursive or constructive $\omega$-rule, the 'real' proof of $\forall x\varphi x$ will still be finitary. Hence the proof system which is actually being used to persuade is still subject to Gödel's theorems.[32]

What this shows is that certain types of finitary reasoning, though proof-theoretically redundant with respect to infinitary systems of sufficient power, are epistemically indispensable in demonstrating that the abbreviated token infinitary proofs really are

---

[31] Where, as in Chapter 4, §III.2, the formal sentence $\sim$Bew($n$, $|G|$) 'says' via diagonalization that $n$ does not code a proof of the Gödel sentence G.

[32] Thanks to Dag Prawitz for pressing the sceptic's case in discussion.

proofs. The situation is to be compared with the use of second-order logic or set theory to produce a finitary demonstration that there really is a first-order demonstration of the conclusion of Boolos's Curious Inference from its premises. This epistemically indispensable second-order reasoning does not, of course, show that the first-order derivation as an abstract mathematical object is not really first-order nor does it show that the first-order idealization is not a good idealization of at least some of our informal reasoning. (I say more on this in Chapter 8, §VII.)

The situation is no different in the infinitary case. Just as with Boolos's inference, or the use of informal set theory to characterize Gödel and Rosser sentences 'constructed' via diagonalization, we appeal to abbreviation and use methods not part of the fundamental rules of our idealized framework in producing proof tokens which convince. None of this shows that the tokens are not tokens of an infinitary system, nor that the infinitary rules are illegitimate as idealizations of actual practice nor that the infinitary additions to the finitary logic are redundant. On the contrary, we can prove (concretely) a lot more in the infinitary system.

What reason can the 'Gödelian' proffer for not accepting infinitary languages as actual tools of mathematical practice, languages which have tokens of purported proofs which can be checked for correctness? The unthinking retort—that we cannot physically construct or check such proofs—we have seen to be flawed. For the same is true of nearly all the abstract proofs in finitary systems. But we can construct tokens of some of the infinitary proofs, which get mapped onto the infinitary objects which are the abstract proofs in our idealizations. There will inevitably be recourse to abbreviation in any system and only a very incomplete fragment of the set of proofs will be concretely realized, only a paltry subset of sentences will be concretely decidable. This is the norm in all cases of the relationship between concrete languages and formal languages, including finitary languages.

So why the prejudice against infinitary languages and systems? It cannot be that they cannot fulfil the purposes required of idealization of concrete languages. For let us look again at those goals, the useful functions of formal languages. One is their intrinsic interest as mathematical objects. But infinitary languages fill that role even better than finite ones because of their richer and deeper structure. Moreover, they have, in addition, instrumentalistic value in proving results in other areas of mathematics. Infinitary languages, for example, have long been used to prove important results about large cardinals (compact, supercompact, and so on); see e.g. Drake (1974). A second reason given earlier for idealizing concrete proofs was epistemic, formalization enabling us to increase rigour in the proof of certain more complex propositions. Although current orthodoxy would have it that infinitary logic could play no epistemic role, this is simply false. Finite tokens of infinitary proofs enable us to prove theorems we otherwise are not be able to prove, as we have just seen.

A third fruit of idealization, mentioned in §I, is conceptual innovation. In fact, the modern conception of quantification as it emerged in Peirce, rather than Frege, seems to have arisen via infinitary generalization of conjunction and disjunction, and is often explained this way to logic students. Thus infinitary logic can be, at the least, a route to conceptual innovation.

Finally I mentioned the use of formalization in proving general, systematic results about languages used in mathematical reasoning, results such as soundness, completeness, undecidability, and so forth. But here idealization to infinitary, and not just arbitrarily large finite, proofs really comes into its element. It is true that for the systems which have now become standard—first-order predicate calculus mainly, systems in which proof theory is finitistic but the model theory not, we get not only soundness but also completeness results. But when we move beyond those systems, the mismatch between the infinitary model theory and the finite proof theory can yield, e.g. in standard second-order logic, incompleteness, in the sense of failure of the converse of soundness, and also undecidability in the sense of negation-incompleteness, for important theories such as arithmetic. But these limitations do not necessarily apply when the logic is infinitary. Thus, as is well known, arithmetic is negation-complete when one augments a standard system of Peano arithmetic, even weaker in fact than Q, with an $\omega$-rule of the above form. Indeed, this holds even in cases where the background logic, minus the $\omega$ rule, is non-classical and I will argue in the next chapter that this justifies the use of classical logic in arithmetic.

Gödel's important limitative results depend crucially on the representability of all recursive relations and his demonstration that theoremhood, for the type of systems he considered, is recursively enumerable. They show us not that there are arithmetic truths which are unprovable (granted bivalence) but rather the limitations of a very natural and important subclass of proof-theoretic methods, methods which could be implemented by the idealized computer which is the universal Turing machine.[33] But granted the legitimacy of infinitary logic, the way is open to extend the argument for the determinacy of truth and validity of the law of excluded middle from $\Delta_0$ arithmetic to all of arithmetic.

## §II.4

It may be objected that even if it is plausible to suppose that the algorithms of decimal arithmetic (and perhaps HP or related principles) are part of our intuitive notion of number, the same cannot be said about $\omega$-logic or for that matter, the concepts which feature in many complex proofs of numerical results. I understand Fermat's Last Theorem but not Andrew Wiles's proof. So did Wiles prove the proposition which I understand (did he prove the one Fermat understood)?

This returns us to the question posed in Chapter 4, §II.3: what is it for two mathematical utterances to have the same sense, the same informational content? I promised there a sufficient condition, and offer here this rather vague one:

---

[33] Note, though, that Turing himself investigated more powerful idealized computers, for example his O machines. See Copeland (1998).

Two mathematical utterances u and u', produced by speakers S and S' express the same sense if there is an admissible one:one mapping μ from the language of S to that of S' such that X ⊢$_S$ A iff μ(X) ⊢$_{S'}$ μ(A) and μ(**u**) = **u**′.

A decent account will need to tell us what admissible mappings are; the constraints will be constraints on what makes a translation a good one. Not an easy thing to spell out. But one constraint should be this: if μ maps sentential operator # to !, and # is a logical operator according to the Quinean verdict matrices (conjunction say) then ! is also, according to those matrices, that very operator. Other constraints on terms identified by the syntax for both speakers as function terms will appeal to the notion of meaning-constitutive principles. A murky and vague one, indeed, but pace the Quineans, not a hopelessly empty one. Thus if

$$t*(u*v) = (t*u)*v$$

is a meaning constitutive principle in S's practice, has axiomatic status perhaps, and μ maps it to %, then

$$a\%(b\%c) = (a\%b)\%c$$

should be meaning constitutive for S'.

When we talk of the language of S and S' here, what is meant is their mathematical language at a given time, something which can switch if one switches from decimal to modular arithmetic, for example. Part of the above condition for sameness of content, then, is that the derivability relations of the two calculi (under an acceptable translation from one to the other) are exactly the same. I suggest making that a necessary condition on sameness of informational content for mathematical utterances, that the underlying derivability relation, in the formal idealization of course, be the same.

Thus just as two projective utterances can differ in metaphysical content but have the same informational content, so too can two mathematical utterances. What makes-true $56 \times 843 = 47208$ as uttered by me is the EXISTENCE of structures which are, (or could, by extending equiformity, become) concrete proofs of that string according to rules I follow, perhaps only implicitly. But my children carry out long multiplication and division by a slightly different algorithm from the one I was taught all too many years ago at school. Do we then understand $56 \times 843 = 47208$ differently? Surely not. Computer scientists try to find the most efficient algorithm, relative to the particular type of machine they are dealing with, for calculating a given numerical function. But different machines are still calculating the same numerical function. In the same way, my children and I express the same proposition by '$56 \times 843 = 47208$' because under an acceptable translation, in fact a (more or less) homophonic one which maps tokens of the one tipe '**56** × **843** = **47208**' to each other, what is provable in a legitimate idealization of their decimal arithmetic is the same as what is provable in mine.

In like fashion, the metaphysical content of $x^n + y^n = z^n$, $(n > 2, x,y,z > 0)$ is different for Wiles compared to Weir, since Wiles operates a much more sophisticated calculus $W_1$ than Weir's primitive $W_2$. But the moral of the previous paragraph is that we should not conclude that the string expresses a different proposition for Wiles compared to the one grasped by the lay mathematician. If, under a correct formal idealization of the derivability relation of the Wiles calculus, $W_1$ is the same as that for the Weir calculus $W_2$ then there is no good reason to say that we mean different things by sentences of arithmetic (in the syntactically identical language we both speak). That is to say, if there is a proof of sentence S in a reasonable idealization of $W_1$ just when there is a proof of S in a reasonable idealization of $W_2$ then we are speaking the same mathematical language.

What reason is there to believe that the derivability relation in the formal idealization is the same? If we assume that we have in common the language of first-order arithmetic, that both our calculi for this language are consistent, that the idealizations of both extend first-order (classical) PA and include the $\omega$-rule, then each proves exactly the same theorems, namely the truths of the intended model of arithmetic. Wiles and Weir mean the same thing by their near identical tokens (written, anyway, not spoken) of Fermat's theorem.

What of Fermat's grasp of his conjecture? It may be said that it is absurd to suppose that he, in his arithmetic ratiocinations, was employing a calculus which included the $\omega$-rule, something we can be sure he did not have an inkling of. But what can it mean to talk of the theorems derivable in a system employed by Fermat, or Euler or Euclid? Well, each of these individuals produced a finite output of mathematical utterances. More than this, I argued in the previous chapter, §I.6, that in any reasonable sense of possibility, they could have produced or understood no more than a finite body of utterances. This finite body is not something deserving of the title of a formal system. The formal images of tipes of token concrete proofs which any human could produce form a finite and patchy subset of the infinite set of theorems of any standard formal system.

So when we talk of what is provable in, say, Fermat's system of arithmetic, we are talking about a *formal system* which is a joint product of *Fermat's* actual practice, corrected for errors of performance, and the appropriate techniques of idealization.[34] Who decides what these are? We do of course; clearly it cannot be Fermat's idealization. In this joint product, neither contributor has a determining say in the result.

Though inevitably it is we who decide what counts as a legitimate idealization, if it is we who are interpreting Fermat, it does not follow that there are no objective criteria for legitimacy which are such that we might get things wrong, by those criteria. But it is hard to make sense of the idea that we might, even after careful and well-informed reflection on the nature of idealization, get the criteria themselves wholly wrong.

What makes our formalization of Fermat's marginal note an idealization of *arithmetic* rather than something else? It is the fact (if it is a fact) that Fermat accepted the same constitutive principles, rules, and algorithms for arithmetic as we do. Of course, we

---

[34] Applied, of course, to a translation of Fermat's seventeenth-century Latin into contemporary English.

cannot idealize someone's mathematical system any old way we like. We have to look in particular to which rules are manifested, in short comprehensible instances, in her practice[35] and build our idealization up from these components together with reasonable structural principles. But if it is unreasonable to impose a requirement of finitude on proof architecture, as I argued above, then bringing the ω-rule to our side of the joint product which is ⌜the formal idealization of $x$'s system⌝, is perfectly legitimate, for any $x$ living or dead.[36]

## §II.5

The focus thus far has been very much on a rather special part of mathematics, namely arithmetic. There we can appeal to the role which the algorithms (recursive equations) for addition and multiplication (and exponentiation) play (or perhaps HP or a suitable set of instances of HP) in corralling a bunch of arithmetic axiom systems of differing strengths together to reveal them each as limited and imperfect realizations of the 'set of truths about a unified domain'. In more legitimate neo-formalist terms, we can gloss talk of imperfect approximation to truths about a unified domain in terms of inadequate specifications of the theorems generated by an intuitive principle or bunch of principles and rules implicit in everyday practice when allied with an appropriate logical framework. But what could play such a role elsewhere, in algebra, differential geometry, or the case heavily studied by philosophers (studied to a harmful excess, according to some), namely set theory?

Frege's Axiom V and the naïve set comprehension principle, to be sure, both have at least some claim to be implicit in our mathematical use of the word set or cognate words. Moreover, we can certainly see set theories such as ZFC, second-order ZFC, ZFC plus strong axioms of infinity, and so on, as a series of incomplete realizations of the set of theorems generated by the naïve principles. The problem, of course, is that in standard logic every sentence is such a theorem and the best known way to block this trivialization, dialetheism, asks us to believe in true contradictions. I have argued against this (Weir 1998c) that naïve set theory is in fact consistent and non-trivial in the setting of the 'right' logic for mathematics. But one thing at a time—attracting converts back to a version of formalism is a stiff enough task on its own without adding naïve set theory into the mix. At present, then, it has to be acknowledged that when one determines a previously indeterminable set-theoretic sentence by strengthening the proof-theoretic basis it is, at the least, not obvious that one is showing determinate the same proposition that the previous formal system left undecided.

---

[35] Here difficult issues concerning rule-following arise which I will studiously ignore in this work.

[36] Even for mathematicians who make substantive use of formal techniques and notations, there will be room for a contribution from the external interpreters in the construction of their formal system (or systems), since many different formal systems will often fit coherently over their actual practice. The only exception would be a fully formalized theorem searcher, prover, and checker, but no human will ever come under that heading (one hopes!).

Nor does the move to infinitary logic provide an instant solution to problems of incompleteness, since there are plenty of reasonable set theories which are incomplete even in infinitary logics. Indeed, we need not stray away from arithmetic to make this point. If we consider not first-order PA but full Hume's Principle in second-order logic, merely adding the ω-rule (as given above but with the canonical numerals defined using bridge principles of Fregean arithmetic) will not enforce negation completeness. Consider

$$nx(x = x) = nx(\exists X(x = nxXx)$$

the claim that the number of things in the universe equals the number of numbers. Since we can construct (standard) second-order models for this language in which this sentence is true (e.g. countably infinite models) and others in which it is false (e.g. models of size $\aleph_1$, the number of cardinal numbers in these is $\aleph_0$), in no sound system can it be either provable or refutable. What can the neo-formalist say about this?

The obvious response here is to reject bivalence, arguing that to do so will not butcher everyday mathematical practice (which carries on in blithe disregard of cardinality questions of the above sort). Is it obvious, at least to someone not utterly convinced by absolutist platonism, that there is a determinate fact of the matter as to whether the number of numbers is the number of all things?[37] But in what cases is it legitimate to abandon bivalence? Moving down to the object theory, is there a principled way we can restrict the law of excluded middle? How can we test whether or not in doing so we will cripple a branch of mathematics which seems to the mathematicians themselves, to whom the philosophers must pay serious, if not uncritical, attention, in perfectly good order? It is to these logical matters that I turn in the final chapter.

---

[37] This question cannot be properly formulated in standard set theory (evidence that the latter is too weak), but in second-order set theory we can ask a comparable question: is there a function from the cardinal numbers onto the universe? This too is deductively independent of standard axiom systems.

# 8

# Logic

## §I. Calculus versus Logic

The G-level calculi underlying mathematical assertions (Chapter 3, §I.2) are in one sense logics. They are systems consisting of formal rules of inference setting out which transformations may, and which may not, be applied to formulae, and perhaps distinguishing a privileged initial set of formulae as axioms. As we have seen, there are no restrictions on which such systems are to be admitted; even trivial calculi in which everything is provable count (if the calculus is a syntactically distinct system from the contentful language). We differentiate them not in point of rationality, as absolutely binding on us, or permissible, or impermissible and so forth, but only in terms of the applicability or inner beauty of the mathematical theories whose truth is grounded in provability in the underlying system.

When we move to C-level language and truth-valued sentences, however, then we are concerned with logic in a much more philosophically important sense than that of a formal calculus, a sense which I will reserve for the term 'logic' from now on. We are concerned with the transmission of truth from premises to conclusions—and equally of falsity from conclusions back to premises. We are concerned with consequence and validity and with what conclusions it is rational to draw from given premises. Not every transformation of a formal calculus is to be accepted as legitimate. Prior's 'tonk' rules applied to C-level conjunction, for example, rules allowing us to conclude A&B from A and also B from A&B, are unsound.

But now a whole range of new questions arises: is there only one sense of logical consequence, or only one important one? Even if there is just one important notion, is there only one correct logic, or can we be pluralists and admit a number of equally legitimate[1] logics which differ over the consequence relation? Can we give an illuminating, non-ad-hoc criterion distinguishing logical constants from non-logical

---

[1] Whatever exactly that might mean in this context—this itself is an important question. For a defence of logical pluralism see Beall and Restall (2006).

constants? Even if there is just one 'true logic', are its rules absolutely binding on us? Indeed, what exactly does it mean for a principle or rule of logic (or rational inference more generally) to be absolutely binding?

These are very large questions which I will not attempt to answer here.[2] Rather I will present a logical system which accommodates nicely the neo-formalist approach to mathematics. I will make some observations designed to give plausibility to the idea that it is at least *a* rationally acceptable system for reasoning, regardless of topic (for I accept the traditional view of logic as topic-neutral). The main focus, however, will be on its suitability as a canon of reasoning in mathematics, and more especially, mathematics construed in a neo-formalist fashion; I will also address its utility in enabling us to 'excise' excluded middle without causing untold damage to standard mathematics (as intuitionism does).

## §II. The Basic Semantics Again

The Basic Semantics account of conjunction, disjunction, and negation (Chapter 2, §II.3) is:

> A conjunction is true iff both conjuncts are true. It is false iff at least one conjunct is false.
> Dually, a disjunction is false iff both disjuncts are false; it is true iff at least one disjunct is true.
> A negation is true iff the sentence it negates is false.

Although, as remarked, this semantics assumes a truth-functional, non-supervaluational account of these logical operators, I take it to be otherwise relatively uncontroversial.[3] It does not impose the requirement that each sentence is either true or untrue nor even that no sentence is both true and untrue. It is reasonable, I believe, to add the latter requirement (Weir 2004*a*). However, the former, a weak form of bivalence,[4] has to be rejected if neo-formalism is right, for there are mathematical sentences which are neither provable nor refutable in formal calculi. One example I gave (Chapter 4, §II.5) was $2 = \{\{\emptyset\}\}$. (See Appendix A.5 for a system containing decimal arithmetic and ZFU set theory in which this identity is an indeterminable.) More generally, reasons to reject bivalence and the related law of excluded middle include

(i) reference failure—it is incorrect to affirm, it may be said, that the greatest prime number is either odd or is not;

---

[2] A sketch of an approach to answering some of these questions is to be found in Weir (2000).

[3] More controversially, I believe that there are natural language expressions which in many contexts express the sentential operators of conjunction, disjunction, and negation.

[4] The stronger form is that every sentence is either true or false. Since falsity is at least a way of being untrue, the stronger form entails the weaker (via a simple application of ∨E).

(ii) vagueness—for example borderline cases in a Sorites sequence for a predicate such as 'bald' where we go from the hirsute to the hairless in a large number of indiscriminably differing stages; the borderline cases may be held to be neither determinately true nor determinately untrue;

(iii) and paradoxicality, as in the (strong) Liar sentence $\lambda:\sim\text{True}(|\lambda|)$ and the 'Russell sentence' $\{x: x \notin x\} \in \{x: x \notin x\}$.

All these examples are controversial but they do indicate that there is a prima facie case for holding that some meaningful sentences which, at least on the surface, can be used to make assertions, fail to be either determinately true or determinately untrue. I have phrased the matter in this rather wordy fashion, in terms of determinate truth, because if we express the rejection of bivalence for a sentence P as:

$$\sim(\text{True}|P| \lor \sim\text{True}|P|)$$

then very obvious de Morgan principles lead us (cf. Williamson 1994, pp. 187–9) to

$$\sim\text{True}|P| \ \& \ \sim\sim\text{True}|P|).$$

For non-dialetheists, this is conclusive reason not to say ⌜P is neither true nor untrue⌝, where, in the context, P expresses a meaningful proposition.

The idea that determinate truth is distinct from mere truth and determinate untruth (which I will equate with determinate falsity) from mere untruth is also controversial, rejected by Williamson for one (1994, pp. 194–5). His sceptical arguments deserve a fuller treatment than is appropriate here. Instead I will try to show how partial or gappy logic can do some positive work in the context of a logical framework for mathematics. For the simplest formal way to handle determinacy is probably by adopting a 'gappist' or 'partial logic' semantics. A determinate truth takes the 'top' value, T or 1, a determinate falsehood the bottom value F or 0. But sentences which are neither determinately true nor determinately false take the other 'gap' value G. I do not, in fact, think this framework is fully adequate, at least with respect to mathematical concepts such as that of 'set'. I employ this three-valued (if one counts the gap state as an extra value) approach rather as a sort of test-bed approximation. I will try out some logical ideas in that framework. If they do not work, it can be abandoned. Even if they do work, the framework may eventually be discarded, not a mere ladder to be thrown away perhaps, but the first stage of a rocket designed to set its payload free of the shackles of earth. A second reason for employing this framework is that it leads to a natural, non-intuitionist way to 'excise' excluded middle.

Throughout I will employ the familiar classical logic in the metatheory, which I will take to be standard set theory namely ZFCI, ZFC, plus the axiom of inaccessibles. Thus the non-classical semantics to be explored in the chapter will be developed from within a framework of conventional set theory, as is almost always the case. Reasoning classically, we establish that every sentence is either true or not, hence either true or gappy or false. I will develop a non-classical notion of logical consequence which I take as a fallible guide to the nature of the correct logic in languages in which there can be indeterminacy. This is as far as I will take things in this work. However, in a fuller treatment of the formal semantics of mathematics,[5] the non-classical logic ought then to be adopted as the logic of the metatheory, though the semantics may not be multi-valued. The process could then be iterated, looking at a different non-classical semantics, perhaps using the first approximation to a non-classical logic.

Now there is a very natural gappy semantics to adopt if one wishes to investigate, in the usual model-theoretic fashion, what notion of consequence flows from the Basic Semantics, namely the Lukasiewiczian, or strong Kleene[6] semantics for conjunction, disjunction, and negation. With T for true, F for false and G for the remaining gappy case this is:

|  | P & Q | Q T | G | F |  |  | P ∨ Q | Q T | G | F |
|---|---|---|---|---|---|---|---|---|---|---|
|  | T | T | G | F |  |  | T | T | T | T |
| P | G | G | G | F |  | P | G | T | G | G |
|  | F | F | F | F |  |  | F | T | G | F |

| P | ~P |
|---|---|
| T | F |
| G | G |
| F | T |

These are the most natural tables if one thinks the Quinean verdict matrices (1960, §13) are meaning-constitutive and one is looking for a fully functional table which settles what Quine sees as the undetermined middle value (both inputs gappy) for conjunction and disjunction. Thus where Quine says a conjunction commands assent when and only when both conjuncts do and commands dissent whenever one conjunct does, the strong Kleene functions yield truth for a conjunction when and only when both conjuncts are true and falsity whenever one conjunct is false.

[5] I reiterate that the neo-formalist is entitled to formal semantics, since it is a branch of mathematics with its own theorems and hence truths. Such semantics can be of enormous technical value, e.g. in telling us things about the strength of the derivability relation, even when one does not think that the language of mathematics is 'about' ANYTHING.

[6] Cf. J. Lukasiewicz (1920) some results of which are presented in Lukasiewicz and Tarski (1930), and Kleene (1952, p. 334). The Lukasiewicz and strong Kleene three-valued systems diverge over the conditional as we shall see.

# §III.  Logical Consequence

However, what we are really after is an account of logical consequence and this cannot be read off the valuation scheme. Thus consider the two standard classical model-theoretic accounts of logical consequence for multiple conclusion systems:

$X \models_1 Y$ iff there is no valuation in which all wffs in X are true and all in Y false.

$X \models_2 Y$ iff in every valuation in which all wffs in X are true, one in Y is true.

Equivalent in classical semantics, these come apart when indeterminacy is taken into consideration,[7] if there are sentences which are indeterminate in every admissible model.[8] Thus let P be true and U be a necessarily gappy sentence; then $\{P\}$ entails$_1$ $\{U\}$ but does not entail$_2$ it. The first account of entailment does not exclude failure of truth-preservation and can surely be set aside for that reason. The second, however, is also too strong as an account of consequence since $\{U\}$ entails$_2$ Q, for Q false, U as before, so that falsity is not preserved upwards.

This is a defect if there is no logical asymmetry between downward truth-preservation and upwards falsity preservation. Arguments with unfalse premises and false conclusions are as bad as arguments with true premises and untrue conclusions.[9] One does not need to be a Popperian to appreciate that rejecting a set of hypotheses, on disconfirming an empirical prediction one derives from the set, is a very important aspect of the rationality of science (even though such a modus tollens type strategy may still leave us in ignorance as to which particular sentence in the set ought to be rejected).

If both these classical accounts are wrong, what can the right notion of logical consequence be? My approach here will be to abandon the rather conservative (in its holding to a form of bivalence) designated/undesignated dichotomy and look to analogies with how one ought to pattern attitudes of acceptance and rejection towards components of inferences. Consider the following 'neo-classical' definition of logical consequence. X logically entails Y $(X \models Y)$ iff :

(a)  For any wff C in Y, in any model M in which all wffs in X are true[10] but all in Y but C are false, C is true in M.

---

[7]  One common response to the failure of bivalence is to define entailment in terms of preservation, from premises to conclusions, not of truth but rather of membership in some set of designated values. However, it is arguable that this approach does not take the failure of bivalence seriously, restoring it at the level of designated versus undesignated value.

[8]  One might suggest here our earlier examples of atomic predications of necessarily empty terms such as 'the greatest prime number' and the Liar and Russell sentences.

[9]  Edgington (1993, p. 195). Halbach and Horsten (2006, p. 690) also give an upwards falsity clause for a multiple conclusion system, but a different one from the neo-classical one to be advanced below.

[10]  When discussing 'true' and 'false' in connection with model-theoretic semantics I am talking of truth-in-a-model or valuation and likewise falsity (that is truth of negation) in a valuation or model, and not ordinary disquotational truth. But rather than write 'true in model M' each time, I will often leave this relativization implicit.

(b)  For any wff P in X, in any model M in which all wffs in Y are false but all in X
but P are true, P is false in M.

For single conclusion logics, and I will largely neglect multiple conclusion logics in
what follows, this amounts to:

X $\models$ C iff in all models M if all of X are true in M then C is true and if C is false and
all of X but P are true, then P is false.

The neo-classical account is motivated by the idea that in, for example, multiple
conclusion ∨E—from A ∨ B conclude A,B—it is perfectly legitimate to accept the
premiss A ∨ B ('The baby will be a boy, or a girl', say) whilst accepting neither
disjunct. But it is not acceptable, while accepting the premiss, to reject one disjunct
unless one accepts the other conclusion. Similarly for &I; one may reject the conclusion ('The baby will be a boy and a girl', for example) without rejecting either
conjunct premiss. But it would be wrong, if one rejected the conclusion, to accept
one premiss unless one rejected the other. That is the intuition underlying the neo-
classical account, at any rate.

However, even if one agrees with the neo-classical condition on acceptability of
inference rules, logic consists in more than one-step inferences: we need *structural* rules
telling us how to put operational rules together to form extended proofs. But consider
now a sentence P which is gappy in some valuation $v$. Since I have eschewed a supervaluational approach in favour of Lukasiewiczian connectives, P & ~P is also gappy so the
entailment P & ~P $\models$ $\perp$ fails neo-classically, where $\perp$ is some necessarily false absurdity
constant. As there are no multiple premisses or conclusions, the neo-classical truth of
the claim that P & ~P entails $\perp$ requires in the upwards falsity-preservation direction that
if $\perp$ is false in valuation $v$, which of course it is, then so is P&~P. But this fails in the model
in question since P&~P is gappy. (Similarly P ∨ ~P fails to be a neo-classical logical truth,
for atomic P, since we could always assign P the gap value.) But despite the neo-classical
falsehood of P & ~P $\models$ $\perp$ there are proofs of P & ~P $\vdash$ $\perp$ in which every step is neo-
classically correct, e.g. the following in a Gentzen-style natural deduction system:

$$\frac{\dfrac{P\&\sim P}{P} \quad \dfrac{P\&\sim P}{\sim P}}{\perp}.$$

&E preserves truth downwards and falsity upwards and so is clearly neo-classically
correct. But so too is the natural deduction ~E rule: from P,~P conclude C, for any C
(including the absurdity constant $\perp$). The truth-preservation direction is trivial (at least
if one is already predisposed to accept ~E)—there is no valuation which makes both
premisses true. In the other direction, neo-classical correctness requires that if $\perp$ is
false, which it is in every valuation, then if P is true, ~P is false and if ~P is true P is
false. But this does indeed hold in every valuation by the Kleene rules for ~. So to
preserve neo-classical soundness globally we have to amend the classical structural rules
which permit us to chain together the &E and ~E inferences in the above fashion.

Now on the neo-classical account of entailment, $X \models Y$ if in every model the minimum value of X is no greater than the maximum value of Y; call this necessary condition the *minimax* condition. In the single conclusion case (in propositional logic) this means that any rule allowing us to go from the sequent X:A to X:B, where A minimax entails B, preserves neo-classical correctness. We can give a complete set of rules for this minimax transition—de Morgan rules, associativity, commutativity, distributivity, double negation rules plus the 'Mingle' rule allowing us to go from $(C\&\sim C)$ to $(D\vee\sim D)$. (See further Appendix A.1.) What we have just seen is that there are non-minimax rules such as $\sim$E which are neo-classically sound as single inference steps yet chaining them and minimax rules together by the usual structural principles of (generalized) transitivity leads to unsoundness. Neo-classically, we can have A, B $\models$ C but not A&B $\models$ C.

How, then, should we amend the structural rules to accommodate the neo-classical perspective on entailment? The way that the 'proof' of P & $\sim$P $\vdash \perp$ breaks down suggests placing global restrictions on proof which block the generalized transitivity of entailment. We look, in other words, for a non-transitive notion of logical conse-quence in which transitivity fails in a controlled fashion, holding widely enough to permit that chaining together of proofs which is essential in order to derive the standard results of classical mathematics.[11] If one looks at the problematic proof above, it is noteworthy that, in the counterexample model to neo-classical correctness, an indeterminate, gappy wff, P&$\sim$P, occurred in the overall assumptions on which *both* premises for the minimax unsound $\sim$E were based. My favoured response here (see, for example, Weir, 1998c, 1999, 2005b, §II), is that we rule this out for minimax unsound rules. In any such rules, any wffs which occur in the antecedent of more than one premiss of a sequent system inference rule must be 'determinate'. But character-izing determinacy and investigating the logical issues which flow from that notion will take us too far from our current concerns. So here I will implement a more brutal restriction which yields a weaker logic, but one strong enough for our purposes.

The restriction is that we debar *any* assumption from occurring among the overall assumptions of both the major and the minor premiss of the minimax unsound $\sim$E (or any other minimax unsound rule). Thus the $\sim$E rule in Gentzen–Prawitz proof architecture is:[12]

$$
\frac{\begin{array}{cc} X & Y \\ \cdots & \cdots \\ P & \sim P \end{array}}{C}
$$

---

[11]  Other logicians who have mooted or advocated curtailments on transitivity include Tennant (1987, ch. 17), and Smiley, (1959, esp. pp. 233–4 and §2) (following on from work by Geach and von Wright). Dummett considers but rejects abandonment of transitivity of entailment in (1975/78, p. 252).

[12]  See Gentzen (1969, ch. 3, secs. I, II) and Prawitz (1965, (esp. pp. 98–101) for the history of the origins of natural deduction in the work of Lukasiewicz, Jaskowski, and Gentzen), and Tennant (1978).

subject to the global 'no overlap' restriction that $X \cap Y = \emptyset$.

This format makes it clear that the restriction is a global, structural one and that the basic inference step, from P, $\sim$P to C is legitimate. For reasons of convenience in presenting proofs I will use, instead of this natural deduction format, the sequent version in the familiar Lemmon (1978) format, though this obscures somewhat the fact that the restrictions are on the structural, not operational, rules:

$$
\begin{array}{lll}
X & (1)\ P & \text{Given} \\
Y & (2)\ \sim P & \text{Given} \\
X,Y, & (3)\ C & 1,2\ \sim E \text{ where again } X \cap Y = \emptyset
\end{array}
$$

Thus though we have *ex contradictione quodlibet* in the form P, $\sim$P $\vdash$ C, the classical proof of an arbitrary sentence Q from P&$\sim$P is invalid and transitivity fails since we have P&$\sim$P $\vdash$ P, P&$\sim$P $\vdash$ $\sim$P and P, $\sim$P $\vdash$ Q but not P&$\sim$P $\vdash$ Q.

The standard natural deduction introduction and elimination rules for conjunction, and the introduction rules for $\vee$ and for $\sim$, all come out as neo-classically sound since they are minimax sound. In the case of negation, I include both intuitionistic and classical *reductio ad absurdum* rules:[13]

$$
\begin{array}{lll}
X, P & (1)\ \bot & \text{Given} \\
X & (2)\ \sim P & 1\ \sim I \\
X, \sim P & (1)\ \bot & \text{Given} \\
X & (2)\ P & 1\ \sim I_C
\end{array}
$$

The only other restriction we need, for the operators &, $\vee$ and $\sim$, is on the minimax unsound $\vee E$ which we restrict to:

$$
\begin{array}{lll}
X & (1)\ P \vee Q & \text{Given} \\
Y,P & (2)\ C & \text{Given} \\
Z,Q & (3)\ C & \text{Given} \\
X,Y,Z, & (4)\ C & 1,2,3\ \vee E
\end{array}
$$

where we require that $(X \cap (Y \cup Z)) = \emptyset$.

These overlap restrictions apply to the pure logic. But a distinction can be made between premisses, 'mere premisses' as it were, and non-logical axioms, for example mathematical axioms. Should the latter be subject to the overlap restrictions too?

---

[13] Here, in the second form of the rule, we have the classical form of $\sim$I which I accept just as, in the minimax rules, I accept double negation elimination—$\sim\sim$E—allowing the cancellation of double negations. The intuitionist opposes this, of course. Note, though, that accepting $\sim\sim$E, a highly intuitive rule, does not entail the arguably unintuitive result that excluded middle is a logical theorem. I suspect a lot of the otherwise puzzling attraction of intuitionism arises because intuitionists tend to obscure the bizarreness of rejecting $\sim\sim$E by concentrating on the unattractiveness of LEM. (Of course intuitionistic logic is interesting to study as a formal calculus in its own right as well as being useful in studies in proof theory and with respect to issues of computability—though modal logic can be used to serve such purposes instead.) The issue is too complex to resolve here. For further arguments see Weir (1983), (1985), (1986c), (1988), (2000) with contrary arguments in Tennant (1984) and George (1987), (1988).

If one restricts the notion of model to those in which the axioms are true—the 'admissible models'—then one can treat the axioms in question just like logical axioms, that is exempt from the overlap conditions, and the soundness proof still goes through. Hence I will assume that mathematical axioms are not subject to the overlap clauses.

We need, to get things moving, a structural rule embodying the reflexivity of derivability. One such is a rule of hypothesis:

$$X \quad (1)\ P \quad H$$

where $P \in X$; or else we could use the special case where $X = \{P\}$ to which we must then add an expansion or 'thinning' rule:

$$
\begin{array}{lll}
X & (1)\ P & \text{Given} \\
X,Y & (2)\ P & 1\ \text{Exp.}
\end{array}
$$

I have also assumed throughout a truth-constant T true in all admissible models and the absurdity constant $\perp$ featuring in the negation rules and interpreted as false in all models. Theorems are wffs provable from the empty set of antecedents[14] (which I will represent by '—'). It follows from the soundness of the system (see Appendix §A.2) that neither $\sim(P\ \&\sim P)$ nor $(P \vee \sim P)$ are theorems, for atomic P.

Though generalized transitivity (or Cut) fails, the $\vee E$ rule gives us a fairly broad form of transitivity as a derived rule, via a degenerate case with the major premiss taking the form $P \vee P$:

$$
\begin{array}{lll}
X & (1)\ P & \text{Given} \\
X & (2)\ P \vee P & 1\ \vee I \\
Y\ P & (3)\ C & \text{Given} \\
X,Y & (4)\ C & 2,\ 3\ \vee E
\end{array}
$$

subject only to the overlap restriction that $X \cap Y = \emptyset$. This restricted version yields the special case:

A ⊢ B and B ⊢ C then A ⊢ C.

## §IV. The Conditional

Although we have the rules for conjunction, disjunction, and negation, arguably one operator has been left out, namely the conditional. I say 'arguably' because the definition of ⌜if P then Q⌝ by $(\sim P \vee Q)$ (or some equivalent in the language of $\sim$, $\vee$ and &) leads, it has been argued, to many counter-intuitive results (see Read 1988, ch. 2, for a contrary view Rieger 2006).

---

[14]  Or we could have defined the theorems as the set of wffs derivable from any wff or alternatively as the set of wffs derivable from T alone, and altered matters accordingly.

One natural requirement on a conditional → is that it 'internalize' in the object language, as best as possible, the notion of logical consequence. That is, one ought to have as a metatheorem the Deduction Theorem,

If Δ, A ⊢ B then Δ ⊢ A → B.

or something closely approximating that. To be sure, a modal conditional can represent consequence much better than an extensional one. I introduced a neo-classical modal conditional in (1998*c*). However, notwithstanding the persistent use of modal notions of construct*ibility* in mathematics from ancient to modern times, it is very doubtful that a modalized or intensional conditional plays a role in actual mathematical practice. Therefore the simplification which results from considering only an extensional conditional is, I believe, justified.

In the neo-classical context, in order to represent consequence as best we can in an extensional conditional, the conditional must take the broadly Lukasiewiczian form:[15]

|           |   | Q |   |   |
| --------- | - | - | - | - |
| P → Q     |   | T | G | F |
|           | T | T | ? | F |
| P         | G | T | T | ? |
|           | F | T | T | T |

Given that an extensional conditional is true if the antecedent is false or consequent true and false if the antecedent is true and consequence false, the only values which need justifying are the two marked '?' plus the middle value where both inputs are gappy. But since a model in which P and Q both take the gap value is not a neo-classical counterexample to the entailment of Q by P, since indeed the Liar neo-classically entails the Russell sentence, if we assume they are in all circumstances indeterminate, this justifies the Lukasiewiczian assignment of true in the middle case.

What should the value be in the two remaining cases? Since the inference from a true premiss to a gappy conclusion fails to be truth-preserving and so is not neo-classically sound and since similarly an inference from a gappy premiss to a false conclusion fails to preserve falsity upwards, this suggests the correct value in each case should be false, generating a bivalent conditional, bivalent in the sense that no conditional is gappy. On the other hand, if we wish to have gappy conditionals (for example to handle the Curry paradox) we need a non-bivalent conditional in which the remaining cases are assigned the value Gap.

Here we have a case where the three-valued approximation in a classical metatheory creaks under the strain of attempting to model the thoroughly non-classical idea of indeterminacy. My solution is to adopt a 'belt and braces' job, that is to accept only

---

[15] As remarked, the Lukasiewicz and strong Kleene three-valued systems diverge over the conditionals, see Kleene (1952, p. 334).

rules which are sound under *both* interpretations. The following rules meet this requirement (Appendix A.2). Firstly →I:

$$
\begin{array}{lll}
\text{P} & \text{(1) Q} & \text{Given} \\
\hline
& \text{(2) P} \to \text{Q} & \text{1} \to \text{I}
\end{array}
$$

Thus we restrict the usual →I rule by not allowing there to be any auxiliary assumptions in the premiss antecedent, in addition to the discharged assumption which will form the antecedent of the conclusion. For →E we restrict the rule with the same ban on overlap as in ∨E and ∼E:

$$
\begin{array}{lll}
\text{X} & \text{(1) P} \to \text{Q} & \text{Given} \\
\text{Y} & \text{(2) P} & \text{Given} \\
\text{X, Y,} & \text{(3) Q} & \text{1,2} \to\text{E}
\end{array}
$$

with $X \cap Y = \emptyset$. The two conditional rules are sound in the sense that they preserve neo-classical entailment (on either interpretation of the conditional).

Further sound rules, no longer derivable by the standard proofs given the restrictions on →I and →E, are transitivity and contraposition:
Transitivity:

$$
\begin{array}{lll}
\text{X} & \text{(1) P} \to \text{Q} & \text{Given} \\
\text{Y} & \text{(2) Q} \to \text{R} & \text{Given} \\
\text{X, Y,} & \text{(3) P} \to \text{R} & \text{1,2 [3.}i\text{] Trans.}
\end{array}
$$

where $X \cap Y = \emptyset$.
Contraposition:

$$
\begin{array}{lll}
\text{X} & \text{(1) P} \to \text{Q} & \text{Given} \\
\text{X} & \text{(2) } \sim\text{Q} \to \sim\text{P} & \text{1, Contrap.}
\end{array}
$$

(As usual, the biconditional (P ↔ Q) is defined by (P → Q) & (Q → P).)

The whole system of rules introduced thus far is sound relative to the neo-classical definition of entailment (Appendix A.2). A completeness result is provable for the stronger system which incorporates the more subtle determinacy restrictions (Weir 1998*c*, Appendix) but not for the weaker system set out here which I will refer to as 'strict neo-classical logic'. Unless specified to the contrary, '⊢' in what follows is the strict neo-classical derivability relation. The most important feature of this logic for our purposes is that (P ∨ ∼P) is not provable, for atomic P. T ⊨ (P ∨ ∼P) fails since in the model in which P is assigned gap, we go from a true premiss to a gappy conclusion. Hence by soundness, T ⊢ (P ∨ ∼P) fails too. We have excised (lots of instances of) excluded middle but we still have a fairly powerful logic.

# §V*. Quantification and Infinitary Logic

Thus far I have looked at propositional logic, but clearly we need to extend these ideas to predicate calculus. The generalization to a standard first-order calculus is straightforward. One takes over the same $\forall$I, $\forall$E, $\exists$I rules. These are all minimax sound and therefore neo-classically sound, where we consider preservation of truth relative to an assignment to variables (and likewise falsity preservation upwards relative to such an assignment). However, for $\exists$E we must make an alteration corresponding to the overlap restriction in $\vee$E:

| X | (1) $\exists x \varphi x$ | Given |
|---|---|---|
| Y, $\varphi x/t$ | (2) C | Given |
| X,Y, | (3) C | 1,2 $\exists$E |

adding the strict neo-classical condition that $X \cap Y = \emptyset$. We also have, of course, the usual constraints on the parameter t, that is, it must not occur in $\varphi$, C, or any sentence in Y. I will in addition assume, except where otherwise indicated, a standard theory of identity, the =I and =E rules of Chapter 3, §I.3.

Granted the rehabilitation of infinitary calculi as genuine logics urged in the last chapter, an alternative to standard quantification theory is available. We can replace quantification with infinitary conjunction and disjunction (indeed that is how quantification was often interpreted in the earlier phase of the rise of modern logic). Now a standard infinitary language (see Karp 1964, Dickmann 1975) is designated in some such way as $L_{\kappa,\lambda}$ with $\kappa$ a regular infinite cardinal[16] which is a strict upper bound on the cardinality of conjunctions and disjunctions (considered as set-theoretic objects) and $\lambda \leq \kappa$ is the strict upper bound on the length of variable strings allowed in quantifier blocks of the form $\forall x_1, \ldots x_\gamma, \ldots$ or $\exists x_1, \ldots x_\gamma, \ldots$ . However, given a neo-formalist treatment of quantification, in particular the substitutionalist version of Chapter 3, §III.3, we can simplify by dispensing with quantifiers in favour of infinitary regular conjunctions and disjunctions and so work only with languages of the form $L_\kappa$. (I will require also that $\kappa$ is inaccessible in order that the cardinality of the languages is suitable for various mathematical theories to be investigated.[17]) Let us say that the subscript $\kappa$ gives the *index* of the language. For $\kappa$ regular, it also gives the depth of the language, the least upper bound on the depth of wffs in the language. Here depth is the recursively defined degree of wff complexity, atoms being of depth zero, a conjunction of the wffs in X having depth the least upper bound of the depths of the conjuncts in X, and so on.

---

[16] A cardinal $\kappa$ is regular if it is not the union of $\lambda < \kappa$ sets each of cardinality $< \kappa$.

[17] An inaccessible cardinal (sometimes a 'strong inaccessible') is a regular cardinal $\lambda$ such that for all $\alpha < \lambda$, $2\alpha < \lambda$ (usually one adds that $\lambda > \aleph_0$). Standard infinitary propositional logic with 'ordinary' distributive laws is complete for $L_\kappa$, $\kappa$ inaccessible. See Karp (1964, p. 52).

We can suppose that the atomic wffs are finite expression strings defined just as for conventional first-order languages. In particular, for the infinitary languages I will consider I assume that predicates have only finitely many places and so atomic sentences are of finite length. However, if any interesting mathematical theory is to be true, as regimented in such an infinitary language, then there will have to be infinitely many singular terms, given the substitutionalist interpretation of the quantifiers. The 'substitution class' of singular terms determines the size of models; since conjunction and disjunction are the means of generalizing over the domain, the cardinality $\|ST\|$ of the set of singular terms has to be fixed as of cardinality $< \kappa$, the index of the language (and given only finitely many predicates, $\|ST\| < \kappa$ will fix the size of the language as $\kappa$ also, for inaccessible $\kappa$).

The wffs of the language are defined in the usual way as the inductive closure of the atoms under the operations of forming negations, conditionals, and infinitary conjunction and disjunction which will be represented in the metalanguage in such ways as $\wedge(A_\alpha\ _{\alpha<\beta})$ and $\vee(A_\alpha\ _{\alpha<\beta})$, where the ordinal $\beta$ indexes the immediate constituents of the sentences. We can think of these sentences as pairs, $\langle\wedge, X\rangle$ and $\langle\vee, X\rangle$ with X a set of wffs $< \kappa$ in size. Likewise negation and the conditional are pairs and triples[18] of the form $\langle\sim, A\rangle$ and $\langle\rightarrow, A, B\rangle$ for wffs A, B. However I will generally, and with due apologies to Poland, lapse from this notation into bracket notation.

To define the surrogates for quantification in our 'variable-free' language $L_\kappa$, it is useful to have to hand, as it were, an auxiliary language $L_\lambda^*$, $\lambda$ an inaccessible $> \kappa$ but formed in the same way as $L_\kappa$ by adding $\kappa$ new singular terms. An infinitary conjunction $\wedge(A_\alpha\ _{\alpha<\beta})$ is a universal quantification iff

there is a sentence $\varphi$ of $L_\lambda^*$ containing a 'new' singular term t such that each conjunct $A_\alpha$ results from $\varphi$ by uniformly replacing t with a term in ST and every term $u \in ST$ features in a conjunct in this fashion.

Existential quantifications are defined in dual fashion. More restricted generalizations occur when the 'substitution class' for t is narrower, when only terms from some proper subclass of ST feature in the conjuncts (disjuncts) in the above fashion.

We can think of a formula $\varphi$ of $L_\lambda^*$ with a designated new term t as playing the role of an open sentence $\varphi x$, t playing the role of free variable $x$. So although variables are no part of the language, we can abbreviate infinitary conjunctions and disjunctions in a slang form using variables. Thus $\forall x\varphi x$ is a metatheoretic abbreviation of a regular conjunction $\wedge(A_\alpha\ _{\alpha<\beta})$ as above. (Substitutional quantification, from this perspective, can be viewed as 'pushing down' a metalinguistic abbreviation of especially regular forms of infinitary conjunction and disjunction into the object language.) Special variables can also be used where the generalization has a narrower substitution class.

---

[18] Though nothing prevents one introducing infinitary conditionals with infinitely many antecedents (and indeed consequents, when trying to internalize the entailment relation of a multiple conclusion logic) into the object language. See Weir (1999).

Infinitary generalizations of the sentential rules &I, &E, ∨I, and ∨E (see Appendix §A.3) then perform the function of the (unfree) quantifier rules and the Lukasiewicz/ Kleene account of the meaning of these operators generalizes straightforwardly to the infinitary case. Models for these languages are essentially domains such that there is a function from the singular terms *onto* the domain, with predicates interpreted in the usual fashion. Proofs are strings < κ in length, κ the index of the language, built up from axioms by application of the sentential inference rules.

## §VI. Classical Recapture

In neo-classical logic, the law of excluded middle does not hold. True we have special cases such as

$$\vdash(P \to P)\vee \sim (P \to P)$$

as of course ⊢ φ ∨ ∼φ whenever ⊢ φ or ⊢ ∼φ. But no instance of (φ ∨ ∼φ) is a theorem for any φ which can take the gap value in a Lukasiewiczian valuation—and this includes every sentence of the →-free sector of the language. However, do we not need such instances of LEM if, as I claimed in the Introduction, neo-formalism is to be a non-revisionary philosophy of mathematics? Although philosophers should not be afraid in principle to tell mathematicians and scientists that some practice they are following is incoherent, I prudently decline to do so (at least for the most part) in the case of classical mathematics. Yet mathematicians make essential use of excluded middle in the proofs of many standard results, for example the Bolzano–Weierstrass theorem. So how do we get *classical recapture*? How can we get an entitlement to reason classically from safe and familiar axioms systems such as Peano Arithmetic, Analysis, and so forth (or less formal equivalents) if we restrict ourselves to strict neo-classical logic?

For a full neo-classical answer, I would appeal to the notion of *determinacy axioms*. That is, we suppose that there is a set of sentences of the form ⌜Determinately P⌝ or ⌜∼Determinately Q⌝ which in some cases can have a status similar to that of axioms, and which, as it were, boost neo-classical logic up to an equivalence with classical logic over a given sublanguage. (See Weir 2005b, §II.) But it is not necessary to invoke full neo-classical logic in order to see how a neo-formalist might answer the question.

The reason is that changing up a gear to infinitary logic can take us to the promised land of negation-completeness even granted a background of strict neo-classical logic. Peano arithmetic is a classic, as it were, example. Applying a wee bit of overkill, we will start from the language of finitary PA, where = is the only predicate, 0 the only constant, and the usual function symbols S, +, and ×, the only other non-logical constants then expand to an infinitary language $L_{\theta 0}$, where $\theta_0$ is the first inaccessible. The set of singular terms (the substitution class for the quantifiers in effect) is the countable set of all numerical terms, that is the set of all terms built up from the standard numerals, 0, S0, SS0, . . . $S^k 0$ using +, ×, and brackets. We can let $n$ and $m$, with subscripts as necessary, be metalinguistic variables to be used as part of our shorthand for the regular infinitary compounds which play the role of generalization, i.e. $\exists n \Phi n$ is $\vee(\Phi S^k 0_{\ 0 \le k < \omega})$ and similarly for $\forall$. Since the index $\theta_0$ is inaccessible and there are countably many atoms, an induction on the depth of wffs (breaking the language up into sub-languages of depth $\le \alpha < \kappa$) shows that the cardinality of $L_{\theta_0}$ is itself $\theta_0$.

For the proof theory, add to strict neo-classical propositional logic and the standard rules for identity an axiom set which will decide all atomic sentences, all equations holding between numerical terms; call the result infinitary PA, or IPA (a nice acronym!). One such axiom set is this subset of the Q axioms:

(i) $\forall n \ 0 \neq Sn$,

(ii) $\forall n \forall m (Sn = Sm \rightarrow n = m)$,

(iii) $\forall n \ n + 0 = n$,

(iv) $\forall n \forall m (n + Sm = S(n + m))$,

(v) $\forall n \ n \times 0 = 0$,

(vi) $\forall n \forall m (n \times Sm = (n \times m) + n)$.[19]

An inductive proof of essentially the same type as in the $\omega$-rule case shows that every sentence of $L_{IPA}$ is decided.

Thus the inductive step in the proof for disjunction in the negation-completeness proof goes like this:

Suppose a disjunct of $\vee(A_\alpha {}_{\alpha < \beta})$ is provable, without loss of generality let it be $A_\gamma$. Then $\vdash \vee(A_\alpha {}_{\alpha < \beta})$ by $\vee I$. Suppose, then, no disjunct is provable. By inductive hypothesis, $\vdash \sim A_\gamma$ for all $\gamma < \beta$ hence $\vdash \sim\vee(A_\alpha {}_{\alpha < \beta})$ by the strict neo-classical proof:

| | | |
|---|---|---|
| 1 | (1) $\vee(A_\alpha {}_{\alpha<\beta})$ | H |
| 2.$\gamma$ | (2.$\gamma$) $A_\gamma$ | H, $\gamma < \beta$ |
| — | (3.$\gamma$) $\sim A_\gamma$ | Given, $\gamma < \beta$ |
| 2.$\gamma$ | (4.$\gamma$) $\bot$ | 2.$\gamma$,3.$\gamma$ $\sim$E |
| 1 | (5) $\bot$ | 1, 4.$\gamma$, $\gamma < \beta$, $\vee$E |
| — | (6) $\sim\vee(A_\alpha {}_{\alpha<\beta})$ | 5, $\sim$I |

All the overlap restrictions in the applications of the rules of $\sim$E (lines 2.$\gamma$, 3.$\gamma$, $\gamma < \beta$) and $\vee$E, (lines 1 and 4.$\gamma$, $\gamma < \beta$) are met. $\square$

The classical rules for the conditional are also restricted, neo-classically, but the inductive step goes through here too. Inductive hypothesis gives us $\vdash \sim P$ or $\vdash Q$ or

---

[19] Given any atom t = u, we can prove t = $S^k$o, and u = $S^j$o for some $k$, $j$. (Work from minimal occurrences in t and u of $x + y$ and $x \times y$— no + or × in $x$ or $y$— using repeated applications of (iii) and (iv) in the first case and those plus (v) and (vi) in the second, reducing step by step the number of occurrences of the arithmetic operators.) If $k = j$ then the identity rules give t = u, if not then we use (i) and (ii) to reduce t = u to absurdity.

both $\vdash P$ and $\vdash \sim Q$ and in the first two cases we have a strict neo-classical proof of $P \rightarrow Q$, in the third we have $\vdash \sim(P \rightarrow Q)$.

Thus IPA, an infinitary but strict neo-classical system, yields exactly the same theorems as classical PA in finitary logic plus the $\omega$-rule, since both theories are negation-complete.[20] We get classical recapture and, by negation-completeness and $\vee$I, every instance of LEM is provable.

Can we get classical recapture for more extensive systems than arithmetic? Yes, the same idea can be applied to analysis and beyond. Rename $L_{\theta 0}$, the language of IPA, as $L_0$. Form $L_1$ by adding to the non-logical constant $=$ a membership predicate $\in$ and $\theta_0$ new singular terms $\{x: \varphi x\}$, one for each one-place open wff $\varphi x$ of $L_0$.[21] Restrict application of $\wedge$ and $\vee$ in $L_1$ to sets of conjuncts (disjuncts) of size less than $\theta_1$ the second inaccessible; it follows that $L_1$ itself is of cardinality $\theta_1$ as well as of index $\theta_1$. Since we have an expanded class of singular terms, we have new classes of regular infinitary conjunctions and disjunctions to play the role of quantifications over the entire domain; we can indicate these metalinguistically as before in familiar variable-based notation, using variables $x$, $y$, and $z$ to 'range' over the full new substitution class of singular terms.

To the axiomatic base we add firstly an infinite series of negative axioms, negative identity axioms $t \neq u$, wherever it is not the case that either both t and u are set terms or both are numerical terms; and negative membership claims $t \notin u$, wherever either u is a numerical term or t is a set term. For non-negative axioms we have each instance of the extensionality schema for the set terms:

$$\{x : \varphi x\} = \{x : \psi x\} \leftrightarrow \forall n(\varphi n \leftrightarrow \psi n)$$

and each instance of the comprehension schema:

$$\forall n(n \in \{x : \varphi x\} \leftrightarrow \varphi n)$$

where in each case $\varphi x$ and $\psi x$ are open sentences of $L_0$. Here $\forall n$ abbreviates infinitary regular conjunction with substitution class the numerical terms of $L_0$.

The intended model is obvious. We expand the intended domain of $L_0$ by adding to the numbers the (disjoint) continuum-sized set of all sets of numbers. The numerical terms are interpreted as before, whilst $\{x: \varphi x\}$ is assigned the extension of $\varphi x$ in $L_0$.[22] The new axioms are clearly sound on this interpretation.

---

[20] Relative, that is, to a translation between the two languages in which we translate infinitary conjunctions and disjunctions into ordinary quantificational sentences according to the recipe outlined above for generating 'slang' abbreviations, using variables, in the metatheory.

[21] Of course strictly speaking there are no open sentences in our infinitary languages; we assume some expansion of the language with added terms marking variable places as before. We can think of the set terms as complex singular terms in the language itself, formed by means of a set operator, or as metalinguistic abbreviations for simple singular terms correlated one:one with the open wffs of $L_0$.

[22] That is, the set S such that $\alpha$ belongs to S iff there is an extension $I^*$ of the interpretation I of $L_0$ for the language expanded to include term t and such that $\varphi x/t$ is true in $I^*$ with t assigned $\alpha$ as referent.

What of negation-completeness? The inductive steps of the argument are un-changed. For atoms, the negative axioms settle all identity claims except (i) cases of t = u where both are numerical terms; but this is decided in the same way as $L_0$; or (ii) where both t and u are set terms. But since IPA in $L_0$ is negation-complete and the right-hand-side of each extensionality schema is a sentence of $L_0$, this means that each such identity is decided too. Similarly, the negative axioms settle all atomic member-ship claims except positive ones of the form t ∈ {$x$: $\varphi x$}, where t is a numerical term. But this is settled by the relevant instance of the comprehension scheme, given once again that the right-hand side of this biconditional is part of $L_0$ and thus decided.

We can move on from the negation-complete theory for the language $L_1$ to generate a version of simple type theory. For language $L_{n+1}$ we add a level $n+1$ membership predicate $\in_{n+1}$ and $\theta_n$ new set terms of level $n+1$, one for each $L_n$ open sentence, with the expanded regular infinitary conjunctions and disjunctions (of length $< \theta_{n+1}$) constituting generalization over an even wider substitution class. The new axioms parallel those for $L_1$: a set of negative identity axioms t ≠ u, where t and u are of different levels (different set-theoretic levels, or else one is a numerical term, one not); and likewise axioms t $\notin_{n+1}$ u for all pairs of singular terms except the cases where t is a set term of level $n$, u a set term of level $n+1$. The positive axioms are instances of the level $n+1$ versions of extensionality and comprehension schemas, e.g. in the latter case:

$$\forall t(t \in_{n+1}\{x : \varphi x\}_{n+1} \leftrightarrow \varphi t)$$

where the substitution class for $t$ is the set of singular terms of $L_n$ and $\varphi x$ is an open sentence of level $n$. The proof of negation completeness goes through essentially in the same way as at level 1.

The union of all the languages and axioms gives us the language $L_\omega$ and a negation-complete simple type theory; this can be used to model nearly all mathematics, certainly nearly all with practical applications. Still, the hierarchical divisions of simple type theory are awkward and unattractive. Can we do away with them and develop a negation-complete cumulative set theory?

The answer is yes, we can do that by laying down 'list axioms', which are roughly speaking transfinite extensions of the pair set axiom, to yield an infinitary set theory IS. We start from an infinitary language $L_\kappa$, where κ is an inaccessible greater than the second inaccessible $\theta_1$; $L_\kappa$ has $\theta_\alpha$ many singular terms, $\theta_\alpha$ the $\alpha^{\text{th}}$ inaccessible, for some a such that $\theta_0 \leq \theta_\alpha < \kappa$.[23] It has two predicate constants, the identity predicate and the membership predicate. These interact directly in a standard extensionality axiom:

$$\forall x \forall y(\forall z(z \in x \leftrightarrow z \in y) \rightarrow x = y)$$

(ordinary italic variables, as before, abbreviate regular infinitary conjunctions and disjunctions whose substitution class is the set ST of all singular terms).

---

[23] Hence there is an infinity of IS theories—$IS_{\theta\alpha}$, one for each α ≥ 0.

The canonical model for the IS language is $V_{\theta\alpha}$. There is a bijection $h$ from the singular terms of $L_\kappa$ onto $V_{\theta\alpha}$, we write $\mathbf{t}_i$ for $h(t_i)$. Where $t_0$ is the term assigned the empty set, our first list axiom is:

$$\forall x(x \in t_0 \leftrightarrow x \neq x).$$

For every other term $t_i$, let J index the members $\mathbf{u}_j$ of $\mathbf{t}_i$. Then our $i$-th list comprehension axiom is:

$$\forall x(x \in t_i \leftrightarrow \vee(x = u_j)j \in J).$$

We generate in this fashion what, in model-theoretic terms, are canonical names of the members of the pure iterative hierarchy $V_{\theta\alpha}$. Then for any sentence P, IS $\vdash$ P or IS $\vdash$ ~P (Appendix §A.4). Hence classical reasoning is legitimate in IS theory since applying classical rules does not extend the derivability relation and, as with all the theories considered thus far, the standard models will be classical, bivalent ones.

## §VII. Really Existing Mathematics

Have we then achieved an optimal foundation for mathematics, a reasonable idealization of mathematical practice which decides pretty much any mathematical question one is likely to ask? I suspect that there will have arisen by now a strong feeling that the neo-formalist has cheated, if not in the formalization of simple type theory, at least in the IS theory. Part of this feeling might arise simply from fear and loathing of infinitary logic. But even accepting the legitimacy of infinitary logic as an idealization of actual practice, surely something fishy is going on, in the IS theory at least? In that theory one has proofs of all truths about $V_{\theta\alpha}$; but only by building the structure of that hierarchy into the very structure of the theory, in particular into the structural interrelationships of the list axioms. Thus to prove that the Axiom of Choice is provable in $L_\kappa$, we need to assume Choice in the background metatheory which specifies $L_\kappa$, and so on.

IS, indeed all the theories outlined above including the simple type theory and IPA, in idealizing beyond the lowly finite bounds which mark the limits of concrete, comprehensible practice perforce have to treat theories as mathematical objects in their own right. The results often take forms not as closely tailored to actual mathematical practice as simply generalizing inferences such as &I into the transfinite. Thus consider the proof of commutativity:

$$\forall n \forall m(n + m = m + n)$$

in IPA. The direct proof is by $\wedge$I on all the instances of $n + m = m + n$. Each in turn is provable because we have in each case $\vdash n + m = S^k 0$ and $\vdash m + n = S^k 0$, for some $k$, by the method sketched above, §VI. But how do we know there are indeed all these proofs of the instances? The method of reducing arbitrary numerical terms to standard numerals is proven to work by a mathematical induction more complex than the usual proof of commutativity in first order finitary PA, which is by good old-fashioned mathematical induction from the principle:

$$\forall n((\varphi 0 \;\&\; \forall m(\varphi m \rightarrow \varphi Sm)) \rightarrow \varphi n)$$

Moreover, we know that $n + m$ and $m + n$ will always reduce to the same standard numeral because we already know that commutativity holds!

So although the IPA system, with its weaker-than-Q axiom set boosted, to infinity and beyond, by infinitary logic, yields a stronger theory than standard finitary PA, it depends on the latter; PA is not a ladder to be thrown away. I have urged not only that an infinitary formal system is a legitimate idealization, but that infinitely long wffs and proofs are concretely realized, albeit via the ubiquitous device of abbreviation, in tokens of actual practice. Even so, our arithmetic could not exist if only IPA tokens belonged to the corpus of our utterances. On the contrary, many abbreviatory concrete realizations of IPA depend on prior grasp of finitary arithmetic.

None of this, however, threatens the claim that arithmetic, really existing arithmetic, is a negation-complete (and thus neo-formalistically kosher) theory. The question of whether it is negation-complete or not is not a well-posed one, when addressed to a motley of informal practices. It can only be raised once we have carried out our idealized formalization, even though we construct it using the materials of our informal, 'real', mathematical practice. If the attack on proof-theoretic finitism in Chapter 7 is right, and if the infinitary rules are legitimate idealizations of our informal practice, then the upshot for arithmetic is that it is a negation-complete theory.

As regards our understanding of mathematics, the key divide is between structures which are feasibly within our grasp and questions which we, with our actual powers, can decide, on the one hand—and those which are not. Among the former are theorems establishing the existence of formal idealizations of our actual practice. Investigation into proof theory and semantics has to take place at the level of the idealized theory and this goes way beyond what is concretely determinable by us. There are lots of interesting boundaries when we consider formal languages and proof theories: P-decidable, NP-decidable, decidable sentences, finite, infinite, uncountable, inaccessible structures (cf. Chapter 6, §II.2). There is no reason to suppose that any of these divisions marks the boundary between legitimate and illegitimate idealization; not unless one thinks the boundary between explanatory and non-explanatory appeal to supernatural beings is found at one of those joins, and I have argued that this whole way of thinking is misguided.

Negation-completeness also holds of analysis and higher-order analysis, if infinitary simple type theory is a legitimate idealization. Here the formalization may diverge somewhat further from informal practice than IPA and arithmetic. We do not start, for one thing, by simply laying down stipulative axioms for complete ordered fields as is done in some textbook presentations. Nonetheless really existing analysis has developed out of the improvements in rigour and the techniques introduced by Cauchy, Gauss, Weierstrass, Dedekind, and others in the nineteenth century. One of the techniques, Dedekind cuts, albeit not the way the high school mathematician typically thinks of reals (that is surely in terms of infinite decimal strings), is readily implemented in the type-theoretic framework (though more easily still if one starts from a basis of the rational numbers than from the natural numbers of Peano Arithmetic).[24]

Now mathematics is certainly more than just arithmetic, analysis, complex analysis, and higher-order extensions thereof. Indeed it is more than just arithmetic, analysis, and set theory—that much is certainly true in the common complaint that philosophers of mathematics over-concentrate on these areas. In particular, the neo-formalist need not and should not be a set-theoretic imperialist, need not think of set theory as providing *the* foundation for mathematics. The neo-formalist need not believe there is any one mathematical concept or area which is more fundamental than any other, nor believe in Cartesian foundations—mathematical certitudes on which the rest of mathematics is based. The sense in which formalism provides a foundation for mathematics is a metaphysical, rather than a technical or epistemological one. It purports to give a general explanation of what makes-true mathematical utterances, not to favour one particular branch of mathematics over another nor to secure sure and certain freedom from contradiction. So what are we to say of theories in group theory, abstract algebra, topology, differential geometry, statistical theory, and so forth, in particular what do we say of theories which are negation-incomplete in standard logic?

From a neo-formalist perspective, in those cases (the typical ones) in which an inferential calculus is not a game separated from the practice of meaningful assertoric discourse but is tightly allied with contentful mathematics, substantive constraints are placed on the calculus if it is to generate a body of *truths*. In particular, not only must the calculus be consistent, it must satisfy primality conditions. But these, we have seen, may well fail. Will this not force the neo-formalist towards the deep revisionism associated with the intuitionist? Should we send the Logic Police into classrooms to stop in her tracks anyone arguing by cases, say, in a neo-classically illicit fashion? More realistically, should the neo-formalist criticize mathematicians for their use of classical reasoning, for example in the context of negation-incomplete theories?

That they would disdainfully ignore such criticism is no reason on its own not to make it, and indeed in certain cases some reservations as regards the use of classical reasoning are, I will argue, justified. Nonetheless the anti-revisionary promises of the Introduction can, in good conscience, be met with respect to the vast majority of mathematical practice insofar as it can be accommodated, without too excruciating a fitting, into the procrustean bed of simple type theory 'sitting atop' infinitary

---

[24] Frege argued that the theory of real numbers should be developed in a way which reveals its applicability. A brute coupling effected by impure functions from non-physical magnitudes, masses say, onto the real line was for him insufficient. I see no need, though, to seek for anything more than we find in actual scientific practice. Arithmetic is more closely linked with applications because 'the number of . . . ' is a common natural language expression and some sort of weakening or restriction of Hume's Principle is implicit in the everyday practice of numerate individuals. But there is nothing similar with respect to the theory of real or complex numbers. For a defence of a Fregean approach to real numbers, see Hale (2000/1, 2005); see also the discussion in Dummett (1991a, ch. 22), Shapiro (2000a), Simons (1987/95), Wright (2000).

arithmetic. Certainly this would seem to be true for the mathematics needed for empirical applications in science insofar as it is true that mathematicians, applied mathematicians, and scientists could carry out their work 'inside' that theory. Inside, in the sense that they could achieve the results they do achieve using informal versions of the axioms of that theory, in particular the arithmetic axioms together with the restricted comprehension principles plus extensionality which form the axiomatic basis of the set theory of simple type theory. No doubt proof-shortening additional axioms and derived inference rules would be added along the way; and definitions to introduce (or set-theoretically 'reduce') the specific entities of the domain, topology or whatever, under consideration. If the negation-complete infinitary type theory is a legitimate idealization of a feasible way of doing (most of) contemporary mathematics along the above lines (acknowledging here that there is no sharp dividing line between legitimate and illegitimate idealizations) this is an optimal result for a philosophy of mathematics.

But what of those areas where standard axiomatizations, even in the framework of infinitary logic, do not yield negation-complete (or, more weakly, prime) theories, most notably the higher flights of set theory? Two rather different approaches, suited for two rather different scenarios, suggest themselves. In the first scenario, a mathematician or group of mathematicians introduces a new mathematical concept or field of concepts by setting down some rules, axioms, or principles which they take to be comprehensively constitutive of the system of concepts they are introducing. The concepts in question, they maintain, could not survive any extension of the system which introduces them. If the system is a set of axioms, for example, then in any non-redundant extension of the axioms, no predicate of the language can express, they say, any of the concepts introduced.

In the other, 'open-ended' scenario, the existing rules and axioms may well have evolved without any central direction or conscious moulding over a long period, perhaps with origins lost in the mists of time. It may not be fully determinate exactly what rules and axioms are to be taken as constitutive of the concepts in play. Moreover, and crucially, any formalization of the practice is taken to be only partly constitutive of the concepts expressed in the non-logical expressions, the mathematical community being open to extensions of the axiom system. These are not seen as generating a whole new set of concepts but as constituting various ways of 'sharpening' the concepts.

To be sure, the distinction drawn is controversial, the notion of 'constitutive principles' and the question of the identity of concepts through time being problematic. But a wide range of stances on this can be accommodated, aside from, on the one hand, the extremist rejection of analyticity and of concepts found in Quine, at certain stages of his career anyway, and the epistemicist rejection of indeterminacies, of genuine, non-epistemic, blurring of boundaries, on the other. In the middle ground, there is space for the idea that some terms express concepts which are not entirely sharp and are such that developments in our practice with the terms can sharpen, in various ways, the concepts expressed.

The neo-formalist should take different attitudes to the two scenarios sketched above. To the first case, e.g. an axiom system stipulated to be exhaustively constitutive of the mathematical concepts, a revisionary attitude should be adopted, should the formal system be either neo-classically inconsistent or not prime (nor prime–). No coherent, potentially true, mathematical theory is embodied in this system, and it should be abandoned. In the second case, however (by far the more typical case surely), where a reasonable formalization of current practice is non-prime, a much more tolerant attitude is clearly desirable, in terms of peaceful relations with mathematicians. But can it be adopted with a clear neo-formalist conscience?

Well we can appeal to the existence of prime extensions of the theories. If, that is, T has a neo-classical (partial-valued) model, there is a neo-classically satisfiable prime extension $T^*$ of T. Moreover, suppose T is expressed in a $\rightarrow$-free language. (If not, replace all occurrences of $\rightarrow$ by $\supset$ with $P \supset Q =_{df.} \sim P \lor Q$; for standard classical theories this translation is acceptable.) Any such $\rightarrow$-free theory with a neo-classical model (in our Kleene style approximation of indeterminacy) has a classical model and so we can also show by similar methods (familiar from Henkin-style proofs of completeness) that T has a negation-complete extension $T^{**}$ (Appendix §A.5).

Imagine, then, that T is a legitimate formal idealization of an 'open-ended' theory under live investigation by a given mathematical community and that we are able to show that the theory, as it stands, is not prime.[25] In the unlikely event that the logic being used to do the mathematics is neo-classical, why not treat the theory under investigation to be 'any old' prime extension of T? In the more likely event that the natural formalization of the mathematicians' reasoning is classical, why not treat them as implicitly working in some negation-complete extension of (a $\rightarrow$-free version of ) T?[26]

In the latter classical case, sentences of the language fall into three categories:

(i) those which are in all complete extensions of T; these are classical consequences of T, of course;

(ii) those which are classically refutable, whose negations are in all such extensions;

(iii) those which belong to some, but not all, complete extensions of T, the sentences undecidable in T.

Though we have eschewed a supervaluational semantics for the logical connectives, supervaluational ideas do make sense of the notion of determinate truth in this reading. The determinate truths, relative to T, are the sentences provable in all complete extensions, the determinate falsehoods those refutable in all such, the indeterminates

---

[25] If the idealization uses an infinitary logic of the type figuring in this chapter, then the only way for negation incompleteness to arise is if the rules and axioms do not decide some atoms.

[26] I will concentrate largely on classical logic and negation-complete extensions in what remains.

are the rest. Now in deriving P ∨ ~P for such an indeterminable P, in using this instance of LEM in their reasoning and so on, are our classical mathematicians committing an intellectual crime? To boot, affirming that P has a determinate truth-value, when it lacks one? Well, if we have a disquotational truth-predicate Tr in the formalized language, then (Tr|P| ∨ ~Tr|P|) will be a theorem of the complete system taken to include the rules or axioms governing the truth predicate. But to affirm this semantic version of LEM is very far from making the loaded philosophical assertion that P has a determinate truth-value.

Imagine further, then, a happy day when most of the mathematicians are converted to neo-formalism (it takes a big effort, but can be done with practice). Now they will read ⌜P has a determinate truth-value⌝ to mean that P is provable or refutable from the axioms of the theory of which it forms a part. If they are aware of its indeterminability, they will know this is false, so will not affirm it has a determinate truth-value.

Are such neo-formalists, however, justified in affirming (Tr|P| ∨ ~Tr|P|)? Are they justified in affirming any and every classical theorem of T? Does mere acknowledgement of indeterminacy in truth-value for indeterminables buy one rights to use classical logic in negation-incomplete contexts? On the one hand, if the theorems, which will in general contain logical operators which we interpret via the Basic Semantics, are to be thought of as expressing truths, then on the neo-formalist picture the primeness constraints apply; and so the appropriateness of introducing the dis-quotational truth predicate of the preceding paragraph can be challenged.[27] On the other, if the neo-formalist takes the 'open-ended' route above and views the concepts expressed in T as not fully determinate and as open to precisification in a plurality of ways, then one might argue that in affirming such theorems, she is affirming something that she knows will be provable (neo-classically) in every fully determinate development of the system of concepts expressed by the theory she is investigating. Equating truth with provability as the neo-formalist does, what can be wrong in affirming the truth of such theorems?

All depends on how realistic it is to suppose that the current set of practices, incomplete when formalized, might evolve into a set still faithful to the nature of the concepts involved but which is, on a legitimate formalization, complete. There are two possibilities: there is a set of practices which, in a reasonable idealization, consti-tute a neo-classically consistent, negation-complete extension of current practice and is 'within reach'. That is, it is a real, feasible possibility that current mathematicians, with their limited powers and abilities, can adopt the extended practices. Or not; in which case the current theory does not in fact express a body of mathematical truths. The logical operators in its complex sentences do not express truth-functions since the requisite connections between truth and provability are not in place.

---

[27] Cf. the endorsement of Blackburn's worries about brutally quick moves to truth-aptness on the basis of deflationistic views on truth and minimal syntactic criteria—requiring the declarative mood and the like. Chapter 2, §1.

To be sure, the boundary between legitimate and non-legitimate idealization is fuzzy, so really we have 'two-ish' possibilities rather than exactly two sharp alternatives. However a formalization which extrapolates from existing practice simply by allowing for wffs, axioms, rules and proofs which are too long for us to comprehend is clearly legitimate. At the other extreme, stipulating that a non-recursively enumerable, negation-complete set of axioms which we could never grasp is nonetheless implicitly part of the axiom set to which we apply our logic (infinitary as it may be) is not a twilight borderline case of idealization, it is as bad as one can get. That Superman, or some other fictional being could, we declare, grasp this extension is not to carry out a legitimate idealization of practice but to descend into the supernaturalism condemned in the previous chapter. We could as well have declared that finitary PA is 'implicitly' complete because it has complete extensions.

In general, we will not know whether a set of practices which grounds a complete idealization is feasibly in reach or not. So what should our attitude be to those who nonetheless reason classically though ignorant of whether the system could, in our feasible sense, be extended to a complete one? The neo-formalist has to say that it would be wrong to give a completely clean bill of health to our classical mathematicians working in unprime, incomplete theories. Before this is issued, one ought to show that axioms and rules which form part of our actual practice generate, in a legitimate infinitary logic, a prime, or better negation-complete theory, ideally using those axioms and rules in the metatheory (even if some are, like mathematical induction, redundant in the formalized proof theory). But in advance of this, we need not, and arguably should not, advocate closing the whole enterprise down. After all, though tomorrow we may find it is neo-classically inconsistent, for all we currently know it may in future be shown to be a partial realization of a negation-complete, determinately true theory. Perhaps, then, the neo-formalist should issue in these cases only a provisional licence to conduct business to all those mathematicians prepared to listen to philosophical authority (a thoroughly surveyable group whose number can definitely be computed in real time).

Let us look a little more closely at this matter in the more specific, and highly salient, for philosophers anyway? case of set theory. For though the warning against set-theoretic imperialism is certainly to be heeded, there is something to be said for paying close attention to set theory. Set theory can model the structure of just about any other mathematical domain (to speak in formal mode) in pure as well as applied mathematics, certain areas of category theory aside. So can we say that the IS theory vindicates from a neo-formalist perspective real set-theoretic practice, hence essentially all of mathematics, based on classical logic and in just the same way as IPA and simple type theory do for arithmetic and analysis; namely by showing a reasonable idealization of the theories is negation-complete?

The case is surely much less plausible here. Set theorists do not reason in IS theory. They start from ZFC, or ZFC plus some large cardinal axioms, or Scott's iterative set theory (Scott 1974) or some such. Indeed the latter framework, though less common than ZFC, can at least be plausibly thought of as expressing a unitary conception of set. The notoriously tortured history of ZFC (cf. Potter 2004, *passim*) makes it resemble more an ancient city which has evolved to meet each pressing need than a modern city designed from scratch to some fixed plan. For ZFC encompasses different conceptions of set—iterative versus limitation of size (or, some hold, logical versus combinatorial), which do not fit together all that comfortably. Nonetheless, ZFC is really existing set theory, rather than set theory as a philosopher of mathematics might like it to be. And, moreover, limitative results in infinitary logic (see Appendix §A.6) show that pumping up the logic to an infinitary one will not necessarily yield an extension which is negation-complete in classical logic; though the infinitary systems there are somewhat different from those considered in this chapter, the same lesson holds true for neo-classical logic.

   ZFC, as noted above, is not the only theory to be studied seriously (even considering only first-order theories). Many set theorists are eclectic, they like to see what happens when you add this axiom, or subtract that. They do not normally (though see below) treat the consequence relation as an object of study (unless as a means to set-theoretic ends), but empathetically get into the skin of a given theory to see how the set-theoretic world looks from its perspective. And they *use* classical logic when doing so. So the situation is somewhat different from that which obtains for arithmetic. There we start from a 'gold standard' axiom set, the PA axioms, which is widely accepted by professionals, in tandem with rules, algorithms, and principles—the algorithms of decimal arithmetic, Hume's Principle in some form—principles which, in contrast with most of current mathematics, are widespread throughout the population from Auchenshuggle to Zeal Monachorum and indeed beyond. In the set-theoretic case, however, there is more diversity in axiomatic starting points.

   Can we issue a clean bill of health, then, to the set-theorists working on the mainstream theories anyway, on the basis of the negation-completeness of the IS formalization notwithstanding its differences from the various widely adopted theories such as the above? I think the answer is clearly no: we cannot view it as an extrapolation from any extension of current mathematical practice we might reasonably think we could develop. In the case of simple type theory, the axioms include instantiations of comprehension:

$$\forall n(n \in \{x : \varphi x\} \leftrightarrow \varphi n)$$

in which $\varphi$ has $\aleph_\alpha$ symbols, for accessible $\alpha$. That could be quite a lot of symbols. Nonetheless we have here an axiom which is of the same form as instances we can readily grasp, only a bit longer. But in the case of the IS theory it is not just that the instances of our generalization of pair set can be very long sentences. We cannot actually set down the list of axioms unless we know the diagram of the set-theoretic universe $V_{\theta\alpha}$ up to some high cardinality. That is far too close to stipulating, as a legitimate idealization of our practice, that we implicitly work with an axiom set which includes every truth of mathematics as its theorem.

Should the neo-formalist, then, advocate that no one publish proofs in set theory until the reasonable prospect emerges of an axiom set which is, in infinitary idealization, negation-complete (or at least prime, in neo-classical logic)? Working mathematicians are, of course, not going to cramp, or abandon, their practice in response to philosophical edicts. They did not halt all work in progress on calculus in response to Berkeley's criticism. It would have been a mathematical disaster had they done so, of course; on the other hand, it was intellectually scandalous of those aware at the time of his potent critique not to worry about the foundations of the discipline as a result, not to search for ways of answering his criticisms or amending and developing the theory to avoid them. We should view, I suggest, classical mathematics applied to incomplete set theories in a similar light, adopting the 'provisional licence' suggested above. A neo-formalist could engage in standard set theory with a clear conscience if she were to hold out reasonable hopes that a negation-complete successor will come along, one in which the properly classical consequences now being drawn are derived in respectable neo-classical fashion. Current theory is seen as a sort of promissory note, but the cloud hanging over set theory is acknowledged.

The alternative is for the neo-formalist to treat set theory purely as a mathematical object to be studied proof-theoretically. One can then attempt to trace the classical consequences of ZFC or this or that strengthening or variation without affirming them as mathematical truths. The mathematical theory needed to ground ZFC, viewed as a purely proof-theoretic object, is much weaker than ZFC, essentially just Peano Arithmetic, in the finitary case. Something like this attitude to set theory, withholding full assent from at least some of its theses, including assent to excluded middle applied to indeterminable claims, is evident in the reaction of some mathematicians to the undecidability results—for example, the Hilbertian-style formalism of Paul Cohen himself (1971), and of Abraham Robinson (1965, 1969). A similar attitude could be adopted by neo-formalists.

Overall, then, neo-formalists can deflect the charge of being intellectual vandals intent on wanton destruction of vast swathes of perfectly good mathematics. The mathematical practice of the jobbing mathematician is untouched by neo-formalist scruples, by dint of the negation-complete theories which are reasonable idealizations, such as infinitary simple type theory. On the other hand, neo-formalism is not logically or methodologically toothless, as the case of set theory shows. A goal for formalized theories is laid down, namely primeness, before they can be considered truth-apt and ripe for the application of logical reasoning—neo-classical logical reasoning, that is. For classical reasoning to be licit, a stronger requirement is imposed: negation-completeness of a reasonable formalized idealization. Failing this, the body of mathematics in question remains under a cloud, though purely G-level proof-theoretic derivation of results, which can be treated as pro tem uninterpreted formulae, is of course legitimate and may help clarify whether an acceptable extension is available.

Note that within the neo-classical framework of logic, exposing a theory as classically inconsistent does not demonstrate that it must be abandoned (though of course classical reasoning must not be applied to it). Though abandonment of the theory might be the right response in many cases, there may be exceptions. I have in mind, here, of course, naïve set theory. Though orthodoxy has it that the lesson of the paradoxes was duly learnt, and the theory abandoned, this is not really what happened at all. Rather the theory has soldiered on guerrilla-style, hiding behind various euphemisms: naïve sets became 'collections', 'domains', 'indefinite totalities', and the like. Philosophers, and philosophically minded mathematicians, continue tacitly to uphold full naïve comprehension for sets, or rather for 'collections', 'indefinite totalities', or whatever, because they have to, because they cannot reflectively discuss set theory, in particular its semantics, unless they do so. Or so I have argued (Weir 1998*b*) concurring here, of course, with Graham Priest (1987, ch. 2, esp. pp. 47–8). The conclusion I draw, in sharp contradistinction to Priest, is the need to show that naïve set theory, situated in the correct logical framework, is a perfectly consistent theory yet still powerful enough to do what is asked of it. One important thing we can ask of it is to provide a theoretical structure capable of carrying out the semantics of mathematical theories, including itself. A second is to remove the cloud of incompleteness hanging over current set theory. But these are tasks for another day.

# Conclusion

I started from the idea that not all modes of assertion are representational, that one can make judgements which have objective truth-values but are not thereby *about* the mind-independent world. I went on to claim that pure mathematics provides a prime example of this, invoking the distinction between metaphysical and informational content within a tripartite SCW framework for studying language. The metaphysical content of mathematical judgements, I claim, consists in the EXISTENCE or otherwise of concrete proof tokens, though none of this features in the informational content of the typical mathematical utterance.

I will finish with a final comparison of this neo-formalist theory with some other positions in philosophy of mathematics. One indication of the correctness of neo-formalism, it seems to me, is that it combines the plausible aspects of many of the most prominent views in philosophy of mathematics without, I hope, being merely a 'shallow syncretism'. For example, the neo-formalist agrees with the neo-Fregean that mathematical truths are a species of analytical truth, at least if we interpret this to mean that they are truths derivable from axioms which are essentially stipulative and so can be seen as true by definition.

The neo-formalist also agrees with the constructivists that mathematics is a human product and that truth in mathematics is tied to provability. But neo-formalism rejects the claim that because mathematical truth is a human product it is a human *construct*, consciously designed and comprehended in its entirety by us, either singly or in committee. Nor does the fact that mathematics is the product of human activity mean that it is epistemologically accessible any more than facts about human products such as legal systems, languages, technologies, or market economies need be epistemologically accessible. There is no reason, then, for the neo-formalist to deny that mathematical truth can transcend any body of evidence (of the existence of proofs or disproofs) which we, given our practical capacities, could ever muster for it. The neo-formalist, though ontologically anti-realist, can cleave to metaphysical realism for mathematics.

A theological analogy suggests itself here. Theism, according to some critics, is a projection of human characteristics, hopes, and fears onto a mythical, externally existing reality. Certainly for some of the more anthropomorphic forms of theism, this view is extremely plausible whether one is an atheist or not. But the atheist should nonetheless be wary of over-reactions against theism—extreme forms of humanism, for instance, which in effect directly rather than indirectly worship humanity (belief in the perfectibility of man etc.). Similarly the neo-formalist views the platonist as akin to the anthropomorphic theist, projecting the products of human activity and thought—various rule systems, in effect—onto mind-independent reality. But constructivism can be seen to be an error akin to extreme humanism where it supposes all of mathematics is accessible to the human imagination, or that for every class of determinate problems, there is an algorithm for solving them, or that there are no unknowable mathematical truths.

Neo-formalism, though it rejects the hopeless elements of game formalism, bears strong resemblances to it; strong enough to be deserving of the title 'formalist' I believe. The formalists are right to tie mathematical truth to provability and to hold that there is at least an implicit use of mathematical sentences in which they are merely syntactic elements of purely formal calculi which cannot be used to convey truth-bearing assertions. But the game formalists' mistake is to assume that this is also true of typical mathematical practice in general. It is much more plausible to adopt the neo-formalist view that mathematical utterances can be used to make assertions, true assertions in the case of mathematical theorems. More than this, it is impossible, I argued, to explain our grasp of the theoretical concepts of science on a realist basis without assuming that pure mathematics is true. The non-revisionary nature of neo-formalism thus gives it a decided advantage over fictionalism, though clearly in many respects the fictionalist and neo-formalist agree. Both deny that mathematical objects EXIST, or at any rate that we need to assume this to make sense of mathematics.

The neo-formalist agrees with the strict finitist that THERE ARE NO unsurveyable, far less infinite, mathematical domains. It by no means follows, however, pace the strict finitist, that infinitary mathematics is not true or that infinitistic assertions in mathematics have to be rejected or treated differently from finitistic ones. For THERE ARE concrete proofs of infinitary claims (including infinitistic theorems in model theory and proof theory).

The main problem I see as outstanding for neo-formalists concerns set theory, or rather the shadow of naïve set theory which has stalked our discussion in various places. The naïve comprehension principle is the only viable candidate for the role of an intuitive principle which can play the role in set theory of the Peano–Dedekind axioms (or perhaps Hume's Principle) in arithmetic. That is, only it can unify different set-theoretic axiom systems and explain how they all can be seen as inadequate attempts (sometimes rival attempts) to capture a single intuitive mathematical notion. More importantly, naïve set theory provides the only hope of securing closure, of arriving at a fixed-point explanatory theory which can account for itself, as it were, without resting its intelligibility on a stronger theory. But this problem is very far from being one for neo-formalists alone; it faces any non-contradictory account of the nature of mathematics.

The efforts of mathematicians through the generations, the total output of mathematical creativity spread across space and time as sounds in the air, diagrams in the sand, ink marks on paper, and voltage highs and lows in computers, can seem nonetheless paltry compared to the infinite worlds investigated by those very mathematicians in the course of their activities. The neo-formalist, however, sees these 'worlds' as themselves the products of human creativity (which is not to say that numbers would not exist if humans had not, cf. Chapter 3, §I.3). These supposed worlds do not constitute an independent realm before which we should prostrate ourselves in intimidated awe. On the other hand, the totality of human mathematical output is an awesome achievement, far more than can be grasped by any one mathematician or co-operating group of mathematicians. In fact, the possibilities inherent in the complex structures which individual humans, resting on the shoulders of previous giants, have created are, from the point of view of any one given individual, limitless. Like many human products—language, law, economies—mathematics is, to a large extent, an autonomous realm independent of its creators, a fact which is surely responsible, in part, for its great beauty and power.

# Appendix

## §A.1 Minimax Rules

If we take (single conclusion) sequent rules to have the schematic form:

$$\frac{X_1 \Rightarrow P_1, \quad X_2 \Rightarrow P_2, \ldots X_n \Rightarrow P_n}{\underset{0 < i \leq n}{\cup} X_i \Rightarrow C}$$

then a minimax sequent rule is one in which $P_1, \ldots P_n$ minimax entails C—it is not possible (under the Kleene scheme) for the minimum $P_i$ value in a valuation to be greater than the value of C in that valuation. Such rules preserve neo-classical correctness. (The definition of neo-classical entailment, given in Chapter 7, §III, is:

$X \models C$ iff in all models M if all of X are true in M then C is true and if C is false and all of X but P are true, then P is false.)

For if all of $\underset{0 < i \leq n}{\cup} X_i$ are true in valuation $v$ then so are all the $P_i$, since all the premiss sequents are neo-classically correct; hence so is C by the minimax entailment. Whilst if C is false in $v$ but all of the wffs in $\underset{0 < i \leq n}{\cup} X_i$ but A are true in $v$ then since the $P_i$ minimax entail C, at least one of the premiss succeedents is false, say $P_k$; in which case by the neo-classical correctness of $X_k \Rightarrow P_k$, $A \in X_k$ and is false in $v$.

Minimax soundness is a mechanically decidable principle, for finite sequent rules. If we wish to set out rules for it, one set has the general form:

$$\begin{array}{lll} X & (1)\ \varphi & \text{Given} \\ X & (2)\ \varphi[P/Q] & 1\ \text{MM} \end{array}$$

('MM' for Minimax) where $\varphi[P/Q]$ results from $\varphi$ by uniform substitution of a sub-formula P by Q and where

| P is | A | and Q is | ~~A |
|------|---|----------|-----|
| or P is | ~~A | and Q is | A |
| or P is | A & B | and Q is | B & A |
| or P is | A ∨ B | and Q is | B ∨ A |
| or P is | A & B | and Q is | ~(~A ∨ ~B) |
| or P is | ~(~A ∨ ~B) | and Q is | A & B |
| or P is | A ∨ B | and Q is | ~(~A & ~B) |
| or P is | ~(~A & ~B) | and Q is | A ∨ B |
| or P is | (A & (B & C)) | and Q is | ((A & B) & C) |
| or P is | ((A & B) & C) | and Q is | (A & (B & C)) |
| or P is | (A ∨ (B ∨ C)) | and Q is | ((A ∨ B) ∨ C) |
| or P is | ((A ∨ B) ∨ C) | and Q is | (A ∨ (B ∨ C)) |
| or P is | (A & (B ∨ C)) | and Q is | ((A & B) ∨ (A & C)) |
| or P is | ((A & B) ∨ (A & C)) | and Q is | (A & (B ∨ C)) |
| or P is | (A ∨ (B & C)) | and Q is | ((A ∨ B) & (A ∨ C)) |
| or P is | ((A ∨ B) & (A ∨ C)) | and Q is | (A ∨ (B & C)) |

Minimax soundness is easily established by showing that the formula on the left has the same value, in every model, as the formula on the right. In addition standard sequent form natural deduction ∨I, &E and &I rules (without any determinacy restriction on overlapping assumptions in both premiss antecedents) are minimax sound as is the Mingle rule:

$$X \quad (1) \; A \; \& \sim A \quad \text{Given}$$
$$X \quad (2) \; B \lor \sim B \quad 1 \; \text{Mingle}$$

which is a derived rule of the logic RM which extends relevant logic R by addition of the Mingle axiom scheme.[1]

Most of the minimax rules generalize straightforwardly to the infinitary case. (The distributivity rules are an exception: to extend completeness results for standard languages any significant way into the transfinite one needs extra rules such as the 'ordinary' or 'Chang' distributivity laws (Karp 1964, p. 41; Dickmann 1975, p. 421). The distributivity schema, for all $\gamma < \kappa$, $\kappa$ the index of the language, is :

$$\bigvee_{a \; a<\gamma} \; \bigwedge_{\beta \; \beta<\gamma} \; \varphi_{a,\beta}$$

where each $\varphi_{a,\beta}$ is either $\varphi_\delta$ or $\sim\varphi_\delta$, for some $\delta < \gamma$ and for every function $f$ from $\gamma$: $\gamma$ there is an $\varepsilon < \gamma$ such that $\{\varphi_\varepsilon, \sim\varphi_\varepsilon\} \subseteq \{\varphi_{a,f(a)}: a < \gamma\}$.)

## §A.2  Soundness of Strict Neo-classical Logic

The proof is of the usual inductive type. The semantics for the operators is the Lukasiewicz/Kleene semantics of Chapter 7. As illustration, the inductive step for the ∨E rule:

---

[1] See Anderson and Belnap (1975, §29.5), especially the theorem $\sim(A \to A) \to (B \to B)$ together with theorem RM67 (p. 397) $(A \to A) \Leftrightarrow (\sim A \lor A)$.

$$
\begin{array}{lll}
X & (1)\ P \lor Q & \text{Given} \\
Y,P & (2)\ C & \text{Given} \\
Z,Q & (3)\ C & \text{Given} \\
X,Y,Z, & (5)\ C & 1,2,3\ \lor E
\end{array}
$$

where $(X \cap (Y \cup Z)) = \varnothing$ is as follows:

Proof: (i) Truth preservation: this is exactly as in the classical case.

(ii) Falsity preservation (upwards): suppose that C is false in $v$ and all of X,Y,Z, are true in $v$ but A.

Case (a): $A \notin X$. Then, by the (strict) neo-classical correctness of line (1) (inductive hypothesis) $P \lor Q$ is true in $v$ hence one of the disjuncts is; suppose without loss of generality that it is P. By the correctness of line (2) in the rule above, $A \in Y$ and is false.

Case (b): $A \notin Y \cup Z$. By the correctness of lines (2) and (3) both P and Q are false in $v$ hence so is $P \lor Q$. By the correctness of line (1), $A \in X$ and is false in $v$. By the overlap clause $(X \cap (Y \cup Z)) = \varnothing$, these two options are exhaustive.[2]

A similar, somewhat less convoluted, proof establishes the soundness of $\sim$E. The proof for $\lor$E generalizes to the parallel $\exists$E rule:

$$
\begin{array}{lll}
X & (1)\ \exists x \varphi x & \text{Given} \\
Y,\ \varphi x/t & (2)\ C & \text{Given} \\
X,Y. & (4)\ C & 1,2\ \exists E
\end{array}
$$

with the usual clauses on t and where $X \cap Y = \varnothing$. Again truth-preservation is classical.

Falsity preservation. Suppose all of X,Y, but A are satisfied by $\sigma$ (in model M) but C is false relative to $\sigma$.

Case (a) $A \notin X$. Then $\exists x \varphi x$ is satisfied by $\sigma$ hence for some $a$ in the domain of M, $\varphi x$ is satisfied by $\sigma[x/a]$ hence, since t is not in $\varphi$, $\varphi x/t$ is satisfied by $\sigma[t/a]$. Since t is not in Y or C, all of Y but A are satisfied by $\sigma[t/a]$ along with $\varphi x/t$ whilst C is falsified by that variant assignment (this is provable by induction on sentence complexity). Hence by the correctness of line 2, $A \in Y$ and is falsified by $\sigma[t/a]$ hence, using the same lemma, by $\sigma$.

Case (b) $A \notin Y$. Then by the correctness of 2, $\varphi x/t$ is falsified by $\sigma$ hence so is $\varphi x$ (since t is new to $\varphi$) by $\sigma[x/\sigma(t)]$. Since t does not occur in Y or C the same holds

---

[2] In the more liberal system in which we treat axioms as if they were part of the logic (see Chapter 8, §III), the overlap condition is amended to the requirement that only axioms feature in $X \cap (Y \cup Z)$. Since axioms are true in the admissible models (by definition) we can still rule out the third case, in the falsity-preservation direction, that $A \in X \cap (Y \cup Z)$. For then A is an axiom and so true, along with all the other premises, contradicting downward truth-preservation, given the falsity of C. The same argument applies in the other cases.

for any t-variant $\sigma'$ which agrees with $\sigma$ on all variables and parameters except perhaps t. Thus $\varphi x$ is falsified by every $\sigma[x/a]$ for all $a$ in the domain so that $\exists x \varphi x$ is falsified by $\sigma$. By the correctness of line 1, $A \in X$ and is falsified by $\sigma$.

By the overlap clause $(X \cap Y) = \varnothing$, these two options are exhaustive. $\square$

Soundness for the conditional rules is complicated by the fact that we require them to be sound under two interpretations of the conditional. Firstly, the non-bivalent conditional where a conditional with true antecedent and untrue consequent, or false consequent and unfalse antecedent, takes the gap value. Secondly, the bivalent conditional in which, in those two cases, the conditional is false. However the soundness proofs for the strict neo-classical rules:

$\rightarrow$I:

| P | (1) Q | Given |
|---|-------|-------|
| — | (2) P $\rightarrow$ Q | 1 $\rightarrow$ I |

$\rightarrow$E:

| X | (1) P $\rightarrow$ Q | Given |
|---|----------------------|-------|
| Y | (2) P | Given |
| X, Y, | (3) Q | 1,2 $\rightarrow$E |

where as usual $X \cap Y = \varnothing$, goes through in essentially the same way in either case. The non-classical cases are the falsity-preservation clauses:

(a) Falsity-preservation *and* truth preservation, $\rightarrow$I: suppose P $\rightarrow$ Q is untrue in valuation $v$ (in the bivalent case, it will be false). Then either P is true at $v$ and Q untrue, or Q is false at $v$ and P unfalse; both these possibilities contradict the neo-classical correctness of line 1, hence P $\rightarrow$ Q cannot be untrue at $v$.

(b) Falsity preservation $\rightarrow$E: suppose Q is false and all of X, Y, but A are true. Case (*i*): A $\notin$ X. Then, by the correctness of line (1) P $\rightarrow$ Q is true in $v$ so that (on either interpretation) P is false. By the correctness of line (2) in the rule above, A $\in$ Y and is false.
Case (*ii*): A $\notin$ Y. By the correctness of line (2), P is true in $v$. Since Q is false, so too (on either interpretation) is P $\rightarrow$ Q. By the correctness of line (1), A $\in$ X and is false in $v$. This exhausts the possibilities. $\leq$

The two other principles taken as primitive for the conditional[3] are:

Contraposition:

| X | (1) P $\rightarrow$ Q | Given |
|---|----------------------|-------|
| X | (2) $\sim$Q $\rightarrow$ $\sim$P | 1, Contrap. |

---

[3] By complicating the $\rightarrow$ I rule to allow conditional sentences only in the antecedent of the premise we can render the transitivity and contraposition rules redundant whilst preserving soundness.

Transitivity:

| X | (1) P $\rightarrow$ Q | Given |
|---|---|---|
| Y | (2) Q $\rightarrow$ R | Given |
| X, Y, | (3) P $\rightarrow$ R | 1,2 Trans. (where X $\cap$ Y $=$ Ø.) |

Soundness for contraposition is straightforward since the respective succeedents in each rule take the same value in every neo-classical model, on either interpretation. For transitivity, in the truth-preservation direction, suppose all of X, Y, are true in $v$. Then P $\rightarrow$ Q and Q $\rightarrow$ R are true. On either interpretation of $\rightarrow$, if P is true in $v$, so is R, if P is gappy, Q is not false hence neither is R. Thus in either case, and also in the third case in which P is false in $v$, P $\rightarrow$ R is true (again on either interpretation of $\rightarrow$).

For the falsity preservation direction, take the non-bivalent interpretation first of all. If P $\rightarrow$ R is false in $v$ then P is true in $v$, R false. Suppose all of X, Y are true there but A. There are two cases:

Case (i): A $\notin$ X. Then, by the correctness of line (1) P $\rightarrow$ Q is true in $v$ hence so is Q, so Q $\rightarrow$ R is false. By the correctness of line (2), A $\in$ Y and is false.

Case (ii): A $\notin$ Y. By the correctness of line (2), Q $\rightarrow$ R is true in $v$, hence Q is false so by the correctness of line (1), A $\in$ X and is false in $v$. This exhausts the possibilities.

Next the bivalent interpretation of $\rightarrow$. If P $\rightarrow$ R is false in $v$ then P is not false and R not true, nor do they have the same truth value in $v$. There are two cases:

Case (i): A $\notin$ X. Then, by the correctness of line (1) P $\rightarrow$ Q is true in $v$. If P is true, Q is true but R is not hence Q $\rightarrow$ R is false in $v$. If P is gappy, Q is not false but R is hence once again, Q $\rightarrow$ R is false in $v$. Either way, by the correctness of line (2), A $\in$ Y and is false.

Case (ii): A $\notin$ Y. By the correctness of line (2), Q $\rightarrow$ R is true in $v$. Hence Q is not true. If Q is false then since P is not false, P $\rightarrow$ Q is false in $v$. If Q is gappy, R is gappy, hence P is true so once again P $\rightarrow$ Q is false. Either way, by the correctness of line (1), A $\in$ X and is false in $v$. This exhausts the possibilities. $\square$

## §A.3  Infinitary Rules

The infinitary generalizations of &E and $\vee$I are obvious. For the other two rules they are $\wedge$I:

| $X_\alpha$ | (1.a) $A_\alpha$ | Given for all $\alpha < \beta$ |
|---|---|---|
| $\underset{\alpha<\beta}{\cup} X_\alpha$ | (2) $\wedge A_{\alpha\ \alpha\ <\ \beta}$ | 1.a $\alpha{<}\beta$ $\wedge$I |

whilst $\vee$E is:

| X | (1) $\vee A_{\alpha\ \alpha\ <\ \beta}$ | Given |
|---|---|---|
| $Y_\alpha, A_\alpha$ | (2.a) C | Given, $\alpha < \beta$ |
| X, $\underset{\alpha<\beta}{\cup} Y_\alpha$ | (3) C | 1, 2.a, $\alpha < \beta$ $\vee$E |

where $X \cap \bigcup_{a<\beta} Y_a = \emptyset$.

The soundness steps in the soundness proof are straightforward generalizations of the finitary case. Thus for $\vee E$:

(i) Truth preservation is exactly as in the classical case.

(ii) Falsity preservation (upwards): suppose that C is false in $v$ and all of X and all in $\bigcup_{a<\beta} Y_a$ are true in $v$ but P.

Case (a): $P \notin X$. Then, by the (strict) neo-classical correctness of line (1) (inductive hypothesis) $\vee A_{a}$ $_{a < \beta}$ is true in $v$ hence one of the disjuncts is; suppose without loss of generality that it is $A_\gamma$. By the correctness of line (2.$\gamma$) in the rule above, $P \in Y_\gamma$ and is false.

Case (b): $P \notin \bigcup_{a<\beta} Y_a$. By the correctness of all of lines (2.$a$), $a < \beta$, all of the $A_a$, $a < \beta$ are false in $v$ hence so is $\vee A_a$ $_{a < \beta}$. By the correctness of line (1), $P \in X$ and is false in $v$.

By the overlap clause $X \cap \bigcup_{a<\beta} Y_a = \emptyset$, these two options are exhaustive. $\square$

## §A.4 IS

As set out in Chapter 8, §VI, with $h$ a bijection from the $\theta_\beta$-sized set of singular terms of the language $L_\kappa$ of IS onto $V_{\theta\beta}$, we write $\mathbf{t}_i$ for $h(t_i)$. To prove negation-completeness for the atoms of $L_\kappa$ we prove something stronger: that every truth of the diagram of $V_{\theta\beta}$, every atomic truth or falsehood concerning identity or membership, is provable.

Firstly, the positive truths. If $\mathbf{u}_j \in \mathbf{t}_i$[4] then $u_j$ occurs in a disjunct in the right hand side of the $i$th list comprehension axiom:

$$\forall x \big( x \in t_i \leftrightarrow \vee (x = u_j) j \in J \big).$$

We then have $\vdash u_j \in t_i$ by strict neo-classical reasoning using $\vee E$ ($\wedge E$), $=I$, $\vee I$ and $\leftrightarrow E$ (i.e. &E and $\rightarrow$E).[5] Moreover since each set in $V_{\theta\beta}$ has only one name, the positive identity truths are all provable by $=I$, reflexivity of identity.

For the negative truths, we reason by induction on the rank of terms $t_i$ in $u_j \neq t_i$ and $u_j \notin t_i$ (where the rank of $t_i$ is just the rank of $h(t_i)$ in $V_{\theta\beta}$). For rank zero, we have $\vdash t_i \notin t_0$, for all $t_i$ by a strict neo-classically legitimate reductio, using the empty set list axiom and $=I$.

Turning to identity, $\mathbf{u}_j = \mathbf{t}_0$ is false, for all $\mathbf{u}_j$ distinct from the empty set, but in that case $\mathbf{u}_j$ has at least one member $\mathbf{t}_k$ so that $t_k$ features in the right-hand side of the $i$th

---

[4] Here '$\in$' is a term both of the object language and one of the informal metalanguage, with its usual meaning.

[5] I will annotate the derivability of one side of an instance of a comprehension axiom from the other by CE. It is assumed, as before, that the mathematical axioms are immune from the overlap restrictions.

comprehension axiom and we thereby have $\vdash t_k \in u_j$. Since $\vdash t_k \notin t_0$, identity laws and $\sim$I give us a neo-classical proof of $u_j \neq t_0$.

For the inductive step of this part of the proof, we assume completeness for all identity and membership sentences for terms of rank $< a$, $a > 0$, (each is provable if true in $V_{\theta\beta}$); we have then to show (i) $\vdash u_k \notin t_a$ and (ii) $\vdash u_j \neq t_a$, where $\mathbf{u_k} \notin \mathbf{t_\alpha}$ and $\mathbf{u_j} \neq \mathbf{t_\alpha}$, for terms $u_j$ and $u_k$ of rank $< a$.

(i) Since $\mathbf{u_k} \notin \mathbf{t_\alpha}$, $\mathbf{u_k}$ is distinct from every $\mathbf{u_l} \in \mathbf{t_\alpha}$. By IH, $\vdash u_k \neq u_l$ for every such $t_l$, $l \in L$, L indexing the members of $\mathbf{t_\alpha}$. Hence $\vdash u_k \notin t_a$ by the following neo-classically correct proof (here the $a$ comprehension axiom is:

$$\forall x(x \in t_a \leftrightarrow \vee(x = u_l)l \in L)):$$

| I | (1) $u_k \in t_a$ | H |
|---|---|---|
| I | (2) $\vee(u_k = u_l)\, l \in L$ | I CE |
| 3.$l$ | (3.$l$) $u_k = u_l$ | $l \in L$ |
| — | (4.$l$) $u_k \neq u_l$ | Given $l \in L$ |
| 3.$l$ | (5.$l$) $\perp$ | 3.$l$, 4.$l$ $\sim$E |
| I | (6) $\perp$ | 2, 5.$l$ $l \in L$, $\vee$E |
| — | (7) $u_k \notin t_a$ | 6 $\sim$I. |

(ii) If $\mathbf{u_j} \neq \mathbf{t_\alpha}$ then they have different members. Suppose that $\mathbf{t_k} \in \mathbf{u_j}$ but $\mathbf{t_k} \notin \mathbf{t_\alpha}$. By what we have just established, $\vdash t_k \in u_j$ and $\vdash t_k \notin t_a$. A neo-classically reductio establishes $\vdash u_j \neq t_a$. If instead $\mathbf{t_k} \notin \mathbf{u_j}$ but $\mathbf{t_k} \in \mathbf{t_\alpha}$ the argument is the same since $\mathbf{u_j}$ is of rank $< a$. Hence it follows by induction (using symmetry of $=$ and the proof in (i) above for $u_j$, $t_k$ $j > k$) that every atomic sentence and every negation of an atomic sentence, whatever the ranks of the terms in the sentences, is provable when true.

The argument that all $V_{\theta\beta}$ truths are provable generalizes from the proof for atomic sentences by the same inductive argument as in Chapter 8, §VI.

## §A.5  Prime Extensions

Start with a theory T which is satisfied by a neo-classical model M. Then it can be expanded to a prime theory T* also satisfied by M.

Proof: At initial stage $\langle 0,0 \rangle$ we set $\Delta_{\langle 0,0 \rangle} = T$. Well-order all the disjunctions in the language (so we require choice). At stage $\langle 0, a + 1 \rangle$ we consider the $a$th disjunction $\vee P_i$. If $\Delta_{\langle 0,a \rangle} \vdash \vee P_i$ then (using choice again) select an arbitrary disjunct $P_k$ such that $P_k$ is true in M (an arbitrary sentence otherwise—but we will prove there is no otherwise) and let $\Delta_{\langle 0,a + 1 \rangle} = \Delta_{\langle 0,a \rangle}, P_k$. If it is not the case that $\Delta_{\langle 0,a \rangle} \vdash \vee P_i$ then $\Delta_{\langle 0,a + 1 \rangle} = \Delta_{\langle 0,a \rangle}$. At limit stages $\langle 0, \lambda \rangle$ $\Delta_{<0,\lambda>} = \underset{\beta<\lambda}{\cup} \Delta_{<0,\beta>}$ whilst $\Delta_{<1,0>} = \underset{\beta<\kappa}{\cup} \Delta_{<0,\beta>}$.

An inductive proof shows that at each stage $a$ up to and including $<1,0>$ the associated set $\Delta_{<0,a>}$ is satisfied by M and hence if $\Delta_{<0,a>} \vdash \vee P_i$ there always is at least one disjunct $P_k$ such that $\Delta_{<0,a>}, P_k$ is true in M, since $\Delta_{<0,a>}$ is satisfied by M.

IH: We have by IH that $\Delta_{<0,a>}$ is satisfied by M. If it is not the case that $\Delta_{<0,a>} \vdash \vee P_i$ (as before, this the $a^{th}$ disjunction) then $\Delta_{<0,a+1>} = \Delta_{<0,a>}$ and so all its members are true in M. If $\Delta_{<0,a>} \vdash \vee P_i$ then $\vee P_i$ is true in M, hence at least one disjunct is true in M. Whichever true disjunct $P_k$ is selected, $\Delta_{<0,a+1>} = \Delta_{<0,a>}$, $P_k$ is satisfied by M. At limit stages we have by IH that every member of $\Delta_{<0,\lambda>} = \bigcup_{\beta<\lambda} \Delta_{<0,\beta>}$ is true in M hence $\Delta_{<0,\lambda>}$ is satisfied by M, likewise for $\Delta_{<1,0>}$.

At stage $<1,0>$ we proceed as before up to stage $<2,0>$ and so on, with at stage $<\mu, 0>$, $\Delta_{<\mu,0>} = \bigcup_{\eta<\mu,\beta<\kappa} \Delta_{<\eta,\beta>}$. Since our language is of a standard set-theoretic size $\kappa$, cardinality considerations show that we must reach a fixed point $\pi$ such that $\Delta_{<\pi+1,0>} = \Delta_{<\pi,0>}$. Call this theory $\Delta_{<\pi+1,0>}$, which we have seen is also satisfied by M, $T^*$. By dint of the construction, if $T^* \vdash \vee Q_i$, $\vee Q_i$ any disjunction, then for some disjunct $Q_k$, $T^* \vdash Q_k$.

Note that if $\varphi$ is gappy in M then, since $T^*$ is satisfied by M, we have neither $T^* \vdash \varphi$ nor $T^* \vdash \sim\varphi$ nor $T^* \vdash (\varphi \vee \sim\varphi)$ since $T^*$ is prime. As an example, take ZFCU and consider a classical model M (no gaps, so the positive and negative extensions for each predicate exhaust the domain) with a countable infinity of urelements so there is a bijection from the subdomain of urelements onto the natural numbers. Expand the language by adding individual constant 0, one one-place function term S, two two-place functions $+$ and $\times$ and two one-place predicates N and C. Amend M to a neo-classical model $M^*$ by interpreting N and C classically (i.e. with its negative extension the complement of its positive extension) with the urelements as the positive extension of N and the sets as the positive extension of C. Assign $S^n 0$ to the urelement assigned $n$ and interpret $+$ and $\times$ by plus and times (thus as fully defined functions) over the extension of N. Now we reinterpret identity. Its positive extension is to stay the same and for $a$, $\beta$ both sets or both urelements, $<a, \beta>$ is in the negative extension of $=$ iff $a \neq \beta$; otherwise, where one is a set and the other is an urelement, the pair is not in the negative extension.

We thus have to change the theory of identity. We can still have $\forall x \; x = x$ as an axiom but we amend Leibniz' law to:

$$\forall xy((Cx \,\&\, Cy) \rightarrow (\varphi x \,\&\, x = y) \rightarrow \varphi y))$$ ditto for the restriction to N.

We retain the axioms of ZFC but with all quantifiers restricted to C and add the first-order Peano–Dedekind axioms, all quantifiers restricted to N. The resultant theory, call it NS for numbers/sets, is clearly true in $M^*$. By the previous result we can expand it to a prime theory $NS^*$ also satisfied by $M^*$. Since cross-categorical identities such as $SS0 = \{\{\varnothing\}\}$ (set brackets as abbreviations) are indeterminate in $M^*$ all of the following fail:

$$NS^* \vdash SS0 = \{\{\emptyset\}\}; \ NS^* \vdash SS0 \neq \{\{\emptyset\}\};$$
$$NS^* \vdash (SS0 = \{\{\emptyset\}\} \lor SS0 \neq \{\{\emptyset\}\})$$

If our theory T is expressed in a $\rightarrow$-free sublanguage and is satisfied by neo-classical M, there must exist a classical model $M_C$ which satisfies T. This is generated by assigning arbitrarily either T or F to every atom in the language of T which is gappy in M. By the monotonicity of the $\rightarrow$-free language, every sentence with a determinate value in M has the same value in $M_C$. The above Henkin-style construction then generates from $M_C$ a theory $T^{**}$ which is prime and which proves every instance of LEM (since $M_C$ is classical) hence is negation-complete.

## §A.6  Limitative Results in Infinitary Logics

There are pleasing completeness results for some infinitary languages, for example completeness results for standard infinitary propositional languages $L_\kappa$, $\kappa$ inaccessible (Karp 1964, §5.5, pp. 51–3) and for (objectual) quantifier languages of the form $L_{\kappa,\kappa}$ (again $\kappa$ inaccessible—Karp 1964, p. 131)[6] and also, a rather special case, $L_{\omega 1,\omega 0}$. Nevertheless, as remarked Chapter 8, §VII, limitative theorems such as Scott's Undefinability Theorems (Scott 1965; Karp 1964, ch. 14) hold for many other cardinals (e.g. successor cardinals $\kappa^+$). Scott's theorem says that, for these languages, the set of all (codes) of logically true formulae of the language is indefinable in the language and this in turn (given that the length of proofs is bounded above by the index of the language) renders the systems incomplete.

One important point to make is that one necessary condition of application for Scott's results, the definability of the basic syntactic notions inside the object language itself, does not apply in our quasi-substitutional case, essentially generalized propositional logic. Although there is no inconsistency in the neo-formalist engaging in some model theory, for example assigning a domain of referents for each singular term in $L_\kappa$, note that every such domain of individuals must be of cardinality $< \kappa$. For generalizations are infinitary regular conjunctions and disjunctions and each such is of length $< \kappa$.

Since the cardinality of any such language, the number of its wffs, is $\geq \kappa$ ($= \kappa$, for $\kappa$ inaccessible) this means that we cannot characterize the syntax of the language up to isomorphism by a theory expressible in the language: we cannot even quantify over all symbols or terms of the language. What this shows is that the neat generalization of first-order language to the vastly more expressive infinitary languages $L_\kappa$, $\kappa$

---

[6] These results depend on extensions of distributivity principles (laws of dependent and independent choices) to govern the interaction between quantifiers and sentential operators.

inaccessible, has come, in our case, at a lethal cost. We patently can describe the syntax of English in English (albeit our theories thereof are far from perfect) and construct self-referential 'diagonalization' attributions. Hence the languages $L_\kappa$ fail to regiment crucial aspects of real language. The paradoxes are not even stateable. Again the moral I draw is the need to return to naïve set theory.

# Bibliography

Anderson, Alan and Belnap, Nuel, 1975: *Entailment Volume I* (Princeton, NJ: Princeton University Press).

Anderson, Alan, Belnap, Nuel and Dunn, Michael, 1992: *Entailment Volume II* (Princeton, NJ: Princeton University Press).

Armstrong, D. M., 1997: *A World of States of Affairs* (Cambridge: Cambridge University Press).
—— 2004: *Truth and Truthmakers* (Cambridge: Cambridge University Press).

Balaguer, Mark, 1998: *Platonism and Anti-platonism in Mathematics* (Oxford: Oxford University Press).

Baumann, J. J., 1868: *Die Lehren von Zeit, Raum und Mathematik*, vols. 1 and 2 (Berlin: Erdmann).

Beall, J. C. and Restall, Greg, 2006: *Logical Pluralism* (Oxford: Clarendon Press).

Benacerraf, Paul, 1965: 'What Numbers Could Not Be', *Philosophical Review* 74, pp. 47–73.
—— 1973: 'Mathematical Truth', *Journal of Philosophy* 70, pp. 661–79.

Bergström, Lars, 1993: 'Quine, Underdetermination, and Skepticism', *Journal of Philosophy* 90, pp. 331–58.
—— 2004: 'Underdetermination of Physical Theory', in Roger Gibson 2004, pp. 91–114.

Black, Max and Geach, Peter, 1980: *Translations from the Philosophical Writings of Gottlob Frege* (Oxford: Blackwell, third edition).

Blackburn, Simon, 1984: *Spreading the Word* (Oxford: Clarendon Press).
—— 1993a: *Essays in Quasi-Realism* (Oxford: Oxford University Press).
—— 1993b: 'Realism, Quasi, or Queasy?', in Haldane and Wright 1993, pp. 365–83.
—— 2006: 'The Semantics of Non-Factualism, Non-Cognitivism, and Quasi-Realism', in *The Blackwell Guide to the Philosophy of Language* (ed.) Michael Devitt and Richard Hanley (Oxford: Blackwell), pp. 244–51.

Boghossian, Paul, 2005: 'Is meaning normative?', in A. Beckermann and C. Nimtz (eds.), *Philosophy—Science—Scientific Philosophy* (Paderborn: Mentis), pp. 205–18.

Boolos, George, 1975: 'On second-order logic', *Journal of Philosophy* 72, pp. 509–27.
—— 1987/98: 'A Curious Inference', page reference to the printing in Boolos, 1998, pp. 376–82, first published in the *Journal of Philosophical Logic* 16 (1987), pp. 1–12.
—— 1989/98 'Iteration again', *Philosophical Topics*, 17, pp. 5–21, page reference to the printing in Boolos 1998, pp. 88–104.
—— 1990: 'The Standard of Equality of Numbers'. Page references to the printing in Boolos (1998) pp. 202–19. [First published in G. Boolos (ed)., *Meaning and Method: Essays in Honour of Hilary Putnam* (Cambridge: Cambridge University Press, 1990).]
—— 1993: *The Logic of Provability* (Cambridge: Cambridge University Press).
—— 1998: *Logic, Logic and Logic* (Cambridge, Mass.: Harvard University Press).

Boyd, Richard, 1983: 'On the Current Status of Scientific Realism', *Erkenntnis* 19, pp. 45–90.

Brock, Stuart and Mares, Edwin, 2007: *Realism and Anti-Realism* (Stocksfield: Acumen).

Bundy, Alan, 2005: (ed.), *Philosophical Transactions of the Royal Society A* October, 15, 2005. doi: 10.1098/rsta. 2005.1651.

——Jamnik, Mateja, and Fugard, Andrew, 2005: 'What is a Proof?', in Bundy 2005, pp. 2377–91.

——Green, Ian, and Jamnik, Mateja, 1997: 'Automation of Diagrammatic Proofs in Mathematics', in M. E. Pollack, (ed.), *Proceedings of the 15th International Joint Conference on Artificial Intelligence*, 1 (San Francisco: Morgan Kaufmann), pp. 528–33.

Burgess, John and Rosen, Gideon, 1997: *A Subject with No Object* (Oxford: Clarendon Press).

——Hazen, Allen and Lewis, David, 1991: 'Appendix on Pairing' in Lewis (1991), pp. 121–49.

Butterworth, Brian, 1999: *The Mathematical Brain* (London: Macmillan).

Cappelen, Herman and Lepore, Ernie, 2005: *Insensitive Semantics* (Oxford: Blackwell).

Carnap, Rudolf, 1934/7: *Logische Syntax der Sprache* (Vienna: Springer); translated A. Smeaton, *The Logical Syntax of Language* (London: Kegan, Paul, Trench, Trubner & Co. 1937).

Cartwright, Nancy, 1983: *How the Laws of Physics Lie* (Oxford: Clarendon Press).

——1999: *The Dappled World* (Cambridge: Cambridge University Press).

Chihara, Charles, 1973: *Ontology and the Vicious Circle Principle* (Ithaca, NY: Cornell University Press).

——1990: *Constructibility and Mathematical Existence* (Oxford: Clarendon Press).

Chisholm, R. M., 1957: *Perceiving* (Ithaca, NY: Cornell University Press).

Chomsky, Noam, 1980: *Rules and Representations* (Oxford: Blackwell).

Clark, Stephen, 1993: 'Where Have All the Angels Gone?', *Religious Studies* 28, pp. 221–34.

Clifford, W. K., 1877/1999: 'The Ethics of Belief', 1877, originally published in *Contemporary Review*, 1877, reprinted in *The Ethics of Belief and Other Essays* (New York: Amherst: Prometheus Books, 1999).

Cohen, Paul, 1971: 'Comments on the Foundations of Set Theory', in Dana Scott (ed.), *Axiomatic Set Theory: Proceedings of Symposia in Pure Mathematics*, vol. 13 (Providence: American Mathematical Society), pp. 9–15.

Colyvan, Mark, 2001: *The Indispensability of Mathematics* (Oxford: Oxford University Press).

Copeland, B. J., 1998: 'Turing's O-machines, Searle, Penrose, and the Brain', *Analysis* 58, pp. 128–38.

Corfield, David, 2001: 'Bayesianism in Mathematics', in D. Corfield and J. Williamson (eds.), *Foundations of Bayesianism* (Dordrech: Kluwer), pp. 175–201.

Currie, Gregory, 1990: *The Nature of Fiction* (Cambridge: Cambridge University Press).

Curry, Haskell, 1951: *Outlines of a Formalist Philosophy of Mathematics* (Amsterdam: North Holland).

Davidson, Donald, 1968/84: 'On Saying That', first published in *Synthèse* 19, 1968, page references to the version in Davidson 1984, pp. 93–108.

——1984: *Inquiries into Truth and Interpretation* (Oxford: Clarendon Press).

Davies, Martin, 1981: *Meaning, Quantification, Necessity* (London: Routledge and Kegan Paul).

Davis, Martin, 2005: 'What did Gödel believe and When Did He Believe It?', *The Bulletin of Symbolic Logic* 11, pp. 194–206.

Descartes, René, 1628/1911: 'Rules for the Direction of the Mind', translated in Haldane and Ross (eds.), *The Philosophical Works of Descartes Vol. I* (Cambridge: Cambridge University Press, 1911), pp. 1–77.

Detlefsen, Michael, 1986: *Hilbert's Program* (Dordrecht: Reidel).

Detlefsen, Michael, 2005: 'Formalism' in Stewart Shapiro (ed.), *The Oxford Handbook of Philosophy of Mathematics and Logic* (Oxford: Oxford University Press).

Devitt, Michael, 1984: *Realism and Truth* (Oxford: Blackwell).

Dickmann, M. A., 1975: *Large Infinitary Languages* (Amsterdam: North Holland).

Divers, John and Miller, Alexander, 1999: 'Arithmetical Platonism: Reliability and Judgement-Dependence', *Philosophical Studies* 95, pp. 277–310.

Drake, Frank, 1974: *Set Theory: An Introduction to Large Cardinals* (Amsterdam: North Holland).

Dummett, Michael, 1963/78: 'Realism'; a talk first published in Dummett 1978, pp. 145–65.

——1963b/78: 'The Philosophical Significance of Gödel's Theorem', Dummett 1978, pp. 186–201. Originally published in 1963 in *Ratio*, V.

——1973/78: 'The Philosophical Basis of Intuitionistic Logic', Dummett (1978), pp. 215–47. Originally published in H. E. Rose and J. C. Shepherdson (eds.), *Logic Colloquium '73* (Amsterdam: North Holland, 1975), pp. 5–40.

——1975/78: 'Wang's Paradox', *Synthese* 30 (1975), pp. 301–24; references are to the printing in Dummett 1978, pp. 246–68.

——1976: 'What is a Theory of Meaning II?', in G. Evans and J. McDowell (eds.), *Truth and Meaning* (Oxford: Oxford University Press, 1976), pp. 67–137.

——1978: *Truth and Other Enigmas* (London: Duckworth).

——1981a: *Frege: Philosophy of Language* Second Edition (London: Duckworth).

——1981b: *The Interpretation of Frege's Philosophy* (London: Duckworth).

——1982/92: 'Realism', *Synthese* 52, pp. 55–112, page references to the reprint in Dummett (1993, pp. 230–76).

——1991a: *Frege: Philosophy of Mathematics* (London: Duckworth).

——1991b: *The Logical Basis of Metaphysics* (Cambridge, Mass.: Harvard University Press).

——1993: *The Seas of Language* (Oxford: Clarendon Press).

Edgington, Dorothy, 1993: 'Wright and Sainsbury on Higher-order Vagueness', *Analysis* 53, pp. 193–200.

Enderton, Herbert, 1977: *Elements of Set Theory* (London: Academic Press).

Evans, Gareth, 1982: *The Varieties of Reference* (Oxford: Clarendon Press).

Field, Hartry, 1980: *Science without Numbers* (Oxford: Blackwell).

——1989: *Realism, Mathematics and Modality* (Oxford: Blackwell).

Fine, Kit, 2005: 'Our Knowledge of Mathematical Objects', in Tamar Szabó Gendler and John Hawthorne (eds.), *Oxford Studies in Epistemology*, vol 1, pp. 89–109 (Oxford: Oxford University Press).

Fisher, Alec, 1988: *The Logic of Real Arguments* (Cambridge: Cambridge University Press).

Føllesdal, Dagfinn, 1973: 'Indeterminacy of Translation and Under-determination of the Theory of Nature', *Dialectica* 27, pp. 289–301.

Frege, Gottlob, 1879: *Begriffsschrift: eine der arithmetischen nachgebildete Formelsprache des reinen Denkens.* (Halle: L. Nebert).

——1884/1953: *Die Grundlagen der Arithmetik: eine logisch-mathematische Untersuchung über den Begriff der Zahl* (Breslau: W. Koebner, 1884). Translated as The Foundations of Arithmetic: A Logico-Mathematical Enquiry into the Concept of Number, by J. L. Austin (Oxford: Blackwell, 1953).

——1903: *Grundgesetze der Arithmetik, begriffsschriftlich Abgeleitet*, vol. 2 (Pohle: Jena: Pohle). Reprinted 1962 (Hildesheim: George Olms).

—— 1903/1980: 'Frege Against the Formalists: Vol II of Frege 1903, §§86–137)', in Black and Geach 1980, pp. 162–213.

—— 1918/97: 'Thought'—'Der Gedanke', *Beiträge zur Philosophie des deutschen Idealismus I* (pp. 58–77), translated by Peter Geach and R. H. Stoothoff; page references to the printing in *The Frege Reader* ed. Michael Beaney (Oxford: Blackwell, 1997).

—— 1979: *Posthumous Writings*, eds. Hermes, Kambartel, Kaulbach with the assistance of Gabriel and Rödding; translated by Peter Long and Roger White with the assistance of Roger Hargreaves (Oxford: Blackwell).

Geach, Peter, 1957: *Mental Acts* (London: Routledge and Kegan Paul).

—— 1965: 'Assertion', *Philosophical Review* 74, pp. 449–65.

Gentzen, Gerhard, 1969: *The Collected Works of Gerhard Gentzen* edited by M. E. Szabó (Amsterdam: North Holland).

George, Alexander, 1987: 'Reply to Weir on Dummett and Intuitionism', *Mind* 96, pp. 404–6.

—— 1988: 'Intuitionism, Excluded Middle and Decidability: A Response to Weir on Dummett', *Mind* 97, pp. 597–602.

Giaquinto, Marcus, 1992: 'Visualizing as a Means of Geometrical Discovery', *Mind and Language* 7, pp. 381–401.

—— 1994: 'Epistemology of Visual Thinking in Elementary Real Analysis', *British Journal for the Philosophy of Science* 45, pp. 789–813.

—— 2002: *The Search for Certainty* (Oxford: Clarendon Press).

Glüer, Kathrin and Wikforss, Åsa, 2009: 'Against Content Normativity', *Mind* 118, pp. 31–70.

Gödel, Kurt, 1930: 'Die Vollständigkeit der Axiome des logischen Functionenkalküls', *Monatshefte für Mathematik und Physik* 37, pp. 349–60.

—— 1931: 'Über formal unentscheidbare Sätze der *Principia Mathematica* und verwandter Systeme, I', *Monatshefte für Mathematik und Physik* 38, pp. 173–98.

—— 1936: 'Über die Länge von Beweisen', *Ergebnisse eines mathematischen Kolloquiums* 7, pp. 23–4.

Goodman, Nelson and Quine, W. V., 1947: 'Steps towards a Constructive Nominalism', *Journal of Symbolic Logic* 12, pp. 97–122.

Halbach, Volker and Horsten, Leon, 2006: 'Axiomatizing Kripke's Theory of Truth', *Journal of Symbolic Logic* 71, pp. 677–712.

Haldane, J. and Wright, C. (eds.), 1993: *Reality: Representation and Projection* (Oxford: Oxford University Press).

Hale, Bob, 1984: 'The Compleat Projectivist': Critical Notice of S. Blackburn, *Spreading the Word*, *Philosophical Quarterly* 36, pp. 65–84.

—— 1993: 'On the Logic of Attitudes', in Haldane and Wright 1993, pp. 337–63, 385–8.

—— 2000/01: 'Reals by Abstraction', *Philosophia Mathematica*, Series III, 8 pp. 100–23 reprinted in Hale and Wright 2001, pp. 399–400.

—— 2005: 'Real Numbers and Set theory—Extending the Neo-Fregean Programme Beyond Arithmetic', *Synthese* 147, pp. 21–41.

Hale, Bob and Wright, Crispin, 2001a: *The Reason's Proper Study* (Oxford: Clarendon Press).

—— 2001b: 'To bury Caesar . . . ', in Hale and Wright 2001a, pp. 335–97.

Harris, J. H., 1982: 'What's So Logical about the "Logical" Axioms?', *Studia Logica* 41, pp. 159–71.

Haslanger, Sally, 1995: 'Ontology and Social Construction', *Philosophical Topics* 23 pp. 95–125.

Hattiangadi, Anandi, 2006: 'Is Meaning Normative?', *Mind and Language* 14, pp. 220–40.

Heal, Jane, 1989: *Fact and Meaning: Quine and Wittgenstein on Philosophy of Language* (Oxford: Blackwell).

Heck, Richard, 1992: 'On the Consistency of Second-Order Contextual Definitions', *Noûs* 26, pp. 491–4.

——1996: 'The Consistency of Predicative Fragments of Frege's *Grundgesetze der Arithmetik*', *History and Philosophy of Logic* 17, pp. 209–20.

——1997: 'Finitude and Hume's Principle', *Journal of Philosophical Logic* 26, pp. 589–617.

Hellman, Geoffrey, 1989: *Mathematics without Numbers* (Oxford: Clarendon Press).

——2005: 'Structuralism', in Stewart Shapiro (ed.) 2005, pp. 526–62.

Hogarth, M. L., 1994: 'Non-Turing Computers and Non-Turing Computability'. *PSA* 1, pp. 126–38.

Horgan, Terence, 1994: 'Naturalism and Intentionality', *Philosophical Studies* 76, pp. 301–26.

Hume, David, 1739/1888: *Treatise of Human Nature*, (ed.) L. A. Selby-Bigge (Oxford: Clarendon).

——1748/1975: *Enquiry Concerning Human Understanding* in *Hume's Enquiries* ed. L. A. Selby-Bigge and P. H. Nidditch, 3rd edn. (Oxford: Clarendon Press).

——1751/1975: *Enquiry Concerning the Principles of Morals* in *Hume's Enquiries* ed. L. A. Selby-Bigge and P. H. Nidditch, 3rd edn. (Oxford: Clarendon Press).

Johnston, Mark, 1992: 'Objectivity Refigured: Pragmatism without Verificationism', in Haldane and Wright, 1993, pp. 85–130.

Kamp, Hans, 1971: 'Formal Properties of "Now"', *Theoria* 37, pp. 227–73.

Kaplan, David, 1989: 'Demonstratives', in J. Almog, J. Perry, and H. Wettstein (eds.), *Themes from Kaplan* (New York: Oxford University Press), pp. 481–563.

Karp, Carol, 1964: *Languages with Expressions of Infinite Length* (Amsterdam: North Holland).

Kemeny, J. and Oppenheim P., 1956: 'On Reduction', *Philosophical Studies* 7, pp. 6–18.

Kenny, Anthony, 1968: *Descartes* (New York: Random House).

Kirby, L. and Paris, J., 1982: 'Accessible Independence Results for Peano Arithmetic', *Bull. London Mathematical Society* 14, pp. 285–93.

Kitcher, Philip, 1984: *The Nature of Natural Knowledge* (New York: Oxford University Press).

Kleene, Stephen, 1952: *Introduction to Metamathematics* (Amsterdam: North Holland).

——1967: *Mathematical Logic* (New York: Wiley).

Kölbel, Max, 2002: *Truth without Objectivity* (London: Routledge).

Kreisel, George, 1959: 'Wittgenstein's Remarks on the Foundations of Mathematics', *British Journal for the Philosophy of Science* 9, pp. 135–58.

Kripke, Saul, 1972/80: *Naming and Necessity* (Oxford: Basil Blackwell, 1980), page references to this revised edition, the work being first published in G. Harman and D. Davidson (eds.), *Semantics of Natural Language* (Dordrecht: Reidel, 1972).

——1976: 'Is There a Problem with Substitutional Quantification?', in G. Evans and J. McDowell (eds.), *Truth and Meaning: Essays in Semantics* (Oxford: Oxford University Press), pp. 325–419.

——1982: *Wittgenstein on Rules and Private Language* (Oxford: Blackwell).

Kunen, Kenneth, 1980: *Set Theory: An Introduction to Independence Proofs* (Amsterdam: North Holland).

Lavine, Shaughan, 1994: *Understanding the Infinite* (Cambridge, Mass.: Harvard University Press).

Laymon, R., 1985: 'Idealization and the testing of theories by experimentation', in P. Achinstein, and O. Hannaway (eds.), *Observation, Experiment and Hypothesis in Modern Physical Science* (Cambridge, Mass.: MIT Press).

Lavine, Shaughan, 1994: *Understanding the Infinite* (Cambridge, Mass.: Harvard University Press).

Lemmon, E. J., 1978: *Beginning Logic* (Indianapolis: Hackett).

Lewis, David, 1970/83: 'How to define Theoretical Terms', *Philosophical Papers Vol. 1* (Oxford: Oxford University Press, 1983), pp. 78–95 (originally published in the *Journal of Philosophy 67*, pp. 427–46).

——1976: 'Probabilities of Conditionals and Conditional Probabilities', *The Philosophical Review* 85, pp. 297–315.

——1988: 'Desire as Belief' *Mind* 97, pp. 323–32.

——1991: *Parts of Classes* (Oxford: Blackwell).

——1996: 'Desire as Belief II', *Mind* 105, pp. 303–13.

Linsky, Bernard and Zalta, Edward, 2006: 'What is Neologicism?', *The Bulletin of Symbolic Logic*, 12/1, pp. 60–99.

Logue, James, 1995: *Projective Probability* (Oxford: Clarendon Press).

Lukasiewicz, Jan, 1920: 'O logice trójwartosciowej', *Ruch Filozoficzny* (Lwów) 5, pp. 169–71.

Lukasiewicz, J. and Tarski, A., 1930: 'Untersuchungen über den Aussagenkalkül', *Comptes Rendus des séances de la Société des Sciences et des Lettres de Varsovie* 23, pp. 30–50.

MacBride, Fraser, 2000: 'On Finite Hume', *Philosophia Mathematica* 8, pp. 150–9.

Maddy, Penny, 1988a: 'Believing the Axioms I', *Journal of Symbolic Logic* 53, pp. 481–511.

——1988b: 'Believing the Axioms II', *Journal of Symbolic Logic* 53, pp. 736–64.

MacDonald Ross, George, 1985: 'Angels', *Philosophy* 60, pp. 495–511.

McDowell, John, 1998: *Mind, Value and Reality* (Cambridge, Mass.: Harvard University Press).

McClelland, J. L. and Rumelhart, D. A., 1986: 'On learning the past tenses of English verbs' in McClelland and Rumelhart (eds.), *Parallel Distributed Processing* Vol. 2 (Cambridge, Mass.: MIT Press).

McFetridge, I. G., 1975: 'Propositions and Davidson's Account of Indirect Discourse', *Proceedings of the Aristotelian Society* 76, pp. 131–45.

Mendelson, Elliot, 1979: *Introduction to Mathematical Logic* (New York: Van Nostrand).

Meyer, R. K., 1974: 'New Axiomatics for Relevant Logics—I', *Journal of Philosophical Logic* 3, pp. 53–86.

Miller, Alexander, 2006: 'Meaning Scepticism', in M. Devitt and R. Hanley (eds.), *The Blackwell Guide to the Philosophy of Language* (Oxford: Blackwell), pp. 91–113.

——2008: 'Realism', *The Stanford Encyclopedia of Philosophy (Fall 2008 Edition)*, Edward N. Zalta (ed)., URL = <http://plato.stanford.edu/archives/fall2008/entries/realism/.

Milne, Peter, 2004: 'Classical Harmony: Rules of Inference and the Logical Constants', *Synthese* 100, pp. 49–94.

——2007: 'On Gödel Sentences and What They Say', *Philosophia Mathematica* 15, pp. 193–226.

Moore, Gregory H., 1980: 'Beyond First-Order Logic: The Historical Interplay between Mathematical Logic and Axiomatic Set Theory', *History and Philosophy of Logic* 1, pp. 95–137.

——1988: 'The Emergence of First-Order Logic', in *History and Philosophy of Modern Mathematics*, Minnesota Studies in the Philosophy of Science No. 11 (Minneapolis: University of Minnesota Press), pp. 95–135.

Mostowski, A., Robinson R. M., and Tarski, A., 1953: *Undecidable Theories* (Amsterdam: North Holland).

Mulligan, Kevin, Simons, Peter, and Smith, Barry, 1984: 'Truth-Makers', *Philosophy and Phenomenological Research* 44, pp. 287–321.

Nagel, Ernest, 1961: *The Structure of Science* (London: Routledge and Kegan Paul).

Nagel, Thomas, 1986: *The View from Nowhere* (Oxford: Oxford University Press).

Newton-Smith, W. H., 1981: *The Rationality of Science* (London: Routledge and Kegan Paul).

O'Connor, John and Robertson, Edmund (E-resource): *MacTutor History of Mathematics*: URL: <http//:www-history.mcs.st-andrews.ac.uk/HistTopics/Fermat's_last_theorem.html>.

Parsons, Terence, 1982: 'Fregean Theories of Fictional Objects', *Topoi* 1, pp. 81–7.

Peacocke, Christopher, 1992: 'Sense and Justification', *Mind* 101, pp. 793–816.

Peirce, Charles Saunders, 1933: *The Collected Papers of Charles Saunders Peirce, Vol. IV: The Simplest Mathematics*, (eds.) Charles Hartshorne and Paul Weiss (Cambridge, Mass.: Harvard University Press).

Perry, John, 1979: 'The Problem of the Essential Indexical', *Nous* 13, pp. 3–21.

Potter, Michael, 1993: 'Iterative Set Theory', *Philosophical Quarterly* 43, pp. 127–93.

——2000: *Reason's Nearest Kin* (Oxford: Oxford University Press).

——2004: *Set Theory and its Philosophy* (Oxford: Oxford University Press).

Prawitz, Dag, 1965: *Natural Deduction: A Proof-Theoretic Study* (Stockholm: Almqvist & Wiksell).

——1975: 'Ideas and Results in Proof Theory', in J. Fenstad (ed.), *Proceedings of the Second Scandinavian Logic Symposium* (Amsterdam: North Holland), pp. 235–50.

——1977: 'Meaning and Proofs: On the Conflict between Classical and Intuitionist Logic', *Theoria* 43, pp. 2–40.

——1979: 'Proofs and the Meaning and Completeness of the Logical Constants', in J. Hintikka, I. Niiniluoto, and E. Saarinen (eds.), *Essays on Mathematical and Philosophical Logic* (Dordrecht: Reidel), pp. 25–40.

Predelli, Stefano, 2005: *Contexts: Meaning, Truth, and the Use of Language* (Oxford: Clarendon Press).

Price, Huw, 1994: 'A Neglected Route to Realism about Quantum-Mechanics', *Mind* 103, pp. 303–36.

Priest, Graham, 1979: 'Two Dogmas of Quineanism', *Philosophical Quarterly*, pp. 289–301.

——1987: *In Contradiction* (Dordrecht: Nijhoff).

Putnam, Hilary, 1967a/1975: 'The Thesis that Mathematics is Logic', in R. Schoenmann (ed.), *Bertrand Russell: Philosopher of the Century* (Boston: Little and Brown), reprinted in Putnam (1975), pp. 12–42.

——1967b: 'Mathematics without Foundations', *Journal of Philosophy* 64, pp. 5–22. Reprinted in Putnam (1975) pp. 43–59.

——1972: *Philosophy of Logic* (London: George Allen and Unwin).

——1975: *Mathematics, Matter and Method: Philosophical Papers*, vol. 1 (Cambridge: Cambridge University Press).

——1978: *Meaning and the Moral Sciences* (London: Routledge and Kegan Paul).

——1981: *Reason, Truth and History* (Cambridge: Cambridge University Press).

——1983: *Realism and Reason: Philosophical Papers*, vol. 3 (Cambridge: Cambridge University Press).

——1990: *Realism with a Human Face* (Cambridge, Mass.: Harvard University Press).

Quine, W. V., 1936/75: 'Truth by Convention', first published in O. H. Lee (ed.), *Philosophical Essays for A. N. Whitehead* (New York: Longmans, 1936). Page references to the version in W. V. Quine 1975 pp. 77–106.

—— 1940: *Mathematical Logic* (Cambridge, Mass.: Harvard University Press).

—— 1948/53: 'On What There Is', *Review of Metaphysics* 2 (1948), pp. 21–38, page references to the version in Quine 1953, pp. 1–19.

—— 1951/53: 'Two Dogmas of Empiricism', *Philosophical Review* 60, pp. 20–43. Page references to the version in W. V. Quine 1953, pp. 10–46.

—— 1953: *From a Logical Point of View* (Cambridge, Mass.: Harvard University Press).

—— 1953a: 'The Problem of Meaning in Linguistics', in Quine 1953, pp. 47–64.

—— 1960: *Word and Object* (Cambridge, Mass.: MIT Press).

—— 1969: 'Epistemology Naturalized' in W. V. Quine, *Ontological Relativity and Other Essays* (New York: Columbia University Press), pp. 69–90.

—— 1970: *Philosophy of Logic* (Englewood Cliffs, NJ: Prentice Hall).

—— 1974: *The Roots of Reference* (La Salle, Ill.: Open Court).

—— 1975: 'On Empirically Equivalent Systems of the World', *Erkenntnis* 9, pp. 313–28.

—— 1986: 'Reply to Gibson', in L. E. Hahn and P. A. Schilpp (eds.), *The Philosophy of W. V. Quine* (La Salle, Ill.: Open Court), pp. 155–7.

—— 1992: *Pursuit of Truth*, 2nd edn. (Cambridge, Mass.: Harvard University Press).

Read, Stephen, 1998: *Relevant Logic* (Oxford: Blackwell).

—— 2000: 'Harmony and Autonomy in Classical Logic', *Journal of Philosophical Logic* 29, pp. 129–54.

Resnik, Michael, 1980: *Frege and the Philosophy of Mathematics* (Ithaca, NY: Cornell University Press).

Rieger, Adam, 2006: 'A Simple Theory of Conditionals', *Analysis*, pp. 233–40.

Robinson, Abraham, 1965: 'Formalism' in Bar-Hillel et al., *Logic, Methodology and Philosophy of Science* (Amsterdam: North Holland).

—— 1969: 'From a Formalist's point of view', *Dialectica* 23, pp. 45–9.

Rothschild, D. and Segal, G., 2009: 'Indexical Predicates', *Mind & Language* 24, pp. 467–93.

Rumfitt, Ian, 1993: 'Content and Context: The Paratactic Theory Revisited and Revised', *Mind* 102, pp. 429–54.

Russell, Bertrand, 1903: *The Principles of Mathematics* (Cambridge: Cambridge University Press).

—— 1919: *Introduction to Mathematical Philosophy* (London: George Allen and Unwin).

—— 1959: *My Philosophical Development* (London: George Allen and Unwin).

Scott, Dana, 1965: 'Logic with Denumerably Long Formulas and Finite Strings of Quantifiers' in J. Addison, L. Henkin, and A. Tarski (eds.), *The Theory of Models* (Amsterdam: North Holland), pp. 329–41.

—— 1974: 'Axiomatizing Set Theory', in T. Jech (ed.), *Axiomatizing Set Theory: Proceedings of Symposia in Pure Mathematics 13* (Part II) (Providence, RI: American Mathematical Society), pp. 207–14.

Searle, John, 1979: *Expression and Meaning* (Cambridge: Cambridge University Press).

Segal, G., and Speas, M., 1986: 'On saying δ at', *Mind and Language*, pp. 124–32.

Shapiro, Stewart, 1991: *Foundations without Foundationalism* (Oxford: Clarendon Press).

—— 1997: *Philosophy of Mathematics* (New York: Oxford University Press).

Shapiro, Stewart, 1998: 'Incompleteness, Mechanism and Optimism', *The Bulletin of Symbolic Logic* 4, pp. 273–302.

——2000a: 'Frege Meets Dedekind: A Neologicist Treatment of Real Analysis', *Notre Dame Journal of Formal Logic* 41, pp. 335–64.

——2000c: *Thinking about Mathematics* (Oxford: Oxford University Press).

——2000b: 'The Status of Logic', in P. Boghossian and C. Peacocke 2000, pp. 333–66.

——2003: 'Mechanism, Truth and Penrose's New Argument', *Journal of Philosophical Logic* 32, pp. 19–42.

——2005 (ed.), *The Oxford Handbook of Philosophy of Mathematics and Logic* (Oxford: Oxford University Press).

——2007: 'The Objectivity of Mathematics', *Synthese* 156, pp. 337–81.

Sherif, Muzafer, 1935: 'A Study of Some Social Factors in Perception', *Archives of Psychology* 27, pp. 311–28.

Simons, Peter, 1987/95: 'Frege's Theory of Real Numbers', *History and Philosophy of Logic*, 8 (1987), 25–44, reprinted in W. Demopoulos (ed.), *Frege's Philosophy of Mathematics* (Cambridge, Mass.: Harvard University Press, 1995), pp. 358–85.

——2006: 'Real Wholes, Real Parts: Mereology without Algebra', *Journal of Philosophy* 103, pp. 597–613.

Skorupski, John, 1984: 'Dummett's Frege', *Philosophical Quarterly*, 34; page references to the printing in C. Wright (ed.) 1984, pp. 228–43.

Smiley, Timothy, 1959: 'Entailment and Deducibility', *Proceedings of the Aristotelian Society*, pp. 233–54.

Sorensen, Roy, 1988: *Blindspots* (Oxford: Clarendon Press).

Steiner, Mark, 1998: *The Applicability of Mathematics as a Philosophical Problem* (Cambridge, Mass.: Harvard University Press).

Tait, William, 1981: 'Remarks on Finitism', *Journal of Philosophy* 78, pp. 524–46.

Tarski, Alfred, 1936/56: 'Der Wahrheitsbegriff in den formalisierten Sprachen', *Studia Philosophica* 1, pp. 261–405.

——1956: 'The Concept of Truth in Formalised Languages', translation of Tarski 1936 in A. Tarski, *Logic, Semantics, Metamathematics* (Oxford: Oxford University Press), pp. 152–278.

Tennant, Neil, 1978: *Natural Logic* (Edinburgh: Edinburgh University Press).

——1984: 'Were those disproofs I saw before me?', *Analysis* 44, pp. 97–105.

——1987: *Anti-realism and Logic* (Oxford: Clarendon Press).

——1997a: 'On the Necessary Existence of Numbers', *Noûs* 31, pp. 307–36.

——1997b: *The Taming of the True* (Oxford: Clarendon Press).

——2000: 'Deductive versus Expressive Power', *Journal of Philosophy* 97, pp. 257–77.

——2003: 'Theory Contraction is NP-Complete, *Logic Journal of the IGPL* 11, pp. 675–93.

——2004: 'A General Theory of Abstraction Operators', *Philosophical Quarterly* 54, pp. 105–33.

Travis, C., 1997: 'Pragmatics', *A Companion to the Philosophy of Language*, ed. Bob Hale and Crispin Wright (Oxford: Blackwell), pp. 87–107.

Twardowski, Kazimir, 1894: *Zur Lehre vom Inhalt und Gegenstand der Vorstellungen. Eine psychologische Untersuchung* (Vienna). Translated as *On the Content and Object of Presentations. A Psychological Investigation* by R. Grossman (The Hague: Nijhoff, 1977).

Walton, Kendall, 1990: *Mimesis as Make-Believe* (Cambridge, Mass.: Harvard University Press).

Weir, Alan, 1983: 'Truth Conditions and Truth Values', *Analysis* 43, pp. 176–80.

—— 1985: 'Rejoinder to Tennant', *Analysis* 45, pp. 68–72.

—— 1986*c*: 'Dummett on Meaning and Classical Logic', *Mind* 95, pp. 465–77.

—— 1986*a*: 'Against Holism', *Philosophical Quarterly* 35, pp. 225–44.

—— 1986*b*: 'Classical Harmony', *The Notre Dame Journal of Formal Logic* 27, pp. 459–82.

—— 1988: 'Rejoinder to George', *Mind* 97, pp. 110–12.

—— 1991: 'An Instructive Nominalism': Critical Review of H. Field: *Realism, Mathematics and Modality, Philosophical Books* 32, 1991, pp. 17–26.

—— 1993: 'Putnam, Gödel and Mathematical Realism', *International Journal of Philosophical Studies* 1, pp. 255–85.

—— 1994: Review of Simon Blackburn: *Essays on Quasi-Realism, International Journal of Philosophical Studies* 2, pp. 345–7.

—— 1996: Review of Shaughan Lavine, *Understanding the Infinite, Philosophical Books* 37, pp. 136–9.

—— 1998*a*: 'Dummett on Impredicativity', *Grazer Philosophische Studien* 55, pp. 65–101.

—— 1998*b*: 'Naïve Set Theory is Innocent!', *Mind* 107, pp. 763–98.

—— 1998*c*: 'Naïve Set Theory, Paraconsistency and Indeterminacy I', *Logique et Analyse* 161–3, pp. 219–66.

—— 1999: 'Naïve Set Theory, Paraconsistency and Indeterminacy II', *Logique et Analyse* 167–8, pp. 283–340.

—— 2000: 'The Force of Reason: Why Is Logic Compelling?', *Logica Yearbook 1999* (Academy of Sciences of the Czech Republic), pp. 37–52.

—— 2001: 'More Trouble for Functionalism', *Proceedings of the Aristotelian Society*, pp. 267–93.

—— 2003*a*: 'Neo-Fregeanism: An Embarrassment of Riches', *The Notre Dame Journal of Formal Logic* 44, pp. 13–48.

—— 2003*b*: 'Objective Content', *Supplementary Proceedings of the Aristotelian Society* 77, pp. 23–48.

—— 2004*a*: 'There Are No True Contradictions', in G. Priest and J. C. Beall (eds.), *The Law of Non-Contradiction: New Philosophical Essays* (Oxford: Oxford University Press), pp. 385–417.

—— 2004*b*: 'An Ultra-realist Theory of Perception', *The International Journal of Philosophical Studies* 12, pp. 105–28.

—— 2005*a*: 'Naturalism Reconsidered', in Stewart Shapiro (ed.), *The Oxford Handbook of Philosophy of Mathematics and Logic* (Oxford: Oxford University Press, 2004), pp. 460–82.

—— 2005*b*: 'Naïve Truth and Sophisticated Logic', in B. Armour-Garb and J. C. Beall (eds.), *Deflationism and Paradox* (Oxford: Oxford University Press), pp. 218–49.

—— 2006*a*: 'Honest Toil or Sheer Magic', *Dialectica* 61, pp. 89–115.

—— 2006*b*: 'Quine on Indeterminacy', in Ernest Lepore and Barry C. Smith (eds.), *The Oxford Handbook of Philosophy of Language* (Oxford: Oxford University Press), pp. 233–49.

Whiting, Daniel, 2007: 'The Normativity of Meaning Defended', *Analysis* 67, pp. 133–40.

Wickelgren, W. A. (1969): 'Context-Sensitive Coding, Associative Memory and Serial Order in (Speech) Behaviour', *Psychological Review* 76, pp. 1–15.

Wigner, Eugene, 1967: 'The Unreasonable Effectiveness of Mathematics in the Natural Sciences', in his *Symmetries and Reflections* (Bloomington: Indiana University Press).

Williamson, Jon, 2005: *Bayesian Nets and Causality: Philosophical and Computational Foundations* (Oxford: Oxford University Press).

Williamson, Timothy, 1982: 'Intuitionism Disproved?', *Analysis* 42, pp. 203–7.

Williamson, Timothy, 1987/8: 'Equivocation and Existence', *Proceedings of the Aristotelian Society* 88, pp. 109–27.

——1994: *Vagueness* (London: Routledge).

——2000: *Knowledge and its Limits* (Oxford: Oxford University Press).

Wright, Crispin, 1982/93: 'Strict Finitism', originally published in *Synthese* 51 (1992), pp. 203–82, page references to the printing in Wright 1993, pp. 107–75.

——1983: *Frege's Theory of Numbers as Object* (Aberdeen: Aberdeen University Press).

——1984: (ed.) *Frege Tradition and Influence* (Oxford: Blackwell).

——1986: 'Inventing Logical Necessity' in J. Butterfield (ed.), *Language, Mind and Logic* (Cambridge: Cambridge University Press), pp. 187–209.

——1992: *Truth and Objectivity* (Cambridge, Mass.: Harvard University Press).

——1993: *Realism, Meaning and Truth*, 2nd edn. (Oxford: Blackwell).

——1997/2001: 'On the Philosophical Significance of Frege's Theorem', page references to the printing in Hale and Wright 2001, pp. 272–306, first published in R. Heck (ed.), *Language, Thought and Logic: Essays in Honour of Michael Dummett* (Oxford, Clarendon Press, 1997).

——1999/2001: 'Is Hume's Principle Analytic', in Hale and Wright (2001), pp. 307–32; first published in the *Notre Dame Journal of Formal Logic* 40 (1999), pp. 6–30.

——2000: 'Neo-Fregean Foundations for Real Analysis: Some Reflections on Frege's Constraint', *Notre Dame Journal of Formal Logic* 41, pp. 317–34.

Wright, G. H. von, 1951: 'Deontic Logic', *Mind* 60, pp. 1–15.

Yablo, Stephen, 1998: 'Does Ontology Rest on a Mistake?', *Proceedings of the Aristotelian Society, Supplementary Volume LXXII*, pp. 229–61.

——2005: 'The Myth of the Seven', in M. Kalderon (ed.), *Fictionalist in Metaphysics* (Oxford: Oxford University Press).

Yessenin-Volpin, A. S., 1961: 'Le programme ultra-intuitioniste des fondements des mathématiques', in A. Mostowksi (ed.), *Infinitistic Methods* (Warsaw and Oxford: Pergamon Press), pp. 201–23.

# Name Index

# Subject Index